MW00624310

CATHOLICS IN AMERICA

CATHOLICS IN AMERICA

A HISTORY

PATRICK W. CAREY

PRAEGER

Westport, Connecticut
London

Library of Congress Cataloging-in-Publication Data

Carey, Patrick W., 1940–
     Catholics in America : a history / by Patrick W. Carey.
        p.   cm.
     Rev. ed. of: The Roman Catholics. c1993.
     Includes bibliographical references and index.
     ISBN 0-275-98255-6 (alk. paper)
        1. Catholic Church—United States—History.   2. Catholics—United States—
     Biography.   3. United States—Church history.   I. Carey, Patrick W., 1940-
     Roman Catholics.   II. Title.
     BX1406.3.C36 2004
     282′.73—dc22   2004014662

British Library Cataloguing in Publication Data is available.

Library of Congress Catalog Card Number: 2004014662
ISBN: 0-275-98255-6

First published in 2004

Praeger Publishers, 88 Post Road West, Westport, CT 06881
An imprint of Greenwood Publishing Group, Inc.
www.praeger.com

Printed in the United States of America

The paper used in this book complies with the
Permanent Paper Standard issued by the National
Information Standards Organization (Z39.48-1984).

10   9   8   7   6   5   4   3   2   1

To Phyllis

———•◦•———

A Pearl of Great Price

CONTENTS

PREFACE

CONTEMPORARY AMERICAN CATHOLICISM, like its earlier forms, appears to many outside the tradition as a monolithic unity because of its centralized forms of government and its reliance on institutions as signs of its strength and authority. Yet within Catholicism there are movement and change, adaptation and renewal, a manifold and dizzying diversity, and an openness and freedom that challenge neat historical categories. Whether the historian focuses on the elite articulators and institutional implementations of the Catholic tradition or on the people's reception and the popular, or folk, amalgamative appropriations of that tradition, he or she is in constant danger of overlooking or minimizing something that is significant to the total historical experience. History is not an exact science, and that is nowhere more evident than in the attempts to describe religious traditions—and especially in my own attempts here to make sense of American Catholicism.

This text is divided into two sections, the first being a narrative of selected themes and the second a series of biographical essays. The narrative focuses on the themes of continuity and change, unity and diversity, growth and decline, alienation and reconciliation, as these recur in the institutional, intellectual, spiritual, ethnic, and political or social developments of the church. The first section analyzes in particular how the American experience itself (with its predominantly Protestant and republican culture) has influenced the reception and modification of the Catholic tradition.

The second section of this book contains a series of biographical sketches of significant ecclesiastical and lay leaders in American Catholicism. Because of the limits of space, I have selected only those deemed most important to the church's development. Most, although not all, of the individuals included in the biographical sketches are mentioned in the historical narrative, and where a name is first mentioned it is followed by an asterisk.

This volume also contains a basic chronology of the most important historical events in American Catholicism and a selected list of books for further reading and research.

I am indebted to my teachers Colman Barry, O.S.B., Gerald Fogarty, S.J., and Robert Handy in particular for introducing me to the study of the religious and specifically Catholic dimension of American life. Many other teachers and historians also have a share in this work, some are acknowledged in the notes, but many others remain unacknowledged simply because I have, over the years, appropriated so many of their interpretations that I no longer remember where

I first got them and have unconsciously made their insights my own. I hope, however, that I have given proper citation to sources where I have been explicitly aware of my debt.

I am also grateful for grants from Marquette University's Religious Commitment Fund, the Graduate School, and the sabbatical leave program that enabled me to complete this revised text as well as the original on which it is based. I am thankful, moreover, to my chairmen, Philip Rossi, S.J., and John Laurance, S.J., for periodically providing me with a reduced teaching load to complete this text.

In preparing much of the text I had the pleasure of being aided by a number of graduate research assistants. For their help I would like to thank David Schimpf, Dominic Scibilia, Michael Naughton, Rebecca Kasper, Jonathan Zemler, and Pam Young, C.S.J. Nathan Schmeidicke was particularly helpful in preparing the balance of the text for publication.

This text is dedicated to Phyllis, who has been for over thirty years of married life the pearl of great price of which the Book of Proverbs (31:10) speaks: "A perfect wife—who can find her? She is far beyond the price of pearls."

ABBREVIATIONS

AER	*American Ecclesiastical Review*, 1889–1975 (also called *Ecclesiastical Review*, 1905–1943).
CDF	Congregation (Roman) for the Doctrine of the Faith
CH	*Church History*
CHR	*Catholic Historical Review*
CTSA	Catholic Theological Society of America
JCP	*The John Carroll Papers,* ed. Thomas O'Brien Hanley, 3 vols. (Notre Dame, Ind.: University of Notre Dame Press, 1976).
NCCB/USCC	National Council of Catholic Bishops/United States Catholic Conference (1966), successor to NCWC
NCR	*National Catholic Reporter*
NCWC	National Catholic War Council (1917); National Catholic Welfare Council (1919); National Catholic Welfare Conference (1922).
NYT	*New York Times*
PL	*Pastoral Letters of the United States Catholic Bishops*, ed. Hugh J. Nolan, 5 vols. (Washington, D.C.: NCCB/USCC, 1989); *Pastoral Letters and Statements of the United States Catholic Bishops*, vol. 6, *1989–1997*, ed. Patrick W. Carey (Washington, D.C.: NCCB/USCC, 1998)
RACHS	*Records of the American Catholic Historical Society of Pennsylvania*
TS	*Theological Studies*
USCC	United States Catholic Conference, see NCCB/USCC
USCCB	United States Conference of Catholic Bishops (2000), successor to NCCB/USCC
U.S.CH	*U.S. Catholic Historian*

1

---·•·---

COLONIAL CATHOLICISM: 1492–1840

FROM THE SIXTEENTH to the early nineteenth century, Spanish, French, and English missionaries, merchants, explorers, soldiers, governors, and their servants and slaves brought a Catholic presence to the New World. As part of the colonial expansion of their respective empires, the missionaries came to sustain the religious life of their compatriots and to evangelize the newly discovered peoples who inhabited the lands the colonials explored. They intermittently established parishes and missions to the Indians on the southern borderlands of the present United States from Florida to the Southwest, along the California coastland, on the northern borderlands from the St. Lawrence Seaway to the western Great Lakes, down the Mississippi River to New Orleans, and on the Mid-Atlantic coastlands of Maryland and Pennsylvania.

From the mid-sixteenth century onward, Catholicism existed in numerous isolated and loosely organized religious communities shepherded primarily by missionaries who were, until 1790, without the benefit of the episcopacy and other major ecclesiastical institutions. The missionary enterprise was motivated by the long Christian tradition of spreading the faith and by the exploratory, colonizing, commercial, and military aims of the empires it represented. The execution of these mixed motives produced both good and bad results, from the establishment of the first stable Spanish parish and mission in St. Augustine, Florida, in 1565 to the eventual secularization of the Spanish Indian missions in California in the 1830s. Because the missionary efforts were so closely aligned with the strengths and weaknesses of the states they represented, they generally experienced the fate of the political bodies with which they were identified. Spanish and French Catholicism waned as soon as did Spanish and French political power; English Catholicism persisted because it was hitched to Anglo-American fortunes.

SPANISH MISSIONS

On 12 October 1492, under the patronage of the Spanish, the Italian navigator Christopher Columbus and his sailor companions landed on one of the

Bahamian Islands and named it San Salvador. That discovery opened up for the Spanish empire a new era of discovery, colonization, and evangelization, but also expansionism, cupidity, and rapacity. By the mid-sixteenth century, Spanish commercial and military powers as well as a full complement of ecclesiastical institutions (including dioceses, bishoprics, schools, and numerous missions) were well established throughout the Antilles, Mexico, and Central and South America. By that time, too, the Spanish had explored the regions north of their central power bases—from Florida across the southern part of the United States into Texas and Mexico; from Mexico into the northern interiors of New Mexico, Arizona, and Kansas (discovering in the process the Colorado River, the Rio Grande River, and the Grand Canyon); and from Mexico along the California coast to San Francisco.

The Spanish decided to establish military and ecclesiastical institutions on the northern reaches of their southern empire not because they discovered gold or commercial advantage in these lands, but primarily because they feared foreign— French, English, Russian, or American Indian—encroachments upon their southern American empire. In 1565, for example, Spain established a military outpost and a mission at St. Augustine in Florida once it learned that French Huguenots had planted a colony north of St. Augustine. Later, because of the threat of English colonies to the north, Spain sustained St. Augustine as a strategic outpost in the defense of the empire. New Spain established permanent settlements and supported missionary efforts in Texas only at the beginning of the eighteenth century because of French presence at New Orleans and along the Mississippi River. The early establishments in Arizona at the end of the seventeenth and beginning of the eighteenth centuries were in response to the threat of American Indian invasions of Spanish territories further south. The late eighteenth- and early nineteenth-century Spanish movements into Upper California were reactions to the Russian settlements in Alaska. The one exception to this defensive posture appears to be the motivation for building Santa Fe and other New Mexican military and missionary outposts in the early seventeenth century.

The missions to the Indians as well as the presidios were, in Herbert E. Bolton's phrase, "outposts of empire." The intersecting of religious and military objectives was clear in the establishment of these two characteristic institutions of the Spanish empire on the northern frontier.[1] The presidio protected the Spanish empire further south, provided military assistance to the Indian missions, and helped enforce Christian discipline within them. The missions themselves provided the benefits of religion to the military, served as buffer zones between the Spanish military outposts and unfriendly Indians, became listening posts that provided the military with intelligence about warring Indian tribes and the movements of the French and English, and supplied the military with Christianized Indians to wage war against unfriendly Indians and invading foreigners.

For three centuries, Spanish missionaries developed five major mission territories on the North American frontiers and worked to convert the Indians to Christianity. Although the duration of these Indian missions varied from territory to territory, they all passed through three similar phases of historical development: establishment and organization, a golden age of success and prosperity, and, because of various internal and external problems, a period of decline and ruin from which they never rebounded even though some Spanish Catholic influence lingered on in these territories. The Florida missions lasted 198 years (1565–1763), those in New Mexico 230 years (1598–1680; 1692–1840), those in Texas 134 years (1659–1793),[2] those in Arizona 142 years (1700–1842), and those in California 65 years (1769–1834).

The Spanish established the missions to evangelize the Indians and thereby save their souls. To accomplish these goals they frequently sought to separate the Indians from their former way of life and to introduce and incorporate them into Spanish culture. The two complementary methods, separation and incorporation, were so integrally related that it was difficult for the Spanish or the Indians to distinguish between them. The missionaries believed that all people, Indians and Spaniards alike, were subjects of sin and redemption. The missionaries' task was to preach the good news of Christian redemption and free the Indians from their condition of sinful bondage. Many missionaries, however, identified the universal condition of sin with the Indian culture, which they saw as pagan and corrupt. Redemption and conversion meant more to these missionaries than freedom from the universality of sin; it meant that Indian civilization itself had to be replaced by a Christianized Spanish culture.[3] Such a conception of the missionary task remained the dominant tradition among the Spanish from the sixteenth to the nineteenth century.

The Spanish missionaries emphasized not so much individual conversions as the communal means necessary for living a sanctified Christian life. Prior to baptism, the missionaries gave their prospective converts a basic introduction to the *Credo*, believing that such a rudimentary knowledge of Christianity was all that European Catholic peasants possessed. But even this elementary introduction to Christianity could take years, because the missionaries had to learn the Indian languages, discover concepts that could communicate the message of Christian redemption, and convince their prospective converts of the benefits of Christianity.

The missionaries also provided new forms of communal and cultural supports for the Christian neophytes. Once baptized, the Indians were generally separated from their tribes to form new Christian communities. Under the guidance of the missionaries, the new Christians lived a routine quasi-monastic life of worship and work. In this ideal setting they were to experience regular hours of prayer, a cycle of annual liturgical celebrations, a cult of Mary and the saints, seasons of fasting, and daily catechetical instruction. Within such a communal life, the children of the new converts would receive baptism and likewise be nurtured in the Christian life.

Life in an Indian mission also demanded Christian discipline. Those who offended the moral and civil standards of mission life were duly punished, and those who ran away were brought back to the missions by military force. Once baptized and initiated into the Christian community, the converts were expected to live in conformity with Christian and moral standards of Spanish social life.

The Spanish conceived of the Indian missions as transitory institutions that would provide the means of redemption, a basic evangelical introduction to and experience of Christian living, communal support, discipline, and a system for weaning the Christian neophytes away from their former pagan lifestyle. Regular hours for work in fields, tending cattle, preparing food, and building homes, churches, and other institutions for the mission became a significant part of mission life for the Indians and their clergy. Such a sedentary lifestyle fitted the Spanish pattern of civilization and religion, but it was frequently contrary to the nomadic style of life led by many Indians. Although the missionaries learned how the Indians lived off the land, they taught them how to use the implements and arts of Spanish culture to provide for themselves in a Spanish Christian society.

On occasion, some Spanish missionaries adapted themselves to Indian culture as a means of evangelization. This second method, although frequently a part of the practice of separation and incorporation, demonstrated respect for Indian customs and used Indian languages as a means of communicating the Christian gospel. From Bartolomé de Las Casas in the sixteenth century to Eusebio Kino,* S.J., in the eighteenth, moreover, missionaries here and there—horrified by the soldiers' rapacity, the merchants' and traders' cupidity, and the state's destruction of the Indians and their way of life—saw themselves as defenders of the Indians' natural rights and as barriers against the harsh and unjust governmental treatment and official massacres of the Indians. Although some missionaries were rigorous disciplinarians within the Indian missions, they rarely exercised the kind of violence that issued from other quarters of Spanish society. The line between the missionaries' complicity and their actual participation in the demolition of Indian culture was generally very thin, however.

Although the missions had some successes, they did not flourish for long nor did they serve a significant percentage of the Indian population. Eventually they all came to an end. In 1859 John Gilmary Shea, a historian of American Catholicism, wrote that the cause of their annihilation was not some inherent weakness in the mission system. For him, "the interference of government alone crushed them; . . . their ruin is chargeable to the English and Mexican governments, and to the inborn hostility of the Anglo-Saxon race to the Indians."[4] Internal difficulties, however, as well as external forces created, even in times of success, setbacks and eventually a period of decline and ruin.

Most of the missions shared similar internal reasons for their ultimate decline and failure. For almost three hundred years, Catholicism on the northern frontiers of the Spanish empire was much like a preparatory school that had no available higher education. The Spanish Indian missions, although here and there temporarily successful, never developed Indian churches with native dioceses, bishops, parish priests, and all the sacramental and educational means necessary for nurturing and sustaining a mature Christian community. The

Spanish commitment to the missionary efforts on the northern borderlands was never more than tenuous and marginal. Spain did not have the resources or the power to build the institutions necessary to sustain the Catholic Church in North America. The establishment of the Spanish church would have brought with it the full complement of Spanish political, financial, and military power—as it had in Mexico and other Spanish dominions—but this never happened in the North American Spanish colonies. In the larger conception of Spanish policy in the Americas, as Bolton pointed out, the borderland missions were from their origins to their end mere defensive "outposts of empire."

Missionary success, even with the full complement of Spanish resources, would have been limited because of the clash of cultures. The Spanish Christian and the Indian cultures never accommodated themselves very easily to one another. The missionaries, soldiers, and governors, moreover, generally agreed that the best way to Christianize the Indians was to destroy their culture or at least keep the baptized Indians separated from their pagan backgrounds. Frequently the converted Indians living in the sedentary missions felt the pull of their former nomadic way of life and ran away, only to be brought back forcibly by the arm of the law. Some missionaries, though, believed that it was unrealistic to expect the Indians to separate themselves completely from their former cultures. In 1714, Antonio de Miranda, O.F.M., recommended that the missionary have patience in weaning the Indians from their former lifestyles: "Little by little he [the missionary] removes the weeds, and through patience he comes to see the garden free of darnel. But to will that the new plant bear leaves, flowers, and fruit all at once is to will not to harvest anything."[5]

Not all missionaries were as patient or hopeful about Christianizing the Indians or retaining the new converts. Father Joseph Perez, O.F.M., complained in 1817 that, after 130 years of missionary preaching at San Ignacio Mission in Arizona, only those Christian Indians who had died were safe (i.e., saved). "The grownups are full of superstitions, and no matter how the ministers work they do not believe them because they have more faith in their old medicine men."[6] After generations of missionary preaching and teaching, the missionaries could not eradicate the pull of the Indian way of life, and the Indians continued to practice their old religions.

Other internal forces eventually brought the missions to an end. Many missionaries failed to learn the Indian languages and cultures and failed to translate Christianity into Indian ways of thinking. The Indians themselves, because of the harsh treatment they received, periodically rebelled against Spanish military intrusions and missionary tactics. The cycle of revolt and Spanish retaliations increased the instability of mission life and, in many cases, brought about the ruin of the missions. Church–state conflicts, usually between the missionaries and the military governors over jurisdiction and control of the Indians, also contributed to the decline. The inability of the Spanish to provide a constant supply of food and other material benefits, which were used to induce the Indians to remain in the missions, caused Indians to abandon their Christian missions. Deadly diseases, some of them brought by the Europeans, were also frequent visitors at the missions, and many Indians feared that the missionaries and the missions themselves were causes of death.

Even if the missions could have held up under the burdens of their own internal difficulties, they could not withstand the external forces that eventually destroyed them. The Anglo-American military force against the missions in Florida, the constant raids of unfriendly Indian tribes in Texas and the Southwest, the loss of Spanish political power and stability in the eighteenth and early nineteenth century, the Spanish removal of the Jesuit missionaries in the late eighteenth century, the Mexican War of Independence (1810–1820), the struggle for Texas independence (1820–1836), and the Mexican secularization of the California missions in the 1830s–all of these diverted political and economic attention away from the missions, leaving them without the supports necessary for their survival.

In terms of Christian intention, the missions were successful even though they had only a few lasting monuments to their credit. The gospel was preached, the kingdom of Christ was being spread to the "ends of the earth," genuine converts undoubtedly were made, salvation was made possible for numbers of natives, and missionaries fulfilled their own Christian responsibilities with zeal. These kinds of successes are not easily measured by the historian.

Although Spanish Catholicism was unsuccessful in making many Christian converts of the Indians, it did leave a remnant of Catholic presence in the territories the Spanish missionaries originally discovered and evangelized. That remnant became the foundation of an episcopally organized church. Cuba established a diocese in New Orleans in 1793 and sent a bishop, Luis Ignacio Marie de Penalver y Cardenas-Porro, there until 1801; Mexico appointed Francisco Garcia-Diego y Moreno to the two Californias in 1840. For the most part, though, the Americans would be responsible for establishing the institutional church in those areas. They erected dioceses and sent bishops to Galveston in 1842, Santa Fe and Monterey in 1850, St. Augustine in 1857, and Tucson in 1868. That is a story, however, for nineteenth-century American Catholicism.

FRENCH MISSIONS

The acquisition of fish and fur and a desire to spread the faith brought French Catholics to North America in the seventeenth century. From Acadia to the St. Lawrence Seaway to the Great Lakes and down the Mississippi to the Gulf of Mexico, the French established a colonial empire that encircled the English colonies to the south and east and provided a buffer for the Spanish to the west. Although the French built a few missionary outposts within the present boundaries of the United States, they had little success in sustaining them except in New Orleans, where the French presence continued to have a significant impact throughout the eighteenth and nineteenth centuries. Detroit, Vincennes, and St. Louis, too, maintained some French Catholic connections into the early nineteenth century, but for all practical purposes, Americans overtook those towns shortly after the American Revolution. French missionary efforts to evangelize the Indians, although zealous and heroic, also had minimal lasting effects.

After a period of discovery and exploration in the early sixteenth century under Jacques Cartier and a few missionary efforts among the Indians in Acadia in the early seventeenth century, Samuel de Champlain founded Quebec (1608), which became the center of French commercial, political, and ecclesiastical work in the New World. Like Spain, France was a Catholic confessional state. The Gallican church and state enjoyed an alliance in the sixteenth, seventeenth, and eighteenth centuries that made it very difficult at times to distinguish political, commercial, and missionary goals; the three were so intertwined that the successes and failures of one depended on those of the other two. Financial support for the missionaries, for example, periodically depended on their benefit to the state's military and commercial objectives, which periodically warred with religious concerns. Church and state used each other to advance their own causes, even when those causes were not entirely compatible or reconcilable. In such circumstances of alliance, tensions between the church and the state were almost inevitable.

By the end of the seventeenth century, New France had developed both a colonial and a missionary church.[7] The colonial church, an extension of the Gallican church, had its headquarters in Quebec, where the first bishop, François de Montmorency de Laval, was consecrated in 1674 and where the French constructed a number of parishes, hospitals, seminaries, schools, and convents to serve the French and the Indians. Quebec was the structural backbone of the colonial church. Within the present borders of the United States, the colonial church was for the most part far removed from the center of ecclesiastical power and supervision. Parishes for the French were established, for example, in Cahokia (1698), Biloxi (1699), Detroit (1704), Mobile (1710), New Orleans (1718), Vincennes (1734), Duquesne (1754), and a few other places in the Midwest during the mid-eighteenth century. Although the stories of these churches are significant, the most dramatic of the French efforts to plant the church in New France are found in the missionary efforts toward the Indians.

The French developed a missionary church to the Indians alongside and at times as part of the colonial church. French missionaries (Capuchins, Recollects, and especially Jesuits) evangelized, baptized, and established mission stations among the Abenakis in Nova Scotia and Maine periodically from 1610 to 1763, when France ceded Canada to England; among the Indians along the St. Lawrence Seaway (at Tadoussac, Quebec, Sillery, Three Rivers, and Montreal); among the Hurons below the Georgian Bay from 1634 until the Iroquois massacres of 1649; among the upstate New York Iroquois from the early 1650s to the 1680s; among the Hurons and other tribes in the far west at Sault Ste. Marie (Michigan) and Keweenaw Bay on Lake Superior in the 1660s; and, after Louis Jolliet and Jacques Marquette* explored the Mississippi River in 1673, a few missionaries were sent to the Illinois and other tribes in Michigan, Illinois, and Indiana.

Although the French Indian missions had the same ultimate purposes as the Spanish, they did not always engage in the same missionary strategies. At the beginning of the seventeenth century, many of the Jesuit missionaries tried to adapt themselves to the nomadic Indian life, but soon abandoned this procedure because it proved ineffective in establishing a stable Christian life among the tribes. Later they tried to convert the Indians to a sedentary life that would enable the missionaries to evangelize the Indians more effectively, instruct them in the Christian rituals, wean them from customs and practices that were inconsistent with Christian morality, and preserve them in a disciplined Christian way of life. Like the Spanish to the south and like their Jesuit brethren in Paraguay, the French Jesuits built missions they referred to as "reductions" to separate the Christian Indians from the villages of unconverted Indians.[8] The Jesuit missions to the Georgian Bay Hurons, although brief, were the most effective of the French reductions. There the Jesuits built prayer huts (or churches) within the Indian tribal territories and, like the Spanish, tried to develop a regular cycle of Christian life and discipline within a Christian communal context.

Although the French Jesuits in particular accepted and lived with many of the existing Indian customs and sought to show the Christian dimension of indigenous beliefs and morals, they resisted those things in the Indian way of life that they considered contrary to Christianity. Polygamy especially had the force of tradition within the Indian communities and frequently pulled the new converts away from the disciplined Christian life. One Jesuit reported, "of all the Christian laws which we propound to them, there is not one that seems as hard to them as that which forbids polygamy, and does not allow them to break the bonds of lawful marriage."[9] The Indians hated these restrictions on their liberties, and the Jesuits discovered that the Christian Indians often found a monogamous marriage too difficult and frequently entered into scandalous relationships after conversion. The Indians resisted not only assimilation into a French life-style but also into a Christian moral life that conflicted with their own former religious traditions and customs, which had the sanction of their own communities. The Indian missionaries, like their third-century Christian predecessors, tried to separate the newly baptized and the catechumens permanently from former practices and customs that were opposed to Christian tradition, but they were successful only where they were able to sustain a mission for a period of generations.

Even within the sedentary missions, however, the missionaries soon discovered that the strategy of separation would not be effective unless it were accompanied by a genuine attempt to accommodate themselves to those things in the Indian lifestyle that were not inherently repugnant to Christianity. As one Jesuit put it in 1667–1668:

We must then follow them [because we cannot expect to instruct them when they only occasionally come to us] to their homes and adapt [s'accommoder] ourselves to their ways, however ridiculous they may appear, in order to draw them to ours. And, as God made himself man in order to make men Gods, a Missionary does not fear to make himself a Savage, so to speak, with them, in order to make them Christians. *Omnibus omnia factus sum.*[10]

Whatever their methods, the French missionaries believed that God alone was the founder of the Indian as well as the primitive church. The Jesuits in particular believed that martyrdom was the premier providential sign that God was directing the establishment of the churches in the wilderness. In 1639 the Jesuit Jerome Lalemant feared that the missions might be in bad shape because no priest had yet been martyred for the cause.[11] His fear was unwarranted. In subsequent years the *Jesuit Relations* (reports the Jesuit missionaries sent back to France) were filled with accounts of the martyrdoms of the Jesuits Isaac Jogues,* Jean de Brébeuf, and numerous other Jesuits and Indian converts.[12] The story of Indian brutality against Jogues reads like stylized early Christian martyrologies:

> He was greeted with a hundred beatings at the entrance to the Village where he was first conducted; there was no good mother's son who did not fling his paw or claw on this poor victim,—some struck him with heavy blows of cords, others with blows of sticks; some pulled and carried away the hair of his head; others, in derision, tore out the hair of his beard. A woman, or rather a Megera, takes his arm and cuts off, or rather saws off, with knife the thumb of his left hand; she cuts a gash, and goes in quest of the joint, with less skill, but with more cruelty than a butcher exercises upon a dead beast; in short, she lacerates and removes the whole mass of the thumb. Another bites one of the fingers of his right hand, injures the bone, and renders that poor finger crippled and useless; others tear out his nails, then put fire on the end of those poor fingers,—laid bare, in order to render the martyrdom more keenly felt. For all these pains, the poor Father had no other Physician or other Surgeon than patience; no other salve than pain, no other cover than the air which surrounded his wounds.[13]

Jogues found the "Royal Road of the Holy Cross" in the *Imitation of Christ* to be a fundamental source of "great peace, and repose in occasions of suffering."[14] Denying self, taking up the cross daily, and shedding one's blood as a witness to the Christian faith were the means of establishing God's glory in the missions. Repeatedly the missionaries recalled for their French-reading audience the maxim of early Christianity that the "blood of the martyrs is the seed of the church."

Measured by the rod of human efficiency, historical efficacy, and ecclesiological stability and permanence, the French Indian missions within the present borders of the United States were generally failures. They produced few lasting results and collapsed for many of the same reasons that the Spanish missions miscarried. The French efforts were also doomed by the cession of Canada to England in 1763, the decline of Jesuit presence after the papal suppression of 1773, and a more general lack of sufficient personnel to serve the huge geographical expansion from the Niagara to New Orleans. By the end of the eighteenth century, for all practical purposes, the French Indian missions ceased to have any major impact, although a few Indians in the interiors of Indiana and

Illinois throughout the latter half of the eighteenth and early part of the nine-teenth century continued to be served by French priests and would for years carry memories of the French blackrobes within their communities. Measured by the missionaries' standards of Christian witness or by the criterion of human courage and dedication, the Indian missions were a major achievement.

ENGLISH MISSIONS

From 1634 to 1776, English Catholics planted and sustained their religion in the colonies of Maryland and Pennsylvania, and, unlike their Spanish and French neighbors, they did so without the benefit of governmental financial or legal support and without the burden of serving in vast geographical territories. Unlike the Spanish and French, too, English Catholics were geographically sur-rounded by and lived in the midst of Protestants, who had previously built colonies in Virginia and Massachusetts and who were, from the beginning, a majority even within Maryland. Unlike their coreligionists to the north and south, moreover, the English Jesuits very quickly (i.e., by the 1640s) abandoned any efforts to evangelize and serve the Indians in Maryland (even though they originally intended to do so) and concentrated their religious efforts on the Catholic colonists. Catholic presence in the English colonies, furthermore, un-like that of the Spanish and French missions, provided a firm foundation for a lasting influence of Catholicism in the United States.

In 1633 the English Catholic Cecil Calvert,* who had inherited his father George's* possessions and intention to establish a colony in the New World, obtained from King Charles I a charter that acknowledged Cecil's "laudable, and pious Zeal for extending the Christian Religion, and also the Territories of our Empire."[15] The charter made Cecil the sole proprietor. It indicated that Maryland—like other English, Spanish, and French colonies—was established with mixed political, commercial, and religious motivations. Calvert appealed to Protestant and Catholic investors to initiate the Maryland project, but he re-ceived his greatest financial support from seventeen young Catholic gentry. In fact, Catholics had, at least during the seventeenth century, a predominance of financial and political clout in the colony. The charter also gave Calvert the same patronage rights over the colony that the bishop of Durham had over that English province—that is, the power to erect and found all churches and chapels and the exemption from all laws of mortmain. To provide for the religious needs, Calvert invited the Jesuits to join the colony and, appealing to their missionary zeal, indicated that he wanted them to evangelize the Indians.

With these purposes in mind, Calvert's two ships, the Ark and the Dove, set sail and landed in Maryland in 1634. The 150 or so persons on board, mostly Protestant, included Calvert's brother Leonard, who was appointed governor of the new colony, three Jesuits (Fathers Andrew White and John Altham and Brother Thomas Gervase), and a number of young Catholic investors. Although the colony was erected under the authority of a Protestant king, no Protestant ministers came with the first expedition, and in fact, ministers of the Church of England would not appear in the colony until twenty years later.

Throughout the colonial period, the Jesuits provided the only Catholic religious leadership in Maryland and Pennsylvania and, as R. Emmett Curran has noted, "constituted, almost exclusively, the institutional church in British America."[16] During the first 150 years, 113 Jesuit priests and thirty brothers served within the Maryland Province—although no more than five priests and four brothers served at any one time during the seventeenth century. The numbers of priests increased slightly in the eighteenth century, but by 1772 there were only twenty-three priests in the colony.[17] In terms of numbers, the English Catholic colony was far less impressive than the Catholic colonies to the south and north.

The Jesuits built plantation manors, much like those of other Maryland gentlemen, upon lands they received or purchased from the proprietor. Like other gentlemen planters, moreover, they eventually bought and sold black slaves to farm their plantations. By 1785 black Catholics, primarily slaves, made up more than 20 percent of Maryland's total Catholic population.[18] These plantations became the primary temporal support for the Jesuits' religious activities. Although the plantations forced the Jesuits to become involved in managing temporalities, which took time away from their religious mission, they freed the Jesuits from the temporal authority and control of the landed gentry (who had controlled the Jesuits in England) and enabled them to enjoy a certain amount of de facto separation from the proprietor and local Maryland government. This separation also, as Gerald Fogarty has noted, "planted the seeds from which would grow the American Catholic tradition of religious liberty."[19]

The Jesuits were primarily responsible for sustaining and developing Catholic spiritual life not only in Maryland throughout the seventeenth and eighteenth centuries but also in Pennsylvania, where Irish and German immigrants and Maryland migrants had established Catholic communities at Conewago, Goshenhoppen, and Philadelphia during the eighteenth century. Like itinerant preachers in the nineteenth century, the Jesuits carried the chalice and Bible into the outlying regions of Maryland and Pennsylvania. On Sundays, either at the plantations, which became the liturgical centers of Catholic life during the entire colonial period, or at the mission stations outside the plantations, they observed a regular routine of hearing confessions, celebrating Mass, preaching, and giving catechetical instruction to adults and children.

The Jesuits fostered an Ignatian spirituality by leading prominent laity through the *Spiritual Exercises* and by encouraging study, reading, prayer, and meditation. They also tried periodically to establish some schools in Maryland for the education of Catholics, but because of a lack of resources and the penal laws, these schools never lasted beyond a few years. What little religious education there was took place within the manors, at the liturgical centers, and through the lending libraries some Jesuits set up at their plantations. Jesuits circulated Bibles, theology texts, apologetic works, and particularly devotional and spiritual manuals to the laity.[20] They also established religious confraternities to encourage personal meditation, adoration of the Blessed Sacrament, and devotion to the Sacred Heart—traditions that Jesuits had fostered in their European colleges and universities. It appears from some sources that these Jesuits were trying to erect in the Maryland wilderness quasi-collegial Catholic communities. Small prayer groups and reading circles served as cells of Christian growth and development within the larger communities—much like the schools of Lutheran pietism or the class meetings of John Wesley. Building up a devotional elite within the community was consistent with the sixteenth-century Jesuit tradition.

Eighteenth-century Maryland Catholic spirituality, like that in England, was also influenced to a considerable extent by the writings of Richard Challoner, vicar apostolic of London. His *Catholic Christian Instructed* (1737) and *Garden of the Soul* (1740) typified the kind of spirituality that was proposed for eighteenth-century English-speaking Catholics. The *Garden of the Soul* was a spiritual manual intended, as its subtitle indicated, for the English Catholic laity who, "Living in the World, Aspire to Devotion."[21] It prescribed spiritual practices that individuals could perform at home and in the ordinary conditions of their life in English society, and fostered a type of piety that was simple, sober, and unostentatious, befitting cultural circumstances of English and colonial Catholicism. Colonial Catholics did not always have the benefit of clerical and sacramental services, and those who were far removed from the liturgical centers probably conducted their own religious practices and observances within their homes. Colonial religious life was a low-profile experience; Catholics carried on their religious traditions as quietly and privately as possible so as not to offend their neighbors and create a cause for open oppression. As the number of clergy and churches increased in Maryland during the latter half of the eighteenth century, the center of religious life, as Jay Dolan has pointed out, shifted from the home to the parish churches,[22] making the public expression of Catholicism more visible than had been the case earlier.

From the very beginning of the Maryland enterprise, Catholics and other Christians enjoyed an unprecedented degree of religious toleration. In 1632 Cecil Calvert gave his brother Leonard some instructions about conduct on board ship that indicate the low religious profile that would characterize the colony in the future: "be careful to preserve unity and peace amongst all the passengers on Shipp-board." They were to give no offence to Protestants, perform their religious services "as privately as may be," and should not even engage Protestants in discussions of religious matters. Calvert's highest priority as proprietor of the new colony was to maintain the colony's political and social harmony. Religion, he warned, should not be a source of civil disturbance.[23]

Until 1649, religious toleration derived from the proprietor's fiat, and thereafter it became the result of a legal enactment that Cecil Calvert had encouraged the Maryland Assembly to make. In 1649, Calvert argued that God desired unity and peace and "commands us to love one another; Christian Religion teaches us soe to doe for the accomplishment of Eternal happiness and human polity also adviseth it [for] our temporal felicity in this World."[24] Religious toleration was a necessary means to civil peace and was the surest way to secure God's blessings on Maryland. The Maryland Assembly wrote an Act Concerning Religion (1649) that privileged Christianity, provided for toleration of all Christians, and imposed civil penalties and fines for blasphemy, derogatory talk against Mary, the apostles, and the evangelists, and for profanation of the Sabbath.[25] The colonials had learned from experience, as the act indicated, that the legal establishment of religion had frequently "fallen out to be of dangerous Consequence in those commonwealthes where it hath been practiced."[26]

In 1654 a Puritan-controlled assembly revised the Act of 1649, excluding Catholics from general toleration. The revision, however, did not take permanent effect, and the colony continued to enjoy a general toleration for all Christians until the Glorious Revolution, in 1689, when the king replaced the lord proprietor, and gradually thereafter Catholics were excluded from the colony's political life. In 1702 the Church of England was established by law, and Catholics were finally disfranchised in 1718. The Jesuit Peter Attwood complained that the earlier Maryland tradition, unlike that of other colonies, had extended traditional English freedoms to Catholics. The great reversal of that tradition in the aftermath of the Glorious Revolution was a violation of the common law.[27] The complaint was of no avail. Catholics would thereafter become second-class citizens and feel the sting, if not the rigors, of the establishment and penal law system.

From the beginnings of Maryland until the Glorious Revolution, prominent land-owning Catholic families, many related to the proprietor by marriage, had enjoyed social and economic prestige in the colony and an almost privileged status in its political life. These court Catholics helped to preserve Catholic freedoms but also caused a great deal of jealousy within the Protestant majority. Such political circumstances help to explain some of the dynamics behind the great reversal after the Glorious Revolution. Prominent Maryland Catholics continued to maintain some of their social and economic prestige, but because of legal restrictions, they no longer took part in Maryland's political activities. This situation enabled them to develop their plantations and commercial interests. The first Charles Carroll illustrates the point. He came to Maryland in 1688 to be Calvert's attorney general, but because of the revolution he was unable to serve in that capacity. Instead, he began to lay the foundations for what would become a significant fortune for the Carroll family. Prominent land-wealthy Catholics like the Carrolls continued to intermarry and pass on their fortunes to their heirs, giving them economic security in a colony where they did not have much political security or exercise any political functions. It would be from many of these prominent Maryland Catholics that significant support for the American Revolution would come between 1765 and 1776.

In 1765, the year of the Stamp Act, 256 Maryland Catholic gentlemen and in 1773 a few Jesuits, desirous of maintaining their low-profile Catholicism, protested against rumors that the vicar apostolic of London, Richard Challoner, wanted to establish a Catholic bishop in Maryland. They saw such an action as an occasion for increased Protestant opposition to Catholicism.[28] These Catholics, moreover, could not have been unaware of the increasing American resistance to the establishment of an Anglican episcopacy in the colonies. Many Anglo-Americans feared what Sydney Ahlstrom has called the "deeply ingrained 'anti prelatical' bias" that was a part of "the drift of American opinion" during the pre-revolutionary years in the American colonies.[29] The establishment of an Anglican episcopacy would mean, they feared, the imposition of greater restrictions on colonial freedoms. The episcopacy was seen as an instrumental means for reinforcing political oppression, a view that only gradually died out in American consciousness.[30] Maryland Catholics did not have any anti-prelatial biases, but they did fear the Protestant animus against the episcopacy and what that animosity might do to their own already limited liberties within the colony.

By 1773, the year of the Boston Tea Party, Charles Carroll of Carrollton,* the third Charles of that family, emerged as a significant political figure in Maryland. Carroll took up his pen in the *Maryland Gazette* to defend local autonomy and the constitutional rights of the Maryland legislature against what he perceived to be the usurpation of governor Robert Eden's proclamation establishing officers' fees in the colony.[31] Under the pseudonym "First Citizen," Carroll criticized the governor's proclamation as an abuse of power and defended the legislature's constitutional rights.

Daniel Dulany, a Maryland attorney who had supported the governor, took issue with Carroll's position and charged, in ad hominem fashion, that Carroll, a Catholic, was disqualified from the debate. He was legally incapable of belonging to any branch of the legislature, could not even vote for representatives, and in fact was disabled by his own Catholic principles, which were distrusted by the laws, from interfering in the election of members.[32] Carroll shot back that his own "speculative notions of religion" and religious affiliation were private matters that had nothing to do with the interpretation of constitutional principles.[33]

Like other Enlightenment figures, Carroll had clearly separated religion and politics, had done much to raise the issues of natural rights and constitutional procedures, and was hailed as a rising star in the revolutionary generation. The fact that he was a Catholic did not seem to bother those who sided with him. His political prominence in this debate, though, did much to bring about a new era of religious toleration and eventually of religious liberty for Catholics.

Toleration for Catholics, however, was not easily won in America, as evidenced by the American reaction to the British Parliament's Quebec Act of 1774. Among other things, that act officially and legally acknowledged the Catholic Church in Canada, providing Catholics with the full enjoyment of their religious rights. The First Continental Congress of 1774, like the "Suffolk County Resolves," protested against this act, which was interpreted as "dangerous" not only to the Protestant religion but to the "civil rights and liberties of all Americans."[34] The protests manifested the long-standing colonial Protestant antipathy toward Catholicism as well as a fear of the British Parliament's increasing political tyranny.

The American oratory against the act made it impossible for the colonials to win the Canadians over to the cause of the Revolution. In 1776, however, the

Continental Congress appointed a committee of Samuel Chase, Charles Carroll of Carrollton, and Benjamin Franklin to seek an alliance with the Canadians in the revolt against England. They also sent John Carroll,* Charles's cousin and a priest, to accompany the committee, hoping that his Catholicism would help win over the French-Canadian Catholics. The trip was doomed to failure from the start, but it did reveal a growing awareness of the political, if not religious, openness to and perhaps usefulness of Catholics in the war effort. Religious affiliation could not be overlooked entirely in the common project of war and independence.

During and after the Declaration of Independence, a number of Catholics from Maryland and Pennsylvania participated in the war effort and joined in the political process of constitution-building at the state and federal levels.[35] Daniel Carroll II, Charles's cousin and John's brother, was elected a Maryland state senator and, together with fellow Catholic Thomas Fitzsimmons of Philadelphia, served in the U.S. House of Representatives during the formation of the U.S. Constitution and Bill of Rights. Charles Carroll, however, was by far the most significant Catholic involved in the movement toward American liberty. He had written in favor of a constitutional government, acted as an adviser to the Continental Congress since 1774, made a trip to Canada on behalf of the revolutionary cause, helped form the Maryland State Constitution (1776), which acknowledged religious toleration for all Christians, was for a brief period a member of the U.S. Senate, and was a signer of the Declaration of Independence. In 1829, Carroll told a friend that when he signed the Declaration, he had in view "not only our independence of England but the toleration of all sects, professing the Christian religion, and communicating to them all great rights."[36] For many nineteenth-century American Catholics, Carroll was the paramount symbol of the compatibility of American and Catholic identities.

With the end of the war and the beginning of the process of political reorganization, a new era was dawning for American Catholics—one that would bring greater toleration and eventually religious liberty in the states as well as in the nation as a whole.

2

—————

A FREE CHURCH IN A FREE STATE:
1776–1815

FROM 1776 UNTIL 1815, John Carroll was the central figure in the transformation and institutionalization of American Catholicism. Elected as the first American bishop in 1789, he presided over the initial stages of the development of the Catholic community from a tiny, geographically and politically restricted, colonial priestly mission into a free, geographically expansive, and episcopally organized national church. The Revolutionary War, the subsequent establishment of the U.S. Constitution and Bill of Rights, the French Revolution and the consequent arrival of French émigrés, and westward expansion were crucial events in these developments. By 1815 Catholicism had already undergone what Carroll in 1783 had called "a revolution, if possible, more extrordinary [*sic*], than our political one."[1]

The Catholic Church took institutional shape in a new nation that was significantly influenced by the values of the Enlightenment and republicanism. Carroll, too, had been influenced by a moderate Catholic Enlightenment and had adopted the "language of a Republican."[2] Like many other Christian leaders in American society, he rejected what he considered the dangerous tendencies of an excessive rationalism, but he also tried to accommodate Catholicism to those values in the Enlightenment and in republicanism that he found genuinely consistent with the Catholic tradition.

Like the new nation itself, the American Catholic Church was initially shaped in an atmosphere of unprecedented liberty; it became a free church in a free state. This revolutionary and constitutional arrangement meant more than the removal of civil and political restraints on Catholics. It meant that the church was on its own with regard to internal and external operations. The church was free to communicate the gospel, promote its spiritual and liturgical life, teach its distinctive doctrines, organize its institutions, and encourage its membership to support Catholic life and institutions voluntarily. Of its very nature, moreover, voluntaryism in religion demanded a spiritual revival that was built on personal persuasion. Furthermore, Catholic identity, institutions, and particularly the

Catholic understanding of freedom and religious authority would have to be established anew amid the changing political and cultural circumstances.

Catholics such as John Carroll enthusiastically accepted civil and religious liberties not only because they were beneficial to Catholicism but also because they were thought to be based on principles of reason and revelation.[3] Religious liberty and toleration, however, were not something American Catholics could take for granted in the early years of the new republic. A few states (e.g., Massachusetts, Connecticut, New York, the Carolinas), although granting toleration to Catholics, still retained restrictions on full Catholic participation in the political process. Some individuals, too, periodically advocated more rigorous civil and political strictures on Catholics in the new nation. Such circumstances made John Carroll apprehensive and anxious about the future of full religious freedom for Catholics. In the *Columbian Magazine* in 1787, the *Gazette of the United States* in 1789, and in a 1789 joint address with Catholic laity to George Washington,[4] Carroll advocated the full extension of religious liberty in all state constitutions on the grounds that Catholics like other Americans had contributed their blood for the country's independence, and in justice they deserved equal political opportunity under the law.

The American Catholic encounter with modernity in the form of religious liberty, separation of church and state, and voluntaryism was not worked out with systematic reflection. American Catholics simply accepted the new dynamics and principles of the age and began to make the practical adjustments that were necessary to fortify Catholic religious life and institutions.

Like that of many religious leaders in the new nation, John Carroll's first and abiding concern was for a revival of religious practices. In 1785 he reported that the religious vitality of Catholicism was at an ebb. Catholics in Maryland and Pennsylvania were "rather faithful" to their religious obligations. Most of them went to confession and received the Eucharist once a year, fulfilling their Easter duty, but they rarely received the sacraments at other times during the year, and even when they did they had little religious fervor. By comparison, though, the new immigrants in the trading centers were weak Catholics, not even fulfilling their Easter duty. Almost all Catholics in the United States, too, failed to instruct their children and slaves in the basic elements of the faith. Consequently, many of the young were very lax in their morals.[5]

Carroll's extant sermons,[6] his diocesan synod of 1791, and his letters and instructions to his clergy stress the need for a general renewal of American Catholic piety. That reformation, made possible by the new political circumstances, centered on the two things he perceived to be most wanting—namely, the restoration of traditional Catholic practices, especially the frequent celebration of the Eucharist and Penance, and a conversion of the heart that was essential for a fruitful reception of the Sacraments.

The diocesan synod of 1791 gave its highest priority to the revitalization of sacramental practices.[7] Canonical prescriptions, like those of the diocesan synod, indicate the ideals, not the historical reality. Catholics who lived at great distances from the major liturgical centers rarely had the opportunity, because of the scarcity of clergy, of attending Mass and the Sacraments. Many scattered throughout Maryland and Pennsylvania attended Mass only once every other month. Those few families on the frontier settlements in Kentucky, Tennessee, Ohio, Indiana, and Illinois saw a priest perhaps once or twice a year. In those places, the Catholic faith was kept alive, if at all, through family religious services and prayers. Scarcity of clergy, some wandering and inept priests, weakness of Catholic "fervor," and ignorance of the fundamentals of the Catholic religion were continuing obstacles to the realization of the canonical vision. By 1791, however, the simple goals of a religious revival were set. The real work was to instruct the faithful and motivate them to a true conversion of heart.

Catholics needed a host of ecclesiastical and educational institutions as well as competent personnel to help bring about the converted heart. The creation of new structures and an increase in competent personnel were not in themselves the solution to the problem of religious vitality, but they could at least provide instrumental means to aid the revival. American Catholics, like Americans in general, were caught up in the postrevolutionary process of institutionalization—establishing new political institutions to correspond to republican ideology, reforming older models of ecclesiastical polity to adapt to the new political circumstances, and developing new legal institutions and business enterprises for law, order, and prosperity.

Carroll and the former Jesuit priests took some major steps to form a national church in spiritual communion with Rome—analogous to those in France or Spain—but one that would be adapted to the exigencies of the rising new nation. In the early 1780s they already considered themselves a national clergy. They asked Pope Pius VI in 1783, therefore, for an American superior over the missions because they did not want to give any offense to the new civil government by having their own spiritual jurisdiction depend on some foreign ecclesiastical superior.[8] In 1784 Rome appointed John Carroll as the new American superior.

The appointment of a religious superior of the American missions, however, was not sufficient. The presence of some unruly priests, conflicts in some congregations, and distance from Roman jurisdiction made it increasingly evident by 1788, even to those clergy who had originally resisted it, that the church's future depended on the establishment of an American bishop to enforce ecclesiastical discipline and create a truly national church. The clergy, accordingly, petitioned Pope Pius VI to allow them to elect their own bishop in order to "arouse the least suspicion and opposition among those with whom we live."[9]

As was generally the case in the late eighteenth century, Rome permitted the clergy to elect their own bishops, and John Carroll became the first to be elected in the United States. With the episcopacy thus established in 1789, American Catholics had the full institutional presence of Catholicism for the first time in 156 years. This presence stabilized American Catholicism and enabled the systematic development of other institutions that provided for the religious and cultural needs of the new nation. Now American Catholicism was no longer a Jesuit or former Jesuit mission, even though Rome would consider the United States missionary territory until 1908—a fact that periodically irritated some in the American church.

In 1791, after his consecration in England, Carroll convoked a diocesan synod to consult his clergy on a number of issues: the mode for the continuation of the episcopacy, the ordering and uniform administration of the Sacraments and ecclesiastical discipline, the exterior government of the clergy, and the means for a decent support of the clergy.[10] Although Carroll, like other Gallican-trained clergy, repeatedly spoke of a national church, enthusiastically supported American customs and political ideals, and wanted his people to become American Catholics, this did not mean a severance of communion with Rome. His own experience with the dissolution of the Jesuits made him aware of the dangers of an excessive nationalism and how that could and did injure the church. A synod was one way of bringing about uniform Catholic discipline that would provide a foundation for preserving communion with Rome. The Synod of 1791 enacted a number of decrees that would govern the American church for the next thirty-seven years.

After the synod, Carroll wrote American Catholics a pastoral letter, a practice that would continue throughout the nineteenth and twentieth centuries after national episcopal synods and meetings, outlining the deliberations and stressing in particular the fundamental importance of the Christian education of youth. He encouraged parents themselves to train their children in the virtues of morality and religion and urged those with means to send their sons to Georgetown Academy, which had recently opened. Thorough learning would produce increased piety, and from that piety would flow a constant supply of priestly vocations.[11]

Voluntaryism was also a recurring theme in the pastoral. The need for education, schools, seminaries, and clergy demanded increased voluntary financial support from the laity. Carroll noted that voluntary contributions to the clergy and church were a relatively new practice for most American Catholics. In the immediate past, the Jesuits' plantations had supplied resources for the support of the clergy, but this was no longer sufficient to respond to current exigencies. Carroll appealed to biblical injunctions and the practice of primitive Christianity. He reminded his people, in particular, that the ecclesiastical canons of the Catholic tradition had divided voluntary offerings into three parts: the first for the minister, the second for the poor, and the third for the building and repair of churches.[12]

The synod also discussed means for the continuation of the American episcopacy, but apparently nothing was decided. Two options were available: one was to select a coadjutor, the other was to divide the diocese. Carroll preferred division, but Rome decided in favor of a coadjutor, chosen with the consultative voice of the clergy. In 1792, Carroll continued to advocate the election of bishops. Though he was opposed to an "ecclesiastical democracy" of the kind Bishop John Milner of England had likewise opposed, he sincerely wished "that

Bishops may be elected, at this distance from Rome, by a select body of Clergy, constituting, as it were, a Cathedral chapter. Otherwise, we never shall be viewed kindly by our government here, and discontents, even amongst our own Clergy, will break out."[13] For a variety of reasons, not the least of which was Carroll's increasing reluctance to consult a clergy who had opposed him periodically and had been the source of discontent in a few congregations, the clergy did not formally participate in the election of new bishops.

The first major sign of institutional expansion occurred in 1808, when Rome made Baltimore an archdiocesan see, with suffragan dioceses in Boston, New York, Philadelphia, and Bardstown, Kentucky, and appointed new bishops (i.e., John Cheverus, Luke Concanen, O.P., Michael Egan, O.F.M., and Benedict Joseph Flaget, S.S.). Distance of the congregations from Baltimore and Carroll's age (he was seventy-three in 1808) made it impractical for him to continue to administer the loosely organized body. Although the new bishops functioned more like mendicant priests than European princes of the church, they provided the kind of institutional leadership and jurisdiction that promised a permanent Catholic presence in these rapidly developing areas.

Like many leaders of this age of new institutions, Carroll saw the future of the country and the church in terms of education and piety. He became an original member of the boards of trustees for St. John's College in Annapolis, Maryland, and the University of Pennsylvania, both nondenominational schools. He also envisioned and helped to establish Georgetown College. In 1783, he told an English correspondent, "The object nearest my heart is to establish a college on this continent for the education of youth, which might at the same time be a Seminary for future Clergymen."[14] The future of the church, the continuation of the ministry, and the adaptation of Catholicism to American ideals and circumstances depended upon the schools.[15]

Lack of money and adequate teachers, the perennial problem of Catholic schools in the United States, plagued the new educational adventures from the beginnings. Catholic education in a republican environment was the basis of "all our hopes," as Carroll put it. By the end of his episcopacy in 1815, he had witnessed the establishment of three seminaries for the education of priests, three colleges for men, and several academies for young women.

Schools demanded faculty, and Carroll had a difficult time supplying an adequate one. In 1791, fleeing the terror of the French Revolution, the Paris Sulpicians, an order dedicated to the education of Catholic clergy, came to Baltimore to establish the first seminary in the United States exclusively devoted to the theological education of the clergy. The Sulpicians' formation of the American clergy, their membership in the episcopacy, their involvement in missionary activities in the West, and their advice to the archbishops of Baltimore had a significant Gallican influence on the development of antebellum Catholicism.[16] During the Reign of Terror in France, numerous other French clergymen came to the United States for refuge and began to serve the needs of the rising American church, deepening the Gallican dimension of antebellum American Catholicism.

The French émigrés were well educated in languages and theology, and with their contacts in France, the new French bishops in particular were able to enlist significant numbers of French clergy to serve in American dioceses.

From 1776 to 1815, the number of clergy was greatly increased not only because of the French Revolution and its aftermath, but also because of the newly established seminary and the immigration of other clergy from Europe. In 1785, for example, John Carroll counted 24 priests, most of them ex-Jesuits; by 1808, there were 68; and by 1830, there were 232.[17] The rapid growth of clergy in the Maryland diocese, the most populous center of Catholicism, illustrates this point. In 1785, there were 19 priests in Maryland; by 1818, there were 52—14 were French, 12 Americans, 11 Irish, and the remainder from other European countries.[18] During the Carroll years, moreover, a number of other religious orders of men established themselves in the United States, increasing the number of clergy. The Augustinians came to Philadelphia in 1796, the Dominicans established St. Rose's Priory in Kentucky in 1806, and the former Jesuits became affiliated with the unsuppressed Russian branch of their order in 1804 and were fully restored by papal decree in 1815.

Women religious also contributed to the foundation of the American Catholic educational and social mission during the first period of the church's institutional development.[19] The French Ursulines of New Orleans had established a day school and a boarding school for young women as early as 1727, and during Carroll's days, they continued these services once Louisiana became a part of the United States. The Carmelites (1790), a contemplative order of women, the Poor Clares (1790s), the Visitations (1808), and an order of black Catholic Women, the Oblate Sisters of Providence (1828), founded by Mary Elizabeth Lange,* were all established in Baltimore. Mother Elizabeth Seton* founded the Sisters of Charity of St. Joseph in 1808 at Emmitsburg, Maryland, near Mount St. Mary's, a Sulpician college for young men. The Sisters of Charity grew rapidly and eventually erected houses, orphanages, schools, and hospitals in New York, Philadelphia, and Baltimore. The Sisters of Loretto (1812), the Sisters of Charity (Nazareth, 1812), and the Dominicans (1822) were established in Bardstown, Kentucky, as were the Sisters of Our Lady of Mercy in Charleston (1829). Mother Rose Philippine Duchesne and her Religious of the Sacred Heart, a French order of nuns, came to St. Louis in 1818 and by 1829 had founded a number of schools and hospitals from there to New Orleans. The number of women religious increased from none in the 1780s to 1,344 in 1850.[20] Even by 1818, the number of "young American ladies" who aspired to religious life had risen so dramatically that Baltimore's Archbishop Ambrose Maréchal rejoiced while complaining to Rome that he needed to exercise vigilance "lest more than can be cared for be admitted to the monasteries which exist in my diocese."[21] The numerical growth and geographic expansion of convents demonstrated the widespread religious revival that was taking place in early nineteenth-century Catholicism, and manifested the essential role women religious played in the expansion, institutionalization, and Christian nurture of American Catholicism.

Social, ethnic, racial, and political diversity characterized the lay Catholic community from the beginning of Carroll's episcopacy, and that diversity increased dramatically after his death. The most visible and public-minded Catholics were the old-guard Maryland and Pennsylvania families (e.g., the Neales, Brents, Carrolls, Taneys, Fitzsimons, and Barrys), who had land and wealth, commercial enterprises, foreign educations, social prestige, family ties, and close association with the Federalist Party in politics. They were Catholics by birth, family persuasion, and conviction. Their experiences in colonial times had taught them to separate religion and politics, the spiritual from the temporal realm. Like their Protestant neighbors, they rarely doubted their birthright as Americans and, because of their social positions, were engaged in building the new nation.

Some Catholics outside of Maryland were also "Catholic Citizens," as John Tracy Ellis* called them, who participated actively in American public life.[22] Francis Cooper and Andrew Morris of New York, Father Gabriel Richard of Detroit, and William Gaston of North Carolina, for example, were elected either to the U.S. Congress or to local state legislatures. Roger Brooke Taney* of Baltimore was appointed Chief Justice of the U.S. Supreme Court. Mathew Carey* of Philadelphia placed his wealth, talent, and pen at the service of numerous common political, economic, and social causes. Robert Walsh, also from Philadelphia, entered into the spirit of the nation in 1811 when he launched his *Review of History and Politics* to provide a forum for the rise of a national literature that would display the country's genius and promote liberal and useful science. Like others influenced by the spirit of republicanism, he was interested in the common good. Christianity was the fundamental source of this public-spirited mentality, many like Carey thought, and bishops such as John Carroll and Louis William Dubourg repeatedly spoke of the marriage of religious virtue and public life. Bishop John Cheverus of Boston summed up this attitude when he wrote to Irish Catholic immigrants of Hartford in 1823: "Be sober, honest, and industrious; serve faithfully those who employ you, and show that a good Catholic is a good member of society, that he feels grateful to those who are kind to strangers, and sincerely loves his brethren of all persuasions, though he strictly adheres to the doctrines of his own church."[23]

Other older Catholic families in Maryland and Pennsylvania were farmers, small businessmen, and laborers with varying degrees of wealth and different ethnic and racial origins. Some Indian Catholic families, too, lived in Maine and along the Wabash River in the present state of Indiana. Many Catholic congregations, moreover, had their own local elites—men who were generally elected lay trustees and who financed and governed their congregations' temporalities with a sense of their own responsibility for their local churches. These persons, too, wanted to live in peace with their Protestant neighbors and periodically joined them in common civic enterprises.

The ideal of mingling freely in American society was not just the result of an Anglo-Catholic mentality that had arisen in Maryland and Pennsylvania, as some have argued; it was the necessary result of conditions in the early republic.

French, Irish, Italian, German, Spanish, Portuguese, as well as Anglo-Catholics during this period were in tiny Catholic communities that were inevitably a part of the life of their towns and cities. There were not enough Catholics in any single state or city to create a sense of Catholic or ethnic identity separate from their American identity.

Until the 1790s, southern Anglo-Catholics constituted the majority within the Catholic community, even though there were pockets of German, French, and Irish Catholics. After the 1790s, however, the ethnic character of American Catholicism gradually began to change, and with this change came a host of tensions that would continue to disturb the Catholic community throughout the nineteenth and early twentieth centuries. The French Revolution in 1789 and the San Domingo revolt of black slaves in 1791 brought a host of black and white French-speaking Catholics to eastern seaboard cities. In Baltimore, the Catholic population in 1793 was immediately doubled by boatloads of Catholics from San Domingo. Other seaports experienced similar increases. Even before the San Domingo revolution, wealthy Catholic families, anticipating the revolt, had moved to the United States. This was the case with the Jean-Jacques Berard family who moved to New York City in 1787, bringing with them their black household slave Pierre Toussaint* whose exemplary life of charity and holiness has made him a twenty-first century candidate for canonization as a saint. With the Louisiana Purchase in 1803, moreover, the entire lower Mississippi Valley came into the American Catholic communion and significantly increased the number of black and white French- and Spanish-speaking Catholics in the United States.[24]

Irish immigration also began to change the social character of American Catholicism. Between 1785 and 1805, a steady trickle of Irish Catholic immigrants came to Philadelphia, Boston, New York, Norfolk, and Charleston, bringing enough Catholics to the last four cities to begin new Catholic congregations. The Irish Rebellion of 1798 and continuing economic troubles in Ireland increased Catholic emigration to the United States until it became a veritable flood in the 1830s and 1840s. But, before the Irish immigrants would eventually outnumber the Anglo- and French Catholics, they would have little influence on the selection of the American Catholic hierarchy or the direction of American Catholicism. That is a story that remains to be told.

French and Irish Catholic immigration during the Carroll era, although numerically small by comparison to later years, was significant not only because these immigrants established the first new congregations along the eastern seaboard, but also because they were the first Catholics that Americans in those places would come to know. Internal tensions and ethnic hostilities in these first congregations, in John Carroll's estimation, both broke the Catholic bond of peace and created a bad reputation for Catholics in American society. He advised the new immigrants to become "not Irish, nor English, or French congregations and churches, but Catholic-American" ones.[25] Creating Catholic-American congregations was no easy task for the new immigrants, but they did set up patterns of assimilation and lay forms of ecclesiastical organization that would influence

Catholic presence in these cities for years to come. Necessity, remembered Catholic traditions, the spirit of republicanism in American society, and American laws regarding the incorporation of religious societies were combined in the formation of these new congregations. This combination also produced internal tensions within the Catholic community, which will be described later, as the lay Catholic leaders tried to accommodate themselves and their congregations to the ideals and realities of postrevolutionary America.

By the time John Carroll died in 1815, American Catholicism had been significantly transformed. The establishment of the episcopacy, religious orders, schools, and new congregations provided a solid institutional basis for further growth and development. The Catholic population, which John Carroll estimated at twenty-five thousand in 1785, almost quadrupled by 1815 because of natural increase, immigration, and the acquisition of the Louisiana Territory.[26] Catholicism had also expanded geographically. In 1785 Catholics were primarily located in Maryland and Pennsylvania, with a few in New York and throughout Virginia, but by 1815, they were spread along the eastern seaboard from Maine to Florida, and from Detroit to New Orleans. Anglo- and other ethnic Catholics also became a part of the early American movement into the frontiers of upstate New York, western Pennsylvania, Kentucky, and the Ohio River Valley and the Mississippi River Valley where French Catholics had previously established a few pioneer villages. Wherever Catholics went, they intended to preserve the church by establishing as soon as possible the episcopacy as a permanent sign of the church's presence and as a promise of institutional stability, even when numbers did not justify the erection of new dioceses. Frontier Catholicism would develop rapidly in the remaining antebellum period, but during the beginnings of this rapid growth and extension into the West, American Catholics would experience an age of severe crisis that would threaten to shake the foundations that had just been established.

3

INTERNAL CONFLICTS, NATIVISM, AND IMMIGRANT CATHOLICISM: 1815–1866

FROM THE RISE of Andrew Jackson to the end of the Civil War, American society experienced a new age of intellectual ferment, social and religious reform, economic and cultural disruption, conflicts over slavery, and religious and racial antagonisms that challenged the country's republican fiber and tested its own ideals. The first great economic depression, the Mexican-American War of manifest destiny and expansion, the displacement and removals of the Indians, the California gold rush and geographical expansion west of the Mississippi River, the flowering of American Protestant evangelicalism, the rise of Transcendentalism and abolitionism, the tidal waves of Catholic immigration, and the emergence of a virulent anti-Catholic Nativism created conditions for a series of crises in American Catholicism and for its simultaneous growth and social transformation: numerically from one of the smaller American religious communities to the largest single denomination; culturally from an Anglo-American community to a predominantly immigrant community; and religiously from a simple home-centered spirituality to an emotional, highly organized, and ostentatious devotional spirituality that was parish centered.

The most significant crisis before the first provincial council of Baltimore in 1829, and one that was symptomatic of new anxieties in American culture, was lay trusteeism, a Catholic form of popular republicanism that asserted lay rights and powers at the parish level. Lay trusteeism had its roots in Carroll's episcopacy but became much more volatile and assertive after his death, becoming the first major internal test of American Catholic identity in the new republic. How American or how republican and democratic could the ancient Catholic hierarchical institutions become and still retain their continuity with the Catholic tradition? That was the question of the day, particularly from 1815 to 1829. Lay trusteeism arose when Catholic laymen in a few cities and towns formed themselves into voluntary corporations in accordance with the laws of their respective states and/or in conjunction with the ancient Catholic practice of lay patronage in order to purchase property, build churches, and organize their Catholic communities.

Generally, this process put the laymen, who were elected trustees of their churches, in legal control of the church properties. The lay trustees also periodically hired and fired their pastors, created major internal congregational conflicts in their fights with pastors and bishops, and used the American courts and legislatures to win a voice and some legal power within their ecclesial communities. The lay trustees considered themselves the governors of the church's temporalities and generally looked on their clergy as ministers of the church's spiritual affairs, a division of labor that corresponded to the American republican separation of religious and temporal affairs. Many of the articulate trustees argued for the creation of a republican Catholic Church, one that would be significantly accommodated to national principles and practices, believing that the church had in the past always adapted itself to the culture of its people.

Baltimore's archbishop, Ambrose Maréchal, and some of the other French American bishops were not entirely opposed to some form of lay participation within the church, and Bishop John England* even favored some form of diocesan democratic governance that significantly included the lay voice. For the most part, though, bishops and pastors vehemently rejected the trustee form of ecclesiastical republicanism. Most bishops and some pastors entered into a pamphlet war with their lay trustees, periodically took them to the civil courts to settle specific issues, presented petitions before state legislatures, and appealed to the papacy to reinforce the hierarchical nature of the church. When all of these attempts to gain authority over lay trustee–controlled congregations proved ineffective, James Whitfield, Baltimore's archbishop, convoked the first provincial council (1829), where the bishops legislated against the laity holding titles to ecclesiastical properties; reaffirmed the bishop's exclusive right to select, appoint, and remove pastors; and outlawed lay patronage in the United States. Congregational conflicts had produced these provincial decrees against lay control of parish temporalities, and the canonical legislation initiated a gradual transformation of the Catholic Church from a loose confederation of local lay-led congregations under minimal, and at times ineffective, episcopal supervision to a nationally organized denomination under exclusive and forceful episcopal control.

After the Baltimore Provincial Council, a number of bishops petitioned state legislatures to modify state laws on incorporation of church properties. The bishops wanted new laws that reflected canonical regulations on episcopal control of those properties, thereby eliminating the exclusive legal rights of the lay trustees to manage them. In 1833 the archbishop of Baltimore successfully obtained a law in Maryland that made the bishop a corporation sole, enabling him legally to hold and maintain ecclesiastical properties for all the churches in his diocese. The bishop of Chicago and the bishops of California obtained similar legislation in 1845 and 1850, respectively. The struggle to obtain exclusive episcopal control over ecclesiastical properties, making the bishop the legal owner of all titles to properties, demonstrated the new mentality among the bishops with respect to lay involvement in parish affairs, and it became an episcopal trend in the United States throughout the nineteenth century. Some antebellum bishops, however, saw dangers in making the bishops exclusively responsible under the law for church properties. Archbishop Peter Richard Kenrick* of St. Louis complained that exclusive episcopal responsibilities for temporalities made his occupation "more secular than episcopal." Archbishop John Purcell* of Cincinnati anticipated legal problems with legislation that made bishops solely responsible for temporalities in all the parishes. Did the benefits of episcopal control outweigh the risks involved? Purcell worried that corporation sole legislation would make the bishops responsible for debts that local parish priests contracted, because the law might look on the clergy as the bishops' agents, making the bishops legally responsible for clerical actions.[1] By the end of the twentieth century and beginning of the twenty-first century, the limits of such legislation became painfully evident in the legal suits over sexual abuse of some clergy, as the last chapter in this book points out.

Out of the struggle over lay trusteeism came a strong reassertion of episcopal authority and power within the church; the means of asserting that power, the provincial council, initiated a distinctive national episcopal conciliar governing tradition that set the tone and direction for nineteenth-century American Catholicism.[2] Although the provincial council did not in fact bring trusteeism to an end (it would reappear again and again, here and there, throughout the remainder of the nineteenth and early twentieth centuries), it mustered a united and nationally organized episcopal force against it that was difficult, if not impossible, for subsequent lay trustees to resist. Henceforth, too, the bishops would have the major voice in articulating Catholic identity, and they identified Catholicism with a strong hierarchical institution where the lines of authority and power were clearly drawn. By 1829, episcopal authority on the national and local levels called for the creation and assembling of new institutional resources to meet the social and religious needs of a vast immigration. Among other things, the development of Catholic episcopalism produced a violent Nativism that threatened Catholic internal unity and self-identity.

Between 1830 and 1866, at least two distinctive traditions of American Catholicism developed: the immigrant and the Romantic. Although united institutionally, doctrinally, and sacramentally, they had different religious and social sensibilities and distinct ways of perceiving and relating to the world around them. In the course of these thirty-six years, the immigrant tradition would become dominant. Because of the external conditions of Nativism and the internal exigencies of immigrant life, the immigrant form of American Catholicism increasingly developed religious and ethnic solidarity, cultural isolationism, institutional separatism, and an aggressive minority consciousness that was defensive as well as insular. Although immigrant Catholics were segregated from much of mainstream America by choice as well as by the forces of Nativism, they appropriated many values of the host culture and "Catholicized" them in the process, contributing to the larger religious life of American immigrant peoples and to the general social and educational welfare of the country.

The second tradition, a numerical minority impulse, was significantly influenced by a Romanticism that saw in Catholicism the religious, communal, and sacramental sensibilities that could satisfy the human longing for continuity, community, tradition, and authority in a world perceived to be increasingly torn apart by religious individualism and relativism. This tradition was articulated primarily by the converts Isaac Hecker* and Orestes Brownson,* who were at home in the Anglo-American republican tradition and understood Catholicism, when interpreted in the light of their own post-Kantian idealist philosophies, as compatible with American republicanism. Although Hecker and Brownson, like the immigrant Catholics, separated themselves from those elements in American culture that they believed were hostile to the development of a genuine social Christianity, they, unlike the immigrants, encouraged Catholics not simply to preserve Catholicism in its ethnic conclaves but to make America itself Catholic.

The American Catholic population increased by an overwhelming and historically unprecedented 1,300 percent, from about 318,000 in 1830—3 percent of the total American white population—to 4.5 million in 1870, representing about 13 percent of that population.[3] By 1850 Catholicism was the largest single denomination in the country, and although it still represented only a small percentage of the country's total population, it had developed a strong institutional presence from coast to coast. The phenomenal numerical increase and geographical institutional expansion were due to massive immigration, primarily of Irish and German Catholics, the annexation of Texas in 1845, the acquisition of territories in the Southwest and California after the Mexican-American War (1846–1848) and the Treaty of Guadalupe Hidalgo (1848), and the acquisition of the Pacific Northwest territories (1846).

Immigration and geographical expansion significantly increased ethnic and regional diversity within American Catholicism. In addition to the Anglo-Americans of Maryland and Kentucky, American Catholicism encompassed the cultural and religious traditions of the French and Spanish as well as the white and black Creoles in Louisiana; the free and slave blacks throughout the South; the new Irish and German immigrants in the Northeast and Midwest; a few Indians in Maine, the Midwest, Southwest, and Pacific Northwest; some French Canadians in the Northeast and Northwest; and Spanish-speaking peoples in Texas, the Southwest, and California.[4] Especially after the potato famine in the 1840s, waves of Irish immigrants came to America. By 1860, it has been estimated, 63 percent of the Catholic population was of Irish stock.[5] Over 600,000 German Catholic immigrants came to the United States by 1870, when they represented about 15 percent of the Catholic population.[6] Already during the late eighteenth and early nineteenth century, a few had established themselves and their separate national parishes in Pennsylvania, Maryland, and New York City. In the post-1830 period, and especially after the revolutions of 1848, they came in large numbers to Cincinnati, St. Louis, and Milwaukee, the so-called German triangle.[7] By the end of the Civil War, about 78 percent of the Catholic population was of Irish and German heritage, significantly increasing the foreign character of Catholicism. The center of the Catholic population and presence, moreover, had shifted from Maryland to New York, the Northeast, and Midwest.

The rapid increase of Catholic immigrants, the geographical spread of Catholicism, the manifestations of institutional strength and stability, the emancipation of Catholics in England and Ireland in 1829, and traditional Protestant-Catholic theological antagonisms brought about a virulent hostility toward American Catholics, particularly after 1830. Catholic life in this period cannot be understood outside the context of what Ray Allen Billington called "The Protestant Crusade."[8]

This crusade was verbal, militant, and organized—culminating in the Know-Nothing political movement of the 1850s. Catholics were under siege, and their leaders in particular felt the blows of the warfare. In politics, American Nativists charged that Catholicism was an enemy of republican institutions and a friend of foreign despotism. Catholic theology, dogmatic and conciliar statements, as well as papal and episcopal church structures were basically opposed to republicanism, democracy, and civil and religious liberties. In religion Catholics were priest-ridden, intolerant, proscriptive, and against free rational inquiry. Catholicism was also against the spirit of the age, the great foe of progress, and clung to outdated religious forms. It was the religion of a dead tradition, having little interior religious life and little respect for the Bible. In social, economic, cultural, and moral life, Catholicism debased its members, hindered their material prosperity, encouraged ignorance and superstition, and failed to insist on an adequate moral code. In the words of William Ellery Channing, who was in some ways open to and supportive of Catholics, Catholicism belonged to "the dogmatical age of Christianity," an age that was swiftly passing away.[9]

This composite of charges represented a general Protestant assessment of Catholicism that was propagated in secular and religious newspapers, histories, school textbooks, polemical religious debates, and even in some political campaigns. Although most Protestants shared the general assessment of Catholicism, only a few entered into the lurid publishing crusades or into the burning of the Charlestown, Massachusetts, Ursuline convent in 1834, the Philadelphia Bible riots in 1844, and Louisville's "Bloody Monday" battles in 1855.

The Protestant crusade had a considerable effect on the church's defensive and insular posture in theological reflection, apologetics, institution-building, spiritual programs, missionary endeavors, and especially in the indefinable area of the Catholic imagination. The primary agency for the Catholic defense was the newspaper.[10] The American propensity for reading newspapers and the use of them for anti-Catholic propaganda convinced Bishop John England and others after 1820 to publish their own newspapers as a means of communicating their doctrines and defending themselves before the public. Catholics repeatedly asserted their Americanism and increasingly emphasized those distinctive elements in their tradition (e.g., ecclesiastical unity, hierarchical authority, historical continuity) that distinguished and separated them from their Protestant neighbors. Church leaders, moreover, tried to construct a strong internal religious identity that would enable Catholics to withstand assaults from without. At the same time, they retaliated with their own aggressive counteroffensive.

The American Catholic view of Protestantism was as reductive as the Nativist view of Catholicism. Whatever was good in it—that is, the fundamental Christian dogmas—had been retained from the Catholic tradition. Although a number of good people embraced Protestantism, it was a new religious system and a human invention that could not be traced back any further than the sixteenth century. The essence of it was a private interpretation of the Bible, which led inevitably to protesting individualism and ultimately to the breakup of all ecclesiastical unity. And being internally divisive, it could not contribute to social and political unity and stability.

Catholic apologists did not see much good in Protestantism, and if they did, they rarely mentioned it. Bishops and missionaries, though, repeatedly and privately reported to Rome and to European missionary agencies that Protestantism was the dominant force in the United States and that it was able to win over a number of Catholics who did not have sufficient clergy or churches. These Catholics implicitly acknowledged the force of Protestantism, and although they publicly assailed Protestantism for its inability to convert the Indians, they privately feared that it was indeed making successful efforts among Indians, blacks, and even some immigrants. In fact, one of the nineteenth-century motives for missions to the Indians and the westward expansion of Catholicism was the apparent success Protestant missionaries and Bible societies were having in the West.

By the 1850s Catholics were mounting their own crusade to make America Catholic. Few were as bold or, given the Nativist mentality of the times, as arrogant and aggressive as New York's Bishop John Hughes* in articulating the Catholic design. Hughes preached:

> Everybody should know that we have for our mission to convert the world, including the inhabitants of the United States, the people of the cities, and the people of the country, the officers of the navy and the marines, commanders of the army, the Legislatures, the Senate, the Cabinet, the President, and all! . . . There is no secrecy in all this. It is the commission of God to His Church, and not a human project.[11]

Catholics in the United States hardly had the means to serve their own immigrants much less convert others to their cause. Nonetheless, assertions like Hughes's helped to ignite the powder keg of Nativism.

Antebellum Catholic insularity and defensiveness were as much a result of internal demands as a response to external attacks. The almost uncontrollable immigrant invasion and geographical expansion put immediate and massive pressures on the tiny American Catholic communities to absorb the new immigrants, create internal cohesion and religious solidarity among them, develop institutions to meet their spiritual and social needs, and help them preserve their own personal and communal identity while they accommodated themselves to an American way of life that was itself in the midst of movement and change. Preoccupation with the internal life of the Catholic immigrant community, however, was not solipsistic; it was publicly useful to the nation as well as internally necessary. The Catholic Church—especially in its spiritual, educational, and social mission—provided a home and services for the new Americans.

Whether in the East or on the western frontiers, antebellum Catholicism built similar institutions to meet the new immigrants' and pioneers' needs, but the experience of Catholicism in these places was not the same. In the East, Catholics had come into areas where Protestants already had well-established patterns of authority and economics. Most Catholic immigrants were foreign to these established patterns and would fit in only as they gained strength in numbers or were able to develop their own religious, economic, and political support systems. On the western frontiers, the situation was somewhat different. Here, for the most part, Catholics and Protestants settled the new areas together and had equal opportunity for growth and economic development. Even though the old antagonisms between Protestants and Catholics continued to influence life on the frontier, those antagonisms were mitigated by the necessities of building a common life together.

It is sometimes asserted, and with good reason, that the spread of Christianity to the American frontier was primarily the work of Methodists and Baptists. Lay elders and frontier itinerant preachers moved west as the country did and gradually laid the foundations of Christianity there. Catholicism was primarily an eastern and Great Lakes phenomenon that did not have the mobility of ministry that some Protestant churches possessed. Yet Catholics did move into the frontier with amazing speed and established their fledgling institutions sometimes before, but most of the time alongside, those of American Protestantism.[12]

The national expansion and development of Catholicism were directed and controlled primarily by five institutions that molded and shaped American Catholic consciousness and its orientation to American society for years to come: the national episcopal councils, the local episcopacy, the clergy, communities of women religious, and the schools.

Baltimore's seven provincial and three plenary episcopal councils served a number of functions in the American church.[13] They created a uniform national system of ecclesiastical government, became the primary agency for the expansion of bishoprics in the West, defined the nature of episcopal authority in the church, helped to construct a national Catholic identity, provided a code of uniform ecclesiastical discipline, and encouraged the development of Catholic devotionalism and a disciplined moral life.

The territorial or diocesan bishop, the second institution of antebellum Catholicism, was the primary sign and instrument of the presence and development of Catholicism on the midwestern and western frontiers as well as in the East. Immigrant bishops led the multicultural American church. Until 1866, 75 percent of all newly appointed bishops were foreign born. Of the eighty bishops named between 1830 and 1866, 31 percent were Irish, 25 percent American, 20 percent

French, 6 percent German, and the rest from other countries (Spain, Italy, Belgium, Canada, and Mexico).[14] Although the Irish constituted the majority of the Catholic population, they did not dominate the hierarchy in proportion to their numbers, but Irish-born bishops did possess some of the largest eastern and midwestern sees during this period. The disproportionate representation of French and French Canadian–born bishops in the American hierarchy reflected both the church's continuing inability to provide enough qualified native clergy for the episcopate and the generally higher standards of education and leadership that characterized the French missionary clergy. These French bishops were the pioneers of Catholicism in many small new dioceses in the South, Midwest, Southwest, and Pacific Northwest.

Almost all the antebellum bishops appointed for the vast territory from the Midwest to the Pacific Ocean followed a similar pattern in establishing the foundations for Catholicism. Because of their foreign educations, connections in Europe, the scarcity of priests, and the general poverty of the Catholics in these areas, the bishops—many times even before they settled in their dioceses—made a trip to Europe to beg for money and to enlist clergy, seminarians, and religious orders of men and women. Like the seventeenth-century French Jesuits, they tried to stir up the missionary zeal of European Catholics to serve the needs of these new dioceses. In this effort they were largely successful, bringing to the United States hundreds of missionaries and thousands of dollars. Clergy serving in the missions or in the new dioceses also went to Europe on recruiting tours. The Jesuit Pierre De Smet, Indian missionary from St. Louis, went to Europe at least seven times from 1830 to 1870 and brought back over one hundred missionaries for Jesuit enterprises in Missouri and the Northwest.

In spite of their cultural and personal differences, immigrant and American bishops shared a common Tridentine vision about the church. Although they tried to meet the ethnic-based needs of their diverse peoples, they were more concerned about unity and even uniformity of religious life and practice than they were about legitimate cultural diversity.[15] Many bishops also saw themselves as Tridentine reforming bishops. In their reactions to lay trustees, clergy, religious orders, or popular folk religious practices, they intended to establish their own authority and the post-Tridentine parish-centered sacramental tradition of Catholicism.[16]

At the local and congregational levels, the clergy, whether diocesan or members of religious orders, were the third institution to provide for the spiritual and social developments of antebellum Catholicism. The immigrant episcopacy had a predominantly immigrant clergy to assist them in their pastoral initiatives. In 1830, 232 of these priests served about 230 churches; by 1866, 2,770 priests were ministering to 5,067 churches and missions.[17] The greatest number of clergy were from Ireland, and they had, even more so than their bishops, an almost total authority over their Irish people; but that control was dictated not so much by ecclesiastical doctrine or discipline as it was by the Irish veneration of, and attachment to, their priests. Archbishop Gaetano Bedini, on an apostolic mission to the American church, reported in 1853 that the Irish people "see in their priests not a simple minister of Religion; but their father, their magistrate, their judge, their king, their 'Papa,' their idol. This is not an exaggeration."[18]

During the antebellum period, women religious became the backbone of the church's educational and social mission. By 1830, there were approximately five hundred women religious in twelve communities,[19] and between 1830 and 1870, forty-seven new communities of women religious emigrated to the United States.[20] By 1870, well over two thousand women—immigrants and native born—were living a religious way of life in communities across the country, building convents, schools, and hospitals; serving the sick in cities and villages that were periodically plagued with epidemics; becoming the heart of the church's care of orphans; and working to improve the lot of immigrant and pioneer alike. Black women religious—the Oblate Sisters of Providence and the Association of the Holy Family (New Orleans, 1842), German Benedictines (St. Mary, Pennsylvania, 1852), American Dominicans (Kentucky and Ohio, 1820), French Canadian Sisters of Providence (Vancouver, Washington, 1856), and a host of other religious communities provided young women with an opportunity to live an evangelical life and serve real needs in immigrant and pioneer communities. They were an essential part of the church's missionary efforts and an integral part of the institutional means of care and hope. Their social and educational activism was frequently combined with a contemplative quasi-monastic lifestyle (i.e., seclusion in communal convent living, celibacy, retreat from the materialism and acquisitiveness of American life) that made them signs of contradiction in society. They were generally under episcopal and/ or clerical supervision and control, yet they were independent, self-confident builders of the institutions that served the church and the society.

Catholic schools became the fifth institution in which the bishops and their cooperators placed their hopes for the evangelization and education of the people and the continuation of the Catholic tradition. The Catholic school became a primary institutional symbol of the immigrant church, reflecting a symbiotic relationship between Catholicism and American values, simultaneously incorporating purposes of both. It was the church's response to the fundamental need for education in the nation, a defense against the pan-Protestantism of the public schools,[21] an attempt to unite the communication of knowledge with the cultivation of piety,[22] and the means of preserving cultural and religious solidarity. The school, moreover, was another Catholic form of voluntaryism that provided educational alternatives in a religiously pluralistic society. It also furthered the general antebellum American desire to create good and virtuous citizens by means of knowledge and religion.

Although the Catholic schools integrated religion and education, they also separated Catholics, particularly on the East Coast, from the Protestantized Americanism current in common schools, further alienating Nativists and American Protestants who considered them un-American and sectarian. In some places, especially in the Midwest and West, however, Catholic schools were perceived as a major contribution to American public life, because they were the first, and for a while the only, schools available for all children.

The issue of Catholic schools became the focus of Catholic and national attention after a series of antebellum battles between bishops and common school societies. The most publicized of these was the confrontation between Bishop Hughes and the New York Public School Society in the early 1840s. Hughes's controversy set the tone for subsequent school wars in other parts of the country, and began a century of Catholic slurs against public education, a withdrawal of official Catholic support for the improvement of common schools, and a major step toward their secularization.

The New York school controversy was ostensibly a battle over the use of public funds for Catholic schools, but it provided an occasion for Catholics to establish the rationale, as outlined previously, for the very existence of Catholic schools in American society. During the battles Catholics appealed, as they would continue to do for over a century, to the free exercise clause of the First Amendment, and their opponents to the nonestablishment clause. Both the common school proponents and Hughes argued for a link between religion and education, but only the former believed that a true neutrality in regard to religion was possible. For Hughes, neutrality in practice turned out to be religious universalism of the pan-Protestant kind. Although the issues were real for both parties, the controversy itself turned nasty, with a host of hermeneutical suspicions on both sides. The intensity of the verbal battle revealed how significant the school issue was. For both sides the schools helped to define the meaning of America and the specific role of religion in society. Were the schools to be the primary agents of a pan-Protestant Americanism or of a specifically Catholic Americanism?[23]

All bishops shared the desire for Catholic schools, but not all could put that desire into practice. Throughout the nineteenth century, Catholic schools never served more than a very small portion of the Catholic population. It is difficult to say, given the present state of scholarship, just how many were actually established and kept running from 1830 to 1866.[24] Depending on prevailing economic conditions, parishes opened and closed numerous schools during the period. Most orders of women religious who came to this country opened schools for girls, some of which were free and others of which required tuition. The schools provided education and culture for girls and much-needed revenue for the women religious. One report indicates that there were only 20 schools for girls in 1830, but by 1856 the number had increased to 130.[25] This was primarily the result of the arrival of new teaching orders of women religious.

Dominicans, Franciscans, Jesuits, nine teaching orders of brothers, and a number of bishops also established ninety-three new colleges for men in the antebellum period, some of them surviving only a year or two; only twenty-nine are still in existence. Catholic colleges, like many others in the nation, had a very low survival rate throughout the nineteenth century.[26] Generally they had

a threefold religious purpose: to provide a preparatory education for boys as-
piring to the priesthood, to create a center for missionary activities, and to
cultivate moral virtues. The antebellum Catholic colleges often trained boys from
the age of six to twenty, providing elementary as well as higher education.

Antebellum Catholic piety also emphasized Catholic distinctiveness in American society. Increasingly after 1830, the bishops, clergy, and religious orders, in
conjunction with the European Catholic Romantic religious revival, fostered a
multiplicity of traditional Catholic devotional practices and forms of piety that
encouraged the new immigrants to identify their ethnic cultures as well as their
religion as Catholic.

Episcopal conciliar legislation and the subsequent pastorals from 1830 to
1866 reflect a gradual transformation in American Catholic piety. Until the
1830s, the bishops admonished Catholics to develop a spiritual life oriented to
the Sacraments but fundamentally centered in family prayer life. Christian catechesis and spiritual reading in the home were fundamental.[27] Their recommendations reflected the realities of the agrarian and diaspora conditions under
which many Catholics lived, scattered as they were throughout the country,
many times without the benefit of clergy and the regular celebration of the
Sacraments.

After the 1830s the dominant vision of Catholic spirituality shifted gradually,
reflecting new sociological circumstances. The great increase in population, the
migration from peasant agricultural backgrounds to large cities, the loss of control over the means of production and the product produced, the democratic
and republican political atmosphere in which they were living, and the hostility
of a Protestant American environment made Catholics receptive to a spirituality
that corresponded to their new urban situation.

The primary end of Catholic spirituality was the salvation of souls, and the
church was the divinely established means of that salvation. Joseph Chinnici has
argued rightly that the church was the center of this vision of the spiritual life. It
was perceived as the "society whose divinity overshadowed the humanity of its
institutions, its teaching, and practice."[28] The church was also the spiritual
homeland and refuge for uprooted immigrants. John Hughes preached in 1835
that the immigrants, like Abraham, were commanded to "Go forth out of thy
country and from thy kindred, and from thy father's house, and come into the
land that I will show thee. And I will make of thee a great nation, and I will bless
thee and magnify thy name, and thou shalt be blessed" (Gen. 12:1). That "great
nation" was the church, and the providential signs of its identification with
Christ were found in its poverty, suffering, and persecution.[29]

The emphasis on the church as the means of salvation and the spiritual
homeland or refuge for the immigrants was concretely put into practice in a
variety of parish-centered and distinctively Catholic spiritual activities such as
parish missions, pious confraternities, and devotions to the saints. Through
these specific means church leaders hoped to revive the spiritual life of Catholic
immigrants, many (especially the poor Irish peasants in the period before the

Irish Catholic revival of the 1850s) with only a minimal attachment to the church and with inconsistent sacramental practices.[30]

The parish mission was one of the European pastoral activities that produced, according to Jay Dolan's study of the phenomenon, a Catholic revivalism.[31] It was primarily a preserve of the religious orders—particularly the Redemptorists, Passionists, Jesuits, and eventually the American Paulists—and was intended to revive the religious life of local congregations through intensive preaching over a concentrated period of a week or two. The mission emphasized the renewal of the Christian life of baptized Catholics, leading them to a more fervent reception of the Sacraments of Penance and the Eucharist. Although a few parish missions began in the early 1830s, they were flourishing by the hundreds by the 1850s and 1860s. Itinerant preachers from the religious orders had the distinct advantage of coming into a parish, appealing to its congregation to convert, and leaving before their message became routine. Although some sermons were doctrinal expositions, most seem to have been, in Orestes A. Brownson's words, an appeal to the heart as well as head, so that individuals would not only know but also feel sin and grace. The missions awakened the Christian life through "sensible devotions."[32]

Missionaries also enrolled parishioners in pious societies where the revival might be sustained with communal support. The parish missions, moreover, provided parishioners with an opportunity to purchase religious artifacts for their homes and spiritual books and pamphlets for their continued edification. The mission, as Dolan has indicated, was like a Protestant revival, except it was oriented to the sacraments and to identification of individuals with the ongoing religious life of their parishes. Over the course of the nineteenth and early twentieth centuries, immigrants became a faithful, church-going community. How much the missions contributed to this development is difficult to assess, but they seem to have changed the religious habits of a number of immigrants.

The parish mission helped to foster devotional practices within the Catholic community. Some historians, such as Dolan and Ann Taves, have seen devotional Catholicism as the key to the revival of Catholic life during this period. By the mid-nineteenth century devotions to Jesus, the Sacred Heart, the Blessed Sacrament, Mary, and the saints began to flourish in American Catholic piety, replacing to some extent the simple piety of the colonial and early republican age. Devotionalism would continue to characterize Catholic parish piety until the Second Vatican Council in the 1960s, when other forms would replace it. Like other Catholic movements at this time, the devotional development emphasized the unity of the Catholic community in the face of hostility from outside. Indeed, as Taves has argued, devotional Catholicism was another way of separating Catholics from Protestants.[33] Undoubtedly, the devotional revolution fostered closer attachments to ecclesiastical authority, but it was much more than an ideological hammer in the hands of the clergy to promote institutional ends. It was an attempt to revive personal and family piety and reaffirm the traditional Catholic doctrine of the communion of saints, while providing a means of preserving religious and ethnic solidarity.

The revival of devotionalism reinforced the Protestant image of Catholicism as a religion of outward forms rather than interior disposition. Protestants, though, were not entirely alone in their criticisms of Catholic devotional practices. Although some American Catholics, especially the new American converts Hecker and Brownson, accepted in principle the devotions associated with the Catholic doctrine of the communion of saints, they found many practices associated with those devotions to be excessively mechanical and/or so closely tied to ethnic sensitivities that they produced an unnecessary barrier to the development of an American Catholic spirituality. Brownson thought that some devotions to Mary, particularly those recommended by Alphonsus Liguori's *Glories of Mary*, were too effeminate and bathetic for his masculine, Anglo-American heart.[34] At times, too, he charged that some practices associated with the veneration and petitioning of the saints detracted from the central mysteries of Christianity that they were originally intended to illustrate. Some Catholics had an almost superstitious reliance on favorite saints, relics, and sacramentals that made Catholicism particularly unattractive to Protestants, and in fact did a great injustice to the Catholic tradition itself. Catholic spirituality had many times borrowed from the European traditions sentiments that were needlessly alien to American sensitivities, which emphasized the development of personal virtue, liberty, initiative, and responsibility for public life.[35]

In the 1860s Brownson called for a revision of Catholic spirituality that would put it more in accord with the dynamics of American life. The old Catholic spirituality that placed exclusive emphasis on obedience had to be changed in a republican age that demanded an integral relationship between obedience and liberty.[36] Contemporaries, he wrote, "demand personal conviction,—to appropriate, to assimilate to themselves the truth which authority teaches, so that they may have in themselves as Catholics unity of thought and life, and speak from their own thoughts, convictions, and experience as living men, and not merely repeat a lesson learned by rote, and to which they attach no more meaning than the parrot does to her scream of 'pretty pol.'"[37] Here, Brownson was signaling a new development in American Catholicism that had existed alongside and within the immigrant tradition since the 1840s, one that was analogous to the devotionalism that dominated the immigrant church.

This new sensibility, which I have elsewhere called "American Catholic Romanticism,"[38] was part of a much wider European and American spiritual and intellectual impulse. In the United States, the new sensibility exhibited itself in what Sydney Ahlstrom has called "Romantic Religion in New England" and "Catholic Movements in American Protestantism."[39] Out of these American movements, especially Transcendentalism and Tractarianism, came a number of converts to Catholicism who had a significant impact on American Catholic life and thought and whose perspectives and sensibilities were shaped more by the issues coming out of the post-Kantian era than they were by those experiences that conditioned the immigrant Catholics.

The new sensibilities of the Romantic era—for example, the emphasis on religious feelings, the recovery of an incarnational view of the church, an organic approach to history and community, the integration of Christianity and social values, and even the emphasis on authority as necessary for community—appealed to those who converted to Catholicism. To some extent, these elements were also being rediscovered in the popular and institutional religious revival and devotional revolutions that were taking place in European and American Catholicism. But the new converts to Catholicism, especially Hecker and Brownson, revealed a Romantic Catholicism that differed in some major respects from the popular and institutional Catholicism of the immigrant era.

Unlike Hughes, Bishop Martin John Spalding,* Francis Patrick Kenrick,* and other apologists for the immigrant American Catholic vision, Brownson and Hecker possessed a Romantic religious epistemology that emphasized the role of intuition in understanding God and the Catholic tradition. They had been drawn into the modern, post-Kantian religious and philosophical quest to harmonize the subjective and objective dimensions of human and Christian existence. The philosophical and religious questions that were current in New England Unitarianism and Transcendentalism, out of which they emerged, were not even raised in the immigrant community, except to refute them as the wild imaginings of atheistic philosophical geniuses. Brownson and Hecker, on the other hand, took seriously the new religious epistemologies and tried to reconcile intuitive and rational approaches to truth and meaning. What this meant in effect was that both gave far greater significance to the subjective than did their American Catholic coreligionists.

Brownson and Hecker certainly spoke out, like their coreligionists, in favor of ecclesiastical authority, the visible church, the sacramental means of grace, and the communion of saints, but they did so from an intellectual position that differed considerably from the dominant immigrant position. For both men there was a dynamic and harmonious dialectic between subject and object, freedom and authority, nature and grace, church and world that did not enter into the worldview of Hughes, Spalding, and company. For Brownson and Hecker, union with God was individual, activist, and intuitive as well as communal, sacramental, and rational. What made Catholicism so attractive to them was the dialectical harmony of those elements in the Catholic experience of Christianity. This fundamental perspective was at the heart of their understanding of the necessity and role of the church in preserving fundamental American constitutional values and in maintaining freedom, order, and justice in American society. To make America Catholic was a matter, according to Hecker, of demonstrating that those human and universally valid aspirations of American society were grounded in the authentic Catholic tradition.

Although American bishops repeatedly encouraged lay Catholics to good citizenship,[40] they themselves refused to become involved in partisan politics.

Bishops and clergy were extremely sensitive to the Protestant and Nativist criticisms of the church's historical involvement in European politics and to the general republican disdain for clerical interference. In their 1837 pastoral, the bishops made it clear that, unlike some of the Evangelicals who had been organizing for a Christian Party in politics, they refused to identify Catholicism with any political movement.[41] The bishops could count. They knew they could not influence political developments even if they wanted to, and they did not. Catholicism's primary responsibility in the political order was to develop sound moral consciences, not to devise strategies or particular means to achieve penultimate temporal ends.

Slavery was the single economic, political, as well as moral reform issue that divided the nation's conscience perhaps more than any other after 1830. Catholics, like many other Americans, had accepted the institution in practice and in theory. Slavery came with the Spanish Catholics to Florida in the sixteenth century, with the English Catholics to Maryland in the seventeenth, and with the French Catholics to Louisiana in the eighteenth. Catholics throughout the South owned slaves and used them to build their plantations and churches, make their profits, and financially sustain their missionary and evangelical efforts. Large Louisiana and Maryland landowners such as Charles Carroll of Carrollton owned hundreds of slaves, while small farmers in Kentucky and Missouri owned one or two. Lawyers and judges like William Gaston of North Carolina, bishops, priests, and religious orders of men and women bought, sold, traded, and punished their own slaves. Catholics were implicated in the slave business throughout the antebellum period.[42]

Many Catholics not only accepted the American institution of slavery, they also found support for it in Catholic teaching, justifying it on biblical, historical, and theological grounds. In the 1840s, in the midst of a presidential campaign that had raised the issue of abolition, Bishop England gave what amounted to a practical Catholic defense of American slavery.[43] Catholics throughout the South and many in the North periodically repeated England's arguments and shared his view that the legislature had the responsibility for any change in practice. The overwhelming majority of Catholic newspapers, both in the North and South, supported slavery and generally accepted England's argument.

The abolitionist movement, which had in the 1830s and 1840s divided three major Protestant churches, did not affect American Catholic unity. American bishops, individually and as a national body, remained aloof from the moral battles over slavery, except to articulate what they considered to be the traditional Catholic teaching. In fact, their national pastorals never touch on slavery because the bishops considered it a politically divisive issue. The 1852 national pastoral clearly hints that troubles were brewing in the country, but the bishops merely recommended conscientious religious respect for all public authorities.[44] For most articulate American Catholics, slavery was a civil institution, and if there was to be a change in the institution, it would have to come from civil or legislative means.

Traditional Catholic moral theology viewed slavery as a consequence of Original Sin,[45] but the institution of slavery was not itself considered essentially sinful. Nonetheless, there was a moral dimension to slavery, and Catholics, like other American Christians, developed a moral code of the relative rights and duties of masters and slaves.[46] Francis Patrick Kenrick, the most authoritative moral theologian in the antebellum American hierarchy, reinforced the American Catholic position and enshrined it in his *Theologia Moralis* (1841), a textbook used in some seminaries. Like other Catholic moral theologians, Kenrick argued that slavery did not abolish the natural equality of human beings nor did slave-holders have the right to treat slaves as property or animals. Slavery gave the master a right to the use of the slave's services and nothing more. In exchange, the master was to provide due care for his slave and treat him or her humanely.[47] Slaves had a right to a knowledge and practice of religion, lawful and valid marriages, the integrity of family life, and adequate food, clothing, and shelter.[48] No doubt this moral code and the concern for the religious care of slaves was observed in some places, as Stafford Poole and Douglas Slawson have pointed out, but it was by no means uniformly followed.[49]

American Catholics accepted slavery not because they lacked nerve or because of cultural pressure to conform to a dominant tradition; they accepted it willingly and consciously and had a theology and tradition to support it. They were involved in it economically, politically, and culturally. Although the institution was not considered sinful in principle, it was so in concrete practice, and some American Catholics experienced ambivalence and internal conflicts in their acceptance of it because of the moral consequences it produced among the slaves and slaveholders. Catholic ambiguity regarding slavery revolved around the distance between the moral code they themselves accepted and the actual practices that they and their culture observed.

Although the dominant American Catholic tradition accepted slavery and called for the observance of a moral code, a minority of American Catholics rejected American slavery and a few called for its abolition. Mathew Carey of Philadelphia was clearly disturbed by slavery, but his only solution was to support the American Colonization Society for the removal of blacks to Africa. Judge William Gaston of North Carolina, on the other hand, took a prophetic stand on slavery in 1832, calling for the "ultimate extirpation of the worst evil that afflicts the Southern part of our confederacy."[50] During the North Carolina Constitutional Convention in 1835, he also opposed depriving black freeholders of voting for members of the State Senate and House of Commons. Two of his judicial decisions moreover affirmed that even slaves had rights to protect themselves against harsh and murderous assaults.[51] Cincinnati's *Catholic Telegraph* and two of New York's pastors, Jeremiah Cummings and Thomas Farrell, also periodically lectured against slavery and called for its abolition.

Even those Catholics who opposed slavery did not join the abolition movement, for most in both the North and South identified abolitionists with religious bigotry and Nativism. Indeed, a number of abolitionists were anti-Catholic, and some of them made the traditional identification of Catholicism and slavery, see-ing them as "natural allies in every warfare against liberty and enlightenment."[52] In the Catholic mind, abolitionists were associated with all the social and po-litical upheavals in Europe. Catholics periodically called abolitionists Red Repub-licans, socialists, atheists, and revolutionary advocates of a private interpretation of the higher law. A number of abolitionists, however, tried to gain Catholic support and were not the bigoted Nativists many Catholics thought.

The battles over slavery and abolitionism that had split some denominations also split Northern and Southern sympathies more generally and led to the trag-edy of the Civil War. On 4 February 1861, shortly after Abraham Lincoln's election, the South organized the Confederate States of America. Two months later, with the firing on Fort Sumter in Charleston harbor, the war began. Catholics in large numbers came out of their immigrant communities and entered national public life in new and dramatic ways during the war.[53] Southern Catholic leaders almost immediately sided with the Confederacy. In fact, even be-fore the organization of the Confederate States, Bishop Jean-Pierre Augustin Verot of St. Augustine, Florida, had preached a sermon on "Slavery and Abolitionism," which was subsequently printed and distributed throughout the South as a Confederate tract,[54] earning for him the title "rebel bishop." Perceiving a crisis in the public state of affairs and the inevitability of a civil war, he decried the slavery issue as the cause of the present troubles—because one-half of the nation refused to acknowledge the legitimacy of an institution that God, the church, society at all times, and all governments had acknowledged. Most Southerners justified the separation on the basis of a state-rights theory of government and the right to separate from the federal government's aggression on the South.

The process of regional attachment was more gradual in the North. Many Northern Catholics, even those who were against secession as a solution to the problem between the states, had a considerable amount of sympathy for the South. In October 1861, Brownson asserted that he, like most bishops and religious leaders, had for the past fifteen years counseled Catholics to respect and obey the federal government. That government, in Brownson's opinion, was still the legitimate government and "it has never lost its legitimacy by any act of tyranny or oppression . . . . Rebellion against it, therefore, is not only a crime, but a sin." Brownson, however, was disappointed that in the midst of the secession crisis the Catholic population and its leaders had not stood up for the federal government. Of the twelve Catholic newspapers, he could count only two as decidedly loyal, two as occasionally loyal, one that strived to be on both sides, and all the rest as really "secession sheets."[55] Brownson's Yankee American loyalties came to the fore in this assessment, but he also saw a contradiction in those Catholics who were simultaneously siding with Southern revolutionaries while emphasizing in traditional Catholic fashion the authority and unity of the state as well as the church. This did not fit the Catholic pattern.

Some bishops in the North, however, gradually came to share Brownson's view that the Southerners were rebelling against the Constitution and public order. Although Archbishop Kenrick of Baltimore generally stayed out of the battles, Archbishop John Purcell of Cincinnati supported the Union's cause, as did Bishop John Timon of Buffalo and other Northern sympathizers. Hughes won the wrath of the Southern episcopacy by flying the American flag over his cathedral at the commencement of the war.

For Hughes, as perhaps for other Irish supporters of the Northern cause, the war was justified on constitutional grounds; but it was not for him or for many of his Irish people a war to end slavery. Hughes wanted to keep slavery out of the war issue because he believed that Irish Catholics would not support a war to abolish slavery.[56] Hughes, therefore, was particularly disturbed by the Emancipation Proclamation as he privately revealed to William Seward, Lincoln's secretary of state, but he did not express his concerns in public. Such was not the case with James McMaster, editor of the *New York Freeman's Journal*, and with the editor of the *Metropolitan Record*, both of whom expressed racist sentiments and pitted the blacks against the white laboring classes of New York. When the Emancipation Proclamation was followed in 1863 by the enactment of enforced military draft for all those who could not buy their way out with three hundred dollars, the two journals seethed with indignation at the outrage and injustice of the whole thing. These journals either stirred up or expressed a growing class and race hatred that broke out in four days of rioting in New York in 1863.[57]

Catholic sectional patriotism came to the fore during the course of the war, with bishops identifying themselves as citizens of both sections of the country. Patrick Lynch of Charleston and Hughes of New York were both sent on diplomatic missions by their respective governments. In 1861 Lynch went to Rome, hoping to obtain Vatican recognition of the Confederacy; he returned there on a similar mission in 1864, only this time as the Confederacy's official representative. Bishop Hughes acted in a similar fashion for the North. For him, the war was an opportunity for patriotism, and he lost no time in supporting the government's right to conduct war against the rebellion. In 1861 Lincoln and Seward asked Hughes to make a diplomatic mission to Europe with Thurlow Weed to promote "healthful opinions" in France and England in favor of the North. Hughes enthusiastically accepted, traveling to England, France, and Italy as an emissary of goodwill. His mission had very little political influence, but it was a move into the public realm that he interpreted as a sign of the fundamental compatibility of Catholicism and Americanism.[58]

Seventy clergy served in the military chaplaincy on both sides of the war,[59] and many others took care of bereaved families at home. Nursing sisters, too, provided medical aid, constant care, and spiritual comfort to the ill and dying soldiers on the battlefields or confined to military hospitals. A recent scholar estimated that 640 (or 20 percent) of the 3,200 Civil War nurses were nuns.[60]

When the war came to an end, Catholics, like others, tried to interpret its ultimate historical significance. Martin John Spalding saw the "wicked war" as a divine chastisement "for our Sins."[61] Verot saw it and the Southern defeat as divine vengeance on a people who had abused their slaves or who had refused or neglected to provide them with a Christian education.[62] The previous antebellum Catholic ambivalence about slavery was almost totally destroyed as Southern Catholics tried to make some divine sense out of the terrible tragedy. Those like Verot who spoke out after the war did so almost exclusively to remind their people that sin was the cause of it all—not the sin of slavery itself, but of the moral abuses that accompanied it.

Brownson interpreted the war as a major turning point in American political theory and as an opportunity for Catholics to take a leading role in reestablishing national unity and government stability. He believed that a postwar-united Catholicism would be the foremost influence in "forming the character and shaping the future destiny of the American republic." For him, the end of the war demanded that Catholics themselves discover their own universally valid principles and share them with the rest of the country. He believed that Americans, who were not sectarian in their hearts, would respond to a thoroughly catholic (i.e., universal) vision if such a vision could be presented intelligently and responsibly. He wrote *The American Republic* (1866) to argue his case before the American people. The book was also an intellectual peace offering particularly for Southern Catholics who, like himself before the war, had accepted a state-rights view of government. Brownson now rejected that view and called upon Southern Catholics and others to reestablish the metaphysical and theological grounds for national unity and a transcendental source of governmental stability.

The war, Brownson argued, had also brought about a new era of good feeling in American society, perhaps comparable to that following the Revolutionary War. In the midst of the war, he opined that the struggle was making Americans "one people" again.[63] It had made the American people more accepting of Catholics as their fellow citizens, and it had transformed Catholics. He predicted, too, that immigrant Catholics would become Americanized through their participation in the war. Prior to the war those Catholics who were Americanized had been so on the Southern model—a civilization based on slavery, with its center in Baltimore and Virginia. He hoped that the war would Americanize Catholics on the Northern model—a civilization based on constitutional liberty, with Massachusetts as the center.[64]

The need for Catholic unity in the wake of the war was felt in other quarters. In 1865, Archbishop Spalding of Baltimore called a Second Plenary Council in order, among other things, to demonstrate Catholic unity, provide a uniform disciplinary code, and construct some means to evangelize and assist the freed blacks.[65] The call for a council generally resonated well with both Northern and Southern bishops, who were in search of some signs of spiritual and temporal harmony. The archbishop of New Orleans, John Mary Odin, encouraged Spalding's initiative in this regard, remarking, "The holding of a plenary council will be gratifying to all the bishops of the South. Everything seems to be so gloomy in the future, that it will be beneficial for all."[66]

The plenary council focused on internal ecclesiastical and disciplinary matters, leaving little time or energy to discuss the church's responsibility to the freed blacks, about 150,000 of them Catholic. American bishops, however, were not willing or prepared to give them material assistance. The Southern dioceses in particular had been ravaged by the Civil War and were economically and culturally unprepared to care for them. Although one of the council's decrees suggested the establishment of black churches, schools, and orphanages, no specific actions were recommended.[67] The matter was ultimately left up to the individual bishops' consciences. Without any practical organized national effort on behalf of the freed blacks, the Catholic response would continue to be meager and ineffective.

The Civil War and the plenary council represented a major turning point in American Catholicism. The immigrant church would continue on into the twentieth century, but it was significantly transformed by the war. Catholic participation in the war efforts was symbolic of the end of an era of isolation from American public life—at least for some leading Catholics. The participation of large numbers of Northern and Southern Catholic soldiers in the war, the two episcopal diplomatic missions, the contributions of priests and nuns, and the sacrifices on all sides brought Catholics more thoroughly into the nation's life than had been the case throughout the previous thirty years. Catholic immigrants had paid their dues to American society with their services and their blood. They would feel a closer attachment to their country than before the war. Young priests (e.g., James Gibbons,* John Ireland,* Edward McGlynn*), sisters, and immigrant families had all participated in the terrible tragedy, and, in the process, they became more Americanized in their feelings. Nativism, too, had lessened considerably during the war and would not be revived for some years to come—and when it returned it did not have the same virulence as in the antebellum period. If it was an exaggeration to claim, as did James Parton in an 1868 issue of the *Atlantic Monthly*, that the "despised minority" of Catholics was "well on its way to complete acceptance in Protestant American Society," there was at least some truth in the exaggeration.[68]

4

RECONSTRUCTION AND EXPANSION:
1866–1884

FROM THE SECOND (1866) to the Third Plenary Council (1884), American Catholicism, like the nation itself, experienced reconstruction in the South, read-
justment in the North, and continued expansion into the west. It was a period of
transition from the devastation brought about by the Civil War to the beginnings, in the North at least, of economic and social change brought about by
immigration, industrialization, and urbanization. In the midst of these social and
cultural changes, American Catholicism continued to be preoccupied with its
own house, trying to meet its own institutional, social, spiritual, and intellectual
problems—some created by the war and others the result of its own internal
growth and accommodations to changing conditions in society. But, these were
also years of a slow transition from a Catholic antebellum preoccupation with
parochial and diocesan issues to the postbellum emergence of national Catholic
issues and organizations that transcended local concerns. Within this gradual
cultural transformation, the Roman church under Pope Pius IX focused on the
fundamental intellectual threat of naturalism and secularism, and the need to
reassert a Catholic sense of the supernatural. Between the two councils, the
American Catholic Church remained institutionally united; but the visible unity
disguised tensions and unresolved internal problems that would eventually
break out in open conflict by the late nineteenth century.

Although the Second Plenary Council was intended to demonstrate institutional unity in the midst of a society divided by war, it did little to unite
Catholics in the reconstruction of the postwar South. The South was crushed by
the war: Catholic churches and convents had been destroyed, families had been
decimated, orphans abounded, the economy foundered, freed slaves received
little help and much resentment, and Northern Catholics contributed little or
nothing in response to numerous appeals from Southern bishops to help rebuild
Southern Catholic institutions.

Neither Northern nor Southern Catholics pressed reconstructionist policies in
the Southern dioceses[1] or came to the aid of the four million freed slaves.[2] Even
where there was a desire on the part of some white clergy and religious to bring

institutional aid to freed black Catholics—as was the case with the Josephites
(i.e., St. Joseph's Missionary Society, founded in 1871 in England), with Bishop
Verot of Savannah (1861–1870) and of St. Augustine (1870–1876), and a few
others—the means were not available. As a consequence, many of the black
Catholics left the church and became members of the rising black Baptist and
Methodist churches.[3] Lack of financial means, personnel, and, among many,
desire, prevented Catholics from engaging seriously in the post–Civil War
challenge in the South where Catholics were a tiny minority.

The story of Catholicism in the North, Midwest, and far West from 1866 to
1884 differs considerably from that in the South. Although many of these
Catholics, too, were poor and culturally marginalized, they experienced continuing numerical growth and a gradual rise of the American Irish to positions
of leadership in the church, labor, and politics. Between 1860 and 1880, the
Catholic population doubled, from over three million to over six million. Much
of the increase came from the 1.3 million immigrants, about 42 percent of
whom were from Ireland and 29 percent from Germany.[4] This growth neces-
sitated the creation of twenty-four new dioceses (spread throughout the United
States) between 1867 and 1884, and a huge building campaign to accommodate
the new immigrants. Of the sixty-nine new episcopal appointments made during these years, 33 percent had been born in the United States (mostly of Irish
and German ancestry), 21 percent in Ireland, 21 percent in Germany, Austria,
and Switzerland, 10 percent in France, and the remainder in other countries.[5]
The episcopate was becoming increasingly Americanized by the presence of
second- and third-generation Irish and German Americans.

Although most Catholics focused their attention on building institutions at the
local level to meet the needs of the increased Catholic population, a few Catholics
turned their attention to issues that transcended local parishes and dioceses: for
example, lay and clerical rights within the national church, national ethnic and
fraternal associations, national labor unions, politics, and Indian affairs. A
number of articulate clergy in the Northeast and Midwest, for example, became
increasingly discontent about their status and role in the American church, and
protested against the missionary status of the American church and the abnormal
condition of priests who were without permanent canonical rights in the church.[6]
The tensions between bishops and some clergy, however, were not exclusively
related to clerical rights. One small group of Roman-educated clergy in New York
City were convinced that post–Civil War Catholicism needed to be Americanized
rapidly to meet the demands of the new age and to keep culturally progressive
Catholics in the church. They supported ideas and reforms (e.g., radical reconstruction in the South, the Fenian Brotherhood, Irish independence, public
schools for Catholics, revisions in theology, wholehearted Catholic acceptance of
religious liberty and separation of church and state, vernacular liturgies) and
opposed church practices (e.g., the pope's temporal powers, excessive legalism in
the American church, and mandatory celibacy) that the hierarchy in New York
considered dangerously close to anarchy or heresy.[7]

Other tensions were evident among the German clergy and laity who protested that they lacked representation in the hierarchy and that they were considered second-class Catholics in some of the dioceses controlled by Irish bishops. Many German immigrants had migrated to the Midwest, founding *Wahrheitsfreund* (Cincinnati, 1837), a national newspaper, and organizing the German Central-Verein (1855), a national combination of local mutual aid societies; both the newspaper and the Verein manifested a self-conscious national movement toward German solidarity. As Philip Gleason has indicated, the Central-Verein was "part of the search for stability among an immigrant people who were undergoing serious difficulties of adjustment." At first the national federation concentrated on the "mutual support and assistance in cases of poverty or sickness of the individual members," but it gradually developed a consciousness of issues that were more national in scope.[8]

Although the Germans were the first group within the church to develop institutions and organizations with a national rather than a local focus, they were not the only group to do so. Numerous other laity, primarily Irish or Irish Americans, organized what had previously been isolated parish, local, or state benevolent societies into national organizations that reflected the American propensity toward voluntary association and an emerging sense of national identity and mission.[9] The most successful, enduring, and popular of these national lay benevolent societies was the Knights of Columbus, organized in 1882. It eventually became the most efficient and innovative fraternal insurance program in the country. Its purposes, however, went well beyond financial security as it tried to raise the level of awareness of the Catholic contribution to American society, provided laity with an organization in which they could exercise initiative and leadership roles, made effective efforts in organized charity, and supported scholarship and cultural endeavors.[10]

These emerging new lay movements reflected an awareness that the social, cultural, and economic problems the laity faced were not just local but national in scope. These new organizations created a sense of national solidarity and brought about national solutions to common problems. American Protestants, of course, had had nationally organized voluntary religious and reform societies since the early national period. American Catholics came late to this American voluntary tradition. During the antebellum period they had to secure a sense of local identity before they could venture out beyond their parishes. The rise of these national lay organizations testified to an emerging middle class within American Catholicism—a middle-class laity that were aware of their own needs and prosperous enough to devote their time, energies, and monies to attend national meetings and to entertain ways of improving their lot and that of their fellows.

Increasing numbers of Catholic laity also became involved in state and national politics, labor unions, and Indian affairs. This was particularly the case for the postwar rising middle-class Americanized Irish who became involved in state politics or were elected to public office in New York City, Boston, and other cities in the 1870s and 1880s. Although Catholics were not as prominent in politics as their numbers warranted, they were beginning to emerge, and this period is significant for demonstrating that rise. Many Catholic politicians drew a line of demarcation between religion and politics, but they continued to believe that religion was the foundation of morality and good government.[11]

A number of lay Catholic men and women also became active in the rising labor unions as they fought to establish workers' rights, fair wages, decent hours, and favorable working conditions.[12] To protect themselves from the power and resources of the rising capitalists and industrialists, the early labor unions became semi-secret societies and periodically had recourse to labor strikes that crippled the economy and at times produced violence and death. Because they were semi-secret societies and because of the violence associated with them, many priests and bishops opposed the labor unions. Some American Catholic leaders, however, were sympathetic with what they considered the just aspirations of the laboring classes, and some bishops saw the labor unions as one possible means of legitimately articulating labor grievances. In 1869, Baltimore's Archbishop Martin John Spalding told the Vatican Congregation Propaganda Fidei, the Roman office in charge of Catholicism in missionary countries like the United States,

> it is easier and *more common* for employers to commit injuries upon the workers than the contrary. Here, especially, whoever has money believes he can freely oppress the poor, and he does it whenever he can. In all commercial countries, especially Protestant ones, *capital* (money) is the *despotic ruler*, and the worker is its slave. This being the case, I say, leave the poor workers alone—there being little danger that they can do injustice to the tyrannical employers.[13]

Some bishops, as well as clergy and laity, got involved in national Indian affairs during President Ulysses S. Grant's so-called "Peace Policy" (1869–1877), which restructured the way the government related to the Indians. Grant's policy was, according to Francis Paul Prucha, the major linchpin in a program of humanitarian and Christian reform that aimed to Christianize and Americanize the Indians. The original purpose of the policy was to use peaceful methods to put an end to Indian discontent, eliminate the Indian wars, and provide means to civilize individual Indians.[14]

Many Catholics accepted Grant's original objectives because, like many other Americans, they believed Indians needed to be civilized and Americanized, both of which required Christian education and morality, which Grant's policy provided. What disturbed some Catholics about Grant's policy was not the general objectives, but their implementation. Catholics complained, for example, that they were not granted a fair share in the distribution of governmental resources for missionary and educational work. They grumbled, too, as did other religious denominations, that the policy of granting one denomination sole control over missionary activities on some Indian reservations was a distinct violation of the Indian's religious liberty. But Catholics were not so much concerned about the Indian's rights as they were about their own rights to evangelize the Indians freely in those territories where Protestants were in control of the Indian agencies. Oregon City's Archbishop Francis Norbert Blanchet, after repeated attempts to obtain from the government a fair distribution of Indian agencies, charged in 1871 that Grant's policy "has become a dead letter, a mere show of vain words, a perfect deception."[15] Such strong language was characteristic of the Catholic antipathy to what was perceived as unfair treatment. No doubt anti-Catholicism was behind the implementation of the policies, but Catholics themselves did very little to participate in the early formation and execution of Grant's policy.

By the mid-1870s, Francis Norbert Blanchet, his brother Augustine Magloire Alexander Blanchet, bishop of Nesqually, and Jean Baptiste Abraham Brouillet, a missionary with over twenty years of experience among the Indians in the Northwest, awakened eastern bishops to the need of establishing a national agency to represent Catholic Indian interests before the government and the American Catholic people. In 1874, Baltimore's Archbishop James Roosevelt Bayley appointed the Catholic layman General Charles Ewing—son of a distinguished Ohio Catholic senator, a Civil War veteran, and a Washington attorney—as a Catholic Commissioner of Indian Affairs. Through his and Brouillet's efforts, the Bureau of Catholic Indian Missions (BCIM) was established. Throughout the postwar years, the BCIM was able to raise the consciousness of American Catholics about the problems of the Indian missions and represent Catholic interests before the government, enabling the Catholic missions to obtain significant levels of governmental support—especially for contract day and boarding schools. The BCIM was sustained in the early years primarily by the personal contributions of Charles Ewing and his sister, Ellen Ewing Sherman, wife of General William T. Sherman, who, with other Catholic laywomen, organized the Ladies' Catholic Indian Missionary Association (1875) in Washington, D.C. to promote the BCIM and help finance Catholic Indian missions.

While some Catholics were becoming involved in issues of national concern, others were addressing religious and theological issues raised by Charles Darwin and the new sciences of biology and anthropology, which Catholics such as Orestes Brownson saw as manifestations of naturalism—that is, the complete separation of science and thought from faith and divine revelation.[16] Brownson's reactions, and those of other American Catholic intellectuals, were consistent with the theological stance established in Pope Pius IX's papacy. The pope's encyclical *Quanta Cura* (1864) and the attached *Syllabus Errorum* (1864) on the inherent naturalism in modern thought and political practices, and the First Vatican Council (1869–1870) on rationalism, fideism, and papal infallibility set the tone of the papacy against intellectual developments in the modern world. Although American Catholic conservative intellectuals shared the pope's anti-naturalism, they were, unlike the pope, strong advocates of American republicanism and the freedoms associated with modern constitutional government, and, therefore, did not accept the pope's almost universal condemnation of modern political developments.

The *Syllabus of Errors* condemned eighty propositions that were supposedly condensations of prevailing trends in modern thought and practice. The papal document censored, for example, modern rationalism (which denied the authority of revelation and the church), religious liberty, separation of church and state, and freedom of the press. Proposition eighty summarized the position of the papacy toward the modern world. It reprobated those who believed that "The Roman pontiff can and ought to reconcile and harmonize himself with progress, with liberalism, and with modern civilization."[17]

Baltimore's Archbishop Martin John Spalding saw clearly the difficulties the pope's *Syllabus* presented for American Catholics and quickly prepared an encyclical on it. He agreed with the condemnations of pantheism, rationalism, and religious indifferentism, but also pointed out that what the pope had condemned in modern political thought was not the American constitutional arrangements of church and state but the European liberalized and laicized state. In other words, the pope had condemned what any good American would condemn, a view of political liberalism that made the state an absolute in society, restricting human freedoms. "To stretch the words of the Pontiff," he wrote in reaction to some American Protestant interpretations of the *Syllabus*, "evidently intended for the stand-point of European radicals and infidels, so as to make them include the state of things established in this country by our noble constitution, in regard to liberty of conscience, of worship, and of the press [is] manifestly unfair and unjust."[18] Orestes Brownson, like Spalding, distinguished between American and European forms of liberalism and warned that the *Syllabus* itself needed local interpretation: "For the mass of the people, it were desirable that fuller explanations should be given of the sense in which the various propositions censured are condemned, for some of them are not, in every sense, false."[19] This was particularly the case in the papal censures on religious liberty, separation of church and state, and other modern constitutional freedoms—as these were understood in the American Constitution.

The First Vatican Council reinforced the mentality of the *Syllabus* and emphasized a Catholic form of supernaturalism.[20] The Council's first decree, *Dei Filius*, unanimously accepted by American episcopal participants, upheld the dignity and limited efficacy of human reason, underlined the necessity of a supernatural revelation for the attainment of salvation, and attacked modern forms of fideism, rationalism, and naturalism. This decree set the tone for much of American Catholic thinking on the relations of reason and revelation, nature and grace, until the Second Vatican Council (1962–1965). The Council's second decree, *Pastor Aeternus*, declared the pope to possess the charism of infallibility when he explicitly defined matters of faith and morals for the whole church to believe. Prior to and during the Council, American Catholic bishops differed among themselves on the prerogative of papal infallibility,[21] but after the Council, the former anti-infallibilists as well as the infallibilists formally accepted the new decree.[22] Brownson and a few others interpreted the decree on papal infallibility as a victory for the supremacy of the spiritual over the temporal in a world that was increasingly denying the teaching authority of religious sources. Isaac Hecker interpreted the definition as a major turning point in history, bringing to culmination the Catholic Church's efforts since the Protestant Reformation to reassert ecclesiastical authority, but it simultaneously prepared "the way for the faithful to follow, with greater safety and liberty, the inspirations of the Holy Spirit."[23]

Vatican I was indeed somewhat of a turning point in American Catholic consciousness. Most bishops and clergy, already in the antebellum period attached to the papacy as the spiritual center and symbol of Catholic unity and perseverance, became increasingly ultramontane, leaving behind much of their previous quasi-Gallicanism and ecclesiastical localism. Catholics in the future, whether liberal or conservative, would be ultramontanes in their increasing acceptance of papal authority in local American ecclesiastical affairs and would try to use the papacy to fortify their own local agendas. Although the definition of papal infallibility did not necessarily imply greater Roman administrative control of the local or national churches, that was indeed what began to happen, and it was indeed what many bishops felt to be consistent with Catholic teaching.

Vatican I reinforced some previous American Catholic approaches to the modern world. Many clerical and lay leaders in the church believed that a new age of unbelief had arrived in postwar American culture and it was increasingly evident not only in the naturalism of theologians, philosophers, scientists, and politicians, but also in a progressive commercialism and materialism in the mass culture, and a secularism in education.[24] This interpretation, however, was not a wholesale condemnation of modernity. Catholic antinaturalists did not deny the benefits of modern scientific achievements, the progress of technology, or the improvements in communications and transportation; they were extremely apprehensive about the ideological naturalism that was the source and effect of these modern benefits. The church-against-the-world motif, however, was not the only understanding of the church's relationship to modernity in the postwar period.

Hecker's interpretation of Vatican I illustrated a different approach to the modern world, one that was equally antinaturalist, but open to the millennial and pneumatological optimism of the age. For Hecker and his postwar followers the age was full of promise. In the 1880s, Hecker asked, "How can religion be made compatible with a high degree of liberty and intelligence?" More optimistic than Brownson in his understanding of human nature and modern culture, Hecker saw that the development of free civil institutions and the spread of enlightenment had created an atmosphere in the modern world that contributed to "the progress of true supernatural life among men." He argued that modern liberty, so far as true, and the increase of intelligence, so far as "guileless," were invaluable helps to the "spread of Catholicity and the deepening of that interior spirit which is the best result of true religion."[25] Although both Brownson and Hecker saw the necessity of Catholicism becoming incarnate in American culture, their practical judgments differed considerably on the expediency and the methods to be used in accomplishing this goal. Their own differences represented the kind of split that would develop in American Catholicism only after the Third Plenary Council.

In 1884 Rome convoked the Third Plenary Council of Baltimore[26] to respond to grievances it had heard during the postwar years about a host of issues (e.g., clerical rights, the treatment of immigrants, the missions to Indians and black Catholics, Catholic education) and to enact legislation that would govern the American church for years to come. The Council brought to focus many issues of the immediate postwar years but also left an unfinished agenda that would spark new controversies in the subsequent period. It issued a series of legislative decrees[27] that provided, among other things, for some clerical consultation in diocesan administration and for the participation of some clergy in the election of bishops; prohibited clerical involvement in politics (a provision that would have repercussions in subsequent years); and established measures for a uniform national catechism (the *Baltimore Catechism*), for a national collection to assist the missionary efforts among black Catholics and Indians, and for the condemnation of secret societies. One-fourth of the decrees were concerned with Catholic education at various levels.[28] The Council, for example, mandated that bishops establish parochial schools within two years of the promulgation of the decrees and that Catholic parents send their children to these schools, restructured clerical education by requiring two years of philosophy and four years of theology, and initiated plans for the eventual establishment of a national Catholic university.

The Third Plenary Council was the last national legislative council in American Catholic history, the end of episcopal conciliarism, and the last demonstration of national episcopal unity in the nineteenth century. The Council's unfinished business planted seeds for subsequent disunity among the bishops. They failed, for example, to address the immigrant issue adequately, to agree on measures for establishing a Catholic university, and to decide on the principles for determining which secret societies ought to be condemned. The divisive consequences of the unfinished agenda, though, would not become clear until the pressures of subsequent events made them so.

5

———⊶———

AMERICANISM: 1884–1899

FROM THE THIRD Plenary Council (1884) until the papal condemnation of Americanism (1899), American Catholicism experienced a crisis that publicly divided bishops and others into warring factions over how the church should relate to the modern and changing world. These Catholic battles have been tagged "Americanism"[1] because of Pope Leo XIII's apostolic brief *Testem Benevolentiae* (1899), which condemned an excessive accommodationist stance toward American and modern culture. On the one hand, the division was social, reflecting the developing postwar social differentiation within the American Catholic community between the newly arrived immigrants and the increasingly Americanized middle-class immigrants; on the other hand, it was intellectual, embodying two very different evaluations of the modern world. American Catholic leaders in particular broke into at least two major opposing parties in their evaluation of the times and assessments of the proper relationship of the church to the age. The general rupture developed in response to very specific issues: proper pastoral approaches to the immigrants, labor unions, and social justice; the establishment of a Catholic university; the relationship between parochial and public schools; the presence of a Roman apostolic delegate; cooperation with and participation in interdenominational activities; religious liberty and church-state relations; and the relationship between religion and the new sciences.

On the one side were those who wanted to give a Catholic direction to contemporary currents of life and thought by accommodating Catholicism to what was best in the new age while preserving the essentials of faith and ecclesiastical government. This group—variously designated as liberal, Americanist, accommodationist, or transformationist—was led by the archbishop of St. Paul, John Ireland. Associated with him were Bishop John Keane,* Denis J. O'Connell,* Cardinal James Gibbons, the Paulists, the Sulpicians, a few lay and clerical editors and writers, and some professors at the new Catholic University. At times, too, depending on specific issues, Bishop John Lancaster Spalding* of Peoria, Archbishop John Joseph Williams of Boston, and Archbishop Patrick Riordan of San Francisco aligned themselves with this group.

On the other side were those who also accepted the material achievements of the modern age and appreciated the accomplishments of modern science and technology, but were extremely critical of what they perceived to be a spirit behind these developments that was essentially hostile to faith and all religious authority. For them the church could not, without losing its integrity and identity with the apostolic tradition, accommodate itself to the outward forms of modern culture and modern patterns of thought. This group—variously called conservative, anti-Americanist, traditionalist, preservationist, intransigent, *refractaire*—was led by the archbishop of New York, Michael Corrigan.* He was joined and periodically egged on by Bishop Bernard McQuaid* of Rochester and Thomas S. Preston, Corrigan's vicar general. The German clergy and bishops, too, led by Archbishop Frederick Katzer of Milwaukee, resisted the accommodationists and upheld a view of Catholicism as a cultural and religious force against the winds of modernity and secularity. The majority of American and European Jesuits also belonged to this group, as did the theologians Joseph Schroeder and Georges Peries at the Catholic University in Washington, D.C., and St. Louis laymen Arthur Preuss, editor of the *Fortnightly Review*, and Condé B. Pallen, editor of *Church Progress*, who represented the thought of German Catholic lay leadership in the country. Depending on specific issues, this group was joined periodically by Archbishop Patrick Ryan of Philadelphia, Archbishop William Henry Elder of Cincinnati, and numerous writers for the *American Ecclesiastical Review* and *American Catholic Quarterly Review.*

The years 1886 and 1887 were crucial, as Thomas Wangler and others have argued, in the emergence of the Americanist party and in a clear identification of the opposing positions.[2] During a commission to Rome for the American hierarchy in those years, Keane, Ireland, O'Connell, and at times Gibbons developed a self-conscious accommodationist perspective toward the modern world and American culture, a sense of "cause," a realization of a "mission," and the beginnings of a "movement." Keane, O'Connell, and Ireland, in particular, became extremely conscious of their opponents and repeatedly tagged them their "enemies," "*refractaires,*" and/or "conservatives." They began to see themselves as the "advanced" party, the one truly in touch with the modern world. Their enemies were lost in the hopeless battle of preserving a foreign culture.

During the Roman sojourn three specific issues (the German immigrant problem; the condemnations of the Knights of Labor, Henry George, and Edward McGlynn; and the establishment of a Catholic university) split the American hierarchy, and the divisions that originated then would continue and become more public and volatile in subsequent years over other issues. The first problem was the absorption and care of the new immigrants and their adjustment to American conditions. Although much of the national ecclesiastical attention after 1884 was focused on what was called the "German problem," the immigration issue was much larger, as would become increasingly evident. Of the 6.5 million Catholic immigrants who entered the United States from 1880 until 1920, more than 64 percent came from Italy, Poland, and Austria-Hungary and over 365,000 from Mexico. The largest percentage came after 1890, when German and Irish immigration fell off considerably.[3] By 1920 there were almost 20 million American Catholics, representing about 20 percent of the total population and an increase of about 11 million since 1880.

During this period, the Germans were the first to articulate what the immigrant adjustment meant, and what they said in the late 1880s and 1890s would be echoed again and again, with different modulations, by immigrants from French Canada, Mexico, and southern and eastern Europe.[4] German Catholic priests and laity had complained to Rome for some time about their second-class identity in American Catholicism, where they were treated as foreigners, not well represented in the hierarchy, and pressured to Americanize. These complaints came to a head in 1886 when Father Peter Abbelen, vicar general of Milwaukee, presented a memorial to Rome requesting that all German national parishes be acknowledged as legally equal to English-speaking parishes, that all immigrants and all children born to them in the United States be assigned to national parishes, and that immigrants have pastors who understood their language and fostered their customs. He complained about the Irish American Catholic insistence on rapid assimilation, which was dangerous to the faith because particular languages and customs, although not essential to the faith, "foster piety and are so dear and sacred to the faithful that not without great dangers could they be taken away from them." Abbelen believed in the inevitability and desirability of gradual Americanization, but he also feared that those who favored a more rapid assimilation would cause the new immigrants to lose their faith.[5] Ever since the late eighteenth century, German Catholics had here and there built national parishes and organizations separating themselves from English-speaking Catholics and from their German- and English-speaking Protestant neighbors, believing that "language saves faith."[6]

Keane and Ireland countered the Abbelen memorial and his arguments for cultural diversity by preparing an "answer" that revealed very different pastoral priorities concerning the immigrants' and American church's future.[7] The real question in the American church, Keane and Ireland argued, was not between the Irish and the Germans, as Abbelen saw it, but between the use of English, the language of all public life in the United States, and the use of foreign languages, which prevented the new immigrants from entering into and enjoying the benefits of American life. Although Keane and Ireland saw the necessity of immigrant institutions for "the practice of religion in the language most familiar to them," they saw these facilities as transitional elements in the American church. The bishops protested, however, against the overidentification of the German language and culture with faith, because such an identification would force the Americanized immigrants to reject their religion when, as would inevitably happen, they lost their parents' language and culture. For these bishops, history had demonstrated this irreversible process. They saw the transitional necessity of preserving national cultures as a means of preserving faith, but cultural preservation was not the highest pastoral priority because it was all too contingent and not farsighted enough to continue the faith in an American culture. Very much like the Germans, they believed that language and culture were significant bearers of Catholic faith, but the cultural forms that expressed Catholicism most adequately for them were American. Issues involving social justice, however, would soon complicate the differences over pastoral approaches to language and culture.

One of the first of these issues was the church's view of and relations toward labor unions. While in Rome in 1886 and 1887, Keane, Ireland, and Gibbons were forced to articulate their pastoral approaches to labor unions, because in 1885, the Knights of Labor had been condemned as a secret society in Canada. Some in the American hierarchy wanted the prohibition extended to Knights in the United States, whose members were largely Catholic and whose president since 1879 was the Catholic Terence Powderly.[8]

The church, Gibbons argued in a petition to the Vatican, should permit labor unions like the Knights because they were an efficacious, natural, and just means of seeking redress for grievances. The church, too, should be aligned with the laboring classes because Christ himself sent the church to evangelize the poor. Like England's Cardinal Henry Manning, Gibbons maintained that the church was in a new democratic age, one in which the power and influence of the people were providentially rising to new importance. If the church wanted to serve the future, therefore, it had to stand by the people. In fact, for him, "to lose the heart of the people would be a misfortune for which the friendship of the few rich and powerful would be no compensation." A condemnation, he concluded, would be unjust, unnecessary, imprudent, ineffectual, inexpedient, dangerous to the church's reputation, and have financial consequences that would be ruinous for American Catholicism as well as Peter's pence. The Knights were not condemned in the United States.

While in Rome the Americanist prelates also became involved in the internal ecclesiastical affairs of the Archdiocese of New York. New York Archbishop Corrigan had censured Henry George as a socialist and Father Edward McGlynn for disobedience because he publicly supported and stumped for George during the mayoral campaign of 1886. Gibbons petitioned the Roman Propaganda to withhold a condemnation, which was sought by Corrigan and some other American prelates, of George's works.[9] The Americanist prelates, who generally believed that the church should be on the side of the people, also saw in McGlynn a "friend of the people,"[10] even though they believed Corrigan had a just cause for suspending him in 1887. But the Americanist support for George and McGlynn only aggravated the tensions with Corrigan and those who shared his view of the church and society in the United States.

The third divisive issue that came to the fore during Keane and Ireland's 1886–1887 sojourn in Rome was the establishment of a Catholic university, the original intent of their trip. The university eventually won papal approval, opening in Washington, D.C., in 1889 in spite of the opposition of Archbishop Corrigan, Bishop McQuaid, the American Jesuits, many German Catholics, and some opponents within the Propaganda itself. The victory, however, did not settle American discontent. Loss of support from Corrigan and some German bishops in particular had a significant financial effect because New York was the wealthiest diocese and the Germans were among the wealthiest immigrant groups in the country. Lack of financial aid continued to plague the development of the university throughout the late nineteenth century and into the twentieth.

Soon after the successful Roman mission, the whole issue of Catholic education, not just a Catholic university, became a central bone of contention among American Catholics.[11] The issue of parochial schools came to the fore in 1890 when Archbishop Ireland's address to the National Education Association, "The State School and the Parish School—Is Union between Them Impossible?" warmly acknowledged the need for and benefits of public education, admitting that the state had a right and a duty to provide schooling for all the people. He also made the case for Catholic schools but stated, "I sincerely wish that the need for it [the parish school] did not exist. I would have all schools for the children of the people be state schools."[12]

The German bishops, Corrigan, and even Bishop John Lancaster Spalding—all of whom had done much to support and build up parochial schools—fought fiercely against the Ireland proposal. When Ireland tried to implement a cooperative plan with public schools in Fairbault and Stillwater, Minnesota, the German bishops had had enough and delated the whole experiment to Rome for condemnation. Although Rome eventually decided the plan could be tolerated, and that decision ended the debate for the time being, the school question only increased suspicions about a general compromising mentality that existed behind very specific, concrete, Americanist pastoral approaches.

An issue historically and causally connected to the conflict over education was the sending of a Roman apostolic delegate to the United States. In 1893, Pope Leo XIII sent Archbishop Francesco Satolli to Chicago to represent him at the World's Columbian Exposition. Satolli's mission, however, was more permanent: He was also sent to help settle the controversy among the bishops over the education issue and to establish an enduring apostolic delegation. For some time, numerous priests in conflict with their bishops had favored an apostolic delegate as a check on the absolutism of the American episcopacy. Ireland and O'Connell also favored the appointment, because they believed that a Roman delegate would further their accommodationist stance. The sending of an apostolic delegate was therefore the result of developing American-Roman connections, one that both Americanists and their opponents had contributed to by their appeals to Rome to resolve local disputes—but also one that Rome desired. It was a part of Roman centralization that had been taking place increasingly during the nineteenth century, one that developed rapidly after the definition of papal infallibility in 1870.

A great number of archbishops and bishops opposed the appointment of an apostolic delegate.[13] Their opposition was based on a long-standing fear that he would only provide ammunition for a Nativist charge that Catholicism represented foreign interventionism. Some argued, too, that it was imposed on the American bishops without consultation and in opposition to their wishes. This argument was made explicit by McQuaid and especially by Spalding who, in 1894, after the delegation was an accomplished fact, wrote an article for the *North American Review* which charged that in matters of practical ecclesiastical policy, local bishops should make their own decisions.[14]

Another divisive issue was clerical and lay Catholic cooperation with non-Catholics and participation in religious events that were sponsored by either nondenominational groups or by specific Protestant denominations. Participation, cooperation, or even public discussions with Protestants and other non-Catholic religious traditions had, particularly since the days of Pius IX, been discouraged because they were perceived to be actual or potential forms of indifferentism or violations of *communicatio in sacris*, a Catholic prohibition against participating in non-Catholic services. The greatest cause of alarm was Catholic participation in the World's Parliament of Religions, a congress held in conjunction with Chicago's 1893 World's Columbian Exposition. For Archbishop Ireland and a few others, Catholic involvement was an occasion to present in a nonpolemical way the Catholic viewpoint on a variety of issues. At the end of the parliament, Keane addressed the convention, acknowledging that the parliament itself was a living illustration of the "old saying that there is truth in all religions."[15] This statement was in no way indicative of a spirit of indifferentism, because Keane, like most of the other Catholic participants, made clear what the Catholic claims were in regard to Christianity and the Catholic Church, but his statement manifested an attitude that was quickly condemned by his Catholic opponents.

For the conservatives, Catholic participation at the parliament and other overtures of cooperation with non-Catholics were manifestations of indifferentism, dogmatic minimalism, neo-Pelagianism, and ecclesiastical egalitarianism. *Church Progress* and the *Western Watchman*, both of St. Louis, and a host of other newspapers bristled with indignation over this kind of leveling tendency, which they saw now as part of the entire liberal program. By 1895, Bishop McQuaid could not contain his anger over what had been taking place in the American church. In a letter to Cardinal Miecislaus Ledochowski, prefect of Propaganda, he characterized the whole movement in the American church as "liberalism," a term that would have its intended effect in Rome.[16]

The apostolic delegate, Archbishop Satolli, also disapproved of the Catholic participation and requested a ruling from the pope. On 15 September 1895, Leo XIII sent him a decision that Satolli himself had anticipated: "Now, although those general meetings have been tolerated by a prudent silence to this day, it would seem, nevertheless, more advisable for Catholics to hold their own assemblies apart."[17] In their own assemblies they were free to invite other religions to participate. The letter indicated that Satolli and the tide of Roman approval were moving away from the liberal camp. Henceforth, Catholic participation in nondenominationally organized religious discussions would be prohibited.

Church–state issues also divided Americanists and their opponents. On this issue Rome was, from the start, clearly on the side of the conservatives. In 1887, Archbishop Gibbons preached a sermon in Rome that underlined the benefits of the American separation of church and state—at a time when the papacy and some European Catholics were having great difficulties with the anticlerical governments of Germany, Italy, and France. He acknowledged that in the United States, the government protected the church's freedom without interfering in her spiritual mission.[18] For most of those in the Americanist school of thought, separation of church and state was not only beneficial for American Catholics, but it was, according to Spalding, an irreversible modern tendency and an arrangement that all nations would sooner or later assume, just as they would be forced to accept popular rule, the underlying principle of which, equality, "is a truth taught by Christ, is a truth proclaimed by the Church."[19]

American Catholic enthusiasm for separation of church and state was considerably chastened, however, by Pope Leo XIII's encyclical *Longinqua Oceani* (1895), which extolled the virtues of American Catholicism and the practical benefits of separation of church and state, but warned American Catholics that it was "erroneous to draw the conclusion that in America is to be sought the type of the most desirable status of the Church, or that it would be universally lawful or expedient for State and Church to be, as in America, dissevered and divorced." The pope recommended, moreover, that in addition to liberty, the Catholic Church even in the United States would be better off if "she enjoyed the favor of the laws and the patronage of the public authority."[20]

Ireland and other Americanists were stunned by the encyclical, but some conservatives like the Catholic University's theologian Joseph Schroeder shared its vision of the relationship between church and state and, more significantly, saw that vision as a corrective to the modern tendency to divorce religion from social and political life. Conservatives' views of separation, as well as their enthusiasm for the restoration of the pope's temporal powers (lost after Vatican I), were all of a single piece in their understanding of a harmonious relationship between religion and society. Distinguishing between the "thesis" (the normal state of the union of church and state) and the "hypothesis" (the historical necessity and benefit of separation), Schroeder indicated that American separation, though beneficial for Catholics, was not the ideal state of affairs and that even the historical development of church–state relations in the United States could have been better.[21] Many like Schroeder saw separation in principle as a manifestation of social rationalism. When pushed to extremes, separation could ultimately turn into a kind of political atheism in which revelation had absolutely nothing to do with political decisions.

The issue of religion's relationship to critical history and the new sciences also divided some within American Catholicism. From 1895 until the encyclical against theological modernism in 1907, a few scholars at the Catholic University and elsewhere, who were sympathetic to and generally supported by the Americanists, advocated some kind of dialogue with and appropriation of the

new scientific methods and the dynamic worldview of the period. John Zahm*
wrote an extensive study, *Evolution and Dogma* (1895), to demonstrate that an
evolutionary and developmental perspective could reinforce the Christian view
that the world and humankind had an ultimate dignity, purpose, and unity, and
that God was immanent in the processes of history as well as transcendent to the
entire development. John Hogan and Francis E. Gigot, Sulpician priests, wrote in
favor of restructuring seminary education to introduce modern science and to
use the methods of historical criticism in biblical studies.[22]

From the conservative perspective, the dialogue was another form of capitulation to the modern world. The desire to use modern sciences and scientific
methodologies tended to obscure the dangers inherent in such an approach
because it minimized the church's infallible authority and the authority of tradition itself. In 1891, Joseph Schroeder pointed out this tendency with reference
to Canon Bartolo's *I Criteri Theologici*. For him, theologians like Bartolo "started
out with the very best intentions to reconcile the Church and the world
according to their own peculiar ideas, but at last became themselves unable to
keep aloof from the dangerous errors which this spirit hides under the most
specious forms." Rationalism was the spirit behind these tendencies.[23]

Behind all of the specific issues that divided the Americanists and their
opponents were two general conflicting views of the modern age and of how the
church should relate to it. Although the Americanists saw the dangers in modern
society, they emphasized what was good in it. They were sympathetic to the
progressive, optimistic, developmental spirit of the age and saw the Catholic
Church as a fundamental historical force for religious and cultural improvement.
Repeatedly they characterized American culture as democratic, activist, oppor-
tunistic, energetic, and aggressive—values they cherished. They also fostered
and supported individual initiative, a sense of public responsibility, liberty in
politics and religion, and the American constitutional separation of church and
state. Because of American political freedom and increasing economic growth,
moreover, they saw the United States as the future leader of the world and
frequently contrasted the benefits of the New World with the disabilities of the
old. America had its faults, but they were, as Archbishop Ireland frequently said,
the mere accidents of the age; what was essential in American culture and therefore consistent with Catholic traditions belonged to a democratic and progressive
future.

The anti-Americanists' assessment of the modern world, and to a large extent
of American culture, was governed primarily by the views expressed in Pope
Pius IX's *Syllabus of Errors*. In this perspective, the modern world was characterized by "liberalism," that is, a spirit of individualism, rationalism, socialism,
and materialism—and with these aspects of modern culture there could be no
compromise. In politics liberalism meant the absolute separation of church and
state (a condition in which religion no longer had any influence on the political
order—political atheism, as Orestes Brownson had called it), which meant a
historical hostility between church and state. In economics liberalism meant

laissez-faire capitalism or socialism—that is, the attempt to absolutize either the individual or the state. In religious and intellectual life, liberalism meant rationalism, or the divorce of reason from faith, nature from grace. In ecclesiastical life, liberalism meant the attempts not only to restrict the nature and extent of the church's infallibility and authority, but also to accommodate the church to modern culture, ideas, and politics. This group repeatedly criticized modern life, but its members also asserted that they were trying to preserve the primacy of the spiritual order and the absolute necessity of revelation, supernatural grace, and ecclesiastical authority for a proper understanding of the human condition and destiny. They felt these values were severely threatened by developments in modern culture and by those in the church who were sympathetic with them.

Many in the second group saw American culture as part and parcel of liberal modern culture. American culture was primarily Protestant, and Protestantism in their conception was the first historical step toward the rationalism of the Enlightenment and the revolutionary tendencies of modern societies. Americanism was periodically identified with subjectivism, individualism, mammonism, nationalism, and anti-Catholicism. Although they accepted the American constitutional provisions for religious liberty and separation of church and state as beneficial, practical contingencies, members of this group could not see these arrangements as ideal. Although they acknowledged the practical benefits of modern scientific, economic, and technological advances, they could not accept a progressive or developmental view of history that saw the United States as the harbinger of the future. Although they acknowledged a material development, they could not perceive a spiritual evolution of humanity and rejected a progressive interpretation of history that denied, as they thought, the fundamental realities of human sinfulness or the unchanging structures of the human condition. Although they were patriotic Americans, they criticized what they considered an excessive American nationalism and chauvinism that almost made an idol of the nation and national virtues and tended to forget that Catholicism transcended nationalism and was separate from many values in American society. Yet some in this group had their own kinds of cultural nationalism.

From the late 1880s on, the battles between the two worldviews were played out on the European stage as well. The Americanist program became entangled in civil and ecclesiastical politics, especially in Leo XIII's *ralliement* policy with the Third French Republic. In France the Americanists Ireland, Keane, and Gibbons were well received, especially by those who wanted to establish cordial relations between the government and the Catholic Church. The French accommodationists and a few German and Italian sympathizers saw a new religious spirit behind the Americanist programs that they believed was necessary to meet the intellectual and political conditions of modern society. They had some of Ireland's more famous speeches translated into French and Italian and saw the Americanists as members of an international movement to demonstrate the compatibility of Catholicism and modern civilization. The Americanists, too, cooperated and encouraged the cause, speaking in France, attending and participating actively in the International Catholic Scientific Congresses, and working actively in Rome to discredit their opponents' positions and to win Vatican support for their movement. By the mid-1890s Americanism was becoming an international affair and was being used for various purposes in Europe.

The European battle over Americanism became sharply focused after the 1897 French translation of Walter Elliott's *Life of Father Hecker*.[24] The edition was edited for a French audience and contained a preface by Abbé Félix Klein, a professor of literature at the Institut Catholique in Paris, who introduced Hecker as the pioneer of a spirituality that was needed in a modern scientific age, one that emphasized the interior life of the Holy Spirit and had the potential to transform and invigorate the traditional structures of Catholicism. The French translation with Klein's preface was a manifesto for the renewal of Catholicism in France; for the European conservatives it was a revelation that exposed all that was heterodox in the Americanist movement. Throughout 1897 and into 1898, the conservatives mounted a paper warfare against the book. Charles Maignen, a French priest, led the assault with a series of articles in the Parisian daily *La vérité*. For him Heckerism and Americanism represented, among other things, a neo-Pelagian mentality that stressed the superiority of the natural over the supernatural virtues.

The French translation created such a theological and ecclesiastical contro-versy that Pope Leo XIII took the entire issue of Americanism under his own control. The theological charges against Heckerism and Americanism became the catalyst for the final Roman opposition, but the tide had been building for some years in Rome. The Apostolic delegate, Francesco Satolli, had, since the World's Parliament of Religion, turned against the Americanists, and once he returned to Rome in 1895, he joined the Jesuits (e.g., Salvatori Brandi, Cardinal Camillo Mazzella) who had opposed the Americanists from the beginning. The encyclical *Longinqua Oceani*, the removals of Denis O'Connell as rector of the North Amer-ican College in Rome (1895) and of John Keane as rector of the Catholic Uni-versity (1896), and the silencing of John Zahm and forced withdrawal (1898) of his book *Evolution and Dogma* were clear signs of the growing Roman opposition to the Americanists.

The Spanish-American War (April to August, 1898) also intensified the divisions between the Americanists and their European opponents.[25] Some Americanists, even those like Ireland who tried to negotiate peace, saw the war as a manifestation of American superiority over Spain and, by extension, over the entire Old World. Spain just could not compete with American military might and money. The war revealed for the first time that the future belonged to the United States as a world power. Perhaps no one expressed this American chauvinism less guardedly than Denis O'Connell. In a private letter to Ireland, he asserted that for him the real issue in the war was one of the struggle of "two civilizations": one, the European, which was "all that is old and vile and mean and rotten and cruel and false," and the other, the American, which was all that was "free and noble and open and true and humane."[26] Josiah Strong, the late nineteenth-century Evangelical Protestant with American chauvinistic tendencies, could not have been more passionately millennialist.

The European anti-Americanists interpreted the war as another manifestation of aggressive American jingoism and mammonism that were imperialistic and out of control. It was not just a war between two nations, moreover, but between Catholic Spain and Protestant America. The Spanish-American War further fed an appetite for ecclesiastical war that had been going on for some time in Europe and severely discredited the Americanist cause—ecclesiastical as well as political.

The final blow against Americanism came on 22 January 1899, when Leo XIII published *Testem Benevolentiae*.[27] Addressed to Cardinal Gibbons, the brief praised American Catholics for their work in promoting Catholicism and distinguished between a theological Americanism, which he condemned, and a political Americanism, which he lauded because it reflected the characteristic qualities, laws, and customs of the country. For Leo, theological Americanism was characterized by three heterodox tendencies: excessive accommodationism, a spirit of religious subjectivism, and a new form of ecclesiastical nationalism. Without actually condemning anyone for holding such positions, the pope sent the American bishops a warning that such tendencies raised the suspicion "that there are some among you who conceive of and desire a church in America different from that which is in the rest of the world." The old fear of ecclesiastical Gallicanism—this time an American-style ecclesiastical nationalism—was a significant part of his concern.

The reaction to the papal letter was swift. The liberals denied that the condemned opinions were held; the conservatives thanked the pontiff for pointing out dangers that actually existed. For Ireland, the condemned errors were "Maignen's Nightmare."[28] Like Ireland, the other Americanist bishops were angered by the brief, and although thanking the pope for it, they were quick to point out that he was condemning a phantom, an imaginary set of errors.

Two archbishops, Corrigan and Katzer, wrote to the pope in the names of their suffragans to express their full adhesion and to indicate that they believed the letter absolutely necessary to dam up the flood of a false Americanism that would have deluged the country without the papal warning. Corrigan, generally willing to extend the boundaries of ecclesiastical authority, even called the letter "your infallible teaching." He acknowledged that he, as much as anyone else, was proud to be an American and to glory in American institutions, developments, and achievements, but "in the matter of religion, doctrine, discipline, morals and Christian perfection, we glory in thoroughly following the Holy See."[29] Archbishop Katzer and his Milwaukee suffragans told the pope that they were "indignant over the fact" that "not a few" in American Catholicism had accepted the condemnations "but did not hesitate to proclaim again and again, in Jansenistic fashion, that there was hardly any American who had held them and that the Holy See, deceived by false reports, had beaten the air and chased after a shadow."[30]

The papal intervention did not end the differences in the American church, either with regard to basic orientations to the modern world or with regard to judgments of facts. The leading Americanists would continue until their deaths (Spalding in 1916, Keane and Ireland in 1918, Gibbons in 1921, O'Connell in 1927) to believe that their side had been maligned. They would continue to speak out as they had before and insist that their brand of Americanism was not under condemnation. But the Americanists were chastened, and most of them retired from national and international ecclesiastical and political maneuvers. Their legacy, chastised though it was, continued in new forms into the twentieth century, as shall be seen.

The conservatives believed they had won a major victory. They had stuck by the *Syllabus*'s understanding of the dangers inherent in the modern world, and *Testem Benevolentiae* reaffirmed that basic orientation. The leading conservatives died long before their Americanist counterparts (e.g., Corrigan in 1902, Katzer in 1903, McQuaid in 1909), but their legacy would also be continued in new ways by a rising generation of active Jesuits and by a new set of Roman-trained bishops who would gain control of some large dioceses.

6

———•·•———

CATHOLICISM IN THE
PROGRESSIVE ERA: 1900–1920

TESTEM BENEVOLENTIAE HAD at least one major effect on American Catholicism. It ended the intramural battles that had raged through the American hierarchy and Catholic newspapers and journals for the past sixteen years. As American Catholics entered the twentieth century, they could put the old ecclesiastical battles behind them, even if they could not extricate themselves from the different spirits that had been responsible for the battles in the first place. Regardless of their former differences, American Catholic leaders still had to face the problem of providing for the religious needs of their people in the midst of changing American cultural and political circumstances and within the context of a new antimodernist papacy.

Post-Americanist Catholicism developed during the progressive era of American politics—the era of Presidents Theodore Roosevelt, William H. Taft, and Woodrow Wilson. It was a period of moral, political, and social reforms. The progressive movement represented in part a middle-class mentality that feared the concentration of power in Gilded Age trusts on the one hand and radical labor and populist agitations on the other. Progressives also criticized the persistence of corruption in government and aspired to restore the nation's founding democratic ideals in a transformed and industrialized society. They called on government to intervene as a moral agent to regulate, though not dissolve, the power of the trusts for the sake of distributing the benefits of the democratic promise to all. Although they used the government as an agent for moral and social reform, they appealed primarily to the moral individual and to moral institutions as the primary agents for the advancement of the public good.

During this period some American Catholics appropriated the spirit of the Progressive Era, which is usually associated with evangelical Protestant moralism; others rejected that spirit and any form of accommodation to it; still others were not at all involved with the programs of the era, being primarily concerned with the religious needs of immigrant parish communities. The Progressive Era was another period of immigrant growth, continuing Americanization, a series of intellectual and ethnic crises, and a growing realization that American Catholicism had a new social mission in American society and a religious mission in the world at large. By the end of the era, in the face of World War I, the American hierarchy was again united in a common effort to address national interests. Their unity and developed sense of national, over local, interests would have astounded many participants in the late nineteenth-century Americanist conflicts.

Progressive Era American Catholicism also developed within the context of a new papacy that was not only antimodernist in theology but reformist in its approach to a number of internal ecclesiastical issues and religious practices. Pope Leo XIII died in 1903 and was replaced by Pope Pius X. Modernist theologians met forceful resistance in Pius's 1907 decree *Lamentabile* and his encyclical *Pascendi Dominici Gregis*, which condemned modernism as the "synthesis of all heresies." Unlike Leo XIII, Pius X saw irreconcilable differences between the church and the age, believed that a synthesis of theology and modern science was impossible, and thought that Leo's political agenda of *ralliement* had utterly failed. He therefore gave up hope of winning political—French or otherwise—support for the restoration of temporal powers. His encyclical *E Supremi* (1903) outlined his own sense of the church's mission in the modern world to be that of "restoring all things in Christ,"[1] a policy that had ecclesiastical, political, as well as religious implications. On the religious side, the pope intended to revive the church's inner life as a fundamental means of transforming, not accepting, the world. Among other things, he initiated reforms in church music, restoring the primacy of Gregorian chant, and promoted the more frequent reception of the Eucharist, giving the liturgical revival a major new impetus. On the ecclesiastical and political sides, he began to assault all modern developments considered hostile to the church's authoritative and doctrinal integrity. Pius X's Vatican tried to eradicate the evils of the modern world by issuing condemnations of modern errors, as had his predecessor Pius IX, and by organizing ecclesiastical machinery to investigate and eliminate any doctrinal or disciplinary deviance within the church.

Lamentabile and *Pascendi* detailed the errors of the modern mind under the rubrics of "vital immanence," "dogmatic evolutionism," "agnosticism," "subjectivism," "historical relativism," and a symbolic view of doctrine. Modernism within the church was perceived not as an attempt to give Catholic answers to very serious problems raised by modern developments but as a capitulation to a mentality that was inherently opposed to the supernaturally endowed doctrinal tradition. The modern mentality was not just attempting to reconcile faith and science; it was, in fact, subjugating the one to the other. In 1910 the pope followed up his condemnations with *Sacrorum Antistitum*, prescribing that all seminary, college, and university professors of theology take an oath against modernism, thus further institutionalizing the antimodernist stance he had taken.[2]

Although there were not many signs of the existence of theological modernism in the United States,[3] there is no doubt that the papal actions had immediate effects on American Catholicism. They abruptly killed off any historically minded theological and doctrinal research, ended incipient scholarship in biblical studies, caused the cessation of the publication of the *New York Review*, diminished and eventually eliminated the influence of the modernist faculties at Dunwoodie and other seminaries, and created a climate of opinion and oppression that some quasi-modernists, William L. Sullivan and John Slattery, for example, found so objectionable that they left the church.

The reformist papacy created a new American episcopacy during the Progressive Era that was antimodernist in its intellectual orientation, Americanist in its loyalties, and modernist in its consolidating administrative practices. Big-city bishops in particular reflected this combination of Romanization and Americanization. John Murphy Farley was appointed to New York in 1902, James Edward Quigley to Chicago and John Joseph Glennon to St. Louis in 1903, William Henry O'Connell* to Boston in 1906, George William Mundelein* to Chicago and Edward Hanna to San Francisco in 1915, and Dennis Joseph Dougherty to Philadelphia in 1918. Although they were not all cut from the same theological or ecclesiastical cloth, they were all, except for Glennon, educated at some point in Rome and manifested a simultaneous intense loyalty to the Vatican and the United States. All of them, moreover, had been born in the United States, except Farley and Glennon, who were born in Ireland, and Quigley, who was born in Ontario, but all three lived most of their adult lives in the United States.

Big-city bishops of the early and mid-twentieth century were what Edward Kantowicz has aptly called "consolidating bishops." Being Roman to the core did not prohibit them from becoming American and modern in the techniques they used to operate a large institution. Like corporate leaders in American big business, labor, and government, they "brought order, centralization, and business-like administration to their previously chaotic dioceses."[4] Using standards of efficiency, rational control, and pragmatic effect that were characteristic signs of modernity and the rising corporate structures in American society, the bishops began to centralize and control all parish and diocesan matters from their chancery headquarters. These new corporate executive–type bishops were highly visible and triumphalist in their leadership styles, bringing a new respect for and raising the self-image of American Catholicism. They tried to make Catholicism socially self-confident and vigorous both in the United States and at the Vatican. Building big institutions, staging massive public ceremonies, hiring prestigious first-class legal firms, consulting with successful business managers while cultivating their friendship, using the publicity gimmicks of advertising firms to raise much-needed money to finance their building campaigns—all were tactics used by these bishops to create an image of the church that was both Catholic and American. They also worked diligently to Americanize immigrants through schools and other institutions. When they died, they received national media attention that had rarely been accorded their nineteenth-century predecessors. Catholicism was beginning to be acknowledged as a prominent force in American political, cultural, and economic life, and these forceful bishops helped to bring about the change.

The big-city ecclesiastical princes sponsored a practical, not a theoretical, Americanism that steered away from much systematic reflection on the relationship of Catholic doctrine to American individualism, pragmatism, and corporate capitalism. The episcopal attempts to put the Catholic Church on the American map, as Mundelein later phrased it, made them unable or unwilling to think about what values they were incorporating into the church's operational structures.

The episcopal vision and practical implementation of diocesan consolidation, centralization, and control was as American as it was Roman in the early days of the twentieth century, but it was sometimes more vision than reality. Urban, as well as other American bishops, did not always have the effective and pragmatic or charismatic power to fulfill their episcopal designs. The persistence of local autonomy among strong-willed pastors, college presidents, hospital administrators, superiors of women religious, and social agency leaders periodically frustrated the episcopal will and made centralizing tendencies ineffective and practically impotent. The bishops had to face strong American feudalism and local control over large segments of Catholic life. Many had episcopal authority, but they did not always have the power to make that authority effective.[5]

The consolidating bishops did, however, have prominent allies among the early twentieth-century Jesuits in their antimodernist and thoroughly ultramontane ecclesiasticism. Many nineteenth-century Jesuits came from Europe, but by the 1920s their membership was increasingly drawn from second- and third-generation American immigrants. They would gradually have a powerful influence on the educated laity in the American church, primarily because by 1920 they had established and were administering from coast to coast twenty-five colleges and universities, which they were organizing according to the standards of higher education prevalent in American society.

The late nineteenth-century Jesuits had been predominantly anti-Americanists, but their ultramontane Catholicism took a new twist during the early twentieth century, when a few of their leading lights tried to focus Catholic attention on national and international issues—developing in the process a new kind of activist, conservative, and anti-modernist American Catholic tradition. Although they had been in the Anglo-American colonies since 1634 and had started colleges as early as 1789, they had not had much of a national voice in nineteenth-century ecclesiastical or cultural affairs, except for a popular magazine on spirituality, the *Sacred Heart Messenger*. That changed in 1909, when they began to publish *America* as a national weekly journal of Catholic opinion on a variety of national, rather than purely ecclesiastical, issues. The motivating and innovative force behind *America*, as behind a number of other initiatives during the Progressive Era, was the Jesuit John J. Wynne, who became the editor. Wynne's original editorial indicated that it was time American Catholics, in the words of Cardinal John Henry Newman, take "an intelligent interest in public affairs, and not live as a class apart."[6] Coming as it did in the wake of Pius X's *Pascendi*, *America* was thoroughly orthodox and served the traditional apologetical functions of other Catholic newspapers and magazines, but it also had an activist bent that drove the editors to make Catholic principles part of the American and American Catholic intellectual conversation about public issues. The journal would not be a speculative and intellectually innovative enterprise, but a weekly discussion of vital and practical applications of orthodox Catholic views to contemporary social, political, and cultural questions.

Although the editors of *America* were thoroughly antimodernist in Pius X's mold, they were also becoming more concerned than their counterparts in the nineteenth century about guiding Catholics to a redemption of society, again following the lead of Pius X to "restore all things in Christ." *America* was a first step in this process, but it represented a confidence among the conservatives that they did indeed have something to contribute to America. The Jesuit policy was defensive, apologetic, and fiercely antimodernist at first, but it also shifted the conservative focus toward contemporary life—a shift that would much later bring forth Jesuits like John Courtney Murray,* who were not only conversant but also sympathetic with some modern perspectives.

Although there were a few signs that Catholicism was beginning to emerge into American public life, the predominant concerns were still those of the immigrant Catholic communities that were at various stages of settlement, conflict, and development in the large urban areas of Boston, New York, Philadelphia, Baltimore, Chicago, St. Louis, and, to a certain extent, Detroit, Milwaukee, New Orleans, and San Francisco. Southwestern dioceses from Galveston to southern California also experienced a great increase in immigrant population, primarily from Mexico. Until the immigrant restriction laws of the early 1920s, the small southwestern as well as large urban dioceses were in a constant state of flux, trying to absorb the immigrants. The new immigrants brought a rich and dizzying diversity of ethnic Catholic cultures and rites. Each group tried to preserve its own identity and integrity, and each experienced a series of intra-ethnic conflicts, internal church battles, and external hostilities from Nativists.

At times the conflicts became so intense and hostile that they led to permanent schisms—as was the case in the late 1890s with a few Polish Catholics who separated themselves from Catholicism and formed an independent denomination, the Polish National Catholic Church, and as was the case with a number of Byzantine-rite Russian Catholics in Minnesota and elsewhere who permanently separated themselves from the American Catholic Church in the late nineteenth and early twentieth centuries and joined the Russian Orthodox Church. How many individual immigrants left the Catholic Church to become Protestants or enter the long list of the unchurched is uncertain, but surely the tensions and difficulties of adjustment caused some to withdraw from any allegiance.

Although permanent schisms did occur here and there in American Catholicism, they were not the primary focus of Catholic immigrant attention during the first twenty or thirty years of the twentieth century. The primary problem for the numerous southern and eastern European Catholic immigrants was that of preserving their religious and social traditions while they adjusted to new conditions and tried to make a living. Variety characterizes the processes of preservation and accommodation among the different ethnic traditions, but a description of that variety goes beyond the scope of this study. The Irish, Germans, Poles, and French Canadians, for example, brought with them numerous clergy and women religious to help build the institutions that fostered their traditions in the United States and thereby provided institutional means for preservation and assimilation. The Italians, on the other hand, did not bring with them numerous clergy or women religious in the first generation, and consequently their adjustments to American Catholicism were less institutionalized. The Italian peasants, moreover, brought with them various forms of folk Catholicism and an anticlericalism that made their clash with the voluntary and institutional patterns of religious life that had been developing in American Catholicism since the early nineteenth century particularly acute. Intra- and interethnic conflict characterized the Progressive Era, as the new immigrants sought to establish a home within an American Catholicism that was becoming increasingly pluralistic.

Although Progressive Era Catholics focused on the continuing immigrant conditions of their church, they also began to develop new missionary initiatives. At a time when liberal Protestants were calling the Christian missionary enterprise into question, American Catholics started to feel an indigenous missionary zeal that was another sign of the emergence of Catholicism from the self-centered preoccupations of the nineteenth century. In the early twentieth century, American Catholics created some imaginative ventures in home missions to the unchurched Americans and to those in isolated rural areas, and developed entirely new organizations for foreign missions.

New home missionary movements responded to a variety of unmet needs. The heiress of a large Philadelphia banking fortune, Katharine Drexel,* impressed by the Third Plenary Council's call for assistance to Catholic blacks and Indians, established in 1891 the Sisters of the Blessed Sacrament for Indians and Colored People. When she died in 1955, she and her religious order had established fifty-one houses in twenty-one states and the District of Columbia. By then, they also staffed sixty-two schools and had built Xavier University of New Orleans (1925), the only black Catholic university in the country.

Some sought to win Protestants or unchurched Americans over to Catholicism. In 1896 the Paulists, under the leadership of Walter Elliott and Alexander P. Doyle, launched a Catholic Missionary Union, whose fundamental purpose was to win converts by developing evangelical methods that were genuinely persuasive as well as respectful of American religious liberty.[7] The most spectacular of the home missions were the lay-led pioneer adventures in public speaking and street preaching organized by Boston's Martha Gallison Moore Avery and David Goldstein, both of whom were converts from socialism to Catholicism in 1904 and 1905, respectively. From the early twentieth century until World War II, a number of other lay evangelists crisscrossed the country as preachers and apologists for Catholicism.[8] Home missions also received new attention in Francis C. Kelley's Catholic Church Extension Society, organized in

Chicago in 1905 to provide funds and other forms of assistance for rural Catholics.

In the midst of its own continuing dependence on foreign missionaries to serve the pressing problems of urban immigrants and its own inadequate supply of home missionaries for rural peoples, American Catholicism began to send missionaries to foreign lands. By the beginning of the twentieth century, American Protestants had thousands of foreign missionaries and had committed millions of dollars to the endeavor. American Catholics had no more than sixteen religious involved in foreign missions, and their participation was not part of an organized enterprise, but more the result of individual zeal. This situation began to change in 1911 when James A. Walsh* of Boston and Thomas F. Price of Raleigh, North Carolina, established the Catholic Foreign Mission Society of America (Maryknoll), demonstrating again an incipient awareness of the American church's wider role in world Christianity and a new awakening of the missionary spirit. Maryknoll, the first American Catholic foreign mission society, built a seminary, attracted priests and eventually sisters to the new order, and in 1918 sent its first group of missionaries to China.

A few middle-class lay and clerical Catholics also crossed the boundaries of their immigrant conclaves to become involved in the Progressive Era's reformist mentality. Some organized national societies and movements[9] that focused on social, educational, and legislative reforms that were clearly influenced by Pope Leo XIII's perspective on social justice and the common good. Labor priests like Peter Dietz, Catholic socialists like Fathers Thomas McGrady and Thomas J. Hagerty, antisocialists and antiprogressives like Peter Yorke, lay editors and reformers like Milwaukee's Humphrey Desmond, German Christian solidarists like St. Louis's Frederick Kenkel, and sociologists like Father William Kerby worked in a variety of ways to promote very different Catholic visions of social and legislative reforms.

John A. Ryan* was undoubtedly the foremost Catholic representative of the progressive social and economic reformist mentality in the early twentieth century. He created a systematic study of the social question by combining the natural law tradition of the Leonine perspective with an empirical examination of the actual economic conditions in American society. Out of this study came his first major book, which produced arguments and proposals for *A Living Wage* (1906). Richard Ely's introduction called it "the first attempt in the English language to elaborate what may be called a Roman Catholic system of political economy." What impressed Ely most about the book, however, was that it got beyond "vague and glittering generalities to precise doctrine" and passed from "appeals to sentiment to reasoned arguments."[10]

Ryan saw state and later federal legislation as a key practical means to regulate and distribute more equitably the nation's wealth. Although critical of certain economic structures and the legislation that supported them, he was not as unalterably opposed to capitalism as was the German Catholic Central-Verein, and in fact he hoped to work through the capitalist system to transform it in a more democratic direction. His approach to legislation puts him in the camp of some Progressive Age Protestant reformers, but his modified Leonine vision makes his own progressivism distinctively Catholic.

Catholic public opinion on the major social and political issues of the Progressive Era, prohibition and women's suffrage, was as divided as were the perspectives on economic justice. Since the 1840s a few Catholic clerical and lay leaders had been engaged in local parish and state temperance movements, and in 1872 the Catholic Total Abstinence Union (CTAU) was formed as a national movement to promote, exclusively through moral suasion, temperance in the Catholic community. For the exclusive persuasionists, the church and Catholics qua Catholics should stay away from all forms of legislative prohibition. The church should emphasize the supernatural assistance of grace through the sacraments in the reformation of human persons and society. Total legislative prohibition, moreover, was unjustified because drink was not an inherent evil. Perhaps the majority of the CTAU membership opposed reformist movements toward prohibitive legislation, perceiving them to be rooted in Manicheanism, statism or socialism, American activism, pharisaism, and cultural chauvinism.[11] Some bishops, such as Milwaukee's Sebastian Messmer, forbade any priest visiting his diocese to speak in favor of prohibition legislation.

After the early 1880s, some CTAU members began to advocate legislative measures to restrict the sale and licensing of saloons, and by the 1890s, a few Catholics—for example, Fathers George Zurcher of Buffalo, John J. Curran of Wilkes-Barre, Pennsylvania, and James T. Judge of Scranton—were avid prohibitionists. Father James M. Cleary of St. Paul, at one time president of the CTAU, became the first vice president of the Anti-Saloon League. Bishops, too, like Spalding, Keane, and Ireland, favored increasing legislation to limit the availability of liquor.

For Catholic prohibitionists, the evil of intemperance was so pervasive and so destructive of individual, family, and social life that moral persuasion alone would not be effective. The problems were not just individual; they were part of the entire economic and legal structure of society. Legislative as well as moral reforms were needed. Catholic prohibitionists, moreover, not only cooperated with Protestants in suggesting legislation to restrict the use of alcohol but also wanted American Catholicism—which had all too often been identified with "rum and rebellion"—to be identified with the temperance reformist movements.

Catholics, like other Americans, were also divided on the issue of women's suffrage before and after the Progressive Era's ratification of the nineteenth amendment. Social activists Ellen Ewing Sherman, Madaline Vinton Dahlgren, and writers and editors like Katherine E. Conway opposed women's suffrage. Leonora Barry Lake, though, was an active suffragist, as were the pro-labor leader Mary Kenney O'Sullivan and a few other prominent middle-class Catholic women who saw suffrage as a political manifestation and extension of natural equality. Bishops and clergy, too, were divided in their sympathies with the pro- and anti-suffragist movements. Ireland, Spalding, and even the conservative

McQuaid favored the establishment of higher education for women and women's suffrage, while Bishop Joseph Macheboeuf of Denver, many of the German clergy, and even Gibbons railed against the evil effects of women's involvement in politics and opposed the ballot.[12]

Many rejected women's suffrage as a threat to the Christian home and inconsistent with a woman's dignity and role in society. Thomas Francis Lillis, bishop of Leavenworth, Kansas, did not believe that it was the "woman's place to approach the polls and vote."[13] Although, as Bishop Messmer noted in 1913, there was no official Catholic position on women's suffrage and even though it was still an open question, he believed that most Catholic theologians and philosophers, although accepting the natural equality of the sexes, denied the claim to political equality.[14] Cardinal Gibbons, too, had rejected the arguments in favor of suffrage, but once the nineteenth amendment was ratified on 20 August 1920, he encouraged all women to exercise their suffrage "not only as a right but as a strict social duty."[15]

Middle-class Catholics, like many others in the United States, revealed a propensity during the Progressive Era to organize national fraternal and professional societies for a variety of social and reform purposes. The American Federation of Catholic Societies (1901), a national union of various ethnic fraternal, and social societies, was one example of this tendency. The AFCS focused attention on national social and moral issues and provided mutual benefit and support for its members. The national organization of Catholic societies of educators, physicians, historians, philosophers, sociologists, and a host of other professional groups also developed during the Progressive Era and throughout the pre–Vatican II period. These societies tried to create an American Catholic sense of solidarity in responding to professional issues. By organizing themselves nationally, these societies were also adopting a characteristically modern principle of organization in their attempts to improve Catholic performance in their functional specialties, develop intercommunication, and provide a means for coordinated activities. In this respect, these new institutions played a role analogous to that of the consolidating bishops in the large urban dioceses.[16]

This progressive era tendency also contributed toward the development of a national episcopal organization that would be influential in directing Catholic presence throughout the twentieth century. The organization of the National Catholic War Council (NCWC; 1917), although brought about because of the needs of World War I, united bishops and isolated Catholic societies into a national force that was able to respond in organized fashion to the American war effort. The initiative for a united effort to muster Catholic support for the war and supply Catholic soldiers with chaplains and religious services came not from the bishops themselves, but from the Paulist John Burke, editor of the *Catholic World* from 1904 to 1922. He advised the bishops that they must "learn to think nationally."[17] At Burke's suggestion the bishops organized the NCWC as a united Catholic voice—similar to the Federal (later National) Council of Churches of Christ (1908)—capable of asserting Catholic interests in public life. Like some other national Catholic institutions of the period, the NCWC reflected the organizational revolution intrinsic to modernization in the twentieth century.

The NCWC helped the bishops transcend for the moment some of their differences and parochial concerns, and it effectively demonstrated Catholic patriotism. Through the NCWC the bishops helped bring about what Elizabeth McKeown has called "the practical identification of Americanism and Christianity" during the war years.[18] The NCWC also organized an aggressive publicity blitz to broadcast Catholic support for and participation in the war effort and helped to develop lobbying techniques that would serve the bishops well in years to come. Although the council was organized to meet pressing national needs, Burke had, even originally, intended that the national body be more than an ad hoc response. He saw it, or something like it, as a permanent federated Catholic response to public issues.

After the signing of the armistice in November 1918, American bishops decided to form the National Catholic Welfare Council (1919; title changed to Conference in 1922) as a more permanent national body to assist in the postwar reconstruction of American society and meet ongoing concerns of American Catholics. The bishops in particular had become increasingly aware of the growing federal control of American life and wanted an effective agency in Washington to protect and advance Catholic interests.

In the midst of establishing the NCWC, the council's administrative committee issued what has come to be called the "Bishops' Program of Social Reconstruction" (12 February 1919), a detailed proposal for legislation to ensure economic and social justice.[19] Written primarily by John A. Ryan, the program was, in the judgment of Joseph McShane, a synthesis of the Leonine vision of social justice and the progressive reform proposals of the age.[20] Among other things, it called for minimum wage legislation; social insurance for unemployment, old age, and sickness; a national employment agency; low-cost public housing projects; regulation of public utilities and monopolies; establishment of consumers' and producers' cooperatives; and equal wages for women.

Some were shocked by the proposals, tagging them socialistic. A few bishops, such as Cardinal Gibbons, were unprepared for the negative reactions. He insisted that the program was perceived as a novelty because Catholics themselves had not previously communicated their own sense of social justice. "The Church," he told a 1919 national episcopal assembly, "has a great work of social education and social welfare lying before it."[21] Although Gibbons defended the program, other bishops found some of its proposals too daring. But the program itself was a revelation of the new role in moral leadership the bishops were assuming in American society.

American Catholic leaders were optimistic about their role in society. The war had initiated the hierarchy into the national political process and opened the way for their continued leadership in shaping cultural values. Their own federal movement was not only a manifestation of the collegial temper of some nineteenth-century bishops, but an acknowledgment that modern problems demanded a national organization similar to the Federal Council of Churches. Catholic bishops had, perhaps unwittingly, come to terms with some of the dynamics and institutional developments of the Progressive Era, but the Progressive Era was coming to an end.

7

---·•·---

THE ROARING TWENTIES, THE DEPRESSION, AND WORLD WAR II: 1920–1945

AMERICAN CATHOLICS ENTERED the 1920s with a new feeling of their own Americanism and a new confidence in their ability to contribute to the national welfare. The cultural and social changes associated with the Roaring Twenties, the Depression of the 1930s, and the development of totalitarianism and religious intolerance in Russia, Mexico, Spain, and Germany, however, made Catholics aware of their continued alienation from aspects of American and modern life. In the midst of these significant changes, the neo-Thomist philosophical and theological tradition became a serviceable ideology in articulating an American Catholic identity. Catholics were self-consciously searching for a response to the spiritual, cultural, economic, and political anomie of modern American life, producing as a consequence a new kind of Catholic activism in American society, a cautious critique of American Catholic weaknesses, and a discreet call for internal ecclesial reforms. Catholic support for and participation in World War II reaffirmed American Catholic patriotism and nationalism, but it also broke the bonds of a prewar isolationism and laid a foundation for a new kind of internationalism within American Catholic leadership.

In these twenty-five years, according to the *Official Catholic Directory*, the Catholic population increased slowly (only 35 percent, from 17.7 million in 1920 to 23.9 million in 1945), especially in comparison to the previous hundred years of immigrant growth. A population increase of only 5 percent during the 1930s shows that the birth rate suffered considerably from the Depression. The slow population growth was accompanied, however, by a phenomenal 82 percent increase in the number of clergy (from 21,019 in 1920 to 38,451 in 1945), a 140 percent increase in seminarians, and an 83 percent increase in women religious. Prior to the 1920s, the church had been primarily dependent on Europe for clergy and women and men religious; thereafter it developed its own native clergy and religious. The postwar growth in religious vocations corresponded to the needs of the increasing number of schools, colleges, universities, hospitals, and social service agencies. What accounts for the tremendous growth of religious vocations during the period, or what does it signify? It is much easier to point to the fact of the growth than to discover its causes. It seems that the growth was partially the result of a combination of human factors: a concerted effort to recruit young men and women for a religious life, an awareness of the needs within the Catholic community, a growing American Catholic self-confidence, the devastating economic effects of the Depression, and the advantages religious life provided young second- and third-generation immigrants who were conscious of social mobility. Whatever the reasons may have been, there is no doubt that this tremendous growth needs a historian for a more systematic analysis.

The gradual evolution of a pragmatic and institutional Catholic Americanism, which had its origin during the consolidating days of the Progressive Era, continued during the 1920s and 1930s, becoming part of the Catholic defensive reaction to an aggressive postwar Protestant evangelical crusade to promote 100 percent Americanism. The Evangelical battle to protect its long-standing moral hegemony over American culture was an anxious response to the belief that secular values were beginning to threaten the stability and moral integrity of American society, and to the rising visible presence of Catholics and other "foreigners" who challenged Protestant dominance. The campaigns for 100 percent Americanism—for example, the struggle over the justification of Prohibition, the immigrant restriction quotas of 1921 and 1924, the Scopes trial of 1925, Oregon's legislative attempt to eliminate private schools, and Alfred E. Smith's political defeat in 1928—reinforced a Catholic sense of alienation, but stimulated a Catholic crusade to Christianize culture, a crusade that was analogous to the Protestant campaign Catholics opposed.

Ratification of the Eighteenth Amendment was the culmination of the nineteenth-century Protestant struggle for a Christian culture in America. Neither the campaign for legislative prohibition nor the Volstead Act of 1920, however, had been popular among most articulate American Catholics. Many Catholic leaders continued to believe that moral persuasion, rather than legislation, was a more effective remedy against the evils of intemperance and alcoholism. Some prominent Catholics, such as John A. Ryan, had supported the Eighteenth Amendment, but only on the condition that it could be reasonably enforced. By 1927, even supporters like Ryan were beginning to oppose the Volstead Act, because it was becoming increasingly evident that the law was ineffective and unenforceable, thus making a mockery of this law in particular and of all laws in general.[1] Many articulate Catholics also interpreted the Eighteenth Amendment as another manifestation of the increasing and unjustified involvement of "big government" (i.e., socialism) in individuals' lives—a fear that was similarly behind their opposition to federal involvement in education and child labor. The repeal of Prohibition in 1933 brought no resistance from the organs of Catholic opinion in the United States. Although most Catholics probably shared the Protestant concern for a Christian American culture, they did not agree with Prohibition as a means, because according to Catholic moral theology, there was nothing inherently evil in the consumption of alcoholic beverages.

One hundred percent Americanism also manifested itself in the rigorous immigrant restriction quotas enacted by Congress in 1921 and 1924, which were clearly prejudiced against southern and eastern Europeans, many of whom since the 1880s were Catholic. The Catholic press again opposed these measures, interpreting them as disguised prejudice against Catholics in America. John A. Ryan and others in the labor movement, however, saw the restriction laws as necessary legislative enactments to provide better wages for working-class Americans. Ryan also believed that Catholics generally were too quick to raise the anti-Catholic complaint.

Whatever the intent of the immigrant restriction quotas, they did have an unintended benefit within the Catholic community. By restricting the constant flow of immigrants, Congress had provided Catholics, and especially the consolidating bishops, with some time and space to make corporate ecclesiastical planning possible, develop Americanization strategies for the immigrants they had already absorbed into the church, and stabilize a Catholic community that had been in almost constant flux since the 1880s. In spite of the alienation that some Catholics felt because of the restrictions, these quotas, coupled with the rise of the consolidating bishops and creation of the NCWC, made the 1920s the beginning of a period of organizational strength for American Catholicism. That organizational strength gave Catholics a sense of self-confidence.

The issues that aroused the greatest public interest in religion in the 1920s were those connected with schools, the primary American agency for passing on American civilization and culture. In 1925 the widely publicized "Scopes Monkey Trial" in Tennessee and Oregon's attempt to prohibit private schools revealed anxieties about the definition, survival, and transmission of 100 percent (meaning evangelical Protestant, fundamentalist, and xenophobic) American culture. Catholics were affected indirectly by the former and directly by the latter. In reacting particularly to the Oregon school case, they emerged in a new way on the American political scene and helped to reinforce constitutional provisions for religious liberty.

In 1922 Oregon enacted legislation that made public schooling compulsory for all children between the ages of eight and sixteen. Backers of the legislation, including the Ku Klux Klan and Scottish Rite Masons, periodically articulated anti-Catholic slogans in their campaigns to win voters' approval for the legislation. The Oregon law raised the fears of Catholics across the country like nothing else in the most recent past because it challenged the integrity and independence of the entire Catholic school system.

Oregon Catholics, Lutherans, and Seventh-day Adventists, the American Civil Liberties Union, the national office of the Knights of Columbus, the NCWC, and a host of Protestant and liberal secular Americans called for a repeal of the law. Catholics in particular rejected the law because, as they argued in state courts and the U.S. Supreme Court, it violated religious liberty and educational diversity, and reflected a "socialist" movement in society of which Catholics since the mid-nineteenth century had an almost congenital fear.

In *Sisters of the Holy Names v. Pierce et al.* (1925) the U.S. Supreme Court handed down a landmark decision that supported the state's responsibility and rights over education and at the same time protected the rights of private and parochial education.[2] This was a legal victory and a milestone in the interpretation of the Constitution.

Catholic schools continued to expand, particularly during the 1920s, and to symbolize something of the relationship of Catholicism to American culture. During the 1920s and 1930s, they were gradually transformed from agents of separatism to agents of Americanization. Americanization meant that the schools would be used to bring American Catholic immigrant children into the mainstream of American economic and political life. The schools also became increasingly Americanized when they adopted modern methods of education and school administration. Many Catholic educators, like their counterparts in the public school system, began to worship at the shrine of scientific efficiency, believing that standardization, professionalization, state certification of teachers, and bureaucratic centralization were means for improving education. Although American Catholics warred against secularization in the society at large during these two decades, they were themselves captured by the very secular means they adopted in consolidating their dioceses and schools to fight against it.

The 1928 presidential campaign and defeat of the Catholic Alfred E. Smith—like the Oregon school case, immigrant restriction laws, and bigotry of the Ku Klux Klan and other "preservers" of Americanism—reinforced the feeling of alienation for a number of articulate leaders of Catholic public opinion and represented the culmination of threats to Catholic self-confidence in the 1920s. Whatever role religion may have had in Smith's actual defeat—and there is much scholarly dispute about it—there is little doubt that many leading Catholics saw it as a threat to their postwar aspirations of rising out of their nineteenth-century second-class status in America.

Smith's candidacy for the presidency brought to the fore some of the larger issues relative to the relationship of Catholicism to American public and constitutional life. The whole question of double allegiance reasserted itself in the campaign: "Can a Catholic be loyal to his church and, as president, to his country?" Charles C. Marshall, an Episcopal layman and political moderate, articulated the fears of many in 1927 when he concluded that the dogmatic principles of the Catholic Church were antithetical to American constitutional ideals. He asserted that Smith's election, therefore, might "precipitate an inevitable conflict between the Roman Catholic Church and the American State irreconcilable with domestic peace."[3]

Smith responded to Marshall's charges by outlining a religio-political creed that asserted his belief in religious liberty and separation of church and state, and argued that no power in the Catholic Church could overthrow these political realities.[4] But his creed contained a list of Catholic assertions, not rational demonstrations, and they did not persuade the public. Most Catholics in the 1920s, Smith included, resented the fact that they had to demonstrate their allegiance to their country, but most of them also did not perceive how threatening the Roman church's views and alleged political powers were in a liberal society. American fears, moreover, had recently been reinforced by the publication of John A. Ryan and Moorhouse Millar's *The Church and the State* (1922), which asserted that the state had the obligation to make a public profession of religion. It took more than a decade before an American Catholic, John Courtney Murray, S.J., would begin to develop a very different systematic intellectual response to the church–state issues raised by some Catholic teachings and the Smith candidacy.

Many have argued that Smith lost the campaign not only because of his Catholicism, but also because of his urban identification, his stand against Prohibition, Republican prosperity, and Herbert Hoover's popularity. Catholic leaders of public opinion, though, were stung by the charges raised during the campaign and by the subtle yet obvious forms of religious prejudice displayed during it.

Although they felt the sting of cultural alienation during the 1920s and 1930s, a few leading Catholics initiated a number of interlocking reform movements that had as their ultimate goals the development of a specific Catholic culture, the Christianization of American culture, and the revitalization of the economic order according to Catholic principles of justice and the common good. The revival of the Thomistic system of philosophy and theology in the 1920s advanced the cause of creating a specific Catholic intellectual culture. The liturgical movement during the mid-1920s fostered the internal and communal life of the church by recovering the liturgical sense and the doctrine of the Mystical Body of Christ. The neoscholastic and liturgical movements, although different in perspective, were interrelated with various forms of social Catholicism that developed during the period: the black Catholic call for racial justice within church and society; the rising lay consciousness of the "Commonweal Catholics" who published and read *Commonweal* (1924–), a lay Catholic journal of public opinion that nurtured the Catholic sense of lay responsibility for the common good; the increased preoccupations with economic justice during the Depression; the origin of the Catholic Worker Movement (1933–), which tried to restore a sense of Christian personalism by advocating and demonstrating in practice the Christian's personal duty to care for the poor and needy; and various other attempts that called attention to the need for reform in the church as well as society.[5]

The intellectual retrieval of Thomism was indicative of the Catholic search for unity and order within an immigrant church that was socially and culturally diverse and within an American society that was increasingly disillusioned and fragmented.[6] During the 1920s, the Thomist revival, which had been taking place in European Catholicism since the publication of Pope Leo XIII's encyclical *Aeterni Patris* in 1879, became much more self-conscious, systematically organized, and widespread in the United States. That encyclical, the antimodernism of Pope Pius X, and the promulgation of the Code of Canon Law in 1917 officially institutionalized Thomist philosophy and theology as the church's authoritative teaching. The Code of Canon Law, for example, stipulated, "teachers shall deal with the studies of mental philosophy and theology and the education of their pupils in such sciences according to the method, doctrine and principles of the Angelic Doctor and religiously adhere thereto."[7]

In 1921, some Catholic critics such as Virgil Michel,* O.S.B., charged that there was not a single journal devoted to neoscholasticism within the entire English-speaking world and that contemporary Catholics were not conversant enough to engage modern philosophy in discussion and debate.[8] In 1923, things began to change. Pope Pius XI published *Studiorum Ducem* in June to commemorate the six hundredth anniversary of the canonization of St. Thomas Aquinas, calling him the "Common or Universal Doctor of the Church; for the Church has adopted his philosophy for her own."[9] The *American Ecclesiastical Review* celebrated the event in July by calling for an American movement "back to St. Thomas."[10] Two years later, the Jesuits of St. Louis University began publishing the *Modern Schoolman* (1925–), the first *ex-professo* neoscholastic journal. Others followed: *Thought* (1926–), *The New Scholasticism* (1927– , which became the *American Catholic Philosophical Quarterly* in 1990), the *Thomist* (1939–). The American Catholic Philosophical Society was organized in 1926 to bring together Catholic neoscholastic philosophers to discuss and debate the implications of St. Thomas's philosophical system. In 1925, Father Fulton Sheen* published his Louvain doctoral dissertation, *God and Intelligence in Modern Philosophy*, reflecting the rising neoscholastic interests among younger scholars. By the end of the 1920s, a self-conscious intellectual revival was well organized and under way.

In the early 1920s, the Thomist system of philosophy and theology was perceived as a grand synthetic vision, transcending time in its unchangeable truths yet pliable and accommodating in its accidental expressions to the "march of the physical sciences" and to newer philosophical insights.[11] The Thomist revival was, in Philip Gleason's considered judgment, part of the American Catholic search for unity. It was an attempt to establish a synthetic intellectual vision that would demonstrate the integral relationship between reason and faith, religion and life. In fact, the Thomistic vision was a comprehensive philosophy of life that influenced not only philosophy itself, but also sociology, law, morality, politics, education, art, economic justice, exegesis, asceticism, and religion. In a time of intellectual disillusionment, political upheaval, and economic disaster, the Thomist view presented a world of order, balance, and reason capped off with the certitude of faith in an ultimately meaningful human existence. The Thomists reasserted the values of human reason and freedom, but they placed them within the vital context of revelation and faith. Reason, in fact, was ultimately oriented to and capable of discovering God's existence. The Thomist vision, moreover, provided an ideological justification for ecclesiastical authority and became the intellectual equivalent of the movement toward institutional consolidation. The Thomist revival, though, was preeminently an attempt to make the supernatural credible in a world perceived to be running madly toward materialism and naturalism.

The Thomist vision was also antimodernist, and for that very reason it was doubly appealing to many second- and third-generation ethnic American Catholic intellectuals. Individualistic, subjectivist, secularist, relativist, and rationalistic, the modern mind was opposed not only to the Catholic ethnic's sense of tradition and community but also to the antimodernist mentality that had developed in Western Catholicism since the time of Pius IX and was most recently reinforced by Pius X's assault on modern thinking. But the point here is that the antimodernist mind-set in American Catholicism during the 1920s was not something imposed from outside; it was congenial to and almost connatural with the American Catholic experience itself.

The liturgical movement was another major Catholic revival of the 1920s. Like the self-conscious renewal of neoscholasticism, it sought to combat the twin evils of individualism and totalitarian socialism. It, too, was a search for the unity of the Catholic tradition and an attempt to unpack the social and cultural implications of that unity. It found that unity in a concept of the Mystical Body of Christ, the central Catholic doctrine that simultaneously upheld the dignity and worth of the individual and the communal context of all human reality. It was also an attempt to bring about a restoration of a sense of spiritual interiority, organic communion, and the priesthood of the faithful—dimensions that had been diminished, so the liturgical reformers believed, by an individualism that was characteristic of Catholic devotional piety as well as the modern secular mind. A restoration of an active liturgical sense, it was believed, would do much to make American Catholics conscious of their common responsibility for the welfare of American culture and social life.

Virgil Michel was the primary founder and organizer of the movement. Fathers William Busch of St. Paul Seminary in Minnesota, Gerald Ellard, S.J., of St. Louis University, Reynold J. Hillenbrand, rector of Chicago's diocesan seminary, Martin Hellriegel, a St. Louis pastor, and a number of others joined together to promote the liturgical revival. In 1926 Michel, together with Ellard and Hellriegel, established *Orate Fratres* (*Worship* after 1951) as the movement's primary journal. Michel also founded the Liturgical Press at St. John's Abbey in Collegeville, Minnesota, for the dissemination of popular and scholarly works on the liturgical renewal. The publication of *Liturgical Arts* (1931–1972) also raised the consciousness of the importance of art and architecture in American Catholicism. In 1933 Ellard published *Christian Life and Worship*, a textbook used in many Catholic colleges throughout the 1930s and 1940s, to acquaint students with the doctrine of the Mystical Body of Christ and awaken them to the sacramental dimensions of Christian life.

By the time of Michel's death in 1938 the movement, although never more than a minority impulse within American Catholicism prior to the Second Vatican Council, was well organized and beginning to have an effect on some leading thinkers. After Michel's death, leadership of the movement eventually passed to his fellow Benedictine Godfrey Diekmann of St. John's University in Collegeville, a major center of the movement throughout the pre–Vatican II period. After 1940 the liturgical movement was promoted on the national level through the organization of annual Liturgical Weeks and Conferences.

In the midst of the Depression, Pope Pius XI published *Quadragesimo Anno* (1931), and Catholic leaders like Michel began to connect the internal ecclesial liturgical movement with the movement for economic justice. This association of social justice and public worship was, in fact, the distinctive American contribution to a movement that had European origins. For Michel, the German Central-Verein, and a few others, public worship was the practical and sacramental expression of the Mystical Body of Christ, the primary source of the Christian spirit, and the font of Christian social consciousness. As such, the liturgy could inspire and empower Christians to work for social justice in the world—social justice was the virtue that regulated all human actions "in proper relation to the common good."

Like the liturgical reformers, other pioneers promoted a social conscience within American Catholicism during these years. Black Catholics continued to decry racism in church and society and, under the leadership of Howard University biology professor Thomas Wyatt Turner,* organized the Federation of Colored Catholics in the United States (1925–1958), as its 1925 constitution indicated, to unite black Catholics, promote Catholic education for them, and stimulate them to more active participation in the struggle for equality in church and society.[12] The federation invited white clergy and laity as associated members. The Jesuits John LaFarge of Maryland and William Markoe of St. Louis University became active members and eventually made strong appeals to shift priorities from black solidarity to interracial justice. The conflict between Turner's original vision and that of Markoe-LaFarge split the movement in 1933 and for all practical purposes ended its effectiveness. In 1933, the Catholic Interracial Council of the Markoe-LaFarge wing became the primary agency for raising the consciousness of racial injustice in the church and society, but the move toward interracial activity also diminished black leadership in the movement and almost completely eclipsed the aim of black Catholic solidarity.

Through their publications and meetings, locally organized Catholic Interracial Councils were able to keep the issue of racial justice before the Catholic community, but like other movements toward social justice, they were ineffective in making the demands for racial justice a popular movement within American Catholicism. Many, if not all, Catholic colleges, secondary schools, monasteries, convents, and seminaries throughout the 1920s and into the 1930s continued to be segregated.[13] American bishops as a national body, moreover, did not speak out on the constitutional rights of blacks until 1943 and did not make racial discrimination the exclusive subject of a national pastoral letter until "Discrimination and Christian Conscience" in 1958.[14] Desegregation of Catholic institutions would be the work primarily of the post–World War II era.

Other forms of social Catholicism arose during the Depression to deal with economic issues. The 1919 "Bishops' Program of Social Reconstruction" and the NCWC's Social Action Department, under the general guidance of John Burke and the leadership of John A. Ryan and Raymond McGowan, set the tone for a national Catholic social consciousness, but they were not the only forms of social Catholicism during the 1920s and 1930s. The early pastoral and social work of Robert Lucey* in Los Angeles and his later work among Mexican American farm workers in the Southwest, the social activism and labor advocacy of a number of young "labor priests" like Peter Dietz and Francis Haas, the personalism of the Catholic Worker Movement under the leadership of Dorothy Day* and Aristide Peter Maurin,* the social solidarism of the liturgical movement, the social critique and populist polemics of Charles Coughlin* of Detroit, the Jesuit schools of social service, and the advocacy of rural values and the challenge to the government's agricultural policies of the National Catholic Rural Life Conference—these were a few of the individuals and movements that produced a body of literature, a critique of the American social agenda, and a multitude of institutions to foster a Catholic sense of social justice.[15] Although they differed among themselves in selectively appropriating principles from the papal encyclicals and adapting them to the American economic order, they shared a common search for a middle ground between the twin evils of laissez-faire capitalism and socialism. The Catholic vision of social justice upheld simultaneously the inherent dignity and rights of the individual and concern for the common good in the industrial order, themes that were consonant with Pope Leo XIII's 1891 encyclical *Rerum Novarum* and Pius XI's 1931 *Quadragesimo Anno.*

The variety and the specific differences among the diverse kinds of Catholic social reform programs are not easy to depict in a paragraph. John Ryan and the Social Action Department of the NCWC promoted a form of "economic democracy." If the problem, as Ryan saw it, was underconsumption, the solution was an equitable distribution regulated by the government. Ryan's view of the state (especially the federal government after 1930) as a positive agent for social justice corresponded significantly with President Franklin Delano Roosevelt's New Deal—so much so that Charles Coughlin sarcastically referred to Ryan as the "Right Reverend New Dealer." Dorothy Day and the Catholic Workers, on the other hand, encouraged Catholics and others to take personal responsibility for the corporal and spiritual works of mercy. From this initial step, Day and others established Catholic Worker houses of hospitality and soup kitchens in various urban areas throughout the 1930s and 1940s. Charles Coughlin differed from others in his conviction that the central cause of the Depression was a money famine, a conspiracy concocted by international bankers to control and limit the supply of money for their own greedy purposes. Although his diagnosis of the disease was constant, his medicine did vary from time to time, but generally he prescribed an increase in the supply of money. The Catholic Rural Lifers supported a form of Catholic and Jeffersonian agrarianism, believing that a stable and healthy rural economy was a strong support for the entire nation. Most Catholic agrarians favored a decentralized and independent economic system that considered rural life as a whole and not as part of an economic industrial system. In the judgment of Edward Shapiro, they "favored more radical economic and social reforms and were more opposed to big business than the 'liberals' [like Ryan] of the Catholic University of America."[16] Although the Catholic economic reform programs differed, and although the church, American bishops wrote in 1940, did not prescribe "any particular form of technical Teconomic [sic] organization just as she does not prescribe any particular political organization of the state," she taught that every economic system must be in accord with fundamental justice and the common good.[17]

Economic issues and the effects of the Depression on the whole culture were not the only concerns of the American Catholic community. Catholics also became increasingly occupied with national and international politics, and by the end of World War II, some of them had moved into positions of significant political influence that they had not possessed before Roosevelt's presidency. George Q. Flynn has argued convincingly that under Roosevelt and the New Deal, American Catholics were "recognized as a major force in society" and raised to a new level of influence that indicated a transformation in the American political attitude toward the church and in the church's disposition toward the government. Roosevelt placed prominent Catholics (e.g., James A. Farley, Thomas Corcoran, Frank Murphy, Joseph Kennedy, Father Francis Haas) in key administrative positions and courted Catholic favor. Prominent Catholic leaders, on the other hand, accepted much of the New Deal legislation and presented it to American Catholics as an "American version of the papal encyclicals. In this sense the New Deal liberalized American Catholics by showing them the relevance of their Church's teachings on social problems."[18] Catholics also voted in large numbers in support of Roosevelt's four terms. Some studies have revealed that even when other motivational variables like occupation, class, economics, and ethnicity are considered, Catholic votes for Roosevelt and other Democrats during these years were from 27 to 31 percent higher than Protestant votes.[19]

In the realm of international politics, Catholics became increasingly concerned during the 1920s and 1930s with the rise of Russian communism, the Mexican persecution of the church, Spanish communism and fascism, Italian fascism, and German National Socialism. These events reinforced their fears about the disintegration of Western Christian culture. Political divisions among Catholics, however, prevented them—even if they wanted to, and they did not—from mounting a Catholic campaign to influence American foreign policy.[20] Although they were divided among themselves on whether communism or fascism represented the greater threat, they were united in their view that the political, like the economic, order should steer a middle path between the Scylla of secular individualism and the Charybdis of totalitarianism (whether of the communist or fascist kind).

American Catholics' preoccupations with Russian communism and even more with religious persecution in Mexico, Spain, and Germany were motivated primarily by their solicitude for their coreligionists in these countries. The problem of religious persecution, in particular, also flowed from an American view of religious liberty, which they saw violated in these countries. The Catholic campaign against foreign governmental persecution of Catholics was another sign that a few

Catholics were gradually emerging from their nineteenth- and early-twentieth-century conclaves of ethnic Catholicism. The protests laid a broad foundation for a Catholic international perspective that had been developing here and there since the days of Americanism. But the distinctive Catholic concerns for religious liberty at the international level were not widely shared in the American body politic, thus reinforcing the minority status of their own interests.

From 1917 until World War II, Catholic leaders here and there kept alive an opposition to Russian communism, which was generally perceived as totalitarian and antireligious. Although they were united in their anticommunist ideology, American Catholics developed at least three different assessments of communism and different methods of opposing it. Some American Catholics, perhaps the majority, saw their anticommunism as an apocalyptic religious crusade against a diabolic force that could be driven out only by prayer, fasting, and divine intervention. Others—for example, the Catholic Workers, the Commonweal Catholics, and social justice advocates including John A. Ryan, Robert E. Lucey, and Francis Haas—saw the communist critique of unrestrained and individualistic capitalism as valid but sought to combat the appeal of that critique by promoting alternative Christian visions and practices of social justice. Still others, such as Fulton J. Sheen, combined elements of both traditions, but he emphasized the ideological aspects of the Catholic war with communism. For Sheen, communism was an alien philosophy of life that had a messianic religious force in the world because it demanded an absolute submission to the state. The ideological war with communism had to be carried out in publications, sermons, radio lectures, convert lessons, and other forms of communication that could get to the minds and hearts of the people.[21]

From the Mexican Revolution in 1910 to the decline of religious persecutions of Catholics in 1935, leading American Catholics were divided in their assessment of the role they and the American government should play in coming to the aid of their coreligionists. Some, like Cardinal Gibbons in the pre–World War I era and John J. Burke of the NCWC in the 1920s, believed that American Catholics could best help by working quietly and diplomatically through American governmental agencies to put pressure on the Mexican government to modify and eventually eliminate the persecutions. Others, like Francis C. Kelley of the Church Extension Society during the pre–World War I era and Baltimore's Archbishop Michael Joseph Curley during the 1920s and 1930s, believed that the atrocities and fundamental violations of religious liberties ought to be vigorously publicized in the American press, the American government ought to be criticized for its ineffective and inadequate response to the problem, and that violated American sensitivities should be stirred up to put public pressure on the American government to help restore the natural rights of Mexican Catholics.[22] Whether they pursued a diplomatic or heated publishing campaign, American Catholics had little or no measurable effect on public opinion or foreign policy in Mexico, but once again they demonstrated their distress over issues beyond their local churches.

By 1935 American Catholic anxieties over Mexico declined as the persecutions did. From 1936 to 1939 attention shifted to the Spanish Civil War and the persecutions of Catholics in Spain. American Catholics opposed the Popular Front's anticlerical and hostile attacks on the Spanish church and its people and saw the Popular Front as a communist- and secularist-inspired totalitarian regime, operating under the guise of republicanism, but they were divided on the means to preserve the church and its institutions.[23] A public opinion poll taken in 1938 indicated that "39% of Catholics favored Franco; 30% were pro-Loyalist; and 31% were neutral."[24] *America*, the *Tablet, Commonweal* under Michael Williams* (1935–1937), the American bishops' 1937 pastoral "To the Spanish Hierarchy," and a host of diocesan newspapers supported Franco's revolt against the Second Spanish Republic, because they saw him as the protector of the church's interests and the best available agent for the restoration of the church's freedom in Spanish society.

A minority of American Catholic journalists and opinion makers—particularly Dorothy Day, the *Catholic Worker* and *Commonweal* (after 1937)—together with the Italian clerical antifascist Don Luigi Sturzo and the French philosopher Jacques Maritain—believed that Franco's resistance and wartime measures were as cruel and ruthless as those of the so-called Loyalists, and that if Franco did win the war, his totalitarianism would be as objectionable as that of the Popular Front. Support for Franco could thus be interpreted as support for a status quo that was badly in need of social reforms to which fascists like Franco were particularly blind. Catholic support for religious liberty should be closely tied to equally adamant support for social justice in Spain. For the consistent pacifist Dorothy Day, furthermore, the church should condemn violence on all sides and not identify itself with military means to win peace.

Catholics were also somewhat divided in their support for Benito Mussolini and Italian fascism, although there appears to have been more support for Mussolini than for Franco. Since the mid-1920s *America, Commonweal*, and numerous other journals and diocesan newspapers favored Mussolini and Italian fascists because they saw them as the true patriots in the war against Bolshevism and as the strongest allies of the church and family. A 1937 opinion poll demonstrated that when given the hypothetical option of choosing between fascism and communism, 61 percent of all Americans favored fascism. A similar poll in 1939, however, indicated that that support had fallen to 54 percent, but 66 percent of the Catholics in the poll still favored fascism over communism.[25]

But there was also a minority voice in the Catholic community that protested against fascism. Francis Duffy, James Cox, John A. Ryan, and especially the Paulist James Gillis, editor of the *Catholic World*, opposed Mussolini because they rejected his assault on political liberties and his violent undemocratic procedures. After Pope Pius XI's encyclical *Non Abbiamo Bisogno* (1931), an attack on fascist "statolatry" and fascist assaults on Catholic Action in Italy, Gillis charged that too many American Catholic journals had simply "soft pedaled" the encyclical and been blind to fascist injustices and totalitarian designs.[26]

In the late 1930s, some American Catholics also turned their attention to the threat from German National Socialism. For a number of reasons, not the least of which was the 1933 Vatican concordat with Germany, Catholics did not consider Adolf Hitler and Nazi Germany much of a threat until 1935, when Pope Pius XI protested against violations of the concordat and government restrictions on the church's activities.[27] *America*, following in the wake of the papal protests, proclaimed a new Kulturkampf in Germany. By 1936 Catholics such as Sheen were beginning to equate communist Russia with Nazi Germany, the one being as demonic as the other in the denials of religious liberties and basic human rights. In March 1937 Pius XI published his *Mit Brennender Sorge*, condemning the persecution of Catholics in the Reich and protesting against the Nazi divinization of race.[28] Chicago's German-American Cardinal Mundelein followed the pope's encyclical in May 1937 with an attack on the Nazi-style Kulturkampf.[29] In November, American bishops wrote a pastoral "To the German Hierarchy," protesting against the persecution of the church.

Exclusive concern about Nazi persecutions of Catholics made some American Catholics indifferent or numb to Nazi atrocities against the Jews. In 1934 the *Tablet* expressed the opinion of some Catholics when it asked, "Why is it so infamous to restrict certain liberties of 600,000 Jews in Germany and not at all obnoxious to hold in slavery millions of other people in Russia, Mexico, and Spain?"[30] Some Catholics found their own inability to win popular American support for the persecution of their fellow Catholics another sign of the lingering prejudice against them. After 1937 other Catholics, like Coughlin, began to assault Jewish bankers and by implication and direct assertion to justify Hitler's and Mussolini's programs as the inauguration of a new Christian social order. Coughlin and *Tablet* Catholics saw Nazi Germany as a force against the evils of the Depression and the Russian communist revolution, both of which were attributed to Jewish sources.

Others rejected Coughlin's and the *Tablet's* anti-Semitism. In 1938, for example, Msgr. Fulton Sheen, among others, addressed a large New York "rally for American Liberty," declaring, "only those who condemn persecution irrespective of where they find it, have any right to be heard." On another occasion he asserted, "I joined the Jews in New York in their protest against the abominable outrages of Hitler against them and their religion. I only ask now that all who believe in freedom, democracy and religion join us in protest against the Reds."[31] In 1938, the Knights of Columbus protested to President Roosevelt about Germany's persecution of the Jews, expressing "the deepest sympathy for the distressed Jews of Europe," and urged the American government to use its influence to help secure their refuge and protection in Palestine.[32] In 1940 Bishop Robert Lucey of Amarillo, Texas, wrote, "We as Christians, as citizens, as human beings must cry out against the horror of this [Nazi] debauchery [against Jews]." Speaking before the National Conference of Christians and Jews in Dallas that same year, he attacked Hitler and protested against the isolationist mentality in America, warning, "what is happening to the people of Europe is our business."[33]

On 14 November 1941, on the verge of American entrance into the war, the national body of bishops published a pastoral, "The Crisis of Christianity," which condemned religious persecution throughout Europe and singled out the persecutions of the Jews. "We cannot too strongly condemn," they wrote, "the inhuman treatment to which the Jewish people have been subjected in many countries."[34]

Although they protested against religious and civil persecutions in foreign countries, American Catholics, like many other Americans in the late 1930s, remained political isolationists—even after Hitler's rising power, ambitious designs, and military aggression toward Poland, Czechoslovakia, Austria, and other countries. Once Pearl Harbor was bombed on 7 December 1941, however, the isolationism quickly dissipated. Except for Dorothy Day and some Catholic Worker pacifists, most Catholics united with President Roosevelt in the war with the Axis. Although their support was restrained by comparison to that given during World War I, the national body of American bishops placed "our institutions and their consecrated personnel" at the president's disposal for service to the country.[35]

Catholic participation in the war was the culmination of the previous decade's Catholic literary and philosophical assault on totalitarianism, whether in fascist or communist forms. The war brought an end to the Depression, but it produced anxiety and fear at home and abroad about the future of a Christian civilization and the weak possibilities of a just and lasting peace. For many it also brought a common experience of the sacrifice of human life and material goods, a binding together in a united effort to serve the common good, and an idealism about the righteousness of the cause that made the sacrifice and united effort seem redemptive. For many Catholics, in particular, it was another manifestation that they were an integral component of the American system. Fundamental American beliefs and ideals were not only consistent with Catholicism but also ultimately grounded in a transcendental revelatory authority, which the church proclaimed in the modern world.

Between the world wars a number of American Catholics became increasingly interested in issues beyond their parishes and dioceses and emerged into American political life in ways that were unknown before World War I. Although their concerns were still primarily Catholic, their Catholic interests had become more international than previously, and their Catholic political interests were tied significantly to their anxieties about the survival of a Christian culture, not just the Catholic Church. By the end of World War II, Catholics were increasingly preoccupied with world peace, the threat of communism, care and relief of war-torn Europe, and the effects of postwar economic and ecclesiastical expansionism.

8

---·•·---

CATHOLICISM IN THE COLD WAR:
1945–1965

WITH THE END of World War II the United States entered a twenty-year period of unprecedented economic prosperity, worldwide economic and political influence, and a widespread resurgence of religion in the midst of Cold War anxieties over communism. Like many other religious denominations, American Catholicism took advantage of the expanding wealth and built numerous new churches, schools, and other large religious institutions, some of which had been delayed during the previous fifteen years by the Depression and the war. Numerous Catholics, especially the national hierarchy, were convinced that their numerical strength and affluence gave them an exceptional opportunity for moral leadership in American society, but others in American society perceived the increasing Catholic moral crusades as fundamental threats to American democratic liberties. Hopeful, institutionally and numerically strong, and active in the promotion of an American Christian culture, Catholics were withdrawing from their ethnic conclaves, battling each other ideologically, and calling for some moderate reforms in Catholic attitudes and practices. The postwar years began with anxieties about the twin evils of worldwide communism and secularism, and ended with a confidence that Catholicism had finally emerged into American society and the world community with President John F. Kennedy's election and Pope John XXIII's ecumenical council.

Between 1945 and 1965, American Catholicism experienced a phenomenal growth, one significantly unmatched during the previous twenty years and one not repeated in the post-1965 period. The total Catholic population increased by 90 percent, from 23.9 million to 45.6 million. The number of bishops and archbishops increased by 58 percent, clergy by 52 percent, women religious by 30 percent, and seminarians by 127 percent. One hundred and twenty-three new hospitals, 3,005 new Catholic elementary and high schools, and 94 new colleges were built. Enrollments in Catholic elementary and secondary schools increased by 3.1 million—more than 120 percent—and in Catholic colleges and universities, primarily because of the GI Bill, by a whopping 300 percent, from 92,426 to 384,526. Although the schools expanded rapidly to meet the increasing

Catholic population, still they enrolled perhaps no more than 50 percent of all Catholics in primary and secondary education and a significantly smaller percentage in higher education. American Catholics also distributed over $1.35 billion through Catholic Relief Services and the Society for the Propagation of the Faith to aid the world's poor and support missionaries throughout the world. These statistics of numerical and institutional developments and the corresponding increase in financial contributions manifested something not only of the nation's prosperity but also of the general postwar American support for religion and voluntaryism.[1]

The ecclesiastical vision, as officially articulated by the national episcopal pastoral letters from 1945 to 1965, continued to focus on what the bishops repeatedly called the restoration and reconstruction of a "Christian culture" in the United States and the Western world. To restore, preserve, or build a Christian culture meant to permeate civilization with the Christian spirit and struggle against the prevailing and pervasive influences of secularism and communism both at home and abroad. These twin objectives, which had been the focus of various Catholic movements in the 1930s, had percolated up to episcopal consciousness and became the foundation of the bishops' programs. In the postwar situation, bishops increasingly called on all Christians, not just Catholics, to transform society, giving their appeals a more universal ring than they had during the 1930s.

Secularism, the "practical exclusion of God from human thinking and living," was, the bishops wrote in 1947, the historical source of the rise of fascism, Nazism, and communism, and was the root of all of the world's travails. It was doing more than anything else to "blight our heritage of Christian culture." The bishops, acknowledging the limits of the historical order, proclaimed the ideals of Christian culture.[2]

The threat of secularism and its particular manifestation in worldwide communism were evident, the bishops repeatedly charged, in the family (where divorce, birth control, and economic injustices threatened to destroy its unity and stability), the entertainment industry (where materialistic values and sexual promiscuity were being promoted), education (which was increasingly being divorced from a religious vision), the economic order (where either laissez-faire capitalism or totalitarian socialism were destroying the individual's and the family's rights to decent and frugal living), the American courts (where religion was being radically separated from the institutions of American culture, particularly education), and the political order (where individual rights were being smashed by totalitarian communism or where political and legal enactments were divorced from natural law and Christian virtues). These threats were a "menace to our Christian and American way of living."[3] The connection between Christianity and America was in the realm of fundamental values, not in the realm of historical and current practices, but the connection itself revealed how closely the bishops had identified the two.

Marriage and family were issues of primary concern for many postwar Americans, especially Catholics, who saw marriage as a sacrament and the foundation of society. To counteract the forces of secularism (manifested in divorce, birth control, and abortion) that threatened the unity, stability, and fertility of marriage, Catholics since the 1930s, but particularly during the late 1940s and 1950s, had established a number of agencies to nurture married life. In 1931 the NCWC established the Family Life Bureau (FLB) as part of its Social Action Department. The FLB was a national clearinghouse for information and studies on the family and was assigned "to promote a program of action that would encourage the building of successful Christian marriages and wholesome Catholic homes." *Integrity* magazine (1946–1956), founded by Ed Willock and Carol Jackson and later edited by Dorothy Dohen, articulated a radical personalist critique of American individualism and capitalism and fostered a sacramental-personalist approach to family living. The Cana Conference (1943–) and marriage counseling movements sponsored family retreats and days of family renewal to strengthen the spiritual roots of relationships. By the end of the 1940s, moreover, the Christian Family Movement (CFM), under the leadership of Patrick and Patricia Crowley, was organized to reform those conditions in society that wrecked havoc on the integrity of modern family life.[4]

The campaign to maintain and promote a Christian civilization in American society also involved a moral crusade against indecency and immorality in the entertainment industry and modern literature. To combat the increasing threat of obscenity and moral laxity, the American bishops established the League of Decency in 1934 and the National Office for Decent Literature (NODL) in 1938. Both institutions evaluated and published their rankings of movies and pamphlets. These ratings, which started out as moral guidelines for Catholics, soon became in the hands of some church leaders morally binding in conscience. The league, which was an American innovation that Pope Pius XI recommended to the universal church in 1936, also formulated a decency pledge that Catholics took annually during a Sunday liturgy—promising to avoid movies declared objectionable.

Individual bishops and pastors periodically condemned specific movies as occasions of sin and forbade their people to attend them. Urban bishops like Cardinals Francis J. Spellman* of New York and Dennis Dougherty of Philadelphia exercised considerable power in blackballing certain movies. Cardinal Spellman publicly declared that some movies could not be seen "with a safe conscience," and others, like *Baby Doll*, were forbidden "under pain of sin." In 1948 Cardinal Dougherty threatened two theater owners that he would direct all Catholics to boycott their theaters for an entire year if they did not, within forty-eight hours, cease showing *The Outlaw* and *Forever Amber*.[5]

The kind of censorship that was exercised over the entertainment industry was also periodically exercised over the publishing industry. These forms of censorship had as their positive aim the promotion of Christian civilization, but the aggressive and authoritarian tactics that were often used seriously discredited this manifestation of "Catholic action" in the eyes of some non-Catholics and a few articulate Catholic leaders.

The struggle against secularism came out most forcefully in the battles over education. Many Catholic leaders since the 1930s had fought against the increasing secularization of modern American education from the primary to the university levels. Prevailing philosophies of education, debates over federal aid to education, and Supreme Court decisions revealed this trend. At a 1939 conference of the National Catholic Alumni Federation, Geoffrey O'Connell, author of *Naturalism in American Education* (1936), and other Catholic university professors argued that for three decades John Dewey's philosophy of pragmatic secularism had influenced generations of America's public schoolteachers and created a "threat to the Christian cultural education of the youth of our country."[6] A thoroughly Catholic education, integrating the natural and the supernatural, was the only protection against this fundamental menace, and thus Catholics were facing a challenge of unprecedented proportions in the postwar years as they tried to develop their educational philosophy and institutions.

Federal aid to public and private education and various Supreme Court decisions on aid and the role of religion in public education created intense public debate during the period. In the 1920s and 1930s the Catholic bishops had opposed federal aid to public education because they feared that such governmental aid would increase the state's power over education and because they believed that parents by natural law had the primary authority for education. By 1944, however, the bishops supported federal aid to schools for the sake of children in economically depressed areas. Two national episcopal statements (1944 and 1955) on private and public education sought to tie federal aid for health, safety, and welfare to all needy children without regard to color, origin, or creed, and to be equitable, to children in any school that met the requirements of compulsory education.

These appeals and the Supreme Court decision in *Everson v. Board of Education* (1947), allowing New Jersey to use tax funds to bus children attending Catholic schools, created a great deal of consternation among some Americans. Again the cry went up that aggressive Catholic bishops, representing a numerous and increasingly powerful Catholic block, were seeking to destroy the Constitution by uniting church and state. In response to these developments, Protestants and Other Americans United for the Separation of Church and State (POAU) was established in 1948. The organization was another sign of the tensions that were developing between some Protestants and Catholics during the Cold War.

The fear of Catholic cultural and political aggression became most clearly articulated in Paul Blanshard's *American Freedom and Catholic Power* (1949). Blanshard believed that the time was over when Americans could be silent about the threat of powerful Catholic influences in politics, medicine, art, entertainment, literature, scholarship, and education. In all these areas Catholics were using the power of numbers and institutional force to destroy American freedoms.

Blanshard pointed out that he was not against Catholicism or the religious principles of the Catholic people, but against the church's social and political interferences. No doubt there was bigotry in Blanshard's bombshell, but there was also a fundamental difference between his liberal views of the relationship between religion and culture and that of official Catholicism. Blanshard had some historical grounds for asserting that Catholics were politically and culturally aggressive, but he interpreted almost all forms of Catholic action (and the ideology behind it) as censorship because he believed that religion ought to be a private affair of conscience. Few Catholic leaders accepted this perspective.

The reaction to POAU, the Blanshard book, and other criticisms of Catholic intentions was immediate and polemical, intensifying the split in the American religious community. Opposition to Catholics' pleas for state aid for their children or to Catholic attempts to provide moral guidance in the culture was motivated, many Catholic writers thought, either by bigotry, moral laxity, indifference to public and common welfare, or by a secularist mentality that made separation of church and state absolute and reduced religious influence to the privacy of individual conscience and total irrelevance in public life. The Jesuit theologian John Courtney Murray sardonically referred to POAU as "PU," asserting that the real threat in American society was not Catholicism but a progressive secularization "that bears within itself the seeds of future tyrannies."[7] Unlike the old Nativism, which claimed that Catholicism was anti-American because it was not Protestant, Blanshard's "new nativism," according to Murray, saw Catholicism as anti-American because it proclaimed that there was a source of truth beyond democratic majoritarianism and scientific naturalism.[8]

These charges and countercharges stoked the coals of bitterness, but they also provoked questions about the relationship of the Catholic Church to the state and American society, questions that demanded more of an intellectual response than had been provided in the American Catholic past. Out of this experience of conflict and aggressive forms of Catholic action would come a new intellectual struggle (considered later) to define more adequately the Catholic understanding of church–state relations and stimulate more Catholic reflection on the mode of the church's influence in the public forum.

As Catholics criticized the secularization of public education and became involved in the debates over federal aid, their own schools of higher education were undergoing phenomenal changes that made bleak the prospects that Catholic higher education would become the bulwark against naturalism. The postwar expansion of Catholic colleges and universities left little time, financial resources, or energy to scrutinize or develop a Christian educational alternative to the naturalism in secular higher education. Although most administrators within these institutions had a common neoscholastic philosophical orientation, which provided them with an ideological unity and purpose, they concentrated on building up their professional schools to meet increasing demands and simply let the Christian character of the institution take care of itself.

The development of American Catholic intellectual life did not parallel the institutional expansion of education during these years. In 1962 American bishops, meeting in Rome for the Second Vatican Council, complained in their pastoral letter of that year that the American church, despite its tremendous growth and flourishing condition, could not boast of numerous saints, profound scholars, and brilliant writers as could "some of the older centers of Christian culture."[9] Seven years earlier, Msgr. John Tracy Ellis had argued that the immigrant condition of American Catholicism, among other things, had been, but could no longer be, responsible for intellectual narrowness and even anti-intellectualism in education. He and a few others called for more concerted efforts to overcome these conditions.[10]

The primary function of Catholic education, according to some neoscholastic educators, was not intellectual creativity but the communication of the wisdom of the ages. For the Jesuit George Bull, the "humane use of the mind, the function proper to him as man, is contemplation and not research.... In sum, then, research cannot be the primary object of a Catholic graduate school, because it is at war with the whole Catholic life of the mind."[11] How representative Bull's view was is open to question, but it certainly fit in with an unsophisticated scholasticism that tended to dominate Catholic higher education. By the middle of the 1950s though, as indicated, this view was being subjected to considerable internal criticism.

Even prior to the mid-1950s, however, there were some signs of a slowly developing intellectual life within American Catholicism. By the late 1940s, philosophy departments and even a few graduate schools of philosophy were captured by disciples of either Etienne Gilson or Jacques Maritain, two widely acknowledged creative leaders of Thomist philosophy. The liturgical movement, with its origins in the 1920s, was also coming into blossom during the postwar years, fostering a historical study of patristic and liturgical sources and a more adequate biblical knowledge. Too much emphasis in Catholic education on apologetics, individual morality, and the "anti" mentality (e.g., anti-Protestantism, anticommunism, and antisecularism) led, Godfrey Diekmann, O.S.B., asserted, to a neglect of the church's essential life—a situation that the liturgical movement was trying to reverse.[12] Biblical study, still in its infancy at the beginning of the postwar years, was nourished by the establishment of the Catholic Biblical Association and *Catholic Biblical Quarterly* (1938) and encouraged by Pope Pius XII's *Divino Afflante Spiritu* (1943). German refugee Johannes Quasten, who had been teaching at the Catholic University since 1938, advanced significantly historical theology, particularly patristics. Systematic theology received a major new impetus with the publication of *Theological Studies* (1940), the first scientific journal of theology since the *New York Review*, and the organization of the Catholic Theological Society of America (1946).

The stimulation of theological scholarship produced conflicts within the Catholic community, reflecting differences in methodology between the neoscholastic and the historical-critical theologians and biblical scholars. Joseph Clifford

Fenton, for example, a theologian at the Catholic University, took issue with some of the biblical scholars whose advanced ideas on inspiration and historical-critical methods contrasted sharply with his own ahistorical neoscholastic views.[13] Dissensions within the Catholic theological community erupted over a variety of other issues: for example, the kind of theology to be taught at the college level,[14] the possibility of intercreedal cooperation, the understanding of and participation in the ecumenical movement, and the nature of religious liberty and separation of church and state. These incipient postwar theological tensions and diversity would be revealed more fully in the Second Vatican Council. The 1950s neoscholastic accent on a unified Catholic intellectual vision was—in practice, if not yet in theory—gradually being called into question.

Theologians split into two camps over intercreedal cooperation and the ecumenical movement. Murray and Gustave Weigel,* S.J., of Woodstock College argued that circumstances in postwar Europe demanded intercreedal cooperation for the sake of the common good. Such cooperation, countered Fenton, Francis J. Connell, C.SS.R., and Paul Hanly Furfey of the Catholic University, would lead to religious indifferentism.[15] These groups split along the same lines over their approaches to the ecumenical movement: Catholic University professors thought the movement fostered religious relativism, while Woodstock professors considered it necessary to fulfill Christ's will for unity. American Catholic participation in the ecumenical movement, which was predominantly Protestant, was almost nonexistent during these years, except for a very few pioneers who raised the issue of Christian unity to a new level of theological reflection.

The hostilities surrounding the development of POAU and the Blanshard bomb, Protestant suspicions created by certain ill-advised forms of Catholic action, Pope Pius XII's encyclical *Humani Generis* (1950, which was seen as another form of papal repression of theological inquiry),[16] and the papal proclamation of the dogma of Mary's Assumption (1950) curtailed any widespread discussion of Christian unity between American Catholics and Protestants. Nevertheless, in the 1950s, in the midst of these tensions, a few Catholics, including Weigel, George Tavard, A.A., Edward F. Hanahoe, S.A., and John B. Sheerin, C.S.P., began to crack the ice of the cold war between Protestants and Catholics, researching and publishing articles and books on Protestant theology and entering into some pioneering ecumenical activities with the hope of creating convergence among the churches.

In 1960, after Pope John XXIII had convoked the Second Vatican Council, Weigel was appointed consulter to the newly established Roman Secretariat for Promoting Christian Unity, one of four North Americans to receive the appointment.[17] His standing in the American Protestant community was acknowledged in 1962 when Yale University granted him an honorary doctorate, noting, "You have broken through the Reformation wall and pioneered in Catholic-Protestant dialogue."[18] Weigel saw himself as a "middle generation" ecumenist—one who stood between the hostile and closed mentality of the earlier generation and the more advanced ecumenical approaches of those who would be his successors.

The fact that Weigel—along with Murray, Diekmann, and the German theologian Hans Küng—was refused permission to speak at the Catholic University in 1963 indicates that even his moderate openness to the ecumenical movement was throughout the period considered heterodox—in practice, if not in theory.

The most significant and creative theological development of the period, and the one that ran into the most forceful internal opposition, was Murray's views on church–state relations, a perennial problem in American Catholicism. The Catholic understanding of this issue had, of course, been a part of the Protestant-Catholic conflict for generations. The problem of developing an adequate understanding of church–state relations, however, was particularly acute in the postwar years because of what Murray and other Catholics saw as an increasingly secularist interpretation of the First Amendment by the Supreme Court and some liberal Americans like Blanshard—an interpretation that created a virtual wall between church and state, thereby discrediting, if not in fact, at least in theory, any religious influence on society and legislation.

The problem was compounded by the Vatican's understanding of church–state relations (i.e., that the two, although distinct and separate in their ends, belonged ideally in some kind of harmonious institutional union), a view that was contrary to Western political consciousness and institutional developments of the past two centuries. Murray's problem, therefore, was twofold. On the one hand, he wanted to show that a Catholic understanding of church–state was indeed not un-American and, on the other hand, that a true American understanding of the First Amendment need not prohibit Catholics and other religious persons from exercising some influence on the nation's public life. His own perception of the problems that faced Catholics led him to an investigation of historical Catholic sources on church–state and of Western and American constitutional philosophy.

Murray developed a historical interpretation of ancient and recent Catholic teachings and a view of the natural law that supported modern religious liberty, and was critical of the church–state theories that had developed in Catholic thinking since the middle of the nineteenth century. His support of religious liberty as a political immunity was severely criticized by Fenton and Connell in this country and opposed by Cardinal Alfredo Ottaviani, secretary of the Holy Office in Rome. By the middle of the 1950s, Murray's position had become so controversial that he was silenced and refused permission to publish on the issue. During the presidential campaign of 1960, however, he did publish *We Hold These Truths*, an argument that Catholics could, on moral grounds, uphold the constitutional principles and practices of the First Amendment.

Although Murray was under a cloud of suspicion and not at first invited as a theological *peritus* (expert) to the Second Vatican Council, he had the support of Cardinal Spellman, who in 1947 had called for a better Catholic understanding of the relationship between church and state in the United States and who invited Murray as his own theological expert during the council's second session. Murray eventually contributed to the writing of the council's *Declaration on Religious Liberty* (*Dignitatis Humanae*, 1965), vindicating his preconciliar positions.[19]

American Catholics, like many others in the postwar years, experienced a revival of piety. All the measurable indexes of religious participation had increased significantly: church attendance, contributions to religious causes, and publications of religious literature. In 1954, the nation's Catholic bishops noted the increases in church membership, but they were led to question "how significant such mere statistics may be. One looks in vain for any corresponding increase of religion's beneficent influence upon the nation's life."[20] A year later, the sociologist Will Herberg described the renewed interest and activity in institutional religion and President Dwight David Eisenhower's "piety on the Potomac" as superficial, "a religiousness without religion, a religiousness with almost any kind of content or none, a way of sociability or 'belonging' rather than a way of reorienting life to God. It is thus frequently a religiousness without serious commitment, without real inner conviction, without genuine existential decision."[21] By the late 1950s, sociologist Andrew Greeley saw possibilities of a spiritual poverty within a Catholic community that had achieved a postwar suburban economic prosperity: "In the midst of plenty, does not prayer become extremely difficult, if not impossible? Does mortification have any meaning to people who have never known material want? . . . Can man, when he has so many things in this world, seriously long for the next?"[22]

The criticisms of the depth of the revival, however valid they might have been, have obscured something of the variety and indeed vitality of the spiritual movements that were taking place within American Catholicism. During the Cold War years, Catholic piety moved simultaneously in a number of different directions. Catholics in significant numbers continued to be involved in the sacramental life of the church, popular devotional Catholicism persisted with a renewed emphasis on Marian devotions, Jocist cells of reflection and social action persevered, and a liturgically centered piety influenced a few. New styles of Catholic spirituality also arose, with new means of propagating them.

Some Catholics adapted their spirituality to the times, others resisted these efforts as capitulations, still others promoted the retrieval of the contemplative tradition, and many were influenced by the rising missionary consciousness of the postwar period. A few purveyors of piety promoted a revival of spirituality that was particularly adapted to American values and the modern techniques of mass media and advertising. Father Patrick Peyton, C.S.C., for example, organized the nonsectarian "Family Theater Program" (1947) for the Mutual Broadcasting Company and used numerous popular radio and Hollywood stars to promote family prayer with the slogan, "The family that prays together stays together." Bishop Fulton J. Sheen reaffirmed the postwar search for peace and security and stressed the positive influence of religion on the individual and society through his inspirational television program *Life is Worth Living* (1952–1957). The Maryknoll priest James Keller also supported American middle-class values of individualism and activism with his slogan, "It is better to light one candle than to curse the darkness."[23] Keller also used the mass-market techniques of Hollywood and Madison Avenue, radio and TV programs, as well as published pamphlets and books to communicate his message.

Some within the Catholic community thought these popular appeals to the middle class particularly shallow and naive, simply reinforcing a bourgeois mentality and forfeiting any sense of the sacramental, truly personal, and communal dimensions of the Christian tradition. The methods used, moreover, were considered detrimental to the integrity and depth of Christ's message. This critique, articulated by Carol Jackson and others of *Integrity*, was generally followed by a call for a new kind of lay spirituality that connected work and participation in a liturgically centered Catholic spirituality.[24]

The postwar years also saw the revival of contemplation in the Catholic tradition. In the 1940s alone, a Gethsemani, Kentucky, Cisterian monastery of the Strict Observance (i.e., Trappist) established six new Trappist monasteries throughout the United States. The monasteries sponsored weekend and more extended retreats for laypersons, inviting all to share in the fruits of an examined interior life. The postwar retrieval of contemplation and prayerful retreats was most clearly articulated and thereby encouraged by a young convert to Catholicism and monk of Gethsemani Abbey, Thomas Merton.*

Merton came to public notice in 1948 when he published his spiritual autobiography, *The Seven Storey Mountain*, which soon climbed to the top of the best-seller list, indicating that Merton had discovered a spiritual yearning in the American soul. In it and in numerous other publications over the next twenty years, Merton called for a deepening of the contemplative life in everyone, not just in monks and nuns. *The Seven Storey Mountain* made that universal call clear.[25] Merton's interests in and associations with liturgical reformers, Catholic Workers, Catholic pacifists, advocates of social justice, and later with the contemplatives and mystics in the Eastern religious traditions demonstrated something of his own personality and special gifts, but they were also indicative of the wider search for spiritual depth in an American culture beset with Cold War anxieties and organizational and technological manipulations that absorbed the individual in the externals of human and social life. Contemplation, as envisioned by Merton, was neither a panacea for cultural anxiety nor a withdrawal from real social and individual problems, but a way of life that continually called individuals to the center of their existence in order to make them active in transforming the world.

The rise of the United States as a world superpower and the widely publicized accounts of the church's persecution behind the Iron Curtain helped to produce for the first time on an extensive scale a missionary consciousness among American Catholics. Stories of the trials of church leaders and missionaries under communist governments became regular reading in popular Catholic magazines and newspapers. Parish and school programs to rescue "pagan babies," prayers for missionaries and the conversion of Russia, Pope Pius XII's 1951 encyclical on missions (*Evangelii Praecones*), and fund drives to assist missionaries in their work of social amelioraton and evangelization were all part of a massive postwar campaign to create "mission mindedness" among American Catholics.

The promotion of a universal missionary zeal and social consciousness for the poor of the world was tied into a spirituality of the Mystical Body and was another part of the anticommunist motif of the era. The one person most clearly successful in articulating these themes was Bishop Sheen, who from 1950 to 1966 was the national director of the Society for the Propagation of the Faith (SPF). Under his leadership, the SPF became a well-organized national force within American Catholic dioceses. Between 1950 and 1966, Sheen raised more than $100 million to support a network of 300,000 missionaries, 150,000 schools, 26,000 hospitals, 400 leper colonies, and 5,000 orphanages in various parts of the world.[26]

The postwar years also witnessed at least three new major developments in social Catholicism. The fundamental problems in American society continued to be perceived in terms of secularism, communism, and unguarded or unreserved capitalism, but there were also some signs that these problems were not just external threats to a Catholic vision and way of life. Catholics themselves—in their pursuit of suburbia, wealth, respectability, and a place in the American sun—had been influenced to a considerable degree by the spiritual bankruptcy of bourgeois-mindedness. A few Catholics raised their voices not only against a superficial consumer culture but also against those Catholics who had capitulated to it by separating their religious principles and values from their everyday life. During the postwar years, the older forms of social Catholicism that had arisen in the early twentieth century and in the Depression continued, but new forms of social Catholicism developed. Some social Catholics tried to transform their culture, others withdrew from its unholy influence, still others tried to dialogue with what was good in it. The older as well as newer forms of social Catholicism were all variously influenced by a neo-Thomist natural law tradition, a doctrine of the Mystical Body, anticommunism, and the papal social encyclical tradition in their perception of the problems of modern culture and their acceptance of the need for change. Social Catholics, however, differed among themselves in the degree of their hostility to economic lifestyles engendered by American capitalism, in the extent of the reforms needed and in the appropriate means of reform.

Labor problems and just-wage issues continued in the postwar years, but new urban problems shifted the concern of some social Catholics. In the midst of these multiple new urban problems (e.g., urban renewal, housing, redevelopment, racism, movement to the suburbs), a few leading Catholics sought to transform the urban culture in which they lived by getting the church as well as the state to respond to the problems. Chicago, the largest archdiocese in the country, became a virtual seminary for a host of social and religious reform movements that eventually had repercussions throughout American Catholicism. Auxiliary Bishop Bernard Shiel continued to work with the Catholic Youth Organization and transformed it into a movement for social justice. He gathered a number of creative thinkers around himself, delivered numerous talks, and wrote articles on youth, labor justice, neighborhood reclamation, and racism. Reynold Hillenbrand, rector of St. Mary's of the Lake Seminary, formed numerous clergy with a sensitivity to liturgical reform and social justice. Daniel Cantwell and John Egan addressed problems of urban renewal, relocation, and housing for the poor, and lobbied in city and state politics to obtain legislation favorable to persons displaced by urban development.

By 1958 Egan became the executive secretary of the Cardinal's (Albert Meyer) Conservation Committee that, under his leadership, took a more adversarial role toward city officials than had previously been the case among Catholic urban reformers. A few Chicago parish clergy also cooperated with Saul D. Alinsky's "Back of the Yards" movement, organizing laborers and city dwellers to obtain political clout for their neighborhoods. At the invitation of Bishop Shiel, Ann Harrigan established Friendship House in Chicago to serve the needs of black Americans. Patrick and Patty Crowley organized the Christian Family Movement as a Jocist organ for stable family relationships and social action. Edward Marciniak, Frank Delany, and Hillenbrand created the Catholic Labor Alliance and worked for industrial reconstruction according to Catholic social teachings. John Cogley and others worked in the Chicago Catholic Workers' house and contributed to rising lay consciousness. Out of Chicago, too, came George Higgins,* Catholicism's premier "labor priest" between 1944 and his death in 2002. In the postwar years, Chicago Catholicism buzzed with an activism previously unknown in American Catholicism and perhaps not emulated to such a degree anywhere else in the country. This activism represented supreme confidence: These Catholics believed they had something valuable to contribute to the social and political development of the age. They were not "ghetto" Catholics.[27]

A few social Catholics found conditions in America so contrary to the Christian vision that they called for withdrawal from society as a means of transforming themselves prior to transforming the culture. *Integrity* magazine Catholics like Edward Willock and Carol Jackson, and the Grail, a lay apostolate for women, repeatedly railed against the all-pervasiveness of bourgeois, sensate American culture, and charged that American Catholics as well as others had been desensitized by it and were thus unable to embrace poverty voluntarily and identify themselves with the victims of poverty, dislocation, and alienation in industrialized and mechanized American society. These Catholics wanted to re-Christianize America, but they believed that in order to do so, American Catholics like themselves had to withdraw from the corruptions of a consumerist and secularist culture and move into different forms of Christian communalism where they could abandon themselves to the Absolute.[28]

Other social Catholics wanted to dialogue with what they found good in American culture and appropriate elements of the American tradition and experience into their own social vision and practice. In the past, American Catholic social thought was so directed toward the economic plight of workers and critiques of rugged capitalism and socialism that social theorists failed to demonstrate the relevance of Catholic social thought for the professional and entrepreneurial experiences of increasing numbers of postwar Catholics in the fields of medicine, law, dentistry, engineering, and business management. In 1959, a small group of Catholic businessmen who shared a common desire to relate their religious convictions to everyday life formed the National Conference of Catholic (in 1965 changed to Christian) Employers and Managers (NCCEM) to address the common moral and social issues they faced in their own work. The group hoped to develop a continuing exchange with moral theologians so that they could together develop moral guidelines for business and management decisions they were daily called on to make. The group also encouraged business schools in Catholic universities and colleges to apply the social encyclicals to business and management decisions and develop courses in the ethics of business and management. NCCEM ceased to function in 1968, short-circuited by the Second Vatican Council and decreased interest among businessmen and theologians.[29]

A group of lay Catholics who called themselves "liberal Catholics" also articulated an approach to social justice in American society that appropriated liberal democratic procedures into a Catholic social program. Like other Catholics, they accepted fully the Catholic doctrinal tradition, the papal encyclicals on social justice, the dynamics of the liturgical reform movement, and the Mystical Body understanding of the church, but they became increasingly critical of what they perceived to be a "partisan or sectarian [Catholic] spirit."[30] Neither the withdrawal mentality, nor the belief that Catholics had an exclusive corner on social justice, nor an authoritarian crusade to transform culture would in fact change American society. What was needed was a new method of social justice. Catholics had to cooperate democratically with others in American society to bring about justice. Liberal Catholicism was a "spirit and method":

> The use of reason in controversy rather than belligerence, the absence of the chip-on-the-shoulder, the unwillingness to use the truth as if it were one's private possession, the rejection of the sectarian spirit and willingness to deal with others not as if the truth they have were of a different kind from ours or their errors were inevitably born of malevolence—this general approach is often described, in a catch-all word, as liberal.[31]

Catholics, wrote John Cogley, should come forward as individuals, not as a group power block, and play a dynamic role in the "pluralistic" structures of American life.[32] Cogley's recommendation, as Philip Gleason has argued, unwittingly placed more emphasis on individual Catholic participation in American procedural processes than on the substance of one's own Christian commitments.[33] There was no denial of that substance, but there was certainly a shift of emphasis that had implications for weakening individual and communal ties to the content of the tradition.

One of the foremost social justice issues in the postwar era was racial segregation. The large pre- and postwar migrations into urban and industrial areas brought large numbers of urban Catholics into contact with black Americans for the first time. In 1940, for example, black Americans represented 4.1 percent of Chicago's total population; by 1960 they represented 23 percent. This growth in Chicago and elsewhere transformed many Catholic institutions as they responded to the changing urban scene. The migration created a host of negative reactions from white Catholics and others: restrictive housing covenants, violent race riots, institutional and religious segregation, and discrimination policies and practices. The periodic hostilities and racist practices among Catholics were variously motivated by a desire to preserve the value of property, competition in the job market, cultural differences, and long-established and traditional racial attitudes and stereotyping.

In a number of cities, black Catholics were segregated into their own parishes and schools and not allowed into white parishes, parish schools, colleges, hospitals, and other ecclesiastical institutions. As Steven Avella has convincingly demonstrated, postwar episcopal silence on racism provided an atmosphere for systematic discrimination in the Diocese of Chicago, and what took place in Chicago resembled what was occurring in other large urban dioceses.[34] Cardinal Mundelein had established a policy of ecclesiastical segregation in 1919, and in the postwar years that policy remained publicly unchallenged by Mundelein's successor, Cardinal Samuel Stritch. In the midst of discriminatory Catholic practices, however, Bishop Shiel and a number of individual clergy and laity protested against racism in the church and society. After 1945 Stritch, as perhaps a number of other more cautious bishops, made a number of case-by-case decisions for the integration of Catholic institutions, but these decisions were generally communicated through private correspondence and not made a matter of public record. Not until the accession of Cardinal Albert Meyer in 1958 was there any official voice against Catholic discriminatory practices and a public reversal of diocesan policies in Chicago.

The archives in Chicago, as perhaps in a number of other urban Catholic dioceses, contain letters from black Catholics protesting their maltreatment and the discriminatory practices they experienced in Catholic institutions. One black Catholic woman from Chicago's St. Ambrose parish, for example, complained in 1950 about Father Francis Quinn's Sunday sermon in which he was reported to have said:

> The Niggers have taken over Corpus Christi church, Holy Angels and St. Anne'[s] and now they are trying to take over this church; but if its [sic] left to me, they will not. Every time I park my car I'm afraid a Nigger will stab me in the back. Just last week a Nigger from Shakespeare school snatched a white woman's purse and when he was questioned he had snatched several other purses. What's the matter with you white people? Are you yellow? Now all Nigger lovers go back and tell the Niggers what I said. . . . Our forefathers from Ireland came over here and prepared the way for us in this church and the Niggers are not going to run us out.[35]

Quinn did not deny the report when asked to explain himself to the Chicago chancery, but went on to protest: "The next letter of complaint from the negress will be a complaint that I have no negroes in my school. Isn't that just too bad. I cannot begin to care for my white children. When the day comes that you compel me, that will mark the end of St. Ambrose."[36] When Quinn did refuse to allow a black boy into the parish school, the southern-born Stritch responded forcefully, but privately, ordering the priest to accept the student: "The boy is a Catholic boy of your parish. Clearly he is a child of your flock and has a right to enter your school. In admitting Catholic children of your parish into your school there may not be set up a standard of race or color. You are a pastor of all your people. Merely because the child is a negro is no legitimate excuse for refusing him admission."[37] Quinn complied but again protested that the admission was the beginning of the end of the parish, identifying it so much with the white population as he had. In 1956 Quinn resigned; by that time the parish was almost entirely black.

The Quinn case represents the mixture of Catholic responses to the racial urban transformations in the postwar years: overt Catholic racism, black Catholic protests, and official but private reprimands and orders to reverse a standing practice. The pattern in Chicago was perhaps duplicated in many other urban situations where concerned and cautious bishops ruled. This conservative and private approach to racism on a case-by-case basis would also gradually change in the mid-1950s, as more and more bishops would publicly support racial justice and demand integration in Catholic institutions.

St. Louis's Archbishop Joseph Ritter and Washington's Archbishop Patrick O'Boyle in 1947 and 1948 respectively ordered Catholic schools integrated despite loud protests from certain whites in their dioceses. In 1954, prior to the Supreme Court decision in Brown v. Board of Education (ending separate but equal schooling) of the same year, San Antonio's Archbishop Lucey and Raleigh's Bishop Vincent Waters publicly ended segregation in their dioceses, and after the Supreme Court decision a number of other bishops across the country did the same. In 1955, New Orleans's Archbishop Joseph Francis Rummel, with the assistance of his auxiliary John Patrick Cody,* integrated the schools in that diocese and in 1962 excommunicated those Catholics who publicly defied the order.

As a body, the American bishops were slow to register their united voices in support of racial justice. In 1943, the year of the Detroit race riots, the bishops issued a pastoral that supported the constitutional rights of blacks and called on Catholics to work together toward racial peace and harmony.[38] It was not, however, until 1958—after Brown v. Board of Education, the 1955 Montgomery, Alabama, boycott, the 1957 establishment of the Presidential Commission on Civil Rights (one of whose members was Father Theodore Hesburgh, C.S.C., president of the University of Notre Dame), and hosts of public protests over violations of civil rights for black Americans—that the American bishops prepared a pastoral exclusively devoted to the issue of religion and race. That pastoral, "Discrimination and Christian Conscience," forcefully asserted that, "the heart of the race question is moral and religious."[39] Although the statement received a generally favorable response in the American press, some critics, like the Montgomery *Journal*, were quick to point out that the bishops had become publicly vocal on the issue of "race mixing" only after the Supreme Court decision.[40] The bishops' pastoral, though, reflected a growing consciousness in Catholicism of the moral and spiritual damage of racial prejudice in church and society.

In 1963, prior to Dr. Martin Luther King, Jr.'s march on Washington, Catholic leaders in Chicago, together with a number of Protestant and Jewish leaders, organized the first major Conference on Race and Religion. By 1963, Catholics and others were beginning to see the necessity of ecumenical cooperation in resolving a significant social issue that continued to disturb the American soul. By then, too, numbers of sisters, priests, bishops, and Catholic laity were willing to unite in public protests against national and local racial policies and legal practices. Washington's Archbishop O'Boyle, for example, was one of the religious leaders who delivered the invocation just before Dr. King's "I Have a Dream" speech. In 1965, numerous women religious, priests, and a bishop or two joined King's march in Selma, Alabama, despite the disapproval of Thomas Joseph Toolen, the bishop of Mobile-Birmingham. By 1965 there was little doubt about where the church stood on the issue of race, even if all Catholics did not comply with the church's teachings.

Postwar Catholics, benefitting from political developments during the FDR era, rapidly emerged into local and national politics. In 1946 World War II participants like Joseph McCarthy of Wisconsin and war heroes such as John Fitzgerald Kennedy of Massachusetts were elected to the U.S. Senate and House of Representatives, respectively. By 1965 twelve Catholic senators and ninety-one representatives served in Congress, a representation in proportion to their numbers in society.

The political emergence of Catholics was accompanied by a political division in the American Catholic community, one that had been occasionally evident since the days of John Carroll, but one that became much more prominent and vocal during the 1950s, as political conservatives and liberals waged their very different wars against communism and for social justice in American society. The two McCarthys—Joseph R. McCarthy, the junior Republican senator from Wisconsin (1946–1957), and Eugene Joseph McCarthy, the Democratic congressman (1949–1958) and then senator (1958–1970) from Minnesota—symbolized the split in the political allegiances of American Catholics.

The two McCarthys reveal two very different levels of conscious Catholic influence on their political activities and decisions. For Senator Joseph McCarthy, as well as for young Congressman Kennedy, religion was a private and sacramental affair, and politics was largely pragmatic. Both separated their religious from their political life and showed little interest in the intellectual content of their faith or little inclination to probe the political dimensions or implications of their own religious tradition.[41]

Eugene McCarthy, on the other hand, represented a very different kind of Catholic politician. He was a Catholic intellectual, well versed in the tradition of the papal social encyclicals, having taught courses in Catholic social and political thought at St. Thomas College and St. John's University in Minnesota. Although he distinguished between religion and politics, he did not separate the two into independent compartments of his life. His Catholicism, too, was not the Catholicism of novenas, rosaries, and parish bingo, but the Catholicism of the Mystical Body, liturgical movement, rural life movement, and social justice tradition of natural law. Religion was not politics, but politics was a part of one's religious and moral responsibility to provide for individual liberty and the common good. The two McCarthys represent extremes in relating religion to politics; most Catholic politicians were probably somewhere on the spectrum between them.

In the early 1950s, Joseph McCarthy's crusade against internal communism, his army hearings, inquisitorial tactics, and appeals to the fears and anxieties of the age most certainly reflected the postwar religious culture in which he was raised. Polls for the period demonstrate that "Catholic McCarthyites outnumbered the anti-McCarthy Catholics, and his popularity with Catholics was slightly stronger than with the rest of the population."[42] McCarthy's anticommunism, though, was based primarily on appeals to the American political, rather than to the Catholic, tradition.

Within the context of the McCarthy era, a new type of Catholic intellectual conservative emerged. The new political conservatives (e.g., William F. Buckley, Jr., Russell Kirk, Frederick Wilhelmsen, Thomas Molnar, L. Brent Bozell, Arnold Lunn) were not card-carrying Catholics identified with explicit Catholic journals, organizations, or movements, as were many of the Catholic political liberals.[43] Even though they did not always appreciate McCarthy's tactics or agree with his specific accusations, many conservative Catholic politicians and intellectuals shared not only McCarthy's antipathy toward "liberals," whom they considered naive or soft on communism, but also his fears of the socialist tendencies of the welfare state. Unlike McCarthy, however, the new conservatives brought "the insights of their faith and the natural law tradition" to the service of the American political tradition.[44]

Shortly after the Senate's censure of Joseph McCarthy, conservative Catholic intellectuals joined Protestant and Jewish political conservatives to establish the *National Review* (1955) and *Modern Age* (1956). Although not specifically Catholic journals, they became the organs for the revival and dissemination of conservative thought. For most of the new conservatives, McCarthy was right on the one important fact—the peril of totalitarian communism. They attacked the liberals because they lacked fixed and transcendent values by which to judge issues, and because they emphasized almost exclusively procedural, as opposed to substantive, issues. By 1964, some of these new conservatives found a political home with Republican presidential candidate Barry Goldwater. L. Brent Bozell, in fact, became the ghostwriter of Goldwater's *Conscience of a Conservative.*[45]

Although there was considerable support for McCarthy and his anticommunist crusade among American Catholics, a number of American Catholic liberal editors, politicians, educators, labor leaders, and churchmen vehemently opposed his repressive tactics. For them, McCarthyism was a mindless, emotional, superpatriotic, and maliciously conspiratorial hysteria that was destructive of justice, social peace, and the liberal procedures of a democratic society.[46] *Commonweal*—under the liberal leadership of Edward Skillen, John Cogley, James O'Gara, and William Clancy—was in the vanguard of opposition to McCarthyism.[47] Robert C. Hartnett, S.J., editor of *America*, Congressman Eugene McCarthy, Senator Dennis Chavez of New Mexico, Msgr. George Higgins of the NCWC's Social Action Department, and Auxiliary Bishop Bernard Shiel of Chicago were also among the vocal opponents of McCarthy's histrionic methods.

Many Catholic political liberals, like their conservative opponents, were anticommunists for religious as well as political reasons. The anticommunism of the political liberals, however, stemmed more from the papal encyclicals on social justice than from the more explicitly and directly anticommunist papal encyclicals. For the political liberals, the best means for overcoming communism was the promotion of legislative social programs designed to end hunger, disease, deficient housing, and other social and economic ills, all of which were ultimately responsible for the rise of communism and socialism.

Political liberals also saw the rise and spread of totalitarian communism as a fundamental threat to the liberties for which liberalism had traditionally fought—that is, "maximum human freedom under law, social progress and democratic equality."[48] These Catholic liberals, though, were not ideological or philosophical, but procedural liberals. They did not, for example, share the nineteenth-century philosophical liberals' belief in inevitable progress, an overly optimistic view of human nature, or a dogmatic rationalism. They asserted time and again that totalitarian communism and McCarthyism alike had used methods and procedures that threatened the fundamental rights and liberties of the human person under the guise of promoting the public good. In a democratic and pluralistic society, they argued, Catholics should refuse to engage in pressure censorship or to use coercion in religious and cultural matters; instead, they should be tolerant and civil in public debates and support freedom and democratic procedures to secure a political consensus in society. Because they accepted Catholic doctrine and theology, they were suspect among their liberal political friends; because they sided with the liberals in their politics, they were suspect among conservative Catholics.

By the late 1950s, the issue of religion and politics came to the fore once again with the presidential candidacy of Senator John F. Kennedy. By 1959, Kennedy had decided to run, and an interview with him in *Look* (3 March 1959) demonstrated that his Catholicism would be an issue. Kennedy unequivocally supported the separation of church and state and opposed public aid for parochial schools and an American ambassador to the Vatican. One sentence in the interview, however, disturbed some moderate Protestants as well as Catholics. Kennedy was reported to have said: "Whatever one's religion in his private life may be, for the officeholder, nothing takes precedence over his oath to uphold the Constitution and all its parts—including the First Amendment and the strict separation of church and state."[49]

America reacted to Kennedy's "nothing takes precedent" statement by asserting that no religious person—whether Jew, Protestant, or Catholic—could or should reduce religion to the level of private conscience.[50] The Lutheran historian Martin Marty thought that Kennedy's statement revealed an all-too-typical mentality that was "spiritually rootless and politically almost disturbingly secular."[51] The Presbyterian Robert McAfee Brown judged that in Kennedy's effort "to assure his possible constituency that he is just a regular American, he has succeeded only in demonstrating that he is a rather irregular Christian."[52]

Other Protestants were more troubled by Kennedy's Catholicism than by his secularism. Some leaders in the National Evangelical Association, Southern Baptist Convention, Texas Baptist Convention, and newly formed Citizens for Religious Freedom, among others, began to organize against Kennedy, articulating the old anti-Catholic bromides. Other prominent Protestants—among them, Methodist Bishop G. Bromley Oxnam, Eugene Carson Blake, Harold E. Fey, Reinhold Niebuhr, and John C. Bennett, all of whom had intellectual difficulties with Catholic doctrinal and religious positions—called the opposition blindly prejudiced, asserting that these conservative Protestants would oppose any liberal candidate regardless of religious identification.

In the midst of the growing concerns, Kennedy addressed the religion issue directly at a meeting of the Ministerial Association of Greater Houston on 12 September 1960. The talk reaffirmed positions he had taken in the *Look* interview.[53] Although Kennedy's speech may not have eliminated the religious element from the final voting, it went a long way to assuage some people about the dangers of Kennedy's candidacy.[54]

Although Kennedy eventually won the election by a very narrow margin, it was a significant symbolic victory for the American Catholic community, erasing as it did the bitter memory of Al Smith's loss. Catholics who were gradually moving into business, professional life, and politics in ever-greater numbers during the postwar years had eliminated one final barrier to their full civic participation. But what did Kennedy's win really mean for the Catholic community? Was JFK's election simply a sign that religion, not just Catholicism, was no longer a matter of much consequence in American political life? Did his election mean that Catholics had arrived in the pluralistic politics of the age, or did it symbolize a more widespread Catholic capitulation to a secular dynamic in the political arena in order to make it in American society? However one interprets the election, it is clear that it was the culmination of an era of Catholic confidence and transition.

The Second Vatican Council (1962–1965) was another major symbol of the age of Catholic confidence and transition. The council reflected a sense of ecclesiastical stability that allowed the church to produce a new consciousness of itself, bring forth a number of internal ecclesial reforms and changes, call for a new level of ecclesial involvement in society, and articulate a new dialogical attitude toward Protestants and modernity. To some extent, the council confidently put to an end the confrontational or defensive attitude of much of the post-Tridentine era and reflected themes that had been here and there articulated in postwar European and American Catholicism.

On 25 January 1959, just ninety days after he had been elected pope, John XXIII made the surprising announcement that he would call an ecumenical council. After more than three years of preparation it opened on 11 October 1962. Neither American bishops nor laity had any clear ideas of what to expect from a council, and perhaps few saw the necessity for one in the first place. Catholicism in America was strong institutionally. Like Cardinal James McIntyre of Los Angeles, many American Catholics saw "no need for changes."[55]

When the new ecumenical council finally met for the first time, Pope John XXIII made it clear that its primary purposes were pastoral. It was called to revitalize Christian living, reform changeable ecclesiastical practices and structures, nurture Christian unity, engage Catholicism in a compassionate dialogue with the modern world, and promote human dignity and unity, social justice, and world peace.[56]

The council meant free discussion and debate and in fact reflected conflicting theological orientations within the church. The conservative-progressive struggles were closely reported in the press, making many American Catholics significantly aware of ecclesiastical divisions that had previously been hidden in professional journals. When the debates were finished and the votes taken, the council had produced sixteen documents that described in various ways a revitalized understanding of the church's nature and mission in the modern world. The documents on the liturgy, church, revelation, the church's relationship with the modern world, ecumenism, and religious liberty were the most significant of the sixteen. They reflected not only the neoscholastic theological orientations of the immediate past but also the new biblical, historical, and existential theology that had been developing in France and Germany since World War I. The very combination of the differing theological orientations provided grounds for both liberal and conservative postconciliar interpretations of the council's intentions.

The documents, however, reflected and produced a definite shift in Catholic consciousness. Vatican II was the culmination of a twentieth-century Catholic preoccupation with ecclesiology—a view of the church that had moved from a primary emphasis on the institutional and juridical, to the sacramental and spiritual aspects of various Mystical Body theologies, to Vatican II's more comprehensive and multidimensional understanding of the mystery and mission of the church in the world. The council stressed the primacy of the church's mission within the entire economy and mystery of salvation, with Christ as the head and center. Within this context, the church was presented as the "People of God," demonstrating the council's desire to emphasize the historical, human, and communal dimension of the church. The church, moreover, was distinguished from the Kingdom of God, thereby reviving the eschatological dimension of Christian and ecclesial life. The council also acknowledged for the first time in any official Catholic document the ecclesial reality of Orthodox and Protestant churches.

Behind many documents was a renewed sensitivity to the historical and mutable dimensions of human existence and Christian faith, both of which were interpreted existentially as a vocation and a mission. Revelation and salvation were understood historically as a series of events that had a beginning, development, and fulfillment. This historical view of human and Christian existence helped to produce a new consciousness of the church's presence in the world and a new willingness to dialogue with the modern mentality.

The council fathers fostered a spirit of renewal, reform, and change—an élan that Pope John XXIII called *aggiornamento*, a bringing of the church up to date. This emphasis represented a dynamic shift of consciousness, especially for those American Catholics who were accustomed to speaking of the church's irreformable nature and unchanging practices. For many American Catholics, the church had been presented, at least in the most recent past, as the one permanent and stable institution within a world characterized as a chaotic sea of diversity and change.

The council fathers also emphasized the need for accommodation and legitimate diversity within the unity of the faith. Accommodation and variety were clearly possible in liturgical practices, theological conceptualizations, national customs, and forms of spirituality. Although American Catholics had in the past experienced their own kinds of internal Catholic diversity, their most recent ideological emphasis had been on the unity, not the diversity, of the Catholic tradition. The council's deliberations themselves epitomized the real diversity within the church.

The council acknowledged, too, the legitimate autonomy of earthly affairs as a requirement not only of the modern world but also of the Creator's will. Created things and societies enjoy their own laws and values, which must be respected. Religious liberty was one of the manifestations of the developing consciousness of human dignity and autonomy in the modern world that the council also affirmed. The council's *Declaration on Religious Liberty* was the one single document in which the American bishops can claim to have provided some leadership. With the help of Murray, they were able to bring the council to see the religious, moral, and political necessity of recognizing religious liberty in the modern world.

The Second Vatican Council initiated as well a series of internal ecclesiastical reforms and changes at a time in the United States when the church was in a period of institutional strength and stability, and when Catholics were becoming upwardly mobile in American business, professional, and political life. The assassination of President Kennedy (1963), the civil rights movement, and the rising American involvement in Vietnam forecast, however, something of an era of violence in American society that the bishops did not or could not fully discern during the council. The implementation of the conciliar reforms and the communication of a shifting consciousness that accompanied those reforms were to take place in an American cultural, social, and political context that was in the midst of a radical and revolutionary upheaval. The postconciliar church would be different from the preconciliar church.

9

---•---

POST–VATICAN II CATHOLICISM: 1965–1990

THE CATHOLIC COMMUNITY, perhaps more than any other religious community in the United States, experienced the simultaneously stimulating and disintegrating hurricane winds of social and religious reforms and upheavals that blew across the country in the 1960s and early 1970s. The implementation of the Second Vatican Council's liturgical and structural reforms and the corresponding transformation of American Catholic consciousness that accompanied them took place at a time of revolutionary change in American political and cultural life. Radical protests against American involvement in Vietnam, rising racial tensions and hostilities in large urban areas, student rebellions on college campuses, changing sexual morals and movements toward sexual emancipation, and the campaign for women's liberation magnified the impact of Vatican II's institutional reforms. When combined, the religious and cultural reformations produced a period of unprecedented turmoil and change. By the late 1970s and early 1980s some Catholics, like many others in American society, were calling for stabilization and conservation in the political order and for a spiritual revival in the ecclesial realm.

During the first fifteen years after the council, a diversity of institutional reforms, new ways of thinking, internal rebellions, conflicts, closings of numerous institutions, and a dramatic decline in denominational identification shook and transformed an American Catholic community whose most recent experience and memory was one of relative institutional stability, unity, and phenomenal growth. The story of developments since the Second Vatican Council needs more critical analysis than has been given or can be given here, but even a cursory review of those developments demonstrates something of the ambiguities of the religious reforms: continuities in the midst of change, strength in the midst of decline, gains in the midst of losses, cultural and religious amnesia in the midst of so-called historical mindedness, signs of transcendence in the midst of the love of secularity, and a thirst for justice and peace in the midst of cultural and ecclesiastical injustices and inequities.

The conciliar reforms were implemented in American Catholicism between 1964 and 1970. The first, most visible, and tangible signs of change were in the liturgy. The entire Mass was put into the vernacular, the altar was turned around, the priest faced the people, and the laity were visibly and audibly involved in the liturgical action through lectors, offertory processions, congregational singing, and active responses to the liturgical prayers. The liturgical and eventually architectural changes were perhaps the most significant, because they symbolized in very concrete ways the changing consciousness that had taken place at the Second Vatican Council. Whether the changes themselves were implemented in a rapid and uncontrolled pace or haltingly and begrudgingly, they created an atmosphere of reform that was for the most part foreign to the American Catholic experience of the immediate preconciliar era. The liturgy itself had come to symbolize the universal and unchanging nature of the Catholic Church. Liturgical forms had remained fairly constant for four hundred years—at least they had remained relatively unchanged in the memories of most Catholics. Now the church was demonstrating that things once considered permanent were changeable. Some American Catholics resisted the innovations because, like some conservative bishops at the council, they were unprepared and saw no need for any modifications in Catholic forms of religious life. Other Catholics found them desirable. For still others, the liturgical changes led to an increasing expectation and anticipation of innovations in many other areas of moral and ecclesial life. For almost all Catholics, the changes created a new Catholic consciousness about the historically conditioned nature of many things Catholic.

This fundamental shift of consciousness took place gradually, but it was constantly reinforced by changes in pious practices, governance, and Catholic lifestyles. Many signs of a sectarian identity that were so much a part of preconciliar Catholic religious life were eventually eradicated. In a number of churches statues of saints were removed in order to emphasize the centrality of the Eucharistic action within the church and to relegate the cult of the saints to the periphery of Catholic attention. Meatless Fridays, another symbol of Catholic identity in the past, were abrogated; practices of Lenten fasting and abstinence were modified; and the practice of auricular confession, the result of the former emphasis on sin, soon fell into disuse. These mutations were not matters of small consequence, because they touched the lives of many Catholics who had been accustomed to thinking about their religious life and their own religious identity in terms of these daily, weekly, and yearly practices and customs. Whether they resisted these changes or accepted them wholeheartedly, American Catholics were fundamentally aware that change itself was an issue in the post–Vatican II period.

Gradually national, diocesan, and parish structures began to be revised to reflect the council's call for dialogue and shared responsibility. Bishops, clergy, religious, and laity struggled to find instrumental means to implement the council's spirit. Sharing ecclesiastical administration and decision making in the American church was not going to be an easy task for those bishops and priests who had been schooled in a church that emphasized monarchical authority.

But a new style of collegial governance began to be implemented in the years immediately following the council, as the bishops themselves in 1966 reorganized the NCWC, making of that organization two separately incorporated institutions: the National Conference of Catholic Bishops (NCCB), an exclusively episcopal organization that focused its attention primarily on internal ecclesiastical issues, and the United States Catholic Conference (USCC), an episcopal organization that collaborated with lay Catholics and priests to address social and political issues of national and international concern. On the diocesan level, many bishops convoked parish councils, diocesan priests' senates, and diocesan pastoral councils—new institutions that attempted to take into account the voices of priests, religious, and laity in issues of ecclesiastical policy. The restructuring process created a great deal of diversity and tension within the church, as some complained about lay involvement in ecclesiastical matters and others criticized episcopal resistance or lack of real "democratic" procedures at the local level. Internal reorganization in the American church took place at an uneven, slow, painful, and, in many dioceses, not well-thought-out pace. By 1969 the bishops were well aware of the need to provide some new legal instrument for adjudicating differences and conflicting opinions within parishes and dioceses and to provide due process procedures to conciliate, arbitrate, and decide between opposing parties. In that year, therefore, the national bishops prepared "The Resolution on Due Process" in order to protect, as the bishops put it, "human rights and freedoms which should always be among the goals of the Church."[1]

The bishops continued to be the most organized voice for the church at the national level through the yearly meetings of the NCCB. Others in the church, however, also became more fully organized at the national level and issued their own statements that complemented and at times competed with the bishops' voice: the National Federation of Priests' Councils (1968), the National Black Sisters' Conference (1968), the National Black Catholic Clergy Caucus (1968), Priests Associated for Religious, Educational, and Social Rights (PADRES, 1969), the Leadership Conference of Women Religious (1971, formerly the Conference of Major Superiors of Women, 1956), *Consortium Perfectae Caritatis* (1971), Las Hermanas (1971). These new national institutions were created to give voice to special interest groups in the church and were typically American in their emphases on democratic procedures. These representative organizations reflected the diversity of opinion in the church, and at times their competing voices paralyzed decision making and made consensus and common actions impossible except in small groups of very like-minded people. The democratic élan, the aspirations, and the techniques used in these bodies moreover tended to disguise the issue of ecclesiastical authority as defined by the council.

The changing lifestyles of some clergy and women religious, too, became most evident in the replacement of religious habits and clerical collars with secular dress, and in the public involvement of priests and sisters (most of the time dressed in clerical collars and religious habits, respectively) in racial justice marches and in protests against the war in Vietnam. These transformations were not lost on a people very conscious of visible signs. Removing these signs of separation and emphasizing the integration of religion and life influenced the Catholic imagination. The highly visible social and political activism of sisters and priests represented a fundamentally new image of the clergy and religious and symbolized something of the church's involvement in the world's affairs.

Vatican II's openness to other Christians and other religious traditions was soon translated into multiple new symbolic gestures and forms of ecumenical activity that also diminished a separatist mentality and denominational identity. Vatican II's *Declaration on Non-Christian Religions*, for example, stated the new attitude clearly: "The Catholic Church rejects nothing which is true and holy in these religions. She looks with sincere respect upon those ways of conduct and of life, those rules and teachings which, though differing in many particulars from what she holds and sets forth, nevertheless often reflect a ray of that Truth which enlightens all men."[2]

American Protestant theologians who were invited to the council and many others who did not attend welcomed the new Catholic understanding and appreciation of their own ecclesial traditions and the openness to the search for unity. Douglas Horton, one of the Protestant theological observers at the council, expressed the ecumenical warmth of the era when he wrote: "Because you have made us your friends, nothing important to you can be unimportant to us: we shall never again be indifferent (however we may disagree) to anything in your theology, your polity, your liturgy. Let this relationship of simple human friendship be carried from the center you have created here to the boundaries of Christendom and we have at least the beginnings of ecumenism."[3]

The experience at the council was indeed extended by symbolic gestures from the papacy and carried out by ecumenically minded bishops in their own dioceses. In January 1964, even before the conclusion of the council, Pope Paul VI made a trip to Jerusalem and had an amicable meeting with the Orthodox Ecumenical Patriarch Athenagoras. In November 1965 they made a momentous joint declaration lifting the mutual excommunications that the Roman and Orthodox churches issued in 1054. In March 1966 the archbishop of Canterbury, Michael Ramsay, visited the pope, and they agreed to establish a serious theological dialogue that would lead to unity between their two churches. Such gestures and actions demonstrated something of the new atmosphere created by the council itself.

Even before the council, Pope John XXIII had established the Secretariat for promoting Christian Unity, which became the primary Roman organ for the direction of Catholic participation in the ecumenical movement. After the council, the Secretariat established a number of international bilateral dialogues with various Christian churches.[4] In the United States, as in many other countries, the episcopacy formed the Bishops' Committee for Ecumenical and Interreligious Affairs (BCEIA) in 1964 to encourage and advise dioceses about ecumenical activities and to create and coordinate national theological conversations with other Christian and non-Christian religions. These dialogues have been the most sustained form of Catholic ecumenical activity in this country.[5] After years of study and conversation, various bilateral committees have produced common statements that outline their current theological agreements and disagreements.[6]

After 1966 diocesan bishops here and there also organized their own diocesan ecumenical commissions and bilateral conversations. Some parishes, too, continued to observe the Prayer for Unity Octave and engaged other churches in common social service programs. Mutual prayer services in particular flourished in the immediate wake of the council. Laity from the various traditions also became engaged in what were popularly known as "living room dialogues," where lay and clerical participants prayed together, shared experiences of their religious traditions, sought mutual forgiveness, and discussed ways of encouraging religious amity and unity at the local level.[7] Although these dialogues created goodwill, they gradually died out and then ceased to exist by the mid-1970s for lack of interest, energy, and/or direction.

By the 1980s attitudes had changed on many levels, but the movement toward any kind of organic Christian unity had stalled, because the common theological statements of the bilateral commissions were not officially approved by the churches nor received by laypeople, nor were they integrated into the churches' general life, thought, and practice. The ecumenical statements themselves were published but not widely distributed or read and had not even become subjects of much study in religious education programs or in colleges or universities. In the judgment of some ecumenists, "too much has come too soon for too many."[8]

In the midst of simultaneous social and religious tensions and transformations, the Catholic Church, like many other American institutions during the 1960s and early 1970s, suffered for the first time in its history a massive loss of membership, decline in the statistics of institutional identification, and a weakening of authority or influence over significant areas of moral life. The decline took place with the simultaneous social mobility of the Catholic people. Throughout the postconciliar years, Catholics were becoming solidly identified with the American middle class, receiving higher education in large numbers, moving in increasing numbers into the professional and business class, and were prosperous.[9]

Although the *Official Catholic Directory* in 1988 estimated that there were about fifty-three million Catholics (an increase of about eight million since 1965), Gallup and other polls indicated that about sixty-seven million Americans identified themselves as Catholic. This means that about fifteen million Catholics were either lapsed, alienated, or unchurched (i.e., those who were not officially members of the church or who had not attended church in a six-month period).[10] Some surveys revealed that between World War II and 1982, about 17 percent of baptized Catholics had turned to another denomination.[11]

The decline in denominational identification was also measured by other kinds of statistics. Weekly attendance at Mass, the supreme source of Catholic spirituality, was down from 71 percent in 1963 to 52 percent in 1971, and monthly confessions were down from 38 percent in 1963 to 17 percent in 1971.[12] Although the Catholic population increased by 17 percent, the number of clergy actually declined by 8 percent between 1965 and 1988. The decline was due primarily to the 10,000 who left the priesthood and the startling 85 percent decrease in the number of seminarians: from about 49,000 in 1965 to 7,000 in 1988. Disaffection with the church itself, with the exercise of authority, with the clerical or religious lifestyle, with some of the church's teachings on sexual ethics, a desire to marry, or any number of other reasons significantly reduced the number of priests in the church from 1965 to 1975. Shortage of clergy became one of the reasons for the closings of many churches and other ecclesiastical institutions in the inner cities.[13] In the midst of renewal and conflict, women religious experienced a severe 40 percent decline in membership between 1965 and 1988 (from 179,954 in 1965 to 106,912 in 1988). Like the clergy, sisters in over 500 different religious congregations left their communities for a variety of reasons.

Because of the want of clergy and religious, increased costs, lower birth rates, geographical mobility, internal discontent, and a variety of other reasons, the number of Catholic primary and secondary schools also declined. In 1965 there were 13,396 Catholic primary and secondary schools, serving over 5.6 million students. By 1988, the numbers had declined to 9,050 with only 2.6 million students—a decline of 32 percent in the number of schools and 60 percent in the number of students. Similar reductions were registered in various religious education programs outside of the Catholic schools. Between 1976 and 1988, for example, the number of students attending Confraternity of Christian Doctrine (CCD) classes shrank by 1.1 million.

The sociologist Andrew Greeley and his associates argued that the decline in the number of Catholic schools and their enrollment was primarily the responsibility of a Catholic leadership no longer committed to the value of these schools. The fundamental drop in enrollment can be explained, Greeley contended, by a declining birth rate and by a fundamental shift of the Catholic population from the inner cities to the suburbs—and the failure of the church to follow the Catholic population with a school building program. Most of the Catholic laity, he maintained, were as committed as ever to Catholic schooling and were willing to pay for it because they perceived its benefit; but, with a few exceptions, the clergy and bishops lost their nerve in developing the Catholic school system at a time when most of the empirical evidence demonstrated that Catholic school students, whether from middle-class or economically disadvantaged homes, scored higher academically and developed a stronger religious commitment and sense of social justice than their peers in the public school system.[14] CCD programs across the country became the substitute for Catholic schools in religious education, but those programs themselves, according to Greeley, did not prove as effective as the schools in communicating and fostering Catholic attitudes, beliefs, and practices.

As enrollments in Catholic primary and secondary schools declined in the post–Vatican II period, those in Catholic colleges and universities increased by 46 percent—from 384,526 in 1965 to 563,799 in 1988—even though the total number of Catholic colleges actually declined by 23 percent, from 304 in 1965 to 233 in 1988.[15] The continued growth in Catholic colleges and universities reflected the general trend in American higher education in the post–World War II era, when a much higher percentage of high school graduates was going to college as a primary means of advancing professionally and economically in an American society that increasingly demanded skills associated with higher education.

Despite, or perhaps because of, the continuing growth, Catholic colleges and universities experienced a number of crises—raising fundamental questions about academic freedom, participatory democratic governance, and the relationship of the internal governance of Catholic colleges and universities to the external supervision of the church's magisterium. At the heart of many of these issues was the recurring problem of Catholic identity.

The key issue relative to the Catholic identity of higher education—an issue that was symbolic of the wider search in postconciliar American Catholicism— was whether the teaching office of the Catholic Church was effectively present in Catholic institutions of higher education through an individual's conscience or through more formal juridical ties. On 23 July 1967 twenty-six college educators, representing ten institutions of Catholic higher education, signed the so-called "Land O' Lakes Statement."[16] Catholic presence in a university was effective and operative through individual consciences, campus ministry programs, religious practices, and the communal bonds of students and teachers. According to the Land O' Lakes Statement, "to perform its teaching and research functions effectively the Catholic university must have a true autonomy and academic freedom in the face of authority of whatever kind, lay or clerical, external to the academic community itself."[17] Such a position was repeatedly advanced from 1969 to 1989 at numerous national and international meetings sponsored by the National Catholic Educational Association and/or the International Federation of Catholic Universities.

Others within the American Catholic academic community—notably Msgr. George A. Kelly and Joseph T. Cahill, C.M., both from St. John's University in Jamaica, New York—pushed for a more juridical definition of Catholic identity at colleges and universities. While accepting academic freedom, this group emphasized the need for academic responsibility and an institutional identification with the church's teaching office. Cahill, president of St. John's, told his trustees in October of 1965 that a Catholic university "must adhere not only to the highest standards of excellence, but also to the teaching, legislation, and spirit of the Roman Catholic Church."[18] Catholic identity could not be secured effectively and a Catholic sense of freedom preserved without a clear institutional acknowledgment of the legitimacy of the magisterium's rights in doctrinal and moral matters. This group was concerned that the principle of autonomy, legitimate as it was in reference to higher education, was being interpreted too absolutely, without regard for the church's authority.

Both sides in the debate saw the issue of Catholic identity to be tied intrinsically to the issue of ecclesiastical authority, as if such authority, whether perceived as necessary or not, were merely external to the task of teaching and research. Rarely did Catholic educators raise the more fundamental issue of the intrinsic relationship between faith and understanding. That issue came to particular focus in Pope John Paul II's *Ex corde ecclesiae* (1990), an apostolic constitution on the maintenance and promotion of Catholic identity in the colleges and universities. The constitution described the relationship between faith, learning, research, and academic freedom; the distinctive nature and role of Catholic institutions of higher learning; their contributions to the church and to culture, and prescribed certain canonical norms for the preservation of Catholic identity in the future. For the next decade or so, the document was widely discussed and debated particularly in Catholic colleges and universities where it stirred up renewed assessments of the specific contributions Catholic institutions should make in a pluralistic and democratic culture.[19]

Although there were numerous attempts to come to terms with democratization, freedom, and secularity within Catholic higher education in the post–Vatican II era, and although there were numerous attempts to define more precisely what Catholic identity meant on a campus, there was, as Philip Gleason argued, no working consensus among Catholic academics and administrators "about what it means, in intellectual terms, to be a Catholic and about how Catholic faith should influence the work one does as a scholar and teacher."[20] Roman documents, which were once thought to settle disputed issues, no longer had the clout to forge a consensus. Thus Catholic colleges and universities continued to discuss the issues of academic freedom, governance, and identity.

The Catholic universities' desire for prestige and prominence as research and scholarly institutions, and the recurring criticisms of failures to be such,[21] also were symbolic of wider concerns in a postconciliar Catholic community that retained the preconciliar sense of cultural inferiority. For some, though, the concerns also reflected the continuing Catholic desire to influence culture and demonstrate that critical scholarship and authentic research were the hallmarks of higher learning and should complement the traditional religious mission of Catholic higher education.

Defining Catholic identity had been a battleground within American Catholicism since the 1970s not only in Catholic colleges and universities, but also in other Catholic schools, seminaries, hospitals, social agencies, and the NCCB/USCC as well as in ordinary parishes across the country. Catholics were divided over a host of moral and religious issues, including how to interpret the meaning of the Second Vatican Council.

Post–Vatican II American Catholicism experienced an unprecedented period of polarization, conflict, and indeed acrimony as different factions in the church fought with one another over a variety of ecclesiastical, moral, political, and cultural questions. Four issues were particularly divisive: the nature and proper exercise of ecclesiastical authority, social justice, sexual morality and abortion, and the role of religion in politics. Division and conflict, of course, were a part of the much longer history of Christianity. What was particularly new for those whose experience of Catholicism was confined to the relatively halcyon days of the immediate past was not only the widespread and public but also the substantive character of the ecclesial conflicts.

The council had opened up the church to criticism and reform, and during the postconciliar period it seemed that very little in the church's tradition, from the positioning of the altar to moral and doctrinal issues, was free from at least someone's question or criticism. Conflicts within the church were reflective of and exacerbated by the great cultural revolution in the larger American society that protested against all kinds of institutions. Those Catholics who supported long-held values and institutions were in a position of defense; presumption was no longer on the side of tradition and the church's teaching office, as it had been generally in the preconciliar period. Some talked of the "old church" or of "ghetto Catholicism," as if there was very little continuity between pre- and post-conciliar Catholic institutions and experiences. The postconciliar battle was over the definition of precisely what was and what was not continuous and changeable within the Catholic tradition—and it is that character of the battle that helps to explain so much of the acrimony and bitterness that accompanied it.

Conflicts over the nature and extent of ecclesiastical authority recurred periodically throughout the postconciliar period. The authority of the papacy and the Vatican bureaucracy came under repeated attacks within the church. Unpopular papal statements on a variety of sexual ethics issues, jurisdictional debates between American theologians and bishops and Vatican officials over the teaching authority of national episcopal conferences, and the Vatican's disciplining of some American bishops and archbishops created and reinforced tensions within the church and produced at least a psychological distancing between America and Rome. Dissensions between noncollegial bishops and their postconciliar clergy here and there, between noncollegial clergy and their active laity, and between authoritarian bishops and the "new sisters" also reinforced the mentality of conflict and to some extent discredited ecclesiastical authority in general among a large segment of the population.

The most sustained internal conflict was over social justice issues (e.g., war and peace, world poverty, American international aid, other foreign policy questions, the economy, and race). The search for social justice was also one of the defining characteristics of post–Vatican II Catholicism. Although the postconciliar emphasis on social justice had continuities with preconciliar movements in American Catholicism, there were a number of differences: the focus on justice within the church as well as in society; the emphasis on social liberation and a preferential option for the poor over the stress on the economic development of peoples; and human rights perceived in explicitly inclusive terms and in terms of sexual, cultural, and personal empowerments rather than simple immunities. In these emphases, postconciliar American Catholic social thought was modified by its encounter with various liberation movements in North and South American societies.

Following the Second Vatican Council, the Catholic community throughout the world was called on to focus on issues of social justice, but the understanding of what constituted the goal of movements for justice shifted. *Gaudium et Spes*, Paul VI's *Populorum Progressio* (1967), and his establishment of the Pontifical Commission on Justice and Peace (1967) focused on the development of peoples. The Medellin and Puebla Episcopal Conferences in 1968 and 1979, the international episcopal synods on justice (1971), and evangelization of culture (1974) went beyond world development to stress the liberation of peoples as the core of justice. The 1971 International Synod of Bishops in Rome articulated that conviction when it wrote that "action on behalf of justice and participation in the transformation of the world fully appear to us as a constitutive dimension of the preaching of the Gospel." This meant that "the redemption of the human race and its liberation from every oppressive situation" was acknowledged as an integral part of the church's mission.[22]

The American bishops, their advisers at the USCC, and numerous theologians and social activists became major advocates for social justice within the world, focusing in particular on world poverty, the equitable distribution of goods and services, human and civil rights, and a host of other issues involving periodic examinations of American foreign policies. The most extensive and significant of the American episcopal pastorals—*The Challenge of Peace* (1983) and *Economic Justice for All* (1986)—exemplified and epitomized the postconciliar concerns of the official church to demonstrate the interrelated practical, political, and social implications of Christian life and thought. Although these teaching statements were not necessarily indicative or representative of actual and popular Catholic practices and perceptions, they indicated the ideals to which the postconciliar church aspired.

Dramatic and symbolic activities, publications, official ecclesiastical statements, and papal visits focused on Catholic responsibilities to seek peace and justice in the world. Of the 188 official public statements, resolutions, and pastoral letters of the American hierarchy between 1966 and 1988, for example, 52 percent were addressed to issues of national and international social justice. In contrast, only 12 percent focused on sexual morality and abortion. The remainder concentrated directly on internal ecclesiastical issues (e.g., ecumenism, celibacy, Mary, the church, the charismatic renewal, schools and religious education, evangelization).[23]

During the 1960s and early 1970s, the Catholic peace movement took a dramatic turn to radical protests against the war in Vietnam. From 1963 to the Harrisburg Trial in 1972, the so-called Catholic Left, a group of more than 232 Catholics, led high-profile, media-event protests against the war.[24] The demonstrators manifested a sense of unique personal responsibility, an impatience with the established procedures of the peace movement, and a flair for attracting media coverage.

The Catholic Left became effectively organized into local pockets of resistance, particularly after President Lyndon B. Johnson announced the 1965 bombing of Vietnam. The Baltimore four, the Catonsville nine, the Milwaukee fourteen, the Chicago fifteen, the Minnesota eight, the Harrisburg seven, the Camden twenty-eight, the Boston eight, the New York eight, and a host of other groups of local priests, women religious, and laity burned draft cards in defiance of federal legislation, poured blood on draft records, raided corporate headquarters of major industries that supplied the tools of war, burned corporate and federal documents with napalm, and devised other symbolic actions to demonstrate the violence of the war and their abhorrence of it. The most tragic of the protests came on 9 November 1965 when Roger LaPorte, a twenty-six-year-old Catholic Worker volunteer, immolated himself in front of the United Nations building.

In the midst of the protests, a few individuals—the Jesuit Daniel Berrigan, the Josephite Philip Berrigan, Elizabeth McAlister, a Religious of the Sacred Heart, and laymen Michael Cullen and James Forest—became local and national heroes to the movement as they kept up the public pressure against the war, went on trial, and were imprisoned. The 1968 Catonsville trial, brought against nine Catholic protesters who burned draft files, became an international news event, a focal point for rallying the antiwar movement, and the subject of a book, a play, a television documentary, and a movie. This media event became even more dramatic when Daniel Berrigan refused to turn himself in for imprisonment after the trial, went underground as a fugitive from the law, and was not captured by the FBI until 1970. Such actions heightened the movement's visibility and gave it the publicity it sought.

The symbolic and prophetic protests of the Catholic Left represented a new style in the peace movement and a shift in Catholic approaches to social justice—from rational discussion leading to political consensus (à la John Courtney Murray) to passionate witness to gospel values. The Catholic Left was in continuity with the American civil disobedience tradition, but with a Catholic twist that emphasized visible over verbal protests, and in an age of television the Catholic protesters came into their own. The Catholic Left moreover felt no compulsion to demonstrate their Americanism or loyalty, as had many preconciliar Catholic social justice advocates. Their morality of conscience and the higher law was not self-critical or open to the ambiguity of the human situation or drawn from the natural law tradition so much as it was a morality of prophetic witness.

The reaction to the Catholic peace activists varied from outright disdain to conditional support within the American Catholic population. Cardinal Francis Spellman, an ardent supporter of the war in Vietnam, deplored the demonstrators' tactics and had Daniel Berrigan exiled to Latin America for a period.[25] Spellman, however, was not alone in rejecting the protestors' tactics. By 1971, 69 percent of American Catholics, whatever their views on the war (and by 1971 over 50 percent was opposed), believed that Catholics who raided draft boards were not acting as responsible Christians. And despite the widespread publicity given to the Berrigan brothers after 1968, only 38 percent of the Catholic population could identify them.[26] Statistics like these convinced the sociologist Andrew M. Greeley that the Catholic "radicals" made no difference at all in the Catholic community and that "Berrigan-style protests are counterproductive for the causes they support."[27]

A few pacifists like Dorothy Day and Thomas Merton were also critical of the protesters' destruction of property. Although he abhorred the war in Vietnam, Merton believed that the actions of the Baltimore four and the Catonsville nine in seizing and burning draft files in 1968 put the peace movement on "the very edge of violence.... On a long-term basis, I think the Peace Movement needs to really study, practice and use nonviolence in its classic form, with all that this implies of religious and ethical grounds."[28]

By the 1972 Harrisburg trial, the radical Catholic peace movement was already in the midst of decline because of internal tensions and a repetitiveness of symbolic activities that had lost their power to provoke. By the end of the war in 1975, the peace movement may have been somewhat chastened, but it would continue to have an impact within the American Catholic community. According to a Gallup and Castelli study, the peace movement and the bishops' peace pastoral made Catholics "doves for a generation."[29] The value of such social analysis as an indicator of real convictions is doubtful, however, especially in light of the overwhelming American Catholic support for the Gulf War in 1991.

The American bishops' major effort to get the Catholic people involved in issues of justice and peace was the Detroit "Call to Action" Conference (21–23 October 1976). The convention's theme and its name were taken from Pope Paul VI's apostolic letter *A Call to Action* (1971) and the international episcopal synod's *Justice in the World* (1971). Convoked to celebrate the American bicentennial and discover ways by which the Catholic Church could renew itself and translate its faith into forms of justice, this national meeting of American Catholics represented 150 of the 170 dioceses and was composed of 1,340 voting delegates, 47 percent of whom were laity and 53 percent were clergy, including 110 of the nation's 300 bishops.

Cardinal John Dearden,* archbishop of Detroit, presided over the conference. The delegates drew up and sent to the U.S. bishops a set of 182 recommendations, not only on social problems, but on a host of internal ecclesiastical matters: parish life, ministry, education, and church government. Some of the recommendations (e.g., lay involvement in the selection of bishops and pastors, the possibility of a married clergy, the ordination of women) made the experiment in American Catholic democratic action at the national level problematic for the bishops.

The numerous recommendations and the process itself proved to be too all-encompassing, and the conference itself did not have the practical machinery nor indeed a representative American Catholic consensus to make implementation of the recommendations possible. The conference did, however, symbolize a way of life and decision making that would be followed in much smaller ways in various dioceses and parishes throughout the country in the period afterward, as more and more people became involved in social justice and local ecclesiastical affairs.

The NCCB's "Bicentennial Consultation: A Response to the Call to Action" (1977) reaffirmed the national bishops' commitment to the "principle of shared responsibility" in the contemporary church, acknowledged that "Call to Action's" process of consultation was imperfect, and rejected some of the conference's recommendations as contrary to doctrine and current church discipline.[30] In 1978 the NCCB committed itself to a five-year plan (1978–1983) for implementing in the diocesan and national church a six-point program that illustrated central themes of "Call to Action": education for justice, concentration on family life, deepening communal life in parishes and communities, promotion of human rights, and focus on world hunger.[31] That same year the national bishops also created the Secretariat for the Laity as a major institution to advise bishops on lay concerns in the church. Even though "Call to Action" did not produce the kinds of changes in the church that some Catholics envisioned, it did influence the consciousness of a number of bishops, who in subsequent years created structures of greater shared responsibility in their dioceses, diocesan offices of justice and peace, and offices for black and Hispanic concerns.

The long-term effects and implications of "Call to Action" can be seen on the national level in the major pastoral letters that the bishops produced in subsequent years, and more particularly in the processes by which they prepared and wrote those pastorals.[32] The pastorals themselves were significant first of all because they focused national attention on some of the social justice issues identified at Detroit. Second, the process by which the pastorals were written revealed a new approach to Christian teaching in areas of social justice. Prior to writing the pastorals on peace and the economy, the bishops consulted a variety of persons with experience and expertise in politics, education, theology, law, and economics. Various preliminary drafts of the pastorals were discussed among the bishops themselves, and several hearings were held on them throughout the country as the bishops extended their dialogue before they published the final drafts. Third, the pastorals were intended to spark a national discussion on the ethical dimensions of governmental policy in these areas. Fourth, the bishops distinguished those elements in their pastoral teachings that were doctrinal from those applications of Christian principles that were debatable.

The pastorals were widely discussed in the press, professional journals, Catholic schools, and numerous parish and diocesan meetings across the country. Consultation and dialogue were becoming modes of Catholic action, and the issues were substantial, involving the intersection of Christian values and political policies in the country. The pastorals also evoked creative and critical response from other churches and from a number of intellectuals in American society. One group of prominent conservative lay American Catholic entrepreneurs, labor leaders, and intellectuals, for example, issued their own statement on the economy, written primarily by Michael Novak. The lay letter, although in sympathy with many of the bishops' criticisms of the American economy, called for a more affirmative celebration of the benefits of American democratic capitalism than they thought the bishops were willing to acknowledge.[33]

The twenty-year postconciliar emphasis on social justice and liberation seems to have had some impact on American Catholic attitudes. Opinion polls indicated that a substantial majority of Catholics favored a number of the justice and peace issues. According to one study, 84 percent supported a bilateral nuclear freeze, 77 percent increased government spending on social programs, 69 percent the Equal Rights Amendment (ERA), and 68 percent a cut in military spending.[34] By significant margins Catholics were also opposed to President Ronald Reagan's policies in Central America, particularly in providing military aid, and favored greater U.S. pressure on South Africa.[35] On broad economic themes, too, Catholics were in substantial agreement with their bishops, particularly in their perception that the government ought to play a more activist role in the economy, that circumstances many times force people into poverty, and that there was a need for tax reform and an equitable redistribution of wealth and income.[36] These bread-and-butter issues, of course, were a part of the official Catholic view since Leo XIII and the Depression, but the polls demonstrated that even with increased affluence, a majority of American Catholics did not give up their social concerns.

"Call to Action" reflected and further encouraged movements among black and Hispanic Catholics. Justice for blacks in church and society took a new turn in the postconciliar period with the rise of Black Power movements, assassinations, and major urban race riots throughout the country. Black Power movements toward separatism and black nationalism challenged Dr. Martin Luther King Jr.'s leadership role in the black community, as many began to emphasize the self-determination of blacks over integration. With the assassinations of Malcolm X in 1965 and especially of King on 4 April 1968, the fury of frustrations in the black community erupted in a long series of urban riots that threatened the stability of society and dignity of human persons.

Within this context, the American Catholic Church, too, experienced a shift in its approach to racial justice. Some white priests, such as James Groppi of Milwaukee, won the confidence of the black community and led movements for fair housing, jobs, and dignity. The leadership on racism, however, was gradually passing to articulate black clergy and laity as they protested particularly against racism in the church and called for more self-determination within the structures of American Catholicism.[37]

On 18 April 1968, shortly after the assassination of King, more than 50 of the 150 Black Catholic priests met in Detroit, under the leadership of Herman Porter, George Clements, and Rollins Lambert, to prepare "A Statement of the Black Catholic Clergy Caucus," a stinging criticism of racism in the church. The opening sentence declared, "The Catholic Church in the United States, primarily a white racist institution, has addressed itself primarily to white society and is definitely a part of that society." The statement called for more black participation on all levels of decision making in the church, greater efforts to encourage vocations among blacks, more respect for black culture and styles of worship, the establishment of a black-led department within the USCC, and dioceses to set aside funds for a permanent leadership training program for black laypersons. It also called for black assertiveness and self-determination within the

Catholic Church because of the serious defection of black Catholics from it and because the "black community no longer looks to the Catholic Church with hope."[38] The establishment of the National Black Catholic Clergy Caucus (NBCCC, 1968) created a solidarity among the black clergy and a new form of militancy and self-determination that had previously been lacking.

Later in 1968, Sister Martin de Porres Grey, who was present at the NBCCC meeting in Detroit, helped organize a similar institution, the National Black Sisters' Conference. In the same year, the National Black Catholic Seminarians' Association was also founded, and a year later lay Catholics formed a similar national association. In 1970, in response to these solidarity movements, the NCCB established within the USCC a National Office for Black Catholics as a clearinghouse for the black voice in national Catholic affairs.[39]

The militant 1960s and early 1970s did indeed make the national bishops, if not the church as a whole, responsive to the appeals and needs of black Catholics in the United States. In 1965 Harold Perry, S.V.D., was ordained as the first black bishop since the mid-nineteenth century. In 1966, 1968, and 1979, the NCCB published explicit pastoral statements on the issues of racism in church and society. In 1984 the ten black bishops published "What We Have Seen and Heard," a pastoral on the gifts of black Catholicism. The presence of ten black bishops in the American episcopate in 1984 (increased to thirteen in 1988) indicated that the national bishops had also been responsive to the appeals for representation. In 1988, furthermore, Bishop Eugene Marino was appointed archbishop of Atlanta, the first black Catholic archbishop in the nation's history. In 1987 Pope John Paul II gave a special audience to black Catholic leaders during his visit to the United States. That year also saw the National Black Catholic Congress held in Washington, D.C. to articulate concerns.

Although Catholic blacks gained representation within the church, some of them were alienated from Catholicism, as was evident in the separation of Washington, D.C.'s charismatic Father George Stallings from the Catholic Church in 1989, his subsequent ordination as bishop and archbishop of the separatist African-American Catholic Church, and his ordination of black American Rose Vernell, a former sister, as a priest of Imani Temple in Philadelphia.

The Hispanic movement toward civil rights and justice started with migrant farm workers. A steady stream had been coming into California and the Southwest from Mexico since the 1920s, with a veritable flood after World War II. These workers followed the harvest of the crops—particularly grapes, other fruits, and vegetables—receiving in return starvation wages, poor housing, and miserable living conditions, with no promise of financial stability or growth. Most of them were Spanish-speaking Catholics who received little support from their bishops and clergy, with some notable exceptions such as Archbishop Robert Lucey of San Antonio. The workers themselves had little power or recourse against the powerful landowners and growers until, under the leadership of the Arizona-born Mexican American César Chavez, they began to organize themselves in the early 1960s.

Like the peace protests in the East, the farm laborers' protests on the West Coast used united nonviolent symbolic gestures and tactics to accomplish their goals. In 1962 Chavez established the National Farm Workers Association, which in 1965 affiliated with the AFL-CIO Agricultural Workers Organizing Committee. From 1965 to the mid-1970s, Chavez led the workers in a series of strikes against the growers in California and other places, fasted and held prayer vigils to demonstrate the necessity of nonviolence, organized protest marches to reveal the workers' plight, called for and engineered national boycotts of grapes, lettuce, and some California wines, and engaged in a number of successful collective bargaining sessions with the growers that eventually won favorable labor contracts.

The presence of large numbers of Hispanics also called the Catholic Church to respond to the new immigrants. Some estimate that the Hispanic Catholic population grew from about 4.9 million in 1960 to about 13.3 million in 1987, representing in the late 1980s about 20 percent of the American Catholic population.[40] The increasing number of Hispanic immigrants demonstrated clearly that the American Catholic immigrant tradition did not cease in the 1960s, when other American Catholics became solidly identified with middle-class America. A large percentage of this Spanish-speaking population was made up of new immigrants primarily from Mexico, Cuba, Puerto Rico, Spain, South and Central America, and the Dominican Republic. Most of the Hispanics, like other earlier immigrant groups, had low incomes (only 20 percent in 1978 had incomes above $15,000 per year), lacked adequate education and skills, and carried with them particular communal and family traditions and values that clashed with a voluntaristic, technological, urban, and competitive American society. Many also had particular religious sensitivities that did not find ready acceptance in an American Catholic tradition significantly influenced by the republican, Protestant, and capitalistic culture in which it developed.

In the early 1960s there were only a few Hispanics within the priesthood (and none within the episcopacy) to voice the concerns of their peoples. Although the American hierarchy had formed the Bishops' Committee for the Spanish-Speaking in 1945, it was led by Irish-American Catholics. Not until the 1960s did Hispanic leaders begin to protest against the church's inattention to Hispanic concerns and the lack of their representation in the church's hierarchy. In 1969 a number of Hispanic priests, both native born and immigrant, organized in San Antonio (the scene of much support since the days of Archbishop Lucey in the 1940s) PADRES to voice the concerns of their communities. Soon thereafter a number of other local and national Hispanic organizations developed: Las Hermanas (1971), a group of Hispanic sisters; Father Virgil Elizondo's Mexican-American Cultural Center (San Antonio, 1971), which began as a Spanish language institute and developed into a school for Hispanic culture and theology; the Encuentro movement (1972), a campaign to develop a plan for Hispanic ministries; the NCCB's Secretariat for Hispanic Affairs (1974); and Father Allan Deck's Academy of Hispanic Theologians at the Jesuit School of Theology at Berkeley, California (1988).

The Hispanic protests and organizing efforts had some effect. On 5 May 1970 Patricio Flores was ordained a bishop, the first twentieth-century Hispanic to be raised to the episcopacy in the United States. He was later appointed archbishop of San Antonio. By 1988 twenty more Hispanic bishops had been ordained, more than half were immigrants, continuing the immigrant episcopal tradition of American Catholicism. Hispanics had a voice in the church of the 1990s that they never had in the 1960s. They also enriched the American Catholic tradition with their culture by contributing the Cursillo and Marriage Encounter movements, and by reminding American Catholics of their own immigrant roots and the need for equality and justice within the religious community. Some surveys indicated, however, that large numbers of Hispanic Catholics continued to be alienated from the institutional church.[41]

From the 1960s onward, a veritable revolution took place in American society on a variety of moral and lifestyle issues that seriously challenged official Catholic Church teachings. Artificial contraception, premarital sex, abortion, and homosexuality became increasingly accepted by the population at large but created ardent divisions both within the church and society. The media in particular concentrated on the divisions over these issues and focused on the public dissent of theologians within the church and on opinion polls that showed growing differences between official church teachings and the beliefs and practices of ordinary Catholics. The questions were asked repeatedly: "When the official church teaches on these issues, who listens?" "From what source do American Catholics draw their moral values, from the church and its tradition or from their personal experiences and the culture in which they live?" "Does the public dissent within the church create a moral vacuum or at least a moral uncertainty in which individuals are left to their own devices to settle the moral issues without the benefit of an undivided teaching voice in the church?" However the questions were phrased, there was no doubt that the official church's opposition to artificial contraception, premarital sex, abortion, and homosexual activity was countercultural, and, in some circles at least, it reinforced an image of Catholicism as opposed to personal freedoms, women's equality and liberation, and concerns about overpopulation. Although the image did not quite square with the reality, the Vatican did not always make its concern about these issues evident in its own teachings.

The papal encyclical *Humanae Vitae* (1968), prohibiting artificial contraception as immoral, became a major post–Vatican II cause célèbre. It had wide-ranging consequences in the American church because it provoked not only a public opposition among numerous theologians, but also a silent resistance among a growing number of American Catholics and an increasing antagonism to ecclesiastical authority and other church teachings. The encyclical was consistent with *Casti Connubii* (1930), the first major modern papal statement against artificial means of birth control, but it came at a time when there was high expectation that the church was about to change its teaching on the issue. That expectation was created by the general post–Vatican II reform atmosphere and by the fact that Pope John XXIII had created a papal commission on birth regulation in 1962 to reexamine the church's teaching, and Pope Paul VI had broadened the commission's membership during the Second Vatican Council. In 1967 the commission reported a divided opinion to the pope (a report published in the *National Catholic Reporter*): a minority favored retaining the opposition to artificial contraception, while a majority favored changing the teaching. *Humanae Vitae* sided with the minority.

Resistance to the encyclical was immediate in the United States. Theologians at the Catholic University, led by Father Charles Curran, obtained the signatures of eighty-seven theologians who dissented from the papal teaching against artificial contraception. More than six hundred additional theologians and teachers of theology later signed the dissenting statement. Forty priests in the Archdiocese of Washington, D.C., also protested against the encyclical and were swiftly suspended from their clerical duties by Archbishop Patrick O'Boyle.

The theologians' public dissent revealed that a fundamental shift in moral categories was taking place in the postconciliar church: from teleological and essentialist (natural law) categories to personalist and existential categories. Many of the encyclical's theological opponents were proportionalists—that is, those who believed that an action became morally wrong when, all things considered, there was not proportionate reason.[42] The Catholic University theologians and others who signed the dissenting statement were not disciplined immediately, but in 1986, nineteen years after the event, the Roman Congregation for the Doctrine of the Faith (CDF) under Cardinal Joseph Ratzinger declared that Charles Curran could no longer teach at the Catholic University because of his opposition to official church teaching.

The theologians' public dissent unwittingly vindicated a silent sexual revolution that had been going on in American Catholicism since the 1950s, reinforced the contraceptive mentality, and provided warrants for further alienation from the teaching church. Already by 1955, some polls showed, "over four-fifths of Catholic wives capable of conception used some means of birth control, with over one-half of the respondents practicing a method considered immoral by churchmen."[43] Opinion polls from the 1970s to the late 1980s revealed that large numbers of lay Catholics simply ignored the papal ban against contraception. By 1977, one poll demonstrated, 73 percent of Catholics believed that they should be allowed to practice artificial means of birth control.[44]

For the first time in American Catholic history, American Catholics publicly resisted an official church teaching. American Catholics in the past, of course, did not exactly follow the church's teachings in the areas of economic justice, racial discrimination, or even in the areas of sexual morality, but they rarely protested publicly or questioned the church's authority to teach in those areas. Among the host of reasons that motivated elite and then popular resistance or even indifference to church teaching in the area of sexuality morality was a cultural antiestablishmentarianism, an expectation of change created by the council, and a new notion of ecclesiastical authority that had been issued by the council and articulated by postconciliar Catholic theologians and journalists.

Father Andrew Greeley and others have argued that the encyclical was responsible for creating a crisis of authority in the church, alienating many Catholics from it, and for damaging the church's entire sexual ethic. The decline in Catholic opposition to premarital sex[45] seems to provide some evidence for Greeley's claim that the church's general sexual ethic has been damaged, but whether that damage came from the encyclical or from a more general sexual revolution in the culture seems open to question.

Dissent itself became an issue after *Humanae Vitae* and the focus of much discontent among those Catholics who supported the papal teaching and who saw organized public dissent as an imitation of democratic political maneuvering. According to Msgr. George A. Kelly and a number of others, the theologians' dissent was an attempt to establish a second magisterium in the church, but in effect it only created a situation of uncertainty and doubt, which gave rise to a moral relativism and subjectivism. A significant increase in the use of contraceptives can be traced, according to Kelly, to the period of the theologians' published dissent.[46]

If contraception created consternation within the church in the mid-1960s, abortion was to absorb the attention of many Americans after the late 1960s. The push for abortion-on-demand won a major victory in Great Britain when it was legalized in 1967. The movement to abolish state laws in the United States picked up momentum after that victory and became a constant source of concern to American bishops from the late 1960s onward. The campaign to legalize abortion was tied to sexual freedom in general, women's liberation and their right to control reproduction, the problem of unplanned and unwanted children, and the issue of overpopulation. The 1973 Supreme Court decision *Roe v. Wade* abolishing state laws against abortion made it, as some social scientists argued, "one of the most controversial social issues in American society."[47]

Abortion had not been much of an issue at the Second Vatican Council; *Gaudium et Spes* (#27) simply reaffirmed the church's traditional prohibition against it. From the late 1960s onward, the American bishops repeatedly taught against abortion, repudiated the Supreme Court's decision, and argued that society and the state had the moral responsibility to "safeguard the life of every person from the very beginning of that life." The bishops perceived themselves as having a preferential option for those unborn "who are least able to defend themselves." Without denying the pain and suffering associated with illegitimacy, emotional distress, poverty, and a host of other problems legalized abortion was supposed to cure, the American bishops asserted in 1969 that "we find no evidence that easy abortion laws will solve these problems."[48] Papal visits in 1979 and 1987 reinforced this official Catholic teaching, as have numerous postconciliar papal statements.

The abortion issue divided the Catholic Church perhaps more than any other. Numerous church leaders, prominent theologians, and philosophers—for example, James Tunstead Burtchaell, C.S.C., John R. Connery, S.J., William May, Germain Grisez, John Finnis, and Joseph Boyle—although differing among themselves in many particulars, upheld the church's official position and saw abortion primarily as a life-and-death, not a liberation, issue. Other theologians such as Daniel Maguire, however, directly opposed the church's position. And still other theologians, those called proportionalists by theologian Richard A. McCormick, S.J., have argued, "just as not every killing is murder, not every falsehood a lie, so not every... termination of a pregnancy is necessarily an abortion in the moral sense."[49]

Numerous Catholics have been active in the national and local pro-life movements. Marlene Elwell, for example, was prominent in organizing the National Right to Life Committee. On the other hand, Catholic feminists like Eleanor Smeal, the former president of the National Organization for Women (NOW, 1977–1982, 1985–1987), became a vigorous exponent of a woman's right to an abortion.[59] The divided Catholic opinion over abortion was expressed most forcefully during the presidential campaign of 1984. On 7 October 1984 a group of Catholic laity and religious published an ad in the New York Times in support of free choice and legalized abortions. The women religious in the group were subsequently disciplined by ecclesiastical authority, and on 2 March 1986 a Committee of Concerned Catholics published in the Times a declaration of solidarity with those threatened with ecclesiastical discipline for the positions they took, and asked the American bishops "to protect and defend the right of Catholic religious, scholars and activists to speak out on controversial issues of public policy freely, fully and without reprisal." The issue of abortion, like so many issues of the period, again became associated with those of freedom and authority, ecclesiastical discipline, public policy, and the relation of faith to action.

Since 1974 Catholics have registered increasing support for the 1973 Supreme Court decision, while Evangelical American Protestants in general have showed increasing opposition to it. A 1984 Gallup poll disclosed that a majority of Catholics believed that abortion should be legal in cases of rape and incest, but 65 percent opposed abortion-on-demand, and 60 percent supported a constitutional amendment to restrict abortions. Catholic opinion on abortion was not only an indicator that official church teachings had not been fully received, but also a manifestation of the widespread unyielding disagreements on the morality and legality of abortion in American society.[51]

The issue of homosexuality came to the fore in American society in 1969 after the Stonewall Riot in New York, when homosexual men publicly resisted police harassment. Thereafter, the issue of homosexual orientation and lifestyle became matters of some public debate. Catholic teaching, like that of many other religious traditions, had considered homosexual behavior immoral because it was against biblical prescriptions and the natural law. By the early 1970s, though, the American bishops were distinguishing between homosexual orientations (which were not always freely chosen) and homosexual activities (which were prohibited). A few Catholics, however, questioned the absolute prohibition against homosexual activities in the light of scientific evidence.[52]

Pastoral care of homosexuals also became an issue. In 1969 a group of Catholic homosexuals formed the organization Dignity to plead for respect and pastoral care within the church and for the protection of their cultural and civil rights in society. According to some opinion polls, between 1977 and 1985 Catholics became increasingly tolerant of legalizing homosexual relations between consenting adults, supported equal job opportunities for homosexuals (67 percent in favor, 24 percent opposed), believed that homosexuals could be good Christians or Jews (67 percent in favor, 23 percent opposed), but rejected homosexuality as an alternative lifestyle (46 percent in favor, 39 percent opposed).[53]

Catholic Church leaders and politicians as well as many others in American society became acutely aware that many of the moral issues facing American society involved the relationship between religion and politics. For American Catholics in particular, the old debates of the 1940s and 1950s over religious liberty and separation of church and state gave way to new issues after the Second Vatican Council. One of those issues, arising during the presidential campaign of 1984, focused on the responsibilities of a Catholic politician in a democratic society. What was a Catholic politician's specific responsibilities on the issue of abortion? That question came into focus when New York's Cardinal John O'Connor charged that the Democratic vice presidential candidate, Geraldine Ferraro, had given the false impression that the Catholic position on abortion was not monolithic and that "you can be a good Catholic and believe in abortion . . . that there is solid foundations [sic] for a variance in Catholic teaching on abortion."[54] He also criticized her for separating personal conscience from political responsibility. Ferraro held that a Catholic politician, although personally opposed to abortion, could support the political and civil rights of women to make their own decisions and could support legislative programs that funded and supported abortion, because that was part of the American consensus that she and others were called on to represent. In 1982 Ferraro had written a letter to Catholics in Congress suggesting that "the Catholic position on abortion is not monolithic and that there can be a range of personal and political responses to the issue." That position was one advocated by moral theologian Daniel Maguire and Catholics for a Free Choice at a 1982 Washington, D.C., briefing for some members of Congress titled "The Abortion Issue in the Political Process."[55]

The O'Connor-Ferraro conflict had political implications, but it also raised serious issues about the role of religion in politics, issues that New York's Democratic Governor Mario M. Cuomo tried to adjudicate in a speech before a large audience at the University of Notre Dame on 13 September 1984, two days after O'Connor's criticisms of Ferraro's position.[56] Cuomo argued that Catholic bishops had the right to define abortion as immoral for individual Catholics, but that church doctrine did not dictate particular political strategies for converting moral teachings into law. Because law was built upon consensus, and none existed on abortion, the church in the United States should not seek legal remedies for moral problems where there was no consensus. Catholic religious values, he told his audience, need not be the law of the land. The bishops themselves, he opined, had tacitly followed this perspective in the issues of contraception and divorce.

Two weeks after Cuomo's speech, Illinois' Republican U.S. Representative Henry Hyde joined the debate over the role of religion in politics during another Notre Dame convocation. Hyde argued that the abortion issue was distorted if perceived as a personal, religious, or sectarian issue. The issue was one of public morality, and therefore it belonged to those in public service to address it. For him, it was clearly insufficient for a Catholic public official to hold that his or her personal conscientious objection to abortion ended the matter. Law was not simply a matter of public consensus, but had an educative function to lead people to justice and equity in society. Requiring consensus prior to legislation was, moreover, highly selective in some circles. "No consensus was demanded before adopting the Civil Rights Act of 1964 or Fair Housing legislation—they were right and their proponents helped to *create* a consensus by advocacy and example and by understanding that law itself can be an excellent teacher." Therefore, public officials had the responsibility to teach justice, not just to reflect prevailing values. For him, abortion was not a "Catholic issue," but rather a "moral and civil rights issue, a humanitarian issue and a constitutional issue of the first importance." For Hyde, religiously based values must play a role in public life; otherwise the moral foundations of society would continue to erode.[57]

Whether the law should be reflective or creative of a consensus in society, whether politicians should represent the society's prevailing sense of right or teach justice, and whether the abortion issue was one of private and personal morality or a matter of public justice and morality were questions that continued to divide opinion in the church and society.

In the midst of unprecedented decline and conflict within American Catholicism there arose a number of new movements to revive spirituality. A 1976 *Time* cover story, "U.S. Catholicism: A Church Divided," revealed that despite changes and conflicts, the American Catholic people were displaying a "remarkable tenacity" and showing a "spiritual second wind that suggests that U.S. Catholicism might even be on the verge of a new period of vigor."[58] In 1989 Gallup and Castelli, after analyzing recent opinion polls, declared, "American Catholics are in the middle of a religious revival."[59] The revival, though, reflected a shift in Catholic spirituality that took some years to accomplish. It was a revival, moreover, that was continuing simultaneously with the concerns for institutional reforms and in the midst of church divisions.

Although devotional Catholicism continued to characterize the spirituality of many older Catholics during the postconciliar period, it was gradually replaced by a variety of new forms that emphasized the sacramental, communal, and active dimensions thought to be grounded in the public liturgy, the Bible, and the personal experiences of modern Catholics. The ecumenical openness of the Second Vatican Council also encouraged some Catholics to look into forms of spirituality outside of the Catholic tradition.

The charismatic movement was one of the most dramatic, ecumenical, long-lasting, and widespread spiritual movements of the postconciliar period, touching millions of Catholics between 1965 and 1990.[60] The charismatic movement focused attention on the gifts of the Holy Spirit, the necessity of a new experience of spiritual power, and the need to provide individual and communal witnesses to the faith experience. Catholic charismatics differed from classical Pentecostals primarily in their emphasis on the sacramental context of the spiritual gifts, their allegiance to a teaching church, and their willingness to stay within the institutional structures to renew from within.

Another revival of spirituality began to occur during the mid-1970s, when numerous parishes across the country adopted one of any number of parish renewal programs, some of which had been sponsored by the USCC and all of which focused on developing the spiritual life of Catholics at the local level. Perhaps the most successful and widespread of these was RENEW, a diocesan-wide, parish-based pastoral program that originated in the Archdiocese of Newark, New Jersey, in 1976. By 1990 ninety-six dioceses and about one-half of all parishes in the United States had some experience with RENEW.[61]

The national movements toward a recovery of spirituality in American Catholicism were accompanied by a great growth in new and diverse forms of spirituality focused particularly on the special needs of adults, youth, women, divorced people, blacks, and Hispanics. Father Virgil Elizondo's Mexican-American Cultural Center, for example, attempted to formulate a spirituality suited to Hispanics. In the parishes, too, diversity characterized the approaches to extra-sacramental spirituality with an increase in the number of Bible-reading and study groups, prayer groups, and an increased emphasis since the mid-1970s on evangelizing lapsed and/or alienated Catholics. The establishment of the National Organization of Catholic Evangelical Directors in 1982 was one indicator of the increased emphasis placed on evangelization. Older forms of popular Marian piety, too, continued among Hispanics and other groups, and were revived in the 1980s with the alleged Marian apparitions at Medjugorje, Yugoslavia.

Although there were a number of complaints about the institutional church's failures to meet the religious needs of many American Catholics, programs like RENEW, a stabilized (53 percent) Mass attendance by the mid-1970s, widespread participation in prayer meetings, more involvement in church life at parish and diocesan levels, a significant increase in Bible reading, and a large increment in the purchasing and reading of books on spirituality are some of the indicators of a religious revival. Internal disagreements and conflicts, some surveys reported, did not change a sense of belonging to the church. In fact, a 1987 poll found that Catholics had more "confidence in the church than in any other institution," with 85 percent saying that their lifetime experiences in Catholicism had been "overall positive."[62]

In spite of the "overall positive" ratings, serious questions were raised about postconciliar experiences and developments within American Catholicism. Had the unprecedented changes in theological awareness and in ecclesiastical forms brought about a fundamental spiritual regeneration and a new sense of the reality, mystery, and power of God in human lives? Or, had the transformations been simply accommodations to secularity, radical pluralism, and a technological imperative that made ends out of means? Was the selective rejection of official church teachings a new manifestation of basic Christian freedom and personal authenticity, or had it been a sign of American individualism and the decline of faith? Had the decline in identification with and participation in the church been the result of misguided ecclesiastical decisions, radical Catholic aberrations, or the product of a long-standing pretense of belief that was finally shattered once the institutions that supported the pretense began to crumble or show signs of weakness?

Responses to these and a host of other questions produced interpretations and evaluations of postconciliar American Catholicism as varied and as contradictory as the Catholic experiences themselves. In the late 1960s and early 1970s, a number of conservative Catholic groups and individuals rose up in protest against what they perceived to be wrongheaded postconciliar developments. Traditionalist Catholics associated with Father Gommar De Pauw and the French Archbishop Marcel Lefèbvre rejected as invalid the postconciliar liturgical reforms and emphasized the unalterable nature of Tridentine sacramental practices. Others—those associated with the *Wanderer*, Catholics United for the Faith, and a host of other conservative lay Catholic organizations—accepted the conciliar declarations and Vatican-initiated reforms but repudiated the liberal interpretations and abuses and censured unauthorized liturgical experimentations, a resurgence of modernism in catechetics, a weakening of magisterial authority, and the minimizing of the supernatural. They periodically charged some American Catholics with unfaithfulness and some leading bishops with heresy and the abandonment of their authoritative offices.[63]

In the early 1970s and thereafter, a number of conservative intellectuals, groups, and publications began criticizing the disintegration within American Catholicism that had been occurring since the end of the council.[64] Whether they attributed the breakdown and decline in the church to the popular reform mentality that created the "illusion" of a major discontinuity between the preconciliar church and the "New Catholicism," or to the liberal theologians who had blessed an unholy theological pluralism and had capitulated to modernity by collapsing the distinction between the natural and the supernatural, or to the liberal- and reform-minded bishops and clergy who had abdicated their authority in the church, or, in Garry Wills's view, to the fatal insufficiencies in the church's very fabric that had protected a pretense of belief that periodically in the church's history called for reform, these voices reflected discontent with many postconciliar developments. These intellectuals sought to reestablish a sense of the supernatural, reassert the church's interior unity and cohesiveness, and reaffirm loyalty to the church's official magisterium on the ultimate questions concerning God, the human person, and the world. Like the "liberal Catholic" voice of the 1950s, the conservative voice of the 1970s was a minority voice within the Catholic intellectual community. That voice, though, would become more widespread and more moderate in the late 1970s and early 1980s, as the country itself began reacting against the cultural revolution of the 1960s, and the church, under Pope John Paul II and Cardinal Joseph Ratzinger, reinforced traditional Catholic values.

The predominant view of post–Vatican II developments was much more favorable to the consequences of reform, change, and pluralism. That view was articulated by a large group of intellectuals who became advisers and church leaders in a number of national and local ecclesiastical institutions: the bishops' national advisers in the USCC, ecclesiastical leaders of other major national organizations (e.g., LCWR, Network, NFPC, NBCCC, and PADRES), theological leadership (e.g., in the Catholic Theological Society of America, College Theology Society, Catholic Biblical Association, Canon Law Society of America), educational leadership in the Catholic universities and colleges, directors of religious education programs, and some journalists in the major Catholic newspapers and magazines. The reform-minded leaders in the church were at first critical of the slow and uneven pace of the reforms, but they have been generally supportive of what David O'Brien called *The Renewal of American Catholicism* (1972).

The positive evaluations and celebrations of secularity and pluralism (cultural, ecclesiological, and theological) in the early postconciliar period contrasted sharply with the generally negative preconciliar judgments. In 1960, for example, the theologian Joseph Fenton could say without much challenge that the scholastic method and terminology were constants in the Catholic tradition that admitted no substantial change.[65] By 1975, seven years after Fenton's death, David Tracy was affirming "an ever increasing pluralism" in theology and seeing it as the occasion of great promise because it enabled individual theologians to learn from a variety of views of humanity and Christianity.[66] Avery Dulles, S.J., and a whole host of theologians joined Tracy in accepting and celebrating reform, revision, and pluralism within unity as fundamental Catholic values.

The year 1975, however, also marked a turning point in the reformist theological and intellectual community that was symbolic of a wider critique of liberal and reform movements within the church and society. That year twenty-four Protestant, Catholic, and Jewish scholars gathered together at Hartford, Connecticut, and published "An Appeal for Theological Affirmation," which called for a recovery of "a sense of the transcendent" and charged that some contemporary theological projects were "false and debilitating to the church's life and work."[77]

After 1975 a split developed within the reform-minded theological community that was indicative of divisions within the larger Catholic community between moderate reformists like Dulles and revisionist theologians like Tracy who were attempting a "basic revision of traditional Christianity and traditional modernity." By revising both traditions, Tracy intended to demonstrate "that the Christian faith is at heart none other than the most adequate articulation of the basic faith of secularity itself." Thus a revisionist's theology "is best understood as philosophical reflection upon the meanings present in common human experience and the meanings present in the Christian tradition."[68] Some in American Catholicism interpreted such an attempt as capitulation to modernity, others saw it as a dangerous tendency, and still others understood it as the only acceptable way to dialogue with the modern world.

The very diversity of evaluations of postconciliar directions created, especially among some who had adult experiences in both pre- and postconciliar American Catholicism, what Philip Gleason called "psychological marginality." That was the situation of those Catholics who, like new immigrants, belonged to two cultural worlds and felt "semi-detached" from and semi-involved in both worlds simultaneously. Or, as Gleason put it, those who were distanced "from each [culture] by his [and her] attachment to the other."[69] Such Catholics knew and felt the limits as well as the benefits of both past and present assimilationists' and cultural pluralists' experiences and policies within the church. Although they identified totally with neither world and stood in both at the same time, they held in uneasy psychological tension the yearning for God, ecclesial unity and cohesion, and continuity, and simultaneously the desire for freedom, diversity, and change. Such was perhaps the experience of a number of American Catholics.

The first twenty-five years after the Council brought about revolutionary changes in American society and the church. The last decade of the second and the first years of the third millennium brought new hopes for evangelization but also unprecedented troubles in church and society.

10

---·•·---

TROUBLED TIMES: 1990–2003

THE 1990S AND the first years of the third millennium were riddled with wars and terrorism. Americans who grew to maturity in these years experienced the Persian Gulf War, the Oklahoma City bombings of Timothy McVeigh, the Columbine, Colorado, murders of innocent teenagers, the serial sniper killings of random American citizens, the terrible tragedies of 9/11, and the U.S.-led wars against Afghanistan and Iraq. These national calamities were matched by spiraling cycles of violence, civil wars, and their devastating effects on the peoples of the Middle East, various African nations, and countries in Central and South America. In the midst of these worldwide catastrophes, the Catholic Church in the United States encountered its own internal violence in the form of multiple scandalous revelations of clerical sexual abuse of children and adolescents, of episcopal negligence in arresting these crimes, and of numerous civil suits that cost Catholics hundreds of millions of dollars in damages. The times were troubled.

In the midst of these troubled times, Catholics in the pews—continuing their regular cycle of worship and work, raising their children, and experiencing the joys and sorrows of everyday life—faced a host of internal ecclesiastical issues: the need for a new evangelization, women's concerns in the church and society, the continuing shortage of clergy, as well as the crisis of sexual abuse. The American Catholic Church also felt called on to address the issues of justice and peace in national and international affairs. The long-term effects of these and other issues and concerns on the American Catholic community are difficult to determine, and this historical account of them suffers from the historian's nearness to the events.

Taking their cue from the Second Vatican Council, the American Catholic bishops and their collaborators during this period concentrated many of their pastoral efforts, statements, and letters on what Pope John Paul II repeatedly called the "new evangelization." Renewed attention to evangelization was one of the aims of the Second Vatican Council, it was the focus of Pope Paul VI's *Evangelii Nuntiandi* (1975) and of two Roman episcopal synods (1974, 1977). It was a central subject in Pope John Paul II's numerous encyclicals and public statements, and helps to explain the motivation behind the many papal visits to the seven continents. His 1993, 1995, and 1999 trips to the United States, as others during the 1980s, were part of the papal agenda to preach the Gospel and apply it to different national and cultural environments. The new evangelization, as understood by the pope and the American bishops, defined the mission of the Catholic Church in the modern world of the twenty-first century.

In general, the new evangelization was a renewed effort to transform individual persons and modern society and culture into conformity with the word of God. As Pope John Paul II indicated in his Apostolic Exhortation, *Ecclesia in America* (22 January 1999), "to evangelize is the grace and vocation proper to the Church, her most profound identity." Evangelization was "new in its ardor, methods and expression .... In accepting this mission, everyone should keep in mind that the vital core of the new evangelization must be a clear and unequivocal proclamation of the person of Jesus Christ, that is, the preaching of his name, his teaching, his life, his promises and the Kingdom which he has gained for us by his Paschal Mystery."[1] The new evangelization had a particularly Catholic connotation, referring not only to personal conversion but also to liturgy, catechesis, education, and domestic or foreign policy issues that had religious and moral dimensions to them.

Between 1990 and 2003 the NCCB/USCC and its successor, the United States Conference of Catholic Bishops (USCCB) published almost three hundred pastoral letters and statements (many of them very brief) on a host of issues facing the church, American society, and the international community.[2] Behind many of these publications was an integrated vision of the new evangelization. By 1990 it was becoming clear to some bishops that the American church needed to focus on the reevangelization of Catholics, because a large percentage of professed Catholics ignored the Eucharist and other sacraments, and almost seventeen million (of the fifty-seven million who called themselves Catholic) were inactive. By 2003, moreover, the Catholic population had increased to sixty-four million and the problems multiplied. In addition to these internal problems, American materialism, consumerism, and licentiousness, as well as criminal injustices in the business world affected American Catholics.

The struggle for justice for women in society and church was also part of the post–Vatican II experience of Catholicism, as women themselves became the primary voices in the movement for emancipation from traditional cultural, legal, political, ecclesiastical, and theological barriers. The drive for women's liberation had its origins and impetus in secular society, but the Second Vatican Council, as Rosemary Radford Ruether has argued, created an "atmosphere where a discussion among Catholics of women's rights in society and in the Church seemed possible."[3] Vatican II's attention to women's issues was minimal, but it did acknowledge their legitimate social progress and fundamental right to participation in cultural life, and explicitly condemned sex discrimination and prejudices against women as contrary to God's intent. Although the council also admitted that women's roles in the church's mission should be expanded in accord with their greater participation in society, it did not translate that general support into practical reforms.

In the period after the Council, American Catholics became divided politically over the Equal Rights Amendment (ERA) and ecclesiastically over increased participation of women in the church.[4] Sexism in church and society, physical violence against women, the poverty of women and children in single-parent homes, the subordinate roles of women in the church's tradition (particularly in religious orders of women), the struggles among women religious to adapt their religious orders to modern American life and to define new roles for themselves, the use of inclusive language in translations of the Bible, the liturgy, and in church documents, and a host of other issues called for attention within the Catholic Church. Among the questions of prime importance to an increasing number of Catholics was the ordination of women to the priesthood—an issue that arose during the Second Vatican Council and continued into the twenty-first century. During the Council in the early 1960s, a few individual lay Catholic women broached the issue, and even Jean Danielou, a prominent theologian of international stature, indicated that he saw "no fundamental objection" to women priests.[5]

After the Council, the issue of women's ordination became a growing concern here and there among some American Catholics. In 1965, an American branch of the St. Joan's International Alliance—a Catholic organization that advocated, among other things, greater participation of women in all church ministries, including the priesthood—was established. Ten years later, Mary B. Lynch (1925–1979), a Catholic laywoman, founded the Women's Ordination Conference (WOC), a group that expanded throughout the 1970s, 1980s, and 1990s and had the support of a number of prominent American Catholic women theologians and other scholars.[6] Ultimately the organization aimed for a "renewed priestly ministry," meaning that the group sought to reform the worst features of patriarchy, hierarchical authoritarianism, clericalism, and sexism that were attributed to the Catholic hierarchical organization. In 1976 the Detroit "Call to Action" proposed as one of the many agenda items that the church continue to study the issue of women's ordination. In 1978 the Catholic Theological Society of America (CTSA) received a report from one of its committees calling for the ordination of women, and in 1979, the Catholic Biblical Association published a statement asserting that New Testament evidence "while not decisive by itself, points toward the admission of women to priestly ministry."[7] The ordination of women continued to be discussed publicly in the 1980s and 1990s.

Catholic bishops began to respond to women's issues in 1972 when the NCCB created an ad hoc committee on women in society and church, and by 1983 the committee suggested that the American bishops prepare a pastoral letter on women's issues, a pastoral comparable to the successful ones on peace (1983) and the economy (1986).[8] The NCCB formed a commission of women scholars and theologians, clergy, and bishops, and suggested that the committee hold hearings throughout the country prior to the preparation of a pastoral letter.

Between 1988 and 1992, the committee held multiple hearings on the proposed pastoral, published and revised four different drafts, incorporated revisions suggested by the Vatican,[9] and in November 1992, after nine years of preparation, the entire body of bishops voted not to publish it. Such pastorals required a two-thirds majority of episcopal votes, and this draft managed to receive only 137 of the 190 needed to authorize the document as a pastoral. As a compromise, Cardinal Joseph Bernardin* of Chicago proposed that the draft be published as a committee report rather than an official pastoral letter. Even though the draft had raised a number of philosophical and theological issues that needed further study, the draft should be published, he argued, because it contained many sound teachings on women's dignity and a number of helpful pastoral recommendations for the inclusion of women in the church's work. By a vote of 185 to 51, the bishops decided to publish the document as a committee report.[10]

Because of continuing discussion of the ordination of women to the priesthood, Pope John Paul II published an apostolic letter, *Ordinatio Sacerdotalis*, in 1994 that reiterated that there was no grounds for the ordination of women in either Scripture or the church's long tradition and that the ordination of men to the priesthood was a normative part of the tradition, which the church had no authority to change.[11] In response to this document and to the continuing concerns about women's roles in the church, the NCCB published *Strengthening the Bonds of Peace* (1994), a pastoral statement (accepted by a vote of 228 to 10) that reaffirmed the church's teaching on ordination, the church's belief in the equality of men and women, the need for women's leadership roles in the church, and the value of the diversity of gifts within the church.

Even though the Vatican declared repeatedly, most recently in 1995, that the church had no authority to ordain women, some in the church questioned whether or not the Vatican teaching was definitive. In October 1995, the American bishops submitted a question (a "dubium") to Rome on the definitive nature of the church's teaching on the ordination issue. In November 1995, the Congregation for the Doctrine of the Faith (CDF) responded to the "dubium" by reasserting that the church had no authority to ordain women to the priesthood. Bishop Anthony Pilla of Cleveland, president of the NCCB, announced the Roman decision and requested all Catholics to accept this teaching as definitive, saying that it belonged to the deposit of the faith and was "to be held always, everywhere, and by all."[12] The ordination of women was a closed issue and, after 1995, would not be raised again in the NCCB.

In 1997 the CTSA published a statement on "Tradition and Women's Ordination," approved by a vote of the membership present at its June meeting, that questioned whether the Vatican declaration was an infallible teaching of the church's ordinary and universal magisterium and sent their statement to the NCCB.[13] The NCCB's Committee on Doctrine responded, outlining again the church's reasons for denying ordination to women and acknowledging the need for theologians to continue to study, reflect, and discuss the church's definitive teaching because "the theological arguments for the teaching have not yet been fully explored."[14] The issue was aired very publicly through these and other means throughout the postconciliar period. That public discussion came at a time of a severe decline in the number of clergy and seminarians.

Significant segments of the American Catholic women's population supported Pope John Paul II's and the Vatican's teachings on abortion, the ordination of women, and other women's issues. One expression of such support came from Women for Faith and Family. Established in September 1984 in St. Louis by Helen Hull Hitchcock and others, Women for Faith and Family, claiming a membership of over 40,000 by 1994, opposed dissent from church teachings on these issues and asserted that WOC and other liberal women's organizations did not speak for all American Catholic women. Women for Faith and Family affirmed the "intrinsic sacredness of all human life" and rejected as "an aberrant innovation" the idea that the "priesthood is the 'right' of any human being, male or female."[15] Large segments of American Catholics continued to oppose women in the priesthood, but by 1992 a growing majority, according to the opinion polls, favored ordination for women.[16]

The shortage of clergy was becoming increasingly evident as diocese after diocese was forced to close some churches, amalgamate others, and leave some, particularly in parts of the Midwest and West, with only occasional visits from available clergy. Sociological studies in the 1990s, moreover, reinforced what many Catholics believed would be the result of the alarming decline, namely, that many Catholic churches in the future would be without regular sacramental services. The most widely read and generally accepted sociological study, *Full Pews and Empty Altars* (1993), by Richard A. Schoenherr and Lawrence A. Young,[17] predicted that because of the falling number of clergy and the rising number of Catholics, there would not be enough priests to serve the needs of the increasing numbers of Catholics: "The stark facts are that, while the diocesan priesthood population will have declined by 40 percent between 1966 and 2005, the lay population is increasing by 65 percent. The laity-to-priest ratio, a fairly accurate measure of supply and demand, will double between 1975 and 2005 from 1100 to 2200 Catholics per active priest."[18] The predictions were reinforced by the 85 percent drop in the number of seminarians preparing for the priesthood between 1966 and 1993. Such predictions reinforced the calls for opening ordination to married men and women.

In the midst of the priest shortage, women's ordination, and a host of other issues of internal concern and conflict, the American Catholic Church experienced one of the most damaging scandals in its history. From the early 1980s well into the beginning of the twenty-first century, Catholics and others in American society were bombarded with media stories about pedophile priests and other clergy who had committed sexual abuse of minors. An audit conducted in 2003 indicated that over four thousand priests and deacons between 1950 and 2003 (about 4 percent of the active clergy during the period) had violated their vows of celibacy and had committed multiple crimes of sexual abuse of minors under the age of eighteen.[19] A few other priests and even two archbishops were charged with sexual abuse of young girls and women. Amid these disclosures, particularly after 1985, it was learned that some bishops who knew of the charges of pedophilia failed to report them to civil authorities, sent the offenders to therapeutic counseling, and then placed them in new pastoral ministries where some again abused children. The numbers and frequency of the reports of these cases created a national outcry, first in the national Catholic newspapers and then in the secular papers. Many of the victims and their Catholic families pressed charges, civil prosecutors brought the offenders to criminal trials, and families took the offenders and their dioceses to civil court, suing numerous Catholic dioceses across the country for compensatory damages involving court awards of hundreds of millions of dollars from the church's resources, threatening some dioceses with bankruptcy. The problem of pedophile priests and other forms of clerical sexual abuse came to light nationally only in 1985, but some of the abuses, as later testimonies revealed, had been committed in the early 1960s and 1970s.

The history of clerical sexual abuse and of the episcopal responses to the problem is complicated and needs more extensive examination than can be provided here. The episcopal responses to the problem differed from diocese to diocese, making accurate generalizations impossible without detailed study of the 195 dioceses. The precise nature of the problem, too, needs clarity. From an ethical and legal point of view all forms of sexual abuse are immoral and crimes. But one must distinguish between the psychologically addictive and incurable nature of pedophilia (the sexual abuse of pre-pubescent children) that led to recidivism, and the reformable nature of other forms of sexual abuse (of adolescents, other young men, and women) that were not necessarily repetitive. By 1985 many bishops were aware of these different cases of sexual abuse. What they did or did not do with pedophile priests, therefore, needs to be distinguished from what they did with other forms of sexual abuse.

For a variety of reasons the problem of sexual abuse did not receive much national publicity prior to 1985. A general reluctance existed in American society to discuss openly or bring to public notice the issue of sexual abuse by politicians, sports stars, Hollywood celebrities, prominent businessmen, professionals, or the clergy. With respect to priests, moreover, parents and victims were generally unwilling to report sexual abuse cases, and when they did reveal the cases to bishops, many did not want the cases communicated to the police or other civil authorities because of the fear that they and/or their children would be subjected to the publicity that would ensue. Local police, district attorneys, lawyers, and the media, too, were indisposed to deal openly with the issue of clerical abuse because of the scandalous nature of the cases, the desire to protect the church's reputation, the fear of offending public tastes, the dread of public repercussions, or because of some sense of the common good. Professional and scholarly opinion "generally underplayed the significance and harmfulness of 'sex abuse.' "[20] Whatever the reasons, prior to the 1980s there existed a general social disinclination to deal openly with clerical abuse in the courts, or the media. That social reluctance changed gradually in the early 1980s.

Some civil suits against clerical sexual abuse took place in the early 1980s, but they received only local attention. In New Jersey in 1981, the parents of one victim of clerical abuse who had committed suicide in 1979 sued the archdiocese of Newark for damages. The case was eventually dismissed on the grounds that the diocese, as a charitable institution, had legal immunity from such suits. In 1982 a successful suit was brought against a Chicago priest and the Archdiocese of Chicago for sexual abuse of a minor, but when reported in the *Chicago Tribune*, the case was identified simply as one of "moral misconduct."[21] These and other local revelations of clerical abuse of minors did not attract the attention of the national media. Some bishops were aware of the problem locally but did not realize the extent or the extreme seriousness of the problem in the early 1980s.

In 1985 the scandal of pedophile priests hit the headlines of the national newspapers and became an increasing focus of national media attention until the early years of the twenty-first century. Criminal and civil court cases in 1984 and 1985 revealed that a Lafayette, Louisiana, priest, Gilbert Gauthe, had committed multiple crimes of sexual abuse of minors and that Lafayette diocesan officials, who knew of the charges against him, had neglected to prevent the recurring crimes.

The Gauthe case was the first of a number of dramatic revelations about priests who were serial sexual abusers of minors. Gauthe had molested more than one hundred minors in four different parishes to which he had been assigned, even after his initial and continuing abuses had been reported to his diocesan bishop. Gauthe was indicted on thirty-four criminal counts on 24 October 1984, convicted and sent to prison in October 1985. Victims' parents sued the diocese, winning damages amounting to about $4.2 million; one single case was settled in early 1986 for $1.24 million. Gauthe's predatory abuse of minors was reported in local news media in Lafayette, New Orleans, and a few other places in Louisiana, but without much detail. Starting on 23 May 1985, Jason Berry, an investigative reporter and a Catholic, published a three-part serialized account of the affair in the Lafayette *Times of Acadiana*, which received considerable local attention.

In May 1985, during the Gauthe trials and prior to the first major newspaper revelation of clerical abuse as a national problem, two priests and Gauthe's civil lawyer prepared a confidential ninety-two page report, "The Problem of Sexual Molestation by Roman Catholic Clergy: Meeting the Problem in a Comprehensive and Responsible Manner."[22] The report's authors were a Dominican priest, Thomas P. Doyle, a canon lawyer resident in the Apostolic nunciature in Washington, D.C.; Michael Peterson, a priest-psychiatrist and head of a Maryland medical and psychological treatment center for addictive priests; and F. Ray Mouton, a civil lawyer for Gauthe and the diocese of Lafayette. Mouton had an intimate knowledge of the Gauthe case and other sexual abuses scandals in

Lafayette. During 1984 and early 1985 he had consulted with and advised both Doyle and Peterson about the potentially damaging situation in Lafayette and had encouraged them to warn the American bishops about the moral and legal crises they faced not only in the Gauthe case but also in other cases in Lafayette and elsewhere. Prior to writing the May report, the two priests and the lawyer had advised the Apostolic delegate, Archbishop Pio Laghi, Cardinals Bernard Law of Boston and John Krol of Philadelphia, Archbishop Philip M. Hannan of New Orleans, and a few other bishops about the extent and nature of the problem as they saw it. Auxiliary bishops A. James Quinn of Cleveland and William Levada of Cardinal Law's NCCB Committee on Research and Pastoral Practices suggested the kinds of questions and issues the American bishops would likely want the report to tackle. "Law's support," Jason Berry wrote in 1992, "was vital to the document,"[23] a statement that is significant in light of subsequent revelations of sexual abuse in Boston.

"The Problem of Sexual Molestation" outlined the current crisis indicating that clerical abuse was a national problem, that the press had already reported thirty civil court cases against priests involving as many as one hundred children, that one diocese faced $100 million in pending claims, and that within the decade the American church could suffer the loss of as much as one billion dollars in damages. Those clergy accused of sexual abuse crimes, whether substantiated or not, should be suspended immediately from sacramental ministries, and the bishops should report the accusations to the proper civil authorities. Failure to do these things could put dioceses in serious legal, even criminal, trouble. The report also advised the bishops that in most cases of pedophilia they were dealing with "compulsive sexual habits" that must be perceived as "psychiatric disorders" beyond the control of the individual predators. Such kinds of mental sickness could not be treated effectively by the confessional or by private psychotherapy. These offenders needed medical intervention and serious psychiatric institutional care. The victims, furthermore, suffered serious traumatic psychological and spiritual damage from their encounters with priests, and they and their families should be offered psychological and psychiatric as well as spiritual assistance. The report suggested that the American bishops create national policies for dealing with these cases and form a national intervention team (with the three authors of the report as significant members) that could assist dioceses in handling any future cases in the country.

A few bishops were given the "Sexual Molestation" report in June 1985, when the NCCB met at Collegeville, Minnesota. The report, however, was not discussed by the entire body of bishops because not all of them had received it and would not have it until the fall of 1985. At Collegeville, though, the bishops discussed for the first time at a national meeting (in a session closed to the public) the issues of sexual abuse among the clergy after hearing presentations by a psychiatrist, a lawyer, and a bishop on various aspects of child molestation.[24]

While the bishops were meeting in Collegeville, the Gauthe case and that of other pedophiles became a national story when Catholics themselves broke the news to a national audience and revealed for the first time the extent of clerical sexual abuse in the American church. Thomas Fox, editor of the *National Catholic Reporter* (*NCR*), a newspaper with a circulation of about 55,000, published four exposés (one of them by Berry on the Gauthe case) on the multiple instances of clerical pedophilia and abuse of minors throughout the country.[25]

The secular media had at first been reluctant to report on sexual abuse among the clergy unless it was of local interest. In fact, when Berry approached the *New York Times Magazine*, the *Washington Post*, *Rolling Stone*, *Vanity Fair*, the *Nation*, and *Mother Jones* about publishing his story about the Gauthe case, they all declined to report on the case and its significance.[26] Revelations of such cases could have had considerable damaging consequences, either from fear of losing subscribers and advertisers (which did in fact happen to some extent after the *Times of Acadiana* and *NCR* revealed the stories of abuse) or from a general delicacy about the scandalous moral issue. That situation changed once a Catholic newspaper exposed the issue as a widespread national problem. The *New York Times*, the *Washington Post*, and *Time* magazine, among a host of other secular papers, followed the *NCR* story with accounts of their own.[27] Between 1985 and 2003, the issue was treated again and again in national newspapers and other print and visual media as new revelations of clerical criminal behavior came to the fore in court cases throughout the country.

The initial revelations of clerical sexual abuse broke the traditional stigma of reporting these clerical crimes against minors and others, and apparently increased the victims' willingness to report what previously would have been considered a cultural and religious taboo because of the high regard in which clergy were held, particularly in the Catholic community. What came to light in the initial *NCR* stories was a pattern of abuse and "cover-up" that became part of the subsequent national media accounts. Once this newspaper account of the pattern of abuse and neglect became public, prosecutors were more willing to press charges against the offending priests in criminal court cases. Parents or the victims themselves became less reticent to file charges in civil courts against the priests and the bishops who were responsible for reassigning repeat molesters, suing the dioceses for very large sums of money. By the early 1990s the media accused the Catholic bishops of complicity and cover-ups because of their failures to report the crimes that they had known. The NCCB was charged with a lack of leadership in the crisis because of its failure to provide realistic and enforceable disciplinary guidelines for protecting children from pedophiles and other sexual abusers.

The episcopal side of the issue was rarely presented in the media. In response to the criticisms, the NCCB in 1994 published a historical account of their own reactions to the crisis.[28] During the 1980s, the report admitted, the bishops treated the sexual abuse scandals in private and behind closed doors because of the litigious context in which the abuse charges arose, because they desired to protect the priests' as well as the victims' privacy, and because they were not very clear in the mid-1980s about how to approach this very new and unprecedented problem within the church. In fact, none of the NCCB's pastoral letters or other public statements between the years 1983 and 1988 addressed the issue of clerical sexual abuse, and it was not even a topic of consideration in the introduction to a 1989 published collection of those episcopal writings,[29] even though by 1985 pedophilia and ephebophilia among the clergy had been reported in national news media and had become a widespread public scandal. By the end of 1985, though, the USCC had advised bishops to remove alleged offenders from their positions, deal sympathetically with young victims and their families, protect the confidential nature of any claims against the dioceses, comply with the obligations of the civil law, and make appropriate notifications of offenses. Although the bishops did not, as some press reports had it, callously and summarily ignore or reject the information disclosed in the 1985 confidential "Molestation" report, they also did not follow the suggestion that the NCCB establish a national intervention team because dioceses preferred to operate with their own experts who knew the particular local circumstances and the specific laws of their own states.[30]

In the 1980s the NCCB was reluctant to establish national guidelines on sexual abuse because many bishops believed such action would impinge on the rights of individual bishops. That issue of local episcopal autonomy was one that was rarely appreciated or presented in the media because of the media's perception of the Catholic Church as a monolithic institution and the media's failure to understand the independent canonical relationship of the local bishop to the NCCB.

In 1988, the USCC published its first public statement on pedophilia, a document providing primarily legal advice to dioceses on how to handle these cases.[31] The USCC had also provided pastoral directives for dioceses, but those episcopal statements were primarily confidential. Not until the early 1990s did the bishops realize that they could no longer handle the problems in secret and behind closed doors. The problem was a national public scandal, and they needed to make their collective mind known to the public and reveal what they intended to do. The bishops' policy of secrecy, focus on legal issues, and reluctance to establish binding national policies on sexual abuse was flawed, as subsequent events would make abundantly clear.

Between 1989 and 1997, the NCCB issued eight public statements on clerical sexual abuse that dealt openly with the issue, acknowledged the scandalous nature of what was taking place, and assured the public that they would swiftly respond to reported cases.[32] Of the eight documents produced on sexual abuse between 1989 and 1997, "Resolution on Clergy Sex Abuse" (1992) was the first public statement approved by the entire body of bishops.[33] Prior to the publication of the joint episcopal statement, Archbishop Daniel E. Pilarczyk of Cincinnati, president of the NCCB, addressed the bishops in June 1992 on the substance of the "Resolution" statement.[34] He acknowledged that the bishops did not in the early period have a good understanding of what was involved in sexual abuse of minors and admitted that "as our knowledge of this disordered behavior has grown . . . we have tried to refine our policies while redoubling our commitment to prompt action, as well as healing and reconciliation."[35] Increasingly, he acknowledged, medical and sociological knowledge had helped the bishops to see where they could improve the church's response to sexual abuse. He also admitted that mistakes had been made in the past because the bishops did not understand the extent or seriousness of the problem. The "Resolution" summarized the NCCB's concerns and outlined for the public the policy the bishops would follow—although, as future events revealed, some diocesan bishops did not implement this national episcopal policy (which was nonbinding on diocesan bishops). While affirming the goodness, holiness, and dedication of thousands of priests who served faithfully, and while respecting the privacy of individuals, the bishops resolved that they would in each case of sexual abuse deal openly and candidly with the public, respond promptly to all allegations, remove alleged offenders from their positions if evidence was sufficient, comply with civil law in reporting all incidents, and reach out pastorally to all victims. These public resolutions became the cornerstone of all future statements and policies on sexual abuse of minors in the church.

The bishops faced new questions on pedophilia in the 1990s. Their awareness of the compulsive or addictive nature of the problem and the risks of recidivism prompted them to discuss new canonical remedies that might allow for laicization of pedophile priests. The bishops also began to engage other churches, scientists, Rome, and civil servants in a mutual search for solutions to the problem, sharing with others what they had learned and seeking ways to meet the problems in pastorally sensitive as well as legally protective ways for victims and offenders.[36]

In June 1993 the NCCB established a new ad hoc committee on sexual abuse that addressed five areas of concern: (1) pastoral responses to victims and to parishes, (2) emphasis on the well-being of priests and the prevention of abuse, (3) distribution of informative general resources to dioceses, (4) education of church members on the problem, and (5) initiation and support of research that would help not only the church but the wider society. Bishop John F. Kinney of Bismarck, North Dakota, chair of the committee, noted that the media rarely acknowledged the bishops' own regret and sorrow over the cases of abuse and their sympathy for the pain suffered by all involved.[37]

In 1993, while the bishops were acknowledging publicly that they had made mistakes in the past and were about to amend their ways and their policies, one of their own, Cardinal Joseph Bernardin of Chicago, one of the most respected members of the episcopate, was charged (falsely as later events revealed) with the sexual assault of Stephen Cook, a young man who had been a seminarian when Bernardin was archbishop in Cincinnati. Media across the country revealed and repeated the charge and made it sound credible. Within the context of the times in which the charge was made, it was not difficult for the media to believe the allegation. Stephen Cook withdrew the charge in 1994, admitting that an unlicensed hypnotist had induced a false memory of past sexual abuse, and one of

Bernardin's clerical critics had encouraged him to report the incident publicly. Bernardin was devastated by the charge against his good reputation, and once it was proven false, he initiated contact with Cook, seeking reconciliation and healing for both men. Cook had AIDS and Bernardin hoped to, and indeed did, reconcile Cook to the church before he died from the disease.[38]

The false charges against sexual abuse were revealed most dramatically in the Bernardin case, but his was not the only case of false accusation. Other bishops and priests experienced similar false charges. The Bernardin case, though, warned the media and others about too readily accepting accusations in an atmosphere that lent almost immediate credibility to accusers over the accused. But, the charged atmosphere only increased after the Bernardin affair because of more proven cases of sexual abuse among the clergy. Philip Jenkins's *Pedophiles and Priests* (1996), the most thorough systematic study at the time, detailed the ongoing phenomenon of recurring revelations. After his study, moreover, there were other revelations. The diocese of Dallas in 1998, for example, settled sex abuse claims against former priest Rudy Kos for $31 million, and in June of 2003, the Archdiocese of Louisville settled 243 lawsuit claims for $25.7 million. But the most publicized of all the cases, until 2003, occurred in the Archdiocese of Boston.

In January 2002 investigative reporters for the *Boston Globe* revealed the scandalous case of a pedophile priest, John Geoghan, who had for thirty years abused more than 150, mostly prepubescent, boys in six different parishes to which he had been assigned with the archdiocese's knowledge of the accusations of sexual abuse.[39] Since the mid-1990s, more than 130 people reported that Geoghan had allegedly fondled or raped them. Some of these victims had been abused in the 1960s when they were children. Cardinal Law had become archbishop in 1984 and knew then of Geoghan's problems. On a number of occasions between 1980 and 1990, Geoghan was sent to psychological treatment centers for his abuse of children and received clean bills of health from four different therapists. In 1993, after more reports of sexual abuse, Geoghan was finally removed from pastoral duties and placed in a retirement center, but even then he continued to molest some boys. Psychiatric reports in the archdiocesan personnel files from 1995 and 1996 revealed that Geoghan had a deep-rooted sexual perversion.

The *Globe*'s reports appeared prior to the January 2002 criminal court cases against Geoghan for sexual abuse and the civil court cases against the archdiocese for negligence. In the course of investigating the stories of abuse in the archdiocese, the *Globe* sought a court order for the release of all diocesan personnel files relative to the Geoghan case. The court at the end of January 2002 convicted Geoghan and sentenced him to prison. Later, on 25 August 2003, he was murdered in prison by a fellow inmate.

The archdiocese reported in April 2002 that it had released the "name of every living priest known to us against whom there has been a credible allegation of sexual misconduct with a minor" for a period covering fifty-three years. Another of the most perfidious cases that came to light was that of Father Paul Shanley, whose sexual misconduct with adolescent minors since the late 1960s and his public justifications of such conduct horrified many who read about them. In February 2002 one Boston family brought a suit against Shanley for the abuse of their son in the late 1970s and against the archdiocese for its criminal neglect. The victim was reported to have said, "I'm very upset that a lot of people knew about him and what he was doing . . . his 30 year reign of terror, and I hope he rots in hell."[40] The archdiocese released 818 documents from personnel files that revealed what the archdiocese knew about Shanley and what they did or did not do about him. In the files was a letter from a complainant who revealed that Shanley gave a lecture in Rochester, New York, in 1977 in which he stated, "celibacy is impossible . . . He spoke of pedophilia. . . . He stated that the adult is not the seducer—the 'kid' is the seducer and further the kid is not traumatized by the act per se." The archdiocesan files also contained a clipping from *Gaysweek* that told of Shanley's attendance at a "Men and Boys" Conference in Boston in February 1979, where he discussed and justified man-boy love. Cardinal Humberto Sousa Medeiros, at the time archbishop of Boston, reported Shanley's deviant ideas to Rome, removed him from his street-preaching mission, but placed him in St. John the Evangelist parish in Newton, Massachusetts, where he violated other minors. Shanley resigned in 1989, was placed on sick leave, and went to California. In 1990 Bishop Robert Banks, then an auxiliary bishop of Boston, wrote to a priest in the San Bernardino diocese referring to Shanley as a "priest in good standing in the Archdiocese of Boston." In April 2002, after these revelations were reported in the press, Banks stated that he was unaware of any allegations against Shanley. Banks had neglected to consult the personnel files prior to writing the letter. The press and court disclosures about Geoghan and Stanley and a few other deviant Boston clerics, and the charges of criminal negligence against Cardinal Law and the archdiocese, had damaging consequences not only for the Boston archdiocese but for the entire American Catholic Church, the effects of which were not altogether clear at the end of 2003.

Catholics and others were outraged by the crimes against children and the neglect of diocesan officials in failing to protect children from serial sexual abusers. Some victims and their families called for Cardinal Bernard Law's immediate resignation. In December 2002, aware of his inability to provide leadership in the diocese because of the accusations against him, he resigned as archbishop of Boston. In the meantime, lawyers for victims and their families pursued civil trials against the archdiocese, suing for millions of dollars. On 1 July 2003 the Vatican appointed a new archbishop to Boston, Sean Patrick O'Malley, who immediately negotiated to settle the suits. On 9 September 2003 the diocese agreed to pay $85 million to be divided among the 552 people involved in the class action suit. Awards ranged from $80,000 to $300,000 for the victims of sexual abuse, and $20,000 for parents of the minors. The archdiocese also agreed to provide psychological counseling for the victims. The settlement was the largest one ever made against a Catholic diocese.

The Boston crises created an emergency situation for the entire Catholic community and brought forth major new initiatives from members of the Boston Catholic community, from the Vatican, and the national episcopacy.[41] The *Boston Globe* and other press reports made poignant, as never before, the painful trauma suffered by victims of abuse, the criminal nature of the abuse, the extent of the problem, and the negligence of the bishops. The press reports provoked a reconsideration of previous episcopal policies. The NCCB resolutions of 1992 had not been legally binding on dioceses, and individual bishops, as the Boston cases revealed, could choose not to follow the national episcopal recommendations for handling sexual abuse cases. Whatever the bishops had done in the immediate past to meet the decade-long crises was not sufficient to come to terms with the problem. New, more decisive, and legally binding measures were needed.

In April 2002 in response to the Boston disclosures, Pope John Paul II called all the American cardinals and the presiding heads of the USCCB to Rome to discuss more effective means for responding to clerical sexual abuse and ending the crisis. The pope, together with the bishops, reaffirmed Catholic teaching on sexual abuse, stating again that "the sexual abuse of minors is rightly considered a crime by society and is an appalling sin in the eyes of God, above all when it is perpetrated by priests and religious whose vocation is to help persons to lead holy lives before God and men." They also confirmed the need to stand in solidarity with the victims of abuse and their families and to provide appropriate assistance in recovering faith and receiving pastoral care for the physical, psychological, and spiritual damage that they had incurred from priests. The American bishops, moreover, promised to send the Vatican a set of new national standards and policies on how to deal with the crisis after the June meeting of the USCCB in Dallas.[42]

At the June meeting in Dallas the bishops took a number of steps toward a more thorough and forceful response to the crisis. They adopted a "Charter for the Protection of Children and Young People," which was finally approved in their November meeting in Washington, D.C. The charter's preamble acknowledged:

> In the past, secrecy has created an atmosphere that has inhibited the healing process and, in some cases, enabled sexually abusive behavior to be repeated. As bishops, we acknowledge our mistakes and our role in that suffering, and we apologize and take responsibility for too often failing victims and our people in the past. We also take responsibility for dealing with this problem strongly, consistently, and effectively in the future. From the depths of our hearts, we bishops express great sorrow and profound regret for what the Catholic people are enduring.[43]

The charter went on to detail specific measures the bishops were taking to promote healing and reconciliation with victims/survivors, to guarantee an effective response to allegations, to ensure accountability for the episcopal procedures, and to protect the faithful in the future. To ensure public accountability for their own procedures, the bishops created the Office for Child and Youth

Protection within the USCCB to supervise and oversee diocesan compliance with the new policies, and established a National Review Board of primarily lay Catholic experts in various professions and fields of study to assist and monitor the work of the Office of Child and Youth Protection, to commission a comprehensive study of the causes and context of the current crisis, and to create a thorough descriptive national study of the nature and scope of the problem (including statistical data on the perpetrators and victims) in the 195 dioceses and eparchies in the United States. To further secure public accountability for their procedures, the bishops hired the Gavin Group of Boston, a compliance auditing firm, to conduct compliance audits of each and every diocese in the country. In June 2003, the Gavin Group began auditing the dioceses in the United States. Those audit reports were to be submitted to the Office of Child and Youth Protection and to be examined by the National Review Board and then made public. The USCCB also prepared a document, "Essential Norms for Diocesan/Eparchial Policies Dealing with Allegations of Sexual Abuse of Minors by Priests or Deacons," that was reviewed, revised somewhat, and confirmed by the Vatican's Congregation for Bishops on 8 December 2002. The "Essential Norms" then became law for the church in the United States. One of the prominent features of the "Essential Norms" was the immediate removal from pastoral duties of any priest or deacon accused and found guilty of sexual abuse of minors. Bishops, too, were required to report all such crimes to civil authorities for prosecution.[44]

In addition to their formulation of new national policies, bishops across the country actively pursued complaints of abuse. In the year immediately following the Geoghan case, bishops removed at least 325 priests from their pastoral duties because of allegations of abuse. Dioceses that had no previous written policies on sexual abuse formulated them; those with written policies, revised them. The cases of clerical abuse would no longer be dealt with in private. Even one substantiated allegation of abuse would now be dealt with by immediate removal from pastoral duties and, in some cases, by removal from the priesthood.

Although Catholics were universally united in their abhorrence of the crimes against children, they were divided in assessing the causes for the crimes and in suggesting the ecclesiastical reforms necessary to prevent them in the future. Once the initial shock and shame subsided, conservative and liberal Catholics appealed to ecclesiastical agendas of the previous thirty years to try to explain the current crimes in the church. Conservatives saw the causes for the crimes against children in the emergence of liberal moral theology on sexuality, a lack of internal moral discipline within the church, the rise of public dissent against official church teachings, the failures of church leadership to defend those teachings, the post–Vatican II expansion of bureaucratic machinery in dioceses that separated bishops from their supervisory role over seminaries and the clergy, and/or the general sexual license in American culture and the liberal Catholic tendency to accommodate contemporary cultural values. For those who made these judgments, the church needed to shore up its discipline, abide more faithfully by its authentic tradition, and reform seminary life. Some conservative Catholics, however, were not so eager to suggest what needed to be done. They were willing to await the USCCB's own commissioned study to discover the factual evidence for the crisis before suggesting any ecclesiastical reforms.[45]

Liberal Catholics also saw systemic causes for the crisis in the church, but their causes differed dramatically from those of conservative Catholics. Liberal Catholics generally attributed the crisis to the church's discipline of celibacy, its male-only priesthood, its authoritarian structures, its own arrogance and sense of special privilege with respect to civil criminal law, its corporation-sole status in American law, its tradition of secrecy and lack of effective public accountability for church funds, and/or its repressive sexual ethic.[46] Some who saw the crisis in this light called for massive internal ecclesiastical reforms in discipline and structure as a way of preventing the clerical abuses and episcopal negligences in the future.[47]

Throughout the postconciliar period acrimony, distrust, suspicion of motives, and overt hostility had characterized much of the debate in American Catholicism as persons on opposite sides of a host of issues polarized the church. At a press conference in Chicago on 12 August 1996, in the midst of his final battle with cancer, Cardinal Joseph Bernardin launched the Catholic Common Ground Project, which he and others saw as a means for overcoming the acrimonious polarization within the church.[48] Together with Father Philip Murnion of the National Pastoral Life Center in New York City, he produced "Called to be Catholic: Church in a Time of Peril," a document that outlined the general purposes of the new initiative.[49] The project was to be a national forum where radical, conservative, liberal, and moderate Catholics could discuss issues in the church in a way that was creative and faithful to the Catholic tradition and without the distrust, polarization, and entrenchment, or hardening of interpretations that made dialogue and real learning from each other impossible. The project's organizers suggested thirteen possible issues that needed open and honest discussion in the church from a variety of different perspectives, the top three being the changing roles of women, the organization and effectiveness of religious education, and the experiences of Eucharistic liturgy. The focus was primarily on pastoral issues and the attempt to find ways to achieve consensus through discussion.

The Common Ground Project itself generated much positive response, but also opposition in some quarters. Cardinals Law of Boston and James Hickey of Washington, D.C. were among those who expressed doubts about the project. The opponents asserted that the project failed to acknowledge adequately Scripture and tradition as the actual common ground of the Catholic Church, reduced the magisterium to just one of many voices in the church, placed dissent on the same level as truth, appeared to be too ready to compromise the truth for the sake of peace, and insufficiently focused on the centrality of Jesus. At a press conference on 24 October 1996, Cardinal Bernardin responded to the criticisms asserting that the project had no intention of minimizing the doctrinal foundations of the Catholic tradition. He pleaded for a new kind of discussion in the church, not one that envisioned compromise but consensus. The project was Bernardin's last will and testament, as he acknowledged: "A dying person does not have time for the peripheral or the accidental. He or she is drawn to the essential, the important—yes, the eternal. And what is important, my friends, is that we find that unity with the Lord and within the community of faith for which Jesus prayed so fervently on the night before he died. To say it quite boldly, it is wrong to waste the precious gift of time given to us, as God's chosen servants, on acrimony and division."[50] The Common Ground Project continued after Bernardin's death through the National Pastoral Life Center, bringing together Catholics to discuss issues, publishing documents, and suggesting directions for new pastoral initiatives for bishops and congregations.

Throughout the entire period following the Second Vatican Council, the NCCB/USCC (and later USCCB), as the episcopal arm of the Catholic Church in the United States, had published hundreds of statements on American governmental domestic and foreign policies that had moral and religious implications—issues that were part of the public debate and not purely internal ecclesial concerns. Those statements, published in *Origins* or in pamphlet form, focused on the social implications and dimensions of faith, relating a Catholic understanding of Christianity to issues of justice and peace in the world. Bishops and their advisers from the NCCB/USCC also appeared periodically before congressional hearings to focus national attention on the moral dimensions of governmental decisions. Although the bishops and their advisers denied any partisan politics, they took sides periodically on a variety of specific policy choices without indicating that their positions should end the debate.

The bishops spoke out repeatedly on a number of the government's domestic policies relating to economic justice, the dignity of labor and role of labor unions, welfare reform, public education, the natural environment, abortion, euthanasia, capital punishment, general health care reform, pornography and sexual promiscuity, cultural and domestic violence, substance abuse, HIV and AIDS, embryo research, genetic testing and engineering, and the political responsibility of all for the common good.[51] The bishops were aware that in entering the national debates over many of these questions they were involving themselves in issues where medical, moral, legal, scientific, and public policy concerns intersected with faith. The bishops were conscious, too, that in speaking out on public policy and juridical issues they had to define clearly their responsibility to do so and the limits of their authority in a democratic society where all did not share the same faith. While affirming their adherence to the separation of church and state, the bishops reasserted, "the Church has a proper role and responsibility in public affairs flowing from its gospel mandate and its respect for the dignity of the human person."[52] In addressing the public policy and juridical issues surrounding abortion, for example, the bishops not only claimed their First Amendment rights to teach Catholic convictions, but also acknowledged that when they entered the arena of public policy debates they

were "bound by the same rules as other participants. We must present reasons
for our proposals which can be understood and appreciated by people of good
will who may not share our faith convictions."[53] It was reason—not authority—
that the bishops employed in public policy issues. The bishops, in other words,
participated in the public policy debates as concerned citizens applying their
convictions to those issues.

Because they represented tax-exempt institutions, there were certain limits to
their participation in the political process, and they were quite aware of that.
Since the early 1820s, the bishops had avoided anything that might appear as an
official Catholic involvement in partisan political advocacy—so much so that
they had refused to speak out on political as well as moral issues such as slavery.
During each presidential election of the 1990s, the USCC General Counsel sent
the bishops and their advisers a memorandum on political involvement for tax-
exempt organizations, warning them about the fine line between legitimate
political education and illegitimate advocacy for particular candidates.[54]

Bishops and other members of the USCC appeared periodically before various
congressional hearings to speak out on the moral and social implications of
governmental policies and practices. In 1990, for example, Archbishop Roger
Mahoney of Los Angeles and Bishop James Malone of Youngstown called on
members of Congress to put the needs of the poor and vulnerable first in
constructing the 1991 federal budget and suggested other ethical priorities to be
considered in budgetary decisions.[55] In 1991 the USCC sent Bishop Frank
Rodimen of Paterson to testify before a Senate subcommittee on labor in support
of Bill S-55, which would have made it illegal for companies to hire permanent
replacements for striking workers. Rodimen's statement was a powerful testimony for the rights of labor unions. Despite some of the past as well as present
abuses, he argued, unions were sometimes the only protection against certain
destructive corporate tactics.[56]

The USCC General Counsel, too, periodically appeared before the Supreme
Court or district courts, or prepared amicus curiae (friend of the court) briefs
on cases that had moral and religious implications. In 1989, for example, the
USCC's General Counsel filed an amicus brief in the Nancy Cruzan case that was
being tried before the U.S. Supreme Court, arguing for the state's responsibility
to preserve life by continued nutrition and hydration support and against an
individual's or a caretaker's right to choose death.[57] In 1994, the General
Counsel filed another amicus brief before the Ninth Circuit Court of Appeals in
support of Washington State's ban against physician-assisted suicide, a ban that
District Judge Barbara Rothstein had declared unconstitutional in a lower court
decision.[58] When Oregon passed (by 51 percent to 49 percent) the "Death with
Dignity Act," the first law in the United States to authorize physician-assisted
suicide, Judge Michael Hagen of the U.S. District Court of Portland, Oregon,
ruled that the law violated the Fourteenth Amendment's equal protection clause
by discriminating against the dying. Oregon then appealed to the Ninth District
Court to overturn that decision, and the USCC General Counsel, in 1996, filed

an amicus brief in support of the lower court decision, bringing to bear arguments that the General Counsel had used in support of Washington State's law opposing physician-assisted suicide.[59]

The NCCB/USCC also collaborated with other major religious bodies in the United States in preparing joint declarations on issues of public concern. In 1990, for example, the USCC joined with the Jewish Synagogue Council of America in a common statement on "Moral Education in the Public Schools." The common document noted that public educators appeared to be reluctant to teach moral values (e.g., honesty, compassion, integrity, tolerance, loyalty, belief in human worth and dignity). These religious leaders felt compelled to speak out on the necessity of teaching moral values in the public schools because they believed a broad consensus on them existed in society.[60] Again in 1993, the USCC joined together with the National Council of Churches and the Jewish Synagogue Council of America to produce "The Common Good: Old Idea, New Urgency." The general purpose of the joint statement was to help focus the national political debate on a renewed sense of the country's general welfare. To do so, the three religious bodies drew on their common heritage to bring forth a "fresh and empowering vision of the common good." Concern for the common good was not only a moral imperative but also an essential religious calling the statement asserted.[61]

As part of a worldwide communion, the Catholic Church in the United States was vitally interested in international, not just domestic and national, issues that affected Catholics and fellow human beings throughout the world. The church's involvement in global affairs flowed from its identity as a universal communion with a missionary mandate from the Gospel. The bishops in particular shared a collegiality and communication system with other bishops throughout the world, and they periodically shared information about events in various countries. Since the early twentieth century, Catholic missionaries from the United States had established church institutions and humanitarian works in a variety of places throughout the globe. Catholic Relief Services (CRS), founded by the American bishops in 1943, was one of the largest voluntary institutions of humanitarian aid in the United States, providing assistance to the world's poorest. In 2003, because of millions of dollars of contributions from Catholics in the pews, and financial and other support from governmental agencies, CRS provided food, medicine, and volunteer services in over ninety countries, without regard for race, creed, or nationality. CRS afforded not just relief but help for economic development and self-sufficiency programs in those countries.

Because of its identity and its multiple sources of information on world affairs, therefore, the Catholic bishops, representing the Catholic Church in the United States, periodically felt called on to address global issues of justice and peace and to comment as citizens on the moral and religious as well as humanitarian dimensions of American foreign policy and practices. Because of the Gospel mandate, and because of the financial and material resources of the Catholic people and the prosperity of the nation as a whole, the American bishops called on Catholics and other Americans—as believers and fellow human beings—to meet their moral obligations to the less fortunate of the world. It is within this context that one must interpret the American bishops' multiple actions and statements on world affairs between 1990 and 2003.

The episcopal, clerical, and lay members of the USCCB periodically went on fact-finding visits to troubled parts of the world, reported their findings at the national meetings of the American bishops, testified before congressional committees on foreign affairs issues, and in multiple statements encouraged Catholics and others to come to the aid of the world's depressed, and commented on, commended, and at times criticized presidential initiatives and the American government's foreign policies and practices. The USCCB periodically protested against foreign governmental violations of human rights, religious liberty, and human dignity in the Balkan countries, South Africa, Rwanda, Nigeria, the Sudan, Liberia, El Salvador, China, Haiti, Cuba, Iraq, Israel, Palestine, Lebanon, and in a number of other nations, and frequently called on the United Nations, the United States, and other international powers to bring about a progressive nuclear disarmament.[62]

Episcopal statements protested consistently against American foreign aid policies that placed a higher priority on military support than upon economic development. They encouraged the United States to increase its foreign humanitarian aid to address the "scandal of poverty" in certain areas of the world, maintaining, as the bishops wrote in 2001, that the United States "contributes just one-tenth of one percent of its gross national product in official development assistance, as compared with the international development target of 0.7% of GNP, a target endorsed by our country many times."[63] The bishops called for a more comprehensive foreign aid program that emphasized economic and human development, more equitable trade policies, and efforts to relieve the "crushing burden of debt," especially in some Third-World countries. Violence and terrorism, although never justified, many times arose from the intolerable extremes of miserable poverty and abundant wealth in the contemporary world.

After the fall of the "Iron Curtain" in 1989, episcopal statements warned periodically of a growing isolationism and an increasing antiforeigner sentiment in American culture, one that gave rise to movements and policies to restrict immigration and thereby deny refugees from war-torn countries entry into the United States. Quoting Matthew 25:35 ("I was a stranger and you welcomed me"), the bishops called on Catholics and all Americans from 1991 to 2001 to examine their attitudes toward refugee foreigners and the new immigrants, and advocated a "generous and reasonable" U.S. government immigration policy.[64] In 2001 the bishops indicated that the United States had received five million refugees since 1951, and of that number, the Catholic Church through its various agencies (e.g., the USCC's Migration and Refugee Services, the Catholic Legal Immigration Network, Inc., CRS, Catholic Charities, and numerous dioceses and parishes) had assisted more than one million to settle in the United States. Since 1992, the bishops continued, the United States's commitment to refugee protection seemed to be waning as was indicated by the 42 percent drop in refugee admissions at a time in history when the refugee problem was increasing not decreasing. Because of numerous wars and violent revolutions in various parts of the world, the number of refugees increased dramatically between 1981 and 2001, from eight to fourteen million, 80 percent of whom were women and children. The bishops, therefore, called on the American government to reexamine its refugee policies and to continue its long tradition of compassion, thereby honoring its own democratic values.[65]

Wars, rumors of wars, violent uprisings, and terrorism in various parts of the world plagued the 1990s and early part of the twenty-first century, and the United States was a victim of terrorism as well as an active participant in the worldwide violence. In many statements on peace in various parts of the world, the bishops reiterated the principles of their own previous *The Challenge of Peace* (1983), and in *The Harvest of Justice is Sown in Peace* (1993),[66] they renewed their concerns for peace but also addressed more particularly the new situation of bloody regional wars, the lethal arms trade, and the recurring need to provide for sustained development in parts of the world that were racked with poverty and violence.

The USCC's International Policy Committee repeatedly issued statements on specific conflicts throughout the world so that their general concerns for peace and justice were translated into ad hoc statements on very particular and timely topics in international policy. When the Iron Curtain fell in 1989, there was immediate euphoria about the end of the arms race, the cessation of Cold War hostilities between the superpowers, and the restoration of international peace. In 1990, the USCC administrative board seized the day by publishing "New Moment in Eastern and Central Europe," which applauded and supported President Mikhail Gorbachev's policies of *perestroika* and *glasnost*, called the moment a grace-filled advent of a new era, outlined American Catholic responsibilities to help "our brothers and sisters" rebuild their churches, and invited the American people to help revive the countries in the former Soviet Union after the Cold War. The document, however, pointed to the "fragile nature of the present moment."[67] Almost as soon as the statement was published troubles broke out in various parts of the former Soviet Union. The drive for self-determination in places such as Lithuania were followed by increased governmental restrictions on those newly granted freedoms, a situation the American bishops protested in a 1990 letter to the Soviet Ambassador Yuri Dubinin.[68]

The civil wars in El Salvador and Colombia also drew the attention of the American bishops. Many Catholics were aware of the dire situation in El Salvador. The killing there of Archbishop Oscar Romero and four American missionary women in 1980 and six Jesuits in 1989 had been widely reported in the American Catholic press. In the midst of these atrocities, the American bishops were troubled by the U.S. policy toward El Salvador, and in a 1990 letter to President George Bush, they outlined their principal points of concern regarding that policy, requesting, among other things, the government's help to end the pattern of harassment of the Catholic Church in El Salvador and to help establish a cease-fire in the war-ravaged country.[69] In 2000 the chairman of the International Policy Committee, Cardinal Law, focused attention on Colombia, claiming that the forty-year civil war there was to a large degree "due to illegal drug use in the United States." He appealed to the United States and the international community to concentrate not only on destroying the drug traffic that was so much responsible for the economic and military crises in Colombia but also on reforming the economic and juridical infrastructures of Colombian society as the way toward a sustained peace policy.[70]

In the 1990s old hostilities broke out in the Balkans, and the bishops responded by calling for an end to the violence and for the peoples of the West to help rebuild those countries.[71] In 1991 the bishops petitioned the international community to mediate a political settlement to the "unjust war" against the people of Croatia, asserting the necessity of recognizing the independence of Croatia, Slovenia, and other republics in the former Yugoslavia.[72] The nightmarish hostilities in Bosnia-Herzegovina drew from the bishops a strong condemnation in 1993, when they observed that although all parties in the hostilities were guilty of atrocities, the Serbian military forces bore the greatest responsibilities for aggression and abuse. The bishops appealed to the international community to disarm the aggressors and to end the "ethnic cleansing" in the Balkans, but they were not prepared to recommend a military solution to the problem, except where the use of force could be well defined and limited primarily to disarming aggressors. "The world," the bishops lamented, "cannot stand aside as innocent people are destroyed."[73] When some in the United States interpreted the bishops' statement as support for military measures to end the hostilities in Bosnia, the bishops responded that they had not given a general endorsement of U.S. military intervention in Bosnia but had laid down several stringent moral criteria to judge what kind of limited military measures would protect peoples from unjust aggression.[74]

By the late 1990s, the bishops focused their attention on Kosovo. In 1998 Archbishop Theodore McCarrick of Newark, chairman of the USCC's International Policy Committee, visited the war-torn country on a fact-finding mission and consulted with Muslim and Orthodox religious leaders as well as Catholic bishops. On his return he prepared public statements that informed the bishops and others of systematic governmental assaults on ethnic Albanians and others that was "chillingly similar" to the "ethnic cleansing" that had taken place in Bosnia in the early 1990s. McCarrick complained that the international community stood by passively looking on these crimes against humanity. "The question," he wrote, "is not whether a solution is possible. The question is whether the international community has the will to find one now—now before more innocent people are killed, now before more homes and villages are destroyed, now before this smoldering fuse ignites the regional powder keg."[75] In the next two years, the USCC issued ten more statements seeking an immediate end to the killings in Kosovo, a cessation of United Nations' bombings, a negotiated peace, protection and care for more than 230,000 refugees of the conflicts, and for just and balanced international reconstruction efforts to meet basic human needs after the hostilities terminated.[76] In an unusual joint action, the eight American cardinals wrote President Clinton and Yugoslavia's President Slobodan Milosevic on 1 April 1999 imploring them to bring about an immediate cease-fire and a return to negotiations.[77] By the middle of 1999, Archbishop McCarrick supported recent statements by Serbian Orthodox Patriarch Pavle I and Bishop Artemije of Raska-Prizren (Kosovo) who requested the International Criminal Tribunal to bring to public accountability those in Serbian political leadership who were responsible for the systematic and multiple violations of human rights and the horrible atrocities against people.[78]

The bishops kept a watchful eye on developments in Africa, periodically sent members of USCC there on fact-finding missions, and received several reports from African Catholic bishops on conditions there and petitions from them to highlight and respond to the plight of their peoples. In 1993, after consulting Catholic bishops in South Africa, they lifted their own previous support for economic sanctions (which had been imposed in 1986) and encouraged positive economic investment to assist the country's recovery and to help the South African people.[79] In 1994, after three bishops and several others were murdered in the civil war in Rwanda, the American bishops published a statement calling for an end to the conflict and for international intervention and assistance.[80] Violent civil uprisings in Nigeria in 1996 also evoked a response from the American bishops, who joined the Nigerian bishops in calling for political negotiations and peace.[81] In the late 1990s and early 2000s, the USCC prepared a number of statements on the sufferings and deaths of peoples in the Sudan, Kenya, and peoples of the Great Lakes Region (Democratic Republic of Congo, Rwanda, Burundi, Uganda), calling on Catholics and the U.S. government to respond with new political efforts to end civil conflicts, to limit small-arms trade, to reform corrupt governments, and to provide more generous financial assistance, debt relief, education, new health-care initiatives, and more aid for economic development and restructuring of war-ravaged countries.[82]

For more than a decade, the USCCB had tried to focus attention on the plight of African peoples in specific disease-ridden and war-plagued nations. In 2001 the bishops' conference published *A Call to Solidarity with Africa*, a passionate cry for meaningful and supportive solidarity with the 800 million African peoples, multiple millions of whom lived in debilitating starvation, poverty, disease, displacement, and cruel religious, ethnic, and official governmental oppression.[83] Local African tensions and conflicts were in part responsible for the troubles on the continent, but the greed of international corporations and governments and the neglect and indifference of the United States and the international community contributed to the local problems. This document provided statistics analyzing the abusive conditions in various countries. In the Sudan, for example, the document pointed out that over the past eighteen years two million people had died from the internal conflicts and that more than four million were driven from their homes (the largest number of internally displaced peoples in any country in the world). In a previous document on Sudan, the bishops stated, "one of the worst human tragedies of our times has been met with relative indifference by the international community."[84] In response to troubles in Sudan and other places, the bishops called on Catholics, the U.S. government, multinational corporations, and the international community to acknowledge their solidarity with some of the poorest peoples on the globe and to exercise their moral responsibility and contribute their financial resources and technological and political expertise to solve the multiple problems.

A Call to Solidarity asked that Catholics contribute more to Catholic Relief Services, an agency significantly involved in African relief and redevelopment, that major multinational corporations provide economic and technical assistance for social and economic development programs in nations where their companies reaped large profits from the natural resources, and that the U.S. government increase its development assistance to Africa. Contrary to popular opinion, the USCCB asserted, the United States had not contributed its fair share of gross domestic product (GDP) to countries in need of development aid. In fact, among the developed nations of the world, the United States ranked one of the lowest in percentage of GDP it contributed. As one of the wealthiest countries in the world, the United States had a special moral responsibility to assist the poorest peoples in the world. The U.S. government, furthermore, needed to revisit its policies toward Africa.

Of all the tormented regions in the world during the 1990s and early 2000s, the Middle East drew from the USCCB the most numerous and some of the most ardent of its statements for global justice and peace. From the Gulf War of 1991, to the violent terrorist attacks on American soil in 2001, to the United States's retaliatory wars against Afghanistan in 2001 and Iraq in 2003, the bishops in the United States called for peace, peace, but there was no peace.

In 1978 the bishops had published a statement on peace in the Middle East,[85] and in 1989 they renewed that statement in "Toward Peace in Middle East: Perspectives, Principles and Hopes."[86] After describing the historical conditions in the region, particularly with regard to Israel and its conflicts with Lebanon, Syria, other Arabian states, and the Palestinian peoples, the bishops made a series of policy recommendations for the United States. In the course of the next thirteen years, as in the previous twenty, the bishops would return again and again to troubles in the area. In letters to presidents of the United States (George H. W. Bush, Bill Clinton, and George W. Bush), testimonies before congressional committees, consultations with religious leaders in the area, and published statements, the American bishops repeatedly outlined the issues it believed would bring peace to the region: real and guaranteed security for the state of Israel, a viable state for the Palestinians, just resolution of the refugee problem, an agreement on Jerusalem that protected the religious freedom and other basic rights of all religious traditions in the area, an adequate sharing of resources (especially water), and implementation of relevant UN resolutions and other provisions of international law. Such agreements were necessary to end the cycle of violence, terrorism, and wars in the region.[87]

Statements published after the November and June meetings of the American bishops in 2000, 2001, and 2002 called on American Jews, Muslims, Catholics, and other Christians to work jointly to urge the American government toward more effective measures to secure peace between Israel and its neighbors. As they had in many previous statements, the bishops appealed to Catholics in particular to pray, fast, and perform good works as the necessary spiritual means toward universal accord in a world torn apart by the spiral of violence.[88]

Iraq became a central focus of attention on the Middle East after its 2 August 1990 invasion and occupation of Kuwait. After the invasion, the United Nations, at the urging of the United States, called for Iraq's immediate withdrawal, created an economic embargo against Iraq to get it to comply with UN resolutions, and set 15 January 1991 as a deadline for withdrawal. President Bush and his administration, moreover, threatened to use military force against Iraq if it did not obey UN resolutions. This situation led the American bishops to call for political and peaceful measures to secure Iraq's compliance, fearing that war was the inevitable result of escalating American political rhetoric. The bishops asserted, too, that the established deadline did not allow enough time for the embargo to force compliance and avoid war. In response to the emerging crisis, on 7 November 1990, Archbishop Roger Mahony of Los Angeles, chair of the USCC's Committee on International Policy, wrote to James Baker III, secretary of state, outlining Catholic theory on a just war, fearing that the principles of last resort, proportionality, and possibilities of success had not been given sufficient attention in the American march to war.[89] After the November meeting of the American bishops in Washington, D.C., where the bishops discussed the emerging crisis with Iraq, the president of the NCCB, Archbishop Daniel Pilarczyk of Cincinnati, sent President Bush a letter on the Persian Gulf crisis, reiterating principles that Archbishop Mahony had earlier articulated, but indicating that Mahony's position represented that of the American episcopate, not just the concerns of a single bishop.[90] On 6 December 1990 the new chair of the USCC's Committee on International Policy, Archbishop John Roach of St. Paul, Minnesota, testified before the U.S. Senate's Foreign Relations Committee, admitting that Iraq's actions must be opposed, but maintaining that the fundamental issue was how best to oppose those actions and asserting that "modern warfare, even in its conventional version, is very hard to justify morally." The bishops wanted the moral issues discussed more broadly and particularly in Congress.[91] Roach followed up his appearance before the Senate committee with a 7 January 1991 letter addressed to all members of Congress that urged them to seek alternatives to war, even as the U.S.'s machinery of war was being put in place.[92] On 15 January 1991, in a last minute effort to avoid war, Pope John Paul II, wrote to Presidents Bush and Saddam Hussein seeking a peaceful resolution.[93] The appeals for peaceful means to resolve the crisis came to naught, and on

16 January 1991 the United States and coalition forces starting bombing Baghdad and other targets in Iraq to force the withdrawal from Kuwait.

The war was short lived, but had destructive effects on the Iraqi people. Although the bishops had condemned Iraq's aggression against Kuwait, its previous assaults on its neighbors and its own people, and its numerous violations of human rights, many of them had no illusions that the American-led war would restore peace to the Middle East. Bishop Joseph Imesch of Joliet, Illinois, for example, on 25 January 1991 asked people in his diocese: "Is there anyone who seriously believes that our present war will bring peace in the Middle East? We may attain our objective to free Kuwait, but it would be naive to think this action will bring peace."[94] The bishops had opposed war, but once it started they called for prayerful support of the Iraqi people as well as the troops. According to opinion polls, a majority of American Catholics, like a majority of other Americans, supported the war effort, even though the vast majority of their bishops had opposed it. In this, as in a number of other social-political-moral issues, the bishops' teachings, like those of many other religious leaders in the country, were in conflict with generally accepted American cultural attitudes and values.

After the Gulf War, the bishops had second thoughts about their prewar support for the 1990 UN-imposed embargo on Iraq. Originally they saw the embargo as a means of forcing Iraq to withdraw from Kuwait and comply with UN resolutions. But the longer it lasted after the war the more it damaged the people of Iraq. Between 1991 and 2001 the bishops addressed the debilitating effects of the UN embargo. Embargoes, intended to punish unjust governments and/or despotic rulers, had destructive effects on the lives of innocent men, women, and children in the countries affected. Embargoes increased poverty, stopped economic development, and multiplied the miseries under which the people lived. Embargoes were unjust and intolerable means to bring about reforms in tyrannical governments or governments unresponsive to international law, and, as one episcopal statement put it, "embargoes denying basic necessities are never morally acceptable."[95] In November 1997 the bishops promised the Iraqi Patriarch, Raphael Bidawid of Baghdad, that they would continue to provide humanitarian aid to the people of Iraq and to advocate peace policies in the Middle East.[96] After their Washington meetings in November 1998 and 1999, the bishops again urged political not economic sanctions on Iraq and insisted that it was "time for a new approach to Iraq."[97]

The terrorism that had visited so many parts of the world, particularly the Middle East, came down on American shores on the morning of 11 September 2001 when suicide terrorists captured American commercial airlines and guided them into New York City's World Trade Center and Washington's Pentagon, destroying the buildings and murdering thousands, and killing everyone on another airline that crashed in a field in Pennsylvania after passengers overtook the hijackers and thwarted their mission to demolish another target in the United States. The tragic event, immediately etched in the souls of American citizens because of continuous television coverage, bound the nation together in common suffering, grief, and mourning. Thousands of American lives were changed forever, and the nation would no longer feel the security it had felt for so many years. Terrorism, which destroyed so many innocent lives throughout the world, had plundered American peace and security.

The immediate reaction from political leaders, religious leaders, and common American citizens was one of prayer for so many families who lost fathers, mothers, husbands, wives, brothers, sisters, children, relatives, and friends. Immediately Catholic bishops in New York City, Washington, D.C., Philadelphia, and across the country asked their priests to open churches for ecumenical prayer services and for Masses for the dead and suffering. Bishops also prepared statements for the press and for their people on the tragedies of the day, warning against ethnic, religious, or national stereotyping "for what may be the acts of a few irrational terrorists."[98]

When it was learned that Muslim militants were responsible for the planned suicide attacks, President George W. Bush and other political and religious leaders repeatedly asked Americans to distinguish between Muslim religious fanatics who misused their own religious tradition and genuine religious Muslims who abhorred the crime committed. Catholic bishops and other Catholic leaders joined in the chorus calling for religious tolerance and respect for American Muslims in particular, fearing retaliation and vengeance against them. Three days after the tragedy, the USCCB's Committee on Ecumenical and Interreligious Affairs published a joint statement with American Muslim leaders from the Islamic Society of North America, the American Muslim Council, the Islamic Society of North America, the Islamic Circle of North America, and the Muslim American Society deploring the terrorists acts. The statement noted that Catholics and Muslims in the United States had regularly engaged in religious dialogue and had cooperated in many civic projects together. They shared some fundamental beliefs, moreover, that opposed terrorism: "We believe that the one God calls us to be peoples of peace. Nothing in our Holy Scriptures, nothing in our understanding of God's revelation, nothing that is Christian or Islamic justifies terrorist acts and disruption of millions of lives which we have witnessed this week. Together we condemn those actions as evil and diametrically opposed to true religion."[99] Like some other religious leaders, Archbishop William Levada of San Francisco, in a homily on 16 September, protested some popular attempts to demonize whole classes of peoples and called on the president, Congress, and other governmental officials not to lead the United States and the world down the path to war in response to 9/11. He was particularly upset by some local San Francisco alarmist press accounts that asserted irresponsibly that Americans were now in the midst of World War III as a result of terrorism on American shores.[100]

On 7 October 2001, less than a month after the terrorist attacks, President Bush announced that the United States and a coalition of international forces had begun bombing terrorist training camps in Afghanistan. The war with the Taliban leaders of Afghanistan was on. The U.S. government had warned the

Taliban leaders to shut down the al Queda terrorist camps and to hand over Osama bin Laden, the supposed leader of much international terrorism, to the United States for the crimes against humanity carried out in the terrorist attacks. President Bush called this campaign against terrorism "Enduring Freedom," declaring that it was part of a much larger campaign to rid the world of terrorism wherever it existed.

The USCCB responded to the 9/11 attacks and the announced war on Afghanistan with a pastoral message to American Catholics and others of good will after its annual November meeting in Washington, D.C. In "Living with Faith and Hope after September 11," the bishops consoled a grieving nation, provided criteria for moral discernment and judgment, and called Catholics and other Americans to action and solidarity in troubling and challenging times. "The dreadful deeds of September 11," they wrote, "cannot go unanswered." The bishops, therefore, supported "efforts of our nation and the international community to seek out and hold accountable, in accord with national and international law, those individuals, groups and governments which are responsible." Bringing the terrorists to justice by the use of force might be necessary, but the uses of military force had to be governed by traditional moral norms, which the bishops also laid out in their pastoral letter. The bishops were quick to urge restraint in bringing to justice those responsible for the crimes and wanted the nation to focus on the roots of terrorism: "In a world where one-fifth of the population survives on less than $1 per day, where some twenty countries are involved in major armed conflict, and where poverty, corruption, and repressive regimes bring untold suffering to millions of people, we simply cannot remain indifferent." Terrorists themselves exploited these conditions of poverty and injustice with their own immoral means. The nation, and Catholics in particular, should focus on a "more just international political, social and economic order." The American campaign against terrorism would never be successful if it did not attend to the root causes. In the end, the bishops pleaded, "a successful campaign against terrorism will require a combination of resolve to do what is necessary to see it through, restraint to ensure that we act justly, and a long term focus on broader issues of justice and peace."[101]

After the war against Afghanistan and the continuing attempts to uproot the Taliban and hunt down Osama bin Laden, the American government focused on the Iraqi government as a source of systematic terrorism and as a regime unresponsive to international law and the long-term demands of the UN Security Council. President Bush and others in American government spent much of 2003 justifying the use of a preemptive strike against Iraq to remove the regime that had supposedly been illegally creating weapons of mass destruction. Such rhetoric worried many within the American Catholic episcopacy, and in response to it, Bishop Wilton Gregory, president of the USCCB, wrote President Bush on 13 September 2002 to articulate the episcopal concerns. In the name of the bishops, he welcomed Bush's efforts to focus the world's attention on Iraq's eleven-year refusal to comply with UN resolutions and its pursuit of weapons of mass destruction, but he raised serious moral questions about the legitimacy of any preemptive unilateral use of military force to overthrow the Iraqi government. Nothing in the traditional norms for the just use of force supported preemptive warfare.[102] After the 8 November 2002 decision of the UN Security Council against the use of preemptive force and after the USCCB's annual November meeting in Washington, D.C., the bishops published a "Statement on Iraq" that reiterated Bishop Gregory's opposition to any American unilateral action against Iraq: "Based on the facts that are known to us, we continue to find it difficult to justify the resort to war against Iraq, lacking clear and adequate evidence of an imminent attack of a grave nature."[103] The talk of a war against Iraq seemed to violate the principles of a just war: no just cause, not enough consideration of last resort, no legitimate authority (in view of UN resistance to American overtures), no serious consideration of the probability of success and proportionality. The bishops pleaded for the United States to seek alternatives to war and joined Pope John Paul II and bishops from the Middle East and around the world in stating that a resort to such a war with Iraq would not meet these strict conditions in Catholic teaching for the just use of force. Again in February 2003, the bishops reiterated their opposition to American plans for unilateral action against Iraq.[104] In March, Pope John Paul II sent papal envoy Cardinal Pio Laghi to plead with President Bush against war.[105] The pleadings were of no avail. Shortly after the meeting with Cardinal Laghi, President Bush announced that the United States, joined by British forces, had begun bombing Baghdad. The Bush administration did not have the support of the papacy or the American bishops, but, according to opinion polls, it did have the support of large numbers of American Catholics. A few Catholic intellectuals, including Michael Novak and George Weigel, supported the war effort and used moral norms for a just war to back a unilateral preemptive strike against Iraq.[106]

The USCCB's multiple statements on national and international affairs addressed a host of issues that rarely reached the press or received much national attention. The declarations themselves revealed the global concerns of the Catholic Church in the United States, but many of them were buried in periodical literature that was not widely distributed or read by the Catholic laity in general, lay Catholic intellectuals, clergy, and perhaps even some bishops. Of what use, one could ask, are such teachings if they are not widely distributed or read? They reveal, some might say, the exclusive concerns of a hierarchy separated from the everyday concerns of Catholics in the pew. Others might say, and I include myself in this group, they reflect an attempt to apply the gospel to the social, economic, and political conditions in ways that reflect the Catholic Church's mission in a troubled modern world.

The times were indeed troubled and how future historians will assess the turmoil and terror around the globe and in the American Catholic Church during the decade of the 1990s and first years of the twenty-first century remains to be seen. No contemporary historian, and certainly not this one, would care to predict the long-term consequences of the American-led responses to worldwide terrorism or of the revelations and reactions to sexual abuse within the Catholic Church. The sufferings of peoples both within and outside the American borders for more than a decade had been seared into the soul of the American church, and there were some signs that the Catholic people, and the bishops in particular, were in a mood of repentance, conversion, reparation, and healing, but it was not clear at the end of 2003 what would be the result of these experiences.

The new evangelization that focused simultaneously on the social and political implications of the Gospel and on the internal renewal of Catholic life was an ongoing effort within the Catholic community at the beginning of the third millennium. Large numbers of Catholics in the pews continued to be active participants according to sociological surveys, continued to interpret their lives in a troubled world in the light of their personal prayer life, their yearly cycle of liturgical celebrations from Advent to Advent, and their sacramental experiences of baptism, Eucharist, marriage, and death. Many Catholics who came to maturity from the 1930s to the mid-1960s continued to participate in an ecclesial-sacramental-evangelical way of life and found that life credible and meaningful. It remains to be seen how effective the new evangelization efforts will be with a younger generation of Catholics who are coming to maturity in a church that is very different from the one their parents and grandparents had experienced in their youth.

BIOGRAPHICAL
ENTRIES

B

------·•·------

BERNARDIN, JOSEPH (2 April 1928, Columbia, S.C.–14 November 1996, Chicago, Ill.). *Education:* Premedical studies, University of South Carolina, 1944; St. Mary's College, Kentucky, 1945–46; B.A., St. Mary's Seminary, Baltimore, Md., 1947–48; M.A., Catholic University of America, 1952. *Career:* Ordained priest, 1952; assistant pastor, 1952–54, vice chancellor, 1954–56, chancellor, 1956–62, vicar general and diocesan consuler, 1962–64, and assistant to the bishop, 1964–66—in Charleston, S.C.; auxiliary bishop of New Orleans, 1966–68; general secretary of the NCCB, 1968–72; archbishop of Cincinnati, 1972–82; archbishop of Chicago, 1982–96; cardinal, 1982.

After the Second Vatican Council (1962–65), Bernardin rose rapidly to national prominence in the American Catholic Church. Educated in the preconciliar church, he became a consensus-building member of the American Catholic hierarchy in a postconciliar church that was severely divided over a host of religious and moral issues. He came to national notice in 1968 when he was appointed episcopal general secretary of the NCCB, and thereafter archbishop of Cincinnati and of Chicago, the largest Catholic diocese in the United States.

His fellow bishops elected Bernardin president of the NCCB in 1974, demonstrating the confidence the bishops had in his leadership in a period of much turmoil in the Catholic Church. As president of the NCCB and as an archbishop in two different dioceses, Bernardin took a leading role in advancing a number of moral and social issues of local and national concern; he supported, for example, tax increases to foster the public schools in Cincinnati, economic justice for migrant farm workers, and assistance for the homeless. He opposed the war in Vietnam, abortion, and laws favoring euthanasia. In 1983 he chaired the NCCB committee that produced the national episcopal pastoral, "The Challenge of Peace," outlining Catholic thinking on war and peace and condemning the use of nuclear weapons. That pastoral received a significant amount of national discussion in the 1980s, and for his leadership role in promoting it he was given the Albert Einstein Peace Award. Issues ranging from abortion to war received his attention, and during the 1980s, he helped to develop what became known as the consistent ethic of life or the seamless garment approach to many of the significant moral concerns of the times.

Within the church he also tried to build consensus in implementing the reforms of the Second Vatican Council, calling for a collegial approach to problem solving in the dioceses and in the national church. He took a leadership role, too, in advancing the dignity and roles of women in the church, even as he supported the Vatican's official ban against ordaining women to the priesthood. In 1991 he established in Chicago a committee to investigate charges of sexual abuse by priests in his diocese, to discipline the offenders, and to support the victims. He was one of the first bishops in the country to face the scandal publicly and to do something about the problem in his diocese in an open manner.

The last three years of his life received much national attention, as he was falsely accused of sexual abuse in 1993, was diagnosed with pancreatic cancer in 1994, and shortly before his death in 1996, established the Catholic Common Ground Project to heal wounds in the church. His courage and grace in facing death became a lesson in what the mediaeval called the art of dying. In Shakespeare's words: "Nothing in his life became him like the leaving of it."

BROWNSON, ORESTES AUGUSTUS (16 September 1803, Stockbridge, Vt.– 17 April 1876, Detroit, Mich.). *Education:* Studied at Balston Academy, Balston Spa, N.Y., 1818–19. *Career:* Teacher in Detroit, 1823–24, and Elbridge, N.Y., 1824–26; ordained Universalist minister, Jaffrey, N.H., 1826; Universalist preacher in Hartland, Vt., and Lichtfield, Ithaca, Geneva, Auburn, N.Y., 1826– 30; corresponding editor, the *Free Enquirer,* 1829–30; editor, *Genesee Republican and Herald of Reform,* 1829–30; political organizer for Workingman's Party, 1829–30; unaffiliated minister in Ithaca, 1831; founding editor, the *Philanthropist,* 1831–32; Unitarian minister in Walpole, N.H., 1832–34, and Canton, Mass., 1834–36; editor, the *Boston Reformer,* 1836–38; organizer and minister, the Society for Christian Union and Progress, Boston, 1836–38; founding editor, *Boston Quarterly Review,* 1838–42; staff, *United States and Democratic Review,* 1842–44; founding editor, *Brownson Quarterly Review,* 1844–64, 1873–75; independent journalist and author, 1844–76.

Orestes Brownson was the foremost American Catholic lay theologian and philosopher of the nineteenth century. Throughout his life, he was an active and restless religious pilgrim, manifesting something of the diversity of religious options in early nineteenth-century America and the fluidity of ecclesiastical affiliation. He experienced a religious conversion at age 13 during a Methodist revival and in 1822 became a Presbyterian. In 1826, he was ordained a Universalist minister, and in 1829 he rejected his Universalism and joined the Workingman's Party, where he devoted himself to causes of social justice. Influenced by William E. Channing, he became a Unitarian minister in 1832 but left the ministry in 1838, moving more and more in the direction of a religious socialism. In 1844, he converted to Catholicism, and he remained in it for the rest of his life. But even within this tradition, he vacillated between conservatism and liberalism.

In the period before the Civil War he focused on the necessity of the church for salvation and for societal peace and harmony. In the period after the war he, like Pope Pius IX, concentrated his intellectual guns on what he perceived to be a rising secularism in science, politics, and religion. Although he criticized the direction of American society after the war, he emphasized the necessity of preserving in dialectical harmony and tension the American spirit of freedom and the Catholic sense of authority and community.

C

CABRINI, FRANCES XAVIER (1 July 1850, Sant'Angelo Lodigiano, Italy–22 December 1918, Chicago, Ill.). *Education:* Studied under Daughters of the Sacred Heart, Arluno, Italy, 1863–68. *Career:* Teacher in Vidardo, Italy, 1872–74, Cadogno, 1874–80; founder and mother general of Missionary Sisters of the Sacred Heart, 1880–1917.

In 1880 at the age of thirty, Frances Cabrini established the Missionary Sisters of the Sacred Heart to provide spiritual or corporal help primarily to Italian emigrants. Nine years later, at the invitation of Archbishop Michael Corrigan of New York, she emigrated to the United States, where the Missionary Sisters began working for the immigrants in "Little Italy" in New York City. During the first 30 years of their development, the sisters established schools, hospitals, and orphanages and carried on home and prison visitations, teaching basic Christian doctrines and providing needed social services. Mother Cabrini extended this apostolate to the working class beyond New York into New Jersey, Pennsylvania, Louisiana, Mississippi, Illinois, Colorado, Washington, and California.

At her death, 67 missionary communities of over 4,000 women religious could be found not only in the United States, but also in Nicaragua, Chile, and Argentina. Her industry and steadfastness were manifested by her expertise in providing spiritual and human services, and in her abilities in administration and finance. Mother Cabrini was beatified (1938), canonized a saint (1946), the first American citizen to be so designated, and declared "Patroness of Emigrants" (1950).

CALVERT, CECIL (1606, London, England–30 November 1675, London, England). *Education:* Studied at Trinity College, Oxford, 1621. *Career:* Second Lord Baltimore, 1632; proprietor, Colony of Maryland, 1634–75.

Cecil was the eldest son of Anne Myrme and George Calvert, the first Lord Baltimore. In 1632, after his father's death, he inherited the province of Maryland, which King Charles I had granted to his father. Cecil, like his father a Catholic, obtained a charter for the colony, gathered Protestant as well as Catholic investors in the new colony, invited the Jesuits Andrew White and John Altham to provide for the colony's religious needs, appointed his brother

Leonard to be governor of the colony in 1633, and in 1634, sent colonists to Maryland to further his own and his investors' profits, to fortify the English presence in the new world, and to extend Christianity. Cecil also saw the colony as an experiment in religious toleration. Although he invited Jesuits to the colony, he did so on the grounds that they would be financially self-supporting and subject to civilian control. In 1649, after the death of Charles I and seven years of civil and religious war in England, Cecil had prepared for Maryland "The Act Concerning Religion" to protect Catholics as well as others in the free exercise of Christian worship. Calvert twice lost control of the governorship and proprietorship of Maryland to Virginia Puritans, and he spent much of his time in England trying to protect his rights and regain what he had lost. When he died in London in 1675, Maryland was again under his proprietary control.

CALVERT, GEORGE (1580, Yorkshire, England–15 April 1632, London, England). *Education:* B.A., Trinity College, Oxford, 1597; M.A., 1605. *Career:* Clerk of the crown of assize and peace in County Clare, Ireland, 1606; secretary to Lord Robert Cecil, 1606–12; clerk of the privy council, 1613; member of Virginia Company, 1609–20; member of Parliament, 1609–24; knighted, 1617; an undersecretary of state, 1619; baron of Baltimore, Longford County, Ireland, 1625; granted province of Maryland, 1632.

George Calvert was the son of Alice Grosland and Leonard Calvert, Catholics who became Anglicans in the face of penal laws. After his education at Oxford and some experience as a minor government official, he became a Member of Parliament and a staunch defender of King James I's policies. From 1609 to 1625, he served in a number of responsible governmental positions, being appointed, for example, as a special emissary to France in 1610 at the accession of Louis XIII. In 1620, already having been involved in the colonial Virginia Company, he purchased the Colony of Avalon in Newfoundland and tried to establish a colony there in 1623, but it failed. In 1625, the year Charles I became king of Great Britain and Ireland, Calvert returned to the Catholicism of his youth and, because of it, resigned his seat in Parliament and his position as undersecretary of state. In the late 1620s, he petitioned King Charles I for colonial lands near Virginia and, after much opposition from the Virginia Company, the king granted him the colony of Maryland. Calvert died in 1632, however, before the charter for Maryland was finalized. His son Cecil inherited the charter and developed the colony.

CAREY, MATHEW (28 January 1760, Dublin, Ireland–16 September 1839, Philadelphia, Pa.). *Career:* Printer's apprentice, *Hibernia Journal,* Dublin, 1775–79; editor, *Freeman's Journal,* Dublin, 1780–83; founder, *Volunteer's Journal,* Dublin, 1783; founder, *Philadelphia Evening Herald,* 1785; cofounder, *Columbian*

Magazine, 1786; founder, the *American Museum,* 1787–92; established the Carey publishing firm, 1792–93; director, Bank of Pennsylvania, 1802–5; founder, Philadelphia Society for the Promotion of National Industry, 1820.

Born the son of relatively prosperous middle-class, Irish Catholic parents, Christopher and Mary Sheridan Carey, Mathew had the advantage of a good education, and by the age of 15 he was already publishing articles in journals, a practice that he continued for the remainder of his life. At 19, Carey published his first pamphlet, *The Urgent Necessity of an Immediate Repeal of the Whole Penal Code* (1779), and because it disturbed both conservatives and Irish Catholics, he was forced to flee to France, where he met the Marquis de Lafayette and Benjamin Franklin, for whom he worked as a printer's apprentice. He returned to Ireland in 1780, became editor of the *Freeman's Journal,* and established the *Volunteer's Journal,* both of which were pro-American and anti-English. In 1784 the young Carey was imprisoned for publishing an article and cartoon that were considered libelous. After being released from prison he emigrated to Philadelphia.

In Philadelphia Carey continued his publishing interests. In 1786 he cofounded the *Columbian Magazine,* and in 1787 he independently established the *American Museum,* the first nationally distributed literary journal—one that gained for him a national reputation. By 1792 Carey had established a bookstore and shortly thereafter a publishing firm that became the nation's largest in the early nineteenth century. Carey also became prominent in American political discussions, siding with the Madisonian and Jeffersonian pro-French Republicans against the pro-British Federalists after 1792. When Jefferson became president, Carey's fortunes began to rise with his appointment to the board of the Bank of Pennsylvania in 1801. In 1814 he published *The Olive Branch* to reconcile opposing parties during the War of 1812. The book quickly became the most widely read political book since *Common Sense,* going through 10 editions by 1819. On the economic front, Carey supported a strong national bank, wrote at least 40 separate works on protectionism by 1826, and continued to write on national economic issues for the remainder of his life.

Carey was also a supporter of the common good and an advocate of social justice. He helped establish the Hibernian Society (1792) for the relief of Irish immigrants, a Sunday School Society (1796) to promote the religious education of youth, and the Philadelphia Society for the Promotion of National Industry to promote a protection tariff for American workers and small manufacturers. He also wrote numerous essays and pamphlets to promote the establishment of public charities, to advocate justice for poor working women, and to support prison reforms. He was a strong public advocate for political freedom and emancipation for the Irish, Greeks, and Polish. He also published pamphlets favorable to the African Colonization movement of the 1820s. In ecclesiastical affairs he published the first Catholic (Douay) Bible in the United States and numerous Catholic apologetical, doctrinal, and devotional works, and he became involved in the trustee debates over William Hogan. Because of his personal charities and his general involvement in the public life of Philadelphia, his funeral procession in 1839 was, after Stephen Girard's, the longest the city had ever seen.

CARROLL OF CARROLLTON, CHARLES (19 September 1737, Annapolis, Md.–14 November 1832, Baltimore, Md.). *Education:* Studied at Jesuit Bohemian Manor Academy (Md.), 1747; St. Omer's College, Flanders, Belgium, 1748–54; Jesuit college, Rheims, France, 1754–55; law school, Bruges, Belgium, 1756; law school at the Temple, London, 1757–58; College Louis le Grand, Paris, 1759. *Career:* Elected to Maryland provincial convention, 1774; member of Committee of Correspondence, 1775; Maryland Association of the Freeman, 1775; deputy to Maryland State convention, 1775; Continental Congress's mission to Canada with Benjamin Franklin, Samuel Chase, and John Carroll, 1776; signer, Declaration of Independence, 1776; elected to Continental Congress, 1776; appointed to Board of War, 1776; Maryland state senator, 1778; U.S. Senator, Maryland, 1789–92.

Charles Carroll was the son of Elizabeth Brooke and Charles Carroll II of Annapolis, wealthy plantation owners. After receiving a cosmopolitan education in Europe, he returned to Maryland in 1765, where his father gave him Carrollton Manor, a ten thousand-acre plantation. From that time forward he signed his name Charles Carroll of Carrollton to distinguish himself from his father. He married his cousin Mary Darnall in 1768; she gave birth to seven children, two of whom outlived him.

Carroll returned to Maryland at a time of high political turmoil and escalating difficulties with England. By 1770 he became a spokesman for the resistance to what was considered unfair and unjustified colonial taxation. Writing under the pen name "First Citizen" in the *Maryland Gazette,* he protested against the jurist Daniel Dulany's support of new Maryland taxes. Influenced by Enlightenment cries of civil and religious liberties, he supported the people's right to armed resistance and independence from England, becoming a member of the Continental Congress, a signer of the Declaration of Independence, and an instrumental force in Maryland's decision to support independence. Also in 1776, the Continental Congress sent Carroll, his cousin John (a former Jesuit priest), Benjamin Franklin, and Samuel Chase to Canada to solicit support for independence, but the mission failed. Throughout the Revolutionary War he played a major role in the Board of War and in the Maryland State Constitutional Convention as a state senator. After the war he participated in discussions on the U.S. Constitution and the Bill of Rights. Except for his debates with Dulaney, his Catholicism was not a significant issue in his role as political advocate and statesman. As a strong supporter of the Federalist Party, he opposed Thomas Jefferson's election to the presidency in 1800. Although he also opposed the War of 1812, he commented only periodically on political matters after Jefferson's election and withdrew into semiretirement from public life. He died in 1832, the last surviving signer of the Declaration of Independence.

CARROLL, JOHN (8 or 19 January 1736, Upper Marlborough, Md.–3 December 1815, Baltimore, Md.). *Education:* Studied at Jesuit Bohemian Manor Academy (Md.), 1747; St. Omer's Coll., Flanders, Belgium, 1748–53; Jesuit education in philosophy and theology at Watts, Liège, and Bruges, Belgium, 1755–62. *Career:* Entered Society of Jesus and novitiate, 1753–55; ordained, 1761; philosophy teacher, Liège, 1762–67; teacher, Bruges, 1767–69; Jesuit tertianship at Ghent, Belgium, 1770; tutor to Charles-Philip, son of Lord Stourton, 1771–73; missionary priest in Maryland, 1774–83; superior of American missions, 1784; bishop of Baltimore, 1789–1808; archbishop of Baltimore, 1808–15.

In 1774, after 26 years of education and teaching in Europe, 38-year-old John Carroll, saddened and disturbed by the political and ecclesiastical machinations that brought about the papal suppression of the Jesuits, returned home to Maryland to become a former Jesuit missionary. Maryland at the time was in the midst of his cousin Charles Carroll's "First Citizen" debates with Daniel Dulany over taxation and representation, and the country was experiencing the effects of the organization of the first Continental Congress in Philadelphia. John Carroll stayed clear of the debates and served missions in Maryland and occasionally in Virginia. In 1776, however, in the midst of revolutionary talk, he reluctantly accompanied Charles Carroll, Samuel Chase, and Benjamin Franklin on a mission to Canada to solicit support for the Revolution. By the Treaty of Paris in 1783, Carroll and other former Jesuits, reflecting the times in which they lived, were scrambling to establish a quasi-constitutional form of government among themselves to protect their property rights and govern themselves in serving Catholics in a free country where religious tolerance of Catholics had been increasing significantly since the beginning of the Revolution.

As superior of the American missions and first bishop and archbishop of Baltimore, Carroll became the primary organizer of Catholic institutions in the United States and set the tone for the participation of Catholicism in a new and free republican context. He supervised the establishment of Georgetown College (1791), St. Mary's Sulpician Seminary (1791), the first diocesan synod (1791), the diocesan suffragan sees of Boston, New York, Philadelphia, and Bardstown, Kentucky (1808), and Mother Elizabeth Seton's Sisters of Mercy (1809). After the Louisiana Purchase, he also provided ecclesiastical administration for Louisiana and the two Floridas (1805–15) until a new bishop was appointed. He cooperated, too, with Marylanders in founding St. John's College (Annapolis, 1789) and became a member of the board of trustees of Baltimore College (1803).

John Carroll, like many of his fellow Americans, fits into the wide ambit of the Enlightenment. His advocacy of rational religion, the reasonableness of Catholic Christianity, religious liberty, separation of church and state, voluntaryism, ecclesiastical reforms, tolerance of and respect for other religious traditions, and republican political theory reveal some of the dominant concerns of the Age of Reason. Although Carroll wrote no systematic treatises on any of these, many of his personal letters, pastoral programs, and occasional apologetic writings reveal his enthusiastic acceptance of them.

CODY, JOHN PATRICK (24 December 1907, St. Louis, Mo.–25 April 1982, Chicago, Ill.). *Education:* North American College, Rome, 1926–32; S.T.D., J.C.D., Pontifical Institute of the Apollinaris, Rome, 1932. *Career:* Ordained, 1931; staff, Vatican Secretariate of State, Rome, 1933–38; secretary, Archbishop John Glennon, St. Louis, 1938–40; pastoral work in St. Louis, 1938–47; auxiliary bishop, St. Louis, 1947; coadjutor bishop and administrator, St. Joseph, Mo., 1954–55; coadjutor bishop and administrator, Kansas City, Mo., 1956; coadjutor bishop, New Orleans, 1961; apostolic administrator, New Orleans, 1962; archbishop of New Orleans, 1964; archbishop of Chicago, 1965–82; cardinal, 1967–82.

Returning to St. Louis in 1938 after a thorough Roman experience and education, John Patrick Cody eventually became one of the bright, young, ultramontane episcopal leaders of post–World War II American Catholicism. After episcopal duties in the Missouri cities of St. Louis, St. Joseph, and Kansas City, he went to New Orleans where, under Archbishop Joseph Rummel from 1961 to 1965, he became a strong advocate for the rights of blacks within the church's schools. He was also a member of the Second Vatican Council's preparatory Commission on Seminaries, Universities, and Catholic Schools. During the council he made only one speech before the bishops, calling for acceptance of the council's *Declaration on Christian Education* and for the establishment of a postconciliar commission to investigate more thoroughly the problems (peculiar to each nation) of education in the modern world.

From 1965, when he was made archbishop of Chicago, until the end of his life he was the center of controversy in the postconciliar church of Chicago, where his preconciliar exercise of ecclesiastical authority conflicted sharply with new models of episcopal leadership. Although he instituted reforms within diocesan administration (dividing it into 12 vicariates), raised revenues (through "Project Renewal") for the modernization of parishes and schools, and allowed for the establishment of an independent Association of Chicago Priests (1966) and the Presbyterial Senate (1971), his authoritarian style of leadership in dismissing ineffectual pastors and failing to follow the advice of the new clerical associations created an adversarial relationship between him and many of his clergy. The Priests' Association in 1971 voted to censure him and his auxiliaries for not representing their views at the National Conference of Catholic Bishops.

In 1968 Cody provoked some conflict in Chicago when he supported a plan that would bus minority children out of overcrowded, inner-city schools to predominantly white schools in suburban neighborhoods. In 1975 his decision to close several inner-city schools with predominantly minority children for budgetary reasons again brought denouncements on him. His program of associating poor inner-city parishes with wealthier suburban parishes for resource sharing and his overall commitment to the minority community in the inner city brought praise from the archdiocese's black clergy, but his style of leadership did not endear him to the white clergy. When he died in 1982, he was under investigation for improper use of church funds, a charge that was refuted when the grand jury refused to hand down an indictment against him. Although he made great strides in justice and racial equality, his episcopal tenure was challenged by a decline in vocations and respect for episcopal authority, departures from the priesthood, and other difficulties associated with the immediate post–Vatican II era.

COOKE, TERENCE (1 March 1921, Bronx, N.Y.–6 October 1983, New York, N.Y.). *Education:* Preparatory seminary, Cathedral College, New York City, 1934–40; St. Joseph's Seminary, Dunwoodie, N.Y., 1940–45; M.A. Catholic University of America, Washington, D.C., 1949. *Career:* Ordained priest, 1945; assistant parish priest, 1945–47; staff member of Catholic Charities of New York, 1949–54; instructor, Fordham University School of Social Service, 1949–56; secretary to Cardinal Francis J. Spellman, 1957–61; vice chancellor and chancellor of diocese of New York, 1961–65; auxiliary bishop of New York, 1965–68; archbishop of New York, 1968–83; cardinal, 1969.

Cooke served the church of New York during a period of unprecedented turmoil in the nation and decline in the Catholic Church. During the 15 years he served as archbishop, he, like many other bishops across the country, faced the closings of many ecclesiastical institutions and a decreasing level of Catholic participation in church life. In response to problems in the inner-city Catholic communities, he created the Inter-Parish Finance Commission, a local diocesan committee that taxed affluent parishes in order to subsidize churches and parochial schools in disadvantaged neighborhoods. At a time when many dioceses were closing inner-city parishes and schools, Cooke's innovative plan served the needs of inner-city peoples and helped to limit the number of closings. Unlike his immediate predecessor, Cardinal Spellman, he received little national attention for his work and did not play a significant role in the national ecclesial leadership. He faced his death from cancer with dignity, offering the sick and dying an example of the Christian approach to death, as the New York newspapers remarked at the time of his death.

CORRIGAN, MICHAEL A. (13 August 1839, Newark, N.J.–5 May 1902, New York, N.Y.). *Education:* Studied at St. Mary's Coll., Wilmington, Del., 1853–55;

Mount St. Mary's College, Emmitsburg, Md., 1859; D.D., North American College, Rome, 1864. *Career:* Ordained, 1863; professor of dogmatic theology and scripture, Seton Hall College and Seminary, South Orange, N.J., 1864–73; president Seton Hall College, 1868–77; administrator of Diocese of Newark, 1869–70; bishop of Newark, 1873–80; coadjutor archbishop of New York, 1880–85; archbishop of New York, 1886–1902.

As bishop of Newark and archbishop of New York, Michael Corrigan was a vigorous ecclesiastical administrator, a strong disciplinarian, a friend of the immigrants, and a leader of the conservative party in late nineteenth-century American Catholicism. During his Newark episcopacy he consolidated the administration of church properties, fought losing battles to obtain state funds for Catholic institutions, instituted a solemn Roman-style liturgy, increased the number of Catholic schools and other ecclesiastical institutions, and because of the growing number of Catholics in New Jersey, provided for the establishment of a new diocese in Trenton.

After the Third Plenary Council of Baltimore in 1884, Corrigan and Bishop Bernard Joseph McQuaid of Rochester, New York, became the national leaders of a conservative party in the Catholic Church, rejecting an accommodationist stance toward American values and institutions. Corrigan petitioned Rome to condemn the Knights of Labor as a secret society and suspended Edward McGlynn, the popular pastor of St. Stephen's Church, because he had supported and, against canonical legislation, campaigned for the populist and (in Corrigan's view) socialist Henry George when he ran for mayor of New York in 1886. Corrigan also criticized the establishment of the Catholic University of America at Washington, D.C., because he feared its liberal leadership, and was adamantly opposed to Archbishop Ireland's attempts to create a rapprochement between public and Catholic schools. Corrigan believed that those in the Catholic Church who supported these programs were undermining the specific identity of Catholicism, weakening its authority, and confusing its religious aims with specific political and cultural programs and agenda. Corrigan held that American Catholicism could preserve its identity only by staying out of political and social issues, concentrating instead on its religious mission and institutional developments, and reinforcing ecclesiastical and civil authority as a primary means for maintaining the unity and stability of church and society.

Between 1886 and 1899 Corrigan periodically complained to Rome that the pastoral approaches of the "liberal" Americanizing bishops were threatening the foundations of Catholicism in the United States. In 1899, when Pope Leo XIII issued his encyclical *Testem Benevolentiae* condemning the so-called heresy of Americanism, Corrigan rejoiced that ecclesiastical authority had finally intervened to curtail a false Americanism, which, if left unchecked, would have destroyed the American Catholic Church.

COUGHLIN, CHARLES EDWARD (25 October 1891, Hamilton, Ontario–27 October 1979, Birmingham, Mich.). *Education:* Studied at St. Michael's College, Toronto, 1903–7; University of Toronto, 1907–11; St. Basil's Seminary, Toronto, 1911–14, 1915–16; St. Basil's College, Waco, Tex., 1914–15. *Career:* Teacher, Basilian College, Waco, Tex., 1914–15; ordained, 1916; professor of English, Assumption College, Sandwich, Ontario, 1916–23; curate, St. Augustine's Church, Kalamazoo, Mich., 1923; pastor, St. Leo's Church, Detroit, 1923; pastor, Saints Peter and Paul, North Branch, Mich., 1925; founding pastor, St. Therese of the Little Flower of Jesus, Royal Oak, Mich., 1926–66; organizer, National Union for Social Justice, 1934; organizer, Union Party, 1936; founder, *Social Justice,* 1936–42; retirement, 1966–79.

Charles Coughlin rose to national attention as a radio preacher and lecturer who expressed the popular tensions and anxieties of the Depression era. In 1926, he obtained time on Detroit's WJR radio station not only to raise money for his Little Flower parish in a Detroit suburb but also to combat the assaults of the Ku Klux Klan. His broadcasts brought little attention until he began to cover social and political issues at the beginning of the Depression. When he became a forceful supporter and then critic of Franklin D. Roosevelt during the 1930s, he increased his radio audience to an estimated 40 million listeners, many of whom sent him money to continue his Sunday broadcasts excoriating the evil effects of capitalism, the New Deal, and communism.

Coughlin's popularity as a radio preacher encouraged him to form the National Union for Social Justice in 1934. The union was open to all religious traditions and intended to be a populist organization that pushed for the implementation of social justice as defined in the papal social encyclicals and in Midwestern agrarian reforms: for example, a living wage, control of private property for the common good, a fair profit for the farm, the right of labor to organize, absolute government control of all currency, and the priority of human over property rights. By 1935, however, Coughlin's calls for reforms and social justice turned bitterly against President Roosevelt, and in 1936 he instituted *Social Justice,* a journal for expressing his social agenda, and created the Union Party to run against both the Democratic and Republican candidates for the presidency. Running William Lemke for president proved politically disastrous, but it gave Coughlin an opportunity to express his vitriolic attack on the New Deal. By 1938 Coughlin's Christian Front became an anti-Semitic, isolationist, pro-Nazi organization that periodically charged that a Roosevelt-British-Jewish conspiracy would drive the country into ruin, blaming in particular Jewish bankers for the rise of communism and corruptions of capitalism.

In 1942 the government barred Coughlin's journal *Social Justice* from the postal system for violating the Espionage Act, and his new archbishop, Edward Mooney, forced him off the air. He lived in relative obscurity as a parish priest thereafter, retiring in 1966 and dying in Birmingham, Michigan, in 1979. Coughlin saw himself as an advocate for social justice and the people's priest;

many of his opponents saw him as a demagogue and/or populist fascist who provided a link between late nineteenth-century populism and the McCarthyites of the 1950s or the John Birchers of a later period.

CUSHING, RICHARD JAMES (24 August 1895, Boston, Mass.–2 November 1970, Boston, Mass.). *Education:* Studied at Boston College, 1913–15; graduated from St. John's Seminary (Mass.), 1921. *Career:* Curate, Roxbury and Somerville, Mass., 1921–22; assistant and director, Society for the Propagation of the Faith, Boston, 1922–39; auxiliary bishop of Boston, 1939–44; archbishop of Boston, 1944–70; cardinal, 1958–70.

Richard Cushing's education for the priesthood and his early pastoral and episcopal experience took place under the watchful eye of Cardinal William O'Connell, archbishop of Boston, who had made valiant efforts to centralize all ecclesiastical developments in Boston. Under O'Connell's tight control before World War II, Cushing flourished and developed an uncommon clerical interest in foreign missions. As archbishop of Boston he continued that interest, creating the St. James Society in 1958 to allow diocesan priests an opportunity to serve in those foreign territories where there was a shortage of clergy, especially in Latin America. As a priest and later as bishop, moreover, he was an effective fund-raiser not only for diocesan educational and charitable projects but also for foreign missions.

In the 1950s Cushing was acknowledged as one of the leading and most beloved churchmen in American Catholicism. Because of his association with the Joseph Kennedy family, moreover, he was catapulted into the public limelight with the election of John F. Kennedy, a significant social development especially for Boston Catholics, who since the early twentieth century under William O'Connell had tried to demonstrate their Romanism and Americanism.

Cardinal Cushing was present at the Second Vatican Council, but he spoke only three times and did not have much influence on conciliar procedures or results. He was not a theologian, nor was he inclined to theological discussion. In the postconciliar period, however, he became a sensitive reforming bishop, especially in his support of the use of English in the liturgy, a wider participation of the laity in the church, and the church's participation in the wide arena of social justice.

D

DAY, DOROTHY (8 November 1897, Brooklyn, NY.–29 November 1980, New York, N.Y.). *Education:* Studied at University of Illinois, 1914–16. *Career:* Reporter for the *New York Call,* 1917; assistant editor, the *Masses,* 1917; worked on the *Liberator,* 1917–18; reporter, *New Orleans Item,* 1923; cofounder and publisher, *Catholic Worker,* 1933–80; founder, first house of hospitality in New York, 1935; arrested with Cesar Chavez in a farm workers' demonstration, 1973.

After a stormy bohemian and socialist youth that included a sexual liaison that led to an abortion, a marriage that failed, and a common-law relationship that resulted in the birth of a child and subsequent abandonment by the father, Dorothy Day felt the need for religion and was received into Catholicism in 1927. In 1932 she met the French peasant and social philosopher Peter Maurin, who directed her thinking toward the papal social encyclicals and the personalism of Emmanuel Mounier. In the midst of the Depression, Day found her mission in life: personal service to those suffering from unemployment and homelessness. Within this context, she and Maurin began to organize what became known as the Catholic Worker Movement.

On 1 May 1933 she published the first issue of the *Catholic Worker,* calling all Christians to give personal service to society's outcasts, thereby providing personal examples of love in action. For the next 47 years she drew numerous young Catholics to more than 40 Catholic Worker houses of hospitality across the country. In these houses young Catholics were given the opportunity to serve the poor, pray, discuss and clarify Catholic social thought, demonstrate for peace, and live out the spiritual and corporal works of mercy that Day saw as the heart of the Gospel. She and many of her followers were ardent pacifists who were periodically arrested for public demonstrations against militarism, war, and constant preparations for war. She stood steadfast against World War II, the Korean War, the entire Cold War militaristic mentality, and the Vietnam War. She and her workers became the source of Catholic radicalism in the United States, a movement that challenged prevailing moral assumptions in the culture. In the 1990s the Archdiocese of New York initiated procedures for Day's beatification.

DEARDEN, JOHN (15 October 1907, Valley Falls, R.I.–1 August 1988, Southfield, Mich.). *Education:* Studied at St. Mary's Seminary, Cleveland, 1924–28;

North American College, Rome, 1928–32; Pontifical Gregorian University, Rome, 1932–34. *Career:* Ordained, 1932; pastoral work, diocese of Cleveland, 1934–37; faculty, 1937–44, and rector, 1944–48, St. Mary's Seminary, Cleveland; coadjutor bishop of Pittsburgh, 1948–50; bishop of Pittsburgh, 1950–58; archbishop of Detroit, 1958–88; president, National Conference of Catholic Bishops, 1966–71; cardinal 1969–88; retired, 1980–88.

As bishop of Pittsburgh, Dearden was involved, like most American bishops of the 1950s, with numerous building projects to meet the ever expanding educational, religious, and social needs of the rapidly increasing Catholic population. Shortly after he was transferred to Detroit as archbishop in 1958, he became one of three American bishops to be appointed to the Doctrinal Commission on Faith and Practice (known as the theological commission) that Pope John XXIII had established to prepare for the Second Vatican Council.

Dearden came to public prominence and had the greatest influence on American Catholicism during and immediately after the Second Vatican Council. He was a bishop, however, before as well as after the council. From 1959 to 1962 Deardon was involved in the preparation of conciliar documents, and during the council he served on a number of conciliar commissions. After the council Deardon was elected a member of the United States Bishops' Commission on the Liturgical Apostolate and became a national episcopal leader in the implementation of English in the liturgy. Pope Paul VI also appointed him a member of the Secretariate for Non-Christian Religions, where he demonstrated the ecumenical concerns of the council. In 1966, when the American bishops established the National Conference of Catholic Bishops, Dearden was elected presiding bishop, a tremendously significant position, because during the years of his presidency (1966–71) the American church experienced a host of inner conflicts that challenged its authority and tradition. His amicability, conservative theological orientation, and progressive openness to reforming conciliar directions combined to make him a capable leader in times of turmoil and upheaval.

Dearden was instrumental in his diocese and in the American church at large in extending to the laity and clergy a participation in church life and in decisions that had not been common prior to the council. In 1976, after two years of local and national preparations, he presided over the American Catholic bishops' bicentennial convention "Call to Action," held in Detroit. Shortly after "Call to Action," Dearden called his own diocesan synod to involve laity and clergy in discussions of local ecclesiastical life.

Changes in the church and society, a lack of adequate financing, and a loss of commitment forced Dearden to close 56 of the 269 Catholic schools in his diocese. Although these closings and a host of other painful changes in his diocese pleased some Catholics, they angered others. Amid these struggles he was criticized by reformers for not being progressive enough and by conservatives for being a radical innovator. In 1980, because of turmoil and age, he resigned from his see.

DREXEL, KATHARINE (27 November 1858, Philadelphia, Pa.–3 March 1955, Cornwells Heights, Pa.). *Career:* Foundress and mother superior, Sisters of the Blessed Sacrament for Indians and Colored People, 1891–1937; retirement, 1937–55.

Katharine Drexel, the daughter and heiress of a Philadelphia banking family, was raised in luxury, receiving the benefits of private tutoring and the ease of life that immense wealth could bring in the second half of the nineteenth century. On a trip to Rome in the late 1880s, she met Pope Leo XIII, who challenged her to become a missionary to serve the needs of African and Native Americans. In 1889 she joined the Sisters of Mercy of Pittsburgh but left in 1891 to found the Sisters of the Blessed Sacrament for Indians and Colored People. Over the next 46 years, as founder and superior of the new religious order, she distributed over 12 million dollars of her inherited wealth building schools, convents, and social agencies among African and Native Americans throughout the United States. She also provided teaching staff for the schools and nursing sisters for the hospitals. In 1925 she helped establish New Orleans's Xavier University, the first and only Catholic university for blacks. Her benevolence also directly benefited the Bureau of Catholic Indian Missions, John Lafarge's Catholic Interracial Council in New York, black parishes throughout the country, the NAACP, and the 1930s campaign for antilynching legislation in the South.

Her strenuous physical activities were curtailed by a 1935 heart attack, which forced her into retirement in 1937. For the remaining 18 years of her life as a resident in the mother house of her order, she became a contemplative devotee of Eucharistic devotion and an exemplar of diligence in meditation and prayer. When she died in 1955 at the age of 97, she left a legacy of 51 convents in 21 states, 49 elementary and 12 high schools, and one national university. She was canonized a saint in October of 2000.

E

ELLIS, JOHN TRACY (30 July 1905, Seneca, Ill.–16 October 1992, Washington, D.C.). *Education:* B.A., St. Viator College, Bourbonnais, Ill., 1927; M.A., Catholic University of America, 1928; Ph.D., 1930; studied at Sulpician Seminary, Washington, D.C., 1934–38; Harvard University, 1941–42. *Career:* Professor, St. Viator College and College of St. Teresa, Winona, Minn., 1930–34; ordained, 1938; professor, Catholic University, 1938–64, 1977–89; editor, the *Catholic Historical Review,* 1941–64; professor, University of San Francisco, 1964–76; president, American Catholic Historical Society and the American Society of Church History, 1969; retired 1989–92.

John Tracy Ellis started his career as a historian of medieval Catholicism but switched to the history of American Catholicism by the late 1930s, when the Catholic University of America needed a historian to replace Peter Guilday. He became not only the chief historian of American Catholicism during the second half of the twentieth century but also an advocate for change within the Catholic Church. He authored more than 20 studies and historiographic aids and published over 400 articles and essays. His own two-volume biography of Cardinal James Gibbons and his general history of American Catholicism demonstrated his fundamental concern with telling the story of American Catholicism honestly, but with a sense of the usefulness of history for the church's present tasks.

Ellis called on historians of Catholicism to give up the apologetic task in their research and writing, be intellectually honest in uncovering the dark as well as the bright sides of the church's history, subject the church's history to objective scrutiny, and realize in the entire process that there is no absolute objectivity in interpreting history. Ellis wanted to integrate the history of American Catholicism with American history in general, and by doing so he hoped to transform public opinion about the church. He stressed repeatedly how the church had contributed to American life and tried to demonstrate, along the lines of other consensus historians, how Catholics had supported mainstream American values.

In a number of histories and essays he called on the church to reform practices he believed were detrimental to its life and development. He was, for example, an advocate of religious liberty and ecumenical sensitivity prior to the Second Vatican Council and wrote essays to demonstrate the strengths and weaknesses of the American tradition in these areas. He also promoted a more active lay role in the church, more widespread participation in the selection of bishops, the vernacular in the liturgy, and the development of intellectual life in Catholic education. His 1955 essay "American Catholics and the Intellectual Life" blasted Catholic failures to produce national leaders and to exercise commanding influence in intellectual circles. That essay stirred up a major national debate in American Catholicism on academic life and promoted a critical examination of the historical and cultural sources of these failures, an examination that continued into the late twentieth century.

Ellis spent 30 of his 87 years within the context of the Second Vatican Council and postconciliar church. He identified those times as revolutionary. The church was indeed undergoing massive changes, but it had experienced such revolutionary transformations in the past, and therefore there should be no place for Catholic pessimism or despair. Ultimately he believed the church would survive the ecclesiastical and social revolution, not because of its own integrity or skill, but because of a divine promise.

ENGLAND, JOHN (23 September 1786, Cork, Ireland–11 April 1842, Charleston, S.C.). *Education:* Studied at St. Patrick's College, Carlow, Ireland, 1802–8. *Career:* Ordained, 1808; pastoral work in Cork, 1808–12; president, College of St. Mary, Cork, 1812–17; editor, the *Religious Repertory* (1810, 1818) and the *Cork Mercantile Chronicle,* 1814–18; pastor of Bandon, Ireland, 1817–20; bishop of Charleston, S.C., 1820–42.

As a young priest in Ireland and as a bishop in the United States, John England represented that side of late eighteenth- and early nineteenth-century Catholicism that was open and accommodating to an Enlightenment mentality that prized reason, democracy, religious liberty, voluntaryism in religion, and separation of church and state. In Ireland as in the United States, moreover, he fostered a wide participation of clergy and laity in ecclesiastical decision making. In Ireland he supported clerical nominations of bishops and simultaneously opposed the state's veto powers over them. In his diocese of Charleston, South Carolina, he established a constitutional form of government that incorporated laity and clergy in the management and supervision of parish and diocesan temporalities. Like many Gallican-influenced clergy and bishops of his day, he emphasized the rights, dignity, and integrity of the national church, pressuring the archbishops of Baltimore to convoke national councils of bishops to provide a forum for an efficient and effective episcopal governance of the American church.

From 1820 until his death in 1842, England became something of a national spokesman and apologist for the compatibility of Catholicism and American democratic traditions. He was frequently called on to preach in Protestant as well as Catholic churches within and outside of his own diocese. He established the first explicitly national Catholic newspaper in 1822, the *U. S. Catholic Miscellany,* to provide information, defend the church, and give Catholics a voice in national affairs. His national prominence was acknowledged in 1826 when he was invited to address the U.S. Congress, the first Catholic clergyman to do so. The Vatican, too, recognized his skills when it appointed him apostolic delegate to Haiti (1833–37) to reestablish diplomatic relations between that country and the Vatican.

In his own diocese England erected a seminary for the education of native American clergy (1825), a philosophical and classical school for Charleston students (1832), and a school for blacks (1835) that was forced to close because of resistance from prominent Charleston city fathers. He also founded the Sisters of Our Lady of Mercy in Charleston (1827), the Brotherhood of San Marino, the first Catholic society for workingmen in the United States, and an Anti-Duelling Society, and edited catechisms and prepared a new edition of the Missal. Although he considered slavery personally repugnant, he defended the institution itself as compatible with Scripture and the Christian tradition. His ideological support of slavery and his view of the compatibility of Catholicism and American democracy won him many friends in Charleston but also demonstrated clearly the difficulties inherent in his accommodationist stance toward the world in which he lived.

G

GIBBONS, JAMES (23 July 1834, Baltimore, Md.–24 March 1921, Baltimore, Md.). *Education:* Studied at St. Charles College (Md.), 1855; St. Mary's Seminary, Baltimore, 1857–61. *Career:* Ordained, 1861; pastoral work in Maryland, 1861–68; vicar apostolic of North Carolina, 1868–72; bishop of Richmond, 1872–77; coadjutor archbishop of Baltimore, 1877; archbishop of Baltimore, 1877–1921; cardinal, 1886–1921.

Born in Baltimore the son of Irish immigrants, James Gibbons moved to Ireland with his family in 1837, and in 1853, after his father's death, returned to the United States, where they took up residence in New Orleans. After two years as a grocery clerk James returned to Maryland, where he matriculated at St. Charles College and St. Mary's Seminary. Ordained in 1861, he began serving various parishes in the Baltimore area, volunteered as a chaplain to Union troops at Forts McHenry and Marshall during the Civil War, and in 1865 became Archbishop Martin John Spalding's secretary. As assistant chancellor of Baltimore he helped prepare the agenda for the Second Plenary Council of Baltimore (1866). His affability, practicality, and ecclesiastical experience made him a prime candidate for the episcopal office in the post–Civil War period. At the age of 34 he was made the vicar apostolic of North Carolina and became one of the youngest bishops to participate at the First Vatican Council (1869–70).

In 1872 he was made bishop of Richmond, and while there he published *The Faith of Our Fathers* (1876), an introduction to Catholic faith and practice that reflected his missionary experiences among non-Catholics in Virginia and North Carolina. The text was a widely distributed popular and irenic apologetical tract that demonstrated a Catholic acceptance of foundational American institutions and principles.

In 1877 he was appointed archbishop of Baltimore, an office he served for the next 44 years. Throughout these years he became the leading Catholic churchman in the country. In 1884, he was appointed the apostolic delegate to the Third Plenary Council of Baltimore, and after that time he was the symbol of Catholicism in the United States, mediating between Catholic and American values. Although he was known for his "masterly inactivity" in administering national ecclesiastical interests, he was considered a moderate Americanist, fighting against a Vatican condemnation of the Knights of Labor, warding off an official public condemnation of Henry George's works, supporting the establishment of the Catholic University of America, and articulating the value of the American form of religious liberty before Roman audiences.

During the 1890s he sided with the Americanist bishops but was a voice of ecclesiastical moderation, trying to preserve unity among the Americanist and anti-Americanist bishops. When Pope Leo XIII condemned Americanism in 1899, Gibbons argued that no such heresy in fact existed in the United States. In the early twentieth century he was instrumental in establishing the Maryknoll missionaries, preserving the Catholic University from financial failure, and erecting the National Catholic War Council. No other Catholic bishop in the United States during his episcopacy had as much influence on national Catholic life.

H

HECKER, ISAAC THOMAS (18 December 1819, New York, N.Y.–22 December 1888, New York, N.Y.). *Education:* Studied at Redemptorist novitiate, St. Trond, Belgium, 1845–46; Redemptorist training, Witten, the Netherlands, 1846–47; training at Clapham, London, England, 1848–49. *Career:* Ordained, 1849; pastoral work in England, 1849–51; Redemptorist missionary in United States, 1851–57; founder and superior, Congregation of Missionary Priests of St. Paul the Apostle, 1858–88.

In the course of his 45 years as a Catholic, Isaac Thomas Hecker had a significant impact on American Catholic life and thought. After his death, his spiritual legacy continued in the religious order he founded, and his intellectual influence continued in his late nineteenth-century Americanist heirs. He converted to Catholicism in 1844 at the age of 25, and in 1845 became a Redemptorist. After education for the priesthood in Europe he returned to the United States in 1851 to conduct parish missions for non-Catholics as well as Catholics along the East Coast. These missionary experiences made Hecker and other American Redemptorists believe that the German Redemptorists in the United States should establish a branch of the order that would be sensitive to American culture and attractive to young Americans who could carry on an American-style evangelization program among non-Catholics. In 1857 he took this idea to Rome, where he and his American Redemptorist companions were dismissed from the order. Pope Pius IX did, however, allow Hecker and the other former American Redemptorists to establish in 1858 the Congregation of Missionary Priests of St. Paul the Apostle (i.e., Paulists), whose primary mission was the evangelization and conversion of non-Catholics in the United States.

Hecker conducted numerous parish missions throughout the country after 1858, became a theological consultant and adviser to archbishop Martin John Spalding at the Second Plenary Council of Baltimore (1866) and the First Vatican Council (1869–70), published the *Catholic World* (1865–) as a journal of religious thought and opinion, and established the Catholic Publication Society (1866) to distribute to non-Catholics as well as Catholics low-cost Catholic apologetical and spiritual tracts. Throughout the post–Civil War period, he focused his attention and much of his writing on the themes of the compatibility of *The Church and the Age* (1887), the title of an anthology of his significant writings.

Influenced by post-Kantian idealism, Hecker became one of the foremost American Catholic representatives of the Romantic mood in American religion. His concentration on the correlation of the subjective search for meaning and the objective response in the church's sacramental and spiritual tradition helped him develop a new apologetic for Catholicism, one sensitive to the benefits of American cultural and political values. After his death in 1888, his views became the subject of an international ecclesiastical controversy that ended when Pope Leo XIII's encyclical *Testem Benevolentiae* (1899) condemned Americanism as a complex of heretical ideas that some conservative European Catholics had exaggeratedly identified with Hecker.

HIGGINS, GEORGE G. (21 January 1916, Chicago, Ill.–1 May 2002, Chicago, Ill.). *Education:* St. Mary of the Lake Seminary in Mundelein, Ill., 1934–40; M.A. Catholic University of America, 1942; Ph.D., Catholic University of America, 1944. *Career:* Ordained a priest, 1940; staff member, National Catholic Welfare Conference, 1944–80; director, Social Action Department (NCWC), 1954–67; adviser, Preparatory Commission on the Lay Apostolate, Second Vatican Council, 1962–65; retired, 1980–2002.

Higgins was known primarily as the chief "labor priest" in the American Catholic Church from the late 1940s until his death. A champion and promoter of Catholic social thought, Higgins was the point man for the Catholic Church's relations with labor unions and the struggle for human rights and economic justice for all. From his position as director of the Social Action Department of the NCCB/USCC (successor to the NCWC), he not only supported César Chávez and his farm workers movement in the 1960s and beyond, but also employees in Catholic hospitals that resisted union organizations, auto workers, and other lower- and middle-class laborers in the United States. As an adviser to the American bishops and a promoter of their statements on labor and economic justice, he became in the twentieth century, after John A. Ryan, the foremost Catholic advocate of a living wage for laboring families. While promoting the dignity of work, he also lectured in the Catholic University of America's School of Social Science and Department of Theology, wrote a vast number of book reviews, and from 1945 to 2002, prepared a weekly syndicated column, titled "The Yardstick," on international as well as national issues of justice and peace.

In addition to being a primary advocate for labor, Higgins was an active member of several national committees: the NCCB/USCC's Committee on Catholic-Jewish Relations, the Public Review Board, the United Auto Workers of America, American Arbitration Association, the Leadership Conference on Civil Rights, and the United States Delegation to the Belgrade Conference on Human Rights. In 2000, because of the multiple services he performed for laborers and human rights, President Bill Clinton presented him with the Presidential Medal of Freedom. He died on 1 May 2002, the feast of St. Joseph the Worker.

HUGHES, JOHN JOSEPH (24 June 1797, Annaloghan, County Tyrone, Ireland–3 January 1864, New York, N.Y.). *Education:* Studied at Mount St. Mary's College and Seminary (Md.), 1819–26. *Career:* Ordained, 1826; pastor, St. Joseph's Church, Philadelphia, 1827–32; pastor, St. John's Church, Philadelphia, 1832–37; coadjutor bishop of New York, 1838–42; bishop of New York, 1842–50; archbishop of New York, 1850–64.

John Hughes, fourth bishop of New York, was from the beginning of his clerical career in Philadelphia a combative apostle for Catholic doctrines, practices, and institutions. During the 26 years (1838–64) he was bishop of New York, he was perhaps the most visible symbol of Catholicism in the United States. In New York he worked to mold Irish and German immigrants into one Catholic body and defended their rights to exist as Catholics in a rapidly changing American society. His public struggles against the New York lay trustees, the Common School Society of New York, and the "Protestant Crusade" reinforced his authority in the immigrant Catholic community and enabled him to foster an ethnocentric form of Catholicism that was sharply distinguished from the dominant American Protestant community. He resisted Americanizing efforts, stood firm in what he considered the unchanging Catholic tradition, and wanted to Catholicize America. This stance made Hughes severely critical of a number of American values, especially the developing capitalistic system. For him, Protestantism was the root of all contemporary ills; the only solution to present problems, therefore, was to return to the unified Christendom of Pre-Reformation days.

Hughes became a forceful advocate of Catholic schools, giving diocesan priority to school, over church, construction. He also established Fordham College and St. Joseph's Seminary in 1841 and helped found the North American College in Rome in 1859. In 1856 he started construction on St. Patrick's, which was to be the new Cathedral of New York, a church symbolic of the growing wealth and status of the Catholic community in that city.

Hughes had a quasi-despotic control over local ecclesiastical affairs, was a vigorous opponent of lay trusteeism, and was quick-tempered in response to any internal lay or clerical opposition to his rule; but his own forcefulness, ability to excite and control crowds, popularity among the Irish people, and establishment of numerous institutions to serve the immigrants' material, educational, and social needs won him the respect of numerous politicians and the elite in American society, even when they disagreed with his religious perspectives and feared his authoritarian ways. In 1847, in response to the invitation of 54 members of the U.S. Congress, Hughes preached a sermon on "Christianity, the Only Source of Moral, Social, and Political Regeneration" before the Congress. In the midst of the Civil War, President Lincoln sent him on a goodwill mission to Europe to win favor for the Union.

I

IRELAND, JOHN (11 September 1838, Burnchurch, County Kilkenny, Ireland–25 September 1918, St. Paul, Minn.). *Education:* Studied at preparatory seminary, Merimieux, France, 1853–57; Marist seminary, Montbel, France, 1857–61. *Career:* Ordained, 1861; pastoral work, St. Paul, 1861–75; coadjutor bishop of St. Paul, 1875; bishop of St. Paul, 1884–88; archbishop of St. Paul, 1888–1918.

John Ireland, first archbishop of St. Paul, became known in the American hierarchy as the "consecrated blizzard of the Northwest." His zealous advocacy of American values and attempts to get the Catholic Church to assimilate those values made him the chief American Catholic spokesman for harmony between the church and the optimistic Gilded Age.

For 43 years, as bishop and first archbishop of St. Paul, Ireland became a dynamo of institutional Catholicism in the middle Northwest. He built or helped build the College of St. Thomas (1885), St. Thomas Seminary (1894), St. Catherine's College (1905), the Cathedral of St. Paul (1915), and the Basilica of St. Mary (1915). These institutions symbolized his drive to see the development of an educated Catholic elite whose presence in the halls of political and economic power would make a Catholic difference in American society.

Ireland became a national figure of Catholic life because he was an eloquent and gifted orator and because he reflected the progressive and optimistic views of his age. His call for Americanization of the immigrants, Catholic cooperation with the public schools, the establishment of a Catholic University, and his public advocacy of these causes in the press, pulpit, and papal courts made his enemies suspect him of trying to create a schismatic church, one democratic in structure and reductionistic in theology. The Catholic national and international debates over Americanism in the 1890s culminated in the papal condemnation of 1899, ending, for all practical purposes, Ireland's effective ministry at the national level. Thereafter he focused his attention on building the ecclesiastical institutions of his own diocese.

J

JOGUES, ISAAC (10 January 1607, Orléans, France–18 October 1646, Mohawk territory, now Auriesville, N.Y.). *Education:* Jesuit training at Rouen, 1624–46, La Flèche, 1626–29, and Paris, France, 1633–36. *Career:* Grammar instructor at Rouen, 1629–33; ordained, 1636; missionary among Hurons and Iroquois, 1636–46.

At the age of 29, Isaac Jogues, a newly ordained Jesuit priest, emigrated from France to Canada to fulfill his desire to be a missionary among the Native Americans. Like many other young seventeenth-century French Jesuits, he was drawn to the missions. Very conscious of Tertullian's dictum that "the blood of martyrs is the seed of Christianity," the young Jesuits desired to give witness to the Gospel and plant the church among the Native Americans.

For 10 years Jogues traveled throughout the Great Lakes region from Quebec to Sault Ste. Marie and lived among the Hurons and Iroquois, evangelizing and baptizing them. During his first five years in Canada (1636–41) he lived in Jesuit missions and worked among the Hurons in the territory between Montreal and Lake Superior. In 1641, he explored as far as Sault Ste. Marie, giving the place its name. During a 1642 trip back to Jesuit headquarters in Quebec, Jogues, a lay assistant, René Goupil, and a few Hurons were captured by the Mohawks, an Iroquois tribe, and taken to central upstate New York, where Goupil and some of the Huron Christians were killed; Jogues was mutilated and made a slave of the tribe. For about nine months he lived among his captors, evangelizing and baptizing over 60 children, many of whom died. In 1643, with assistance from the Dutch at Fort Orange (Albany, N.Y.), Jogues escaped and was taken to New Amsterdam and eventually back to France.

Jogues returned to Canada in 1644 and, in 1645, became the first Jesuit to reside among the Mohawks, one of whom tomahawked him to death on 18 October 1646. The story of Jogues's martyrdom, told repeatedly in France, reaffirmed the missionary zeal there and continued to be a significant part of the American Catholic consciousness and imagination, particularly in the first half of the twentieth century. In 1925 Jogues was beatified and in 1930 canonized, giving papal confirmation to a cult that began in the seventeenth century.

K

KEANE, JOHN (12 September 1839, Ballyshannon, County Donegal, Ireland–22 June 1918, Dubuque, Iowa). *Education:* Studied at Calvert Hall, Baltimore, Md., 1856; St. Charles College (Md.), 1862; St. Mary's Seminary, Baltimore, Md., 1862–66. *Career:* Ordained, 1866; pastor, St. Patrick's Church, Washington, D.C., 1866–78; bishop of Richmond, Va., 1878–88; rector, Catholic University of America, 1889–96; titular archbishop of Damascus and member of Propaganda, Rome, 1897–1900; archbishop of Dubuque, Iowa, 1900–1911; retirement, 1911–18.

As a young priest, Keane was especially interested in the temperance movement, education, and the formation of young adults—becoming a leader in the formation of the Catholic Total Abstinence Union (1872) and the Catholic Young Men's National Union (1875). As bishop of Richmond he continued the interests of his early priesthood, organized the Confraternity of the Servants of the Holy Ghost, and wrote *A Sodality Manual for the Use of the Servants of the Holy Ghost* (1880) to foster devotion to the Holy Spirit. In 1884 he attended the Third Plenary Council of Baltimore, wrote the council's pastoral, and was appointed to a committee established to found the Catholic University of America.

In 1886, on behalf of the American bishops, he went to Rome to work out arrangements for the establishment of the Catholic University, and while there he, together with Archbishops John Ireland and James Gibbons, fought against the Abbelen memorial and the condemnation of the Knights of Labor and Henry George's published works. That trip to Rome helped transform his consciousness about the church in the United States, and thereafter he was more clearly identified as one of the leading Americanists. In 1889 he was appointed the first rector of the Catholic University of America, a position that allowed him to appoint the faculty and to act as spokesman for the cause of Catholic higher education in the United States.

As a bishop and educator, Keane was ecumenically sensitive, attending and speaking at the World's Parliament of Religions and the World's Columbian Congress in Chicago in 1893, and giving the Dudlean lecture at Harvard. Because of his Americanist activities, however, Pope Leo XIII removed him as rector of the Catholic University in 1896 but gave him a dignified exodus by making him a titular archbishop and assigning him to a consultant position in Rome. After the papal encyclical condemning Americanism in 1899, Keane was appointed archbishop of Dubuque, where he continued to carry out his progressive causes, but failing health caused him to resign his position in 1911.

KENRICK, FRANCIS PATRICK (3 December 1796, Dublin, Ireland–8 July 1863, Baltimore, Md.). *Education:* Studied at Urban College of the Propaganda, Rome, 1814–21. *Career:* Ordained, 1821; theology teacher, St. Thomas Seminary, Bardstown, Ky., 1821–30; coadjutor bishop of Philadelphia, 1830–42; bishop of Philadelphia, 1842–51; archbishop of Baltimore, 1851–63.

Kenrick rose to national prominence in 1830 after he was appointed bishop of Philadelphia. As bishop he brought about a major reformation in Philadelphia Catholicism that included, in addition to his strong sense of episcopal authority, the establishment of the St. Charles Borromeo Seminary (1832) and the *Catholic Herald* (1833). He also supported the founding of the Augustinian Villanova College (1842) and the Jesuit St. Joseph's College (1851). He fought against the so-called Philadelphia Bible Riots of 1844 and sought to establish a strong Catholic school system to counter Nativism in the public schools. Although a forceful and authoritarian reforming bishop, after the model of St. Charles Borromeo, Kenrick was retiring and scholarly. In the late 1830s and early 1840s he published seven volumes of his dogmatic and moral theology for use in American seminaries and a number of apologetic tracts (including his major work on the Roman primacy), and began a new English translation of the Bible. He was the most scholarly and productive of the antebellum bishops.

As archbishop of Baltimore, Kenrick organized and presided over the first Plenary Council of Baltimore (1852), helped promote the establishment of the North American College in Rome (1859), struggled against a virulent Nativist Maryland antipopery campaign in the 1850s, and at the beginning of the Civil War tried to remain politically neutral when the sentiment of a great majority of his flock sided with the South. As the chief moral theologian in the country, Kenrick had held that "under certain protective conditions" the institution of slavery was moral, but he also believed that loyalty to the nation took precedence over loyalty to the state. He died in Baltimore, four days after the Battle of Gettysburg.

KENRICK, PETER RICHARD (17 August 1806, Dublin, Ireland–4 March 1896, St. Louis, Mo.). *Education:* Studied at St. Patrick's College and Seminary, Maynooth, Ireland, 1827–32. *Career:* Ordained, 1832; chaplain, Carmelite Convent, Dublin, 1832; pastoral work, diocese of Philadelphia, 1833–41; coadjutor bishop of St. Louis, 1841–43; bishop of St. Louis, 1843–47; archbishop of St. Louis, 1847–95; retired, 1895–96.

During his long tenure as bishop and archbishop of St. Louis, Kenrick helped to establish and build up numerous institutions to serve the growing number of

German and Irish Catholic immigrants who rushed into the city and diocese. In the early 1840s, his diocese embraced the states of Missouri and Arkansas, the western portion of Illinois, the territories now constituting Kansas, Nebraska, and Oklahoma, and a number of Indian missions in the territory east of the Rocky Mountains. The diocese had about 100,000 Catholics, 65 churches, and 74 priests. Although the geographic size of his archdiocese was reduced substantially by the end of his episcopacy, it had experienced dramatic growth. As metropolitan, he was also instrumental in developing Catholic dioceses and institutions throughout the Midwest, from Wisconsin on the north to Alabama on the south and Santa Fe on the west.

Kenrick was influenced in his early Irish education by a Gallican approach to ecclesiology that emphasized the significance and quasi-autonomy of the national church. In the United States he favored those policies that demonstrated the American character of the Catholic Church and participated actively in the three national Plenary Episcopal Councils of Baltimore in 1852, 1866, and 1884, which set the canonical standards and governing policies for the church. Despite his allegiance to his adopted country, however, he did not accept American policies that he believed were contrary to his people's interests. During the Civil War he refused to fly the U.S flag above the cathedral, and after the war, he refused to abide by the Drake Constitution, which would have required clergymen to swear a special oath of loyalty.

In 1869 and 1870 Kenrick took an active role at the First Vatican Council, where he became the leading American opponent of the definition of papal infallibility, arguing in his *Concio in Concilio Vaticano habenda et non habita* (1870) that the teaching of papal infallibility was a theological opinion, not a definable doctrine, because the evidence from Scripture and tradition was either silent on the issue or opposed to it. Although he eventually accepted the council's definition of papal infallibility, he never repudiated the arguments of his *Concio,* and he refused to make any public statements on his position after returning.

KINO, EUSEBIO FRANCISCO (1 August 1645, Segno, Italy–15 March 1711, Magdalena, Mexico, later Ariz.). *Education:* Entered Jesuit novitiate, Upper German Province, 1665; studied at Freiburg, Ingolstadt, and Munich, Germany, 1665–70; studied theology at Ingolstadt, 1673–77. *Career:* Instructor in grammar, Innsbruck, Austria, 1670–73; missionary in Mexico, 1681–83; missionary and cartographer, Atondo expedition, lower Calif., 1683–85; missionary, Pimeria Alta, Mexico, 1687–1711.

Eusebio Kino, S.J., was the first permanent evangelist and founder of missions among the Pima Indians of northern Mexico and what is now southern Arizona. After finishing a very promising Jesuit education in which he became competent in mathematics and cartography, Eusebio decided to devote his life to the Jesuit missions. He joined the Spanish Jesuits and was sent to Mexico to work among the Native Americans. From 1683 to 1685 he explored lower California, set up mission stations, and tried to evangelize the Indians there, buta drought forced him and the other Jesuits and Spaniards who had joined the exploration to withdraw to Mexico.

In 1687, two years after he left lower California, he was sent to evangelize the Pima Indians of northern Mexico, establishing the first mission at Nuestra Señora de los Dolores, which became the center of missionary activities that extended as far north as the Gila and Colorado rivers. For the next 24 years, he explored the area, made maps and sent them to Mexico City and Spain, discovered that California was not an island, and brought some relative material prosperity to the missions by raising cattle, planting wheat, and providing for relative peace among the warring Indian tribes and Spanish soldiers. Like Spanish missionaries throughout the seventeenth century, he tried to convert the Indians to Christianity by bringing them the benefits of a Spanish culture that valued a sedentary life of steady work in agriculture and/or cattle raising. Throughout his 24 years of missionary service, Eusebio baptized an estimated 4,500 Pima Indians, and by the time he died, he had established seven missions in the area, serving about 2,000 Christianized Indians.

L

LAMY, JEAN BAPTISTE (11 October 1814, Lempdes, France–13 February 1888, Santa Fe, N. Mex.). *Education:* Studied at Royal College, Petite Seminary, and Grand Seminary, Clermont-Montferrand, France, ?–1838. *Career:* Ordained, 1838; assistant pastor, Chapre, France, 1838–39; missionary priest in Ohio and Ky., 1839–50; vicar apostolic of N. Mex., 1850–53; bishop of Santa Fe, 1853–75; archbishop of Santa Fe, 1875–85; retirement 1885–88.

Jean Baptiste Lamy's life as bishop and archbishop of the missionary frontier diocese of Santa Fe became the subject of Willa Cather's best-selling *Death Comes for the Archbishop* (1927). In 1850, after the 1848 Treaty of Guadalupe Hidalgo, Lamy was made the vicar apostolic of Santa Fe, a vicariate that had previously been under the ecclesiastical jurisdiction of the Mexican diocese of Durango. The Santa Fe vicariate included not only New Mexico, but also large parts of Arizona, Nevada, Utah, California, and Colorado. Over the course of the next 35 years, Lamy would help to establish Catholic institutions throughout this large region of the country. His diocese included numerous Native Americans, Hispanics, new immigrants from Ireland and Germany, and a growing number of Protestant American soldiers and politicians who were sent to New Mexico to govern the new American territory and establish the railway and commercial networks that would eventually tie Santa Fe to the East and West coasts. Lamy came into a territory that had about 250 years of Spanish and Mexican Catholic history. His French education and American pastoral experience had not prepared him for the rugged frontier Hispanic culture and folk Catholicism that he met in Santa Fe, nor were the few leading Spanish-speaking priests and people ready to welcome his authority and control after years of ecclesiastical life without episcopal supervision and canonical discipline. His early years in Santa Fe were therefore spent in establishing his authority, canonical discipline, and American-style ecclesiastical institutions for education, social services, and religious ministry. Lamy's importation of French émigré clergy and women religious only helped to increase the clash of cultures on the frontier during his early years.

To help fortify the substructure of Catholic life in the diocese, Lamy secured the assistance of the Sisters of Loretto for Catholic schooling (1852), the Sisters of Charity (1865), who built the first hospital and orphanage west of the Pecos River, the Christian Brothers (1859), and the Society of Jesus (1867), all of whom contributed to his educational and missionary efforts. His public support for spiritual and material developments in the region earned him the respect of Protestants and Jews alike. Their contributions, too, helped to fund the building of the Cathedral in Santa Fe (started in 1869). His rapport with Americans and with the American government, however, remained a continuing irritation and source of contention for those Hispanic Catholics who were pushed aside because of the railway culture that took over the territory after 1850.

LANGE, MARY ELIZABETH (? 1784, Santo Domingo, Haiti–3 February 1882, Baltimore, Md.). *Career:* Founding mother superior, Oblate Sisters of Providence, Baltimore, 1829–32.

Born in what is now the Dominican Republic, Mary Elizabeth Lange and her family moved to Cuba sometime during or after the late eighteenth-century Haitian revolution, and about 1812 they emigrated to the United States. Shortly after their arrival, Elizabeth and two other Haitian women began teaching Haitian children in the lower chapel of St. Mary's Seminary in Baltimore. In 1829 Father Nicholas Joubert, an émigré priest from Santo Domingo, encouraged and helped these women to establish in Baltimore the Oblate Sisters of Providence, the first black order of women religious in the United States. The order received papal approval in 1831, and Mother Mary Elizabeth Lange became the first superior of the small community of three blacks. The primary aim of the new order was to provide Christian education for black children. By 1834, the small community had grown to 12 members, three of whom had been slaves; by the time of Mother Elizabeth's death, the order had grown to about 50. Throughout her life, the sisters established numerous missions and schools in Baltimore and other cities. These schools offered slaves and other black girls courses in "refined and useful education," but many of these schools lasted for only a few years before they were closed because of financial hardship. The sisters also served the sick and dying in the Baltimore community repeatedly during times of cholera epidemics, set up orphanages, and led a communal life of prayer as well as service. In 1991, the Archdiocese of Baltimore initiated procedures for Mother Elizabeth's beatification.

LUCEY, ROBERT EMMET (16 March 1891, Los Angeles, Calif.–1 August 1977, San Antonio, Tex.). *Education:* Studied at St. Vincent's College, Los Angeles, 1905–7; St. Patrick's Seminary, Menlo Park, Calif., 1907–12; S.T.D., North American College, Rome, 1916. *Career:* Ordained, 1916; pastoral work, Diocese of Los Angeles, 1916–34; bishop, Amarillo, Tex., 1934–41; archbishop, San Antonio, 1941–69; retired, 1969–77.

As archbishop of San Antonio, Robert Lucey was a leading social activist in twentieth-century American Catholicism. During World War II and throughout the Truman and Eisenhower administrations, he supported the Allies, was a charter member of the Committee to Defend America, maintained his New Deal pro-labor views, insisted that the church hire only union workers, and became an early and ardent advocate of federal labor regulation and protection of Mexican American migrant farm workers (periodically supporting striking farm workers). Prior to *Brown v. Board of Education* (1954), moreover, he began to integrate the Catholic schools in San Antonio.

Throughout his clerical career he was a promoter of the Confraternity of Christian Doctrine (CCD), believing, as he said at the Second Vatican Council, that many if not most Christians in contemporary society did not know the "eternal truths and the doctrines necessary for salvation." The function of CCD, as organized in the United States, was to use the laity as cells of learning to impart the knowledge and love of Christ. Without a thorough Christian formation program, the work for justice and peace would, he believed, be ineffective and inert.

After returning from the Second Vatican Council in 1965, he became a strong supporter of fellow Texan Lyndon B. Johnson's war on poverty and Vietnam War, becoming a member of the President's National Advisory Council for the war on poverty. Like many other preconciliar bishops, he came into bitter conflict with some of his own priests and laity over ecclesiastical authority and the direction of postconciliar reforms. In 1969, because of pressure from his own younger priests and the apostolic delegate, he resigned his archepiscopal see and retired in San Antonio.

M

MARQUETTE, JACQUES (1 June 1637, Laon, France–18 May 1675, near Ludington, Mich.). *Education:* Entered Jesuit novitiate, Nancy, France, 1654; studied philosophy at Pont-à-Monsson, France, 1657–59; studied Algonkian at Trois Rivières, Canada, 1666–68. *Career:* Ordained, 1665; taught in Jesuit schools in France at Auxerre, 1656–57, Reims, 1659–61, Charleville, 1661–63, Langres, 1663–64, and Pont-à-Monsson, 1664–65; missionary to various North American Indian tribes, 1669–75.

In 1666, after 12 years of formation and teaching in Jesuit schools, the newly ordained Marquette was sent to Trois Rivières in Canada, where he learned the Algonkian language and culture for two years before being sent to Sault Ste. Marie to live with and evangelize the Indian tribes there. After 18 months at Sault Ste. Marie, he moved to the Jesuit mission, La Pointe du Sainte Esprit, on Lake Superior near present-day Ashland, Wisconsin. Because of threats of invasion from the western Dakota Sioux tribes and the belief that his evangelical work was ineffective, Marquette abandoned the mission in 1671 and moved the Huron tribes to the Sault Ste. Marie region, where he established a new mission, St. Ignace, on Mackinac Island. Two years later he joined the Canadian Louis Jolliet and explored the Mississippi River as far as the Arkansas River, determining that the Mississippi flowed into the Gulf of Mexico. Marquette evangelized the Illinois Indians in 1674 but became ill and died on a return trip to St. Ignace in 1675 at the age of 38.

In 1905, after much controversy in Wisconsin, a statue of Marquette, representing the state, was placed in the Washington, D.C., Hall of Statues.

MAURIN, ARISTIDE PETER (9 May 1877, Outlet, France–15 May 1949, Newburgh, N.Y.). *Career:* Novice in the Christian Brothers, Paris, 1893–1903; promoter of the Sillonist social reform in France, 1903–9; homesteader and laborer in Canada and the United States, 1909–33; writer and lecturer for the *Catholic Worker,* 1933–49.

In 1933, Peter Maurin and Dorothy Day cofounded the Catholic Worker Movement and published the *Catholic Worker,* a periodical dedicated to promoting Catholic social teachings. Maurin propagated his ideas of social justice through "Easy Essays," a column in the *Catholic Worker,* and through the example of his simple and unostentatious life of charitable service. Although he was not an organizer, he provided the ideas and inspiration for the establishment of houses of hospitality, farming communes, spiritual retreats, protest movements, and round-table discussions. His decentralized "Christian communism" influenced Dorothy Day and a host of other young Catholics, who spearheaded a number of radical peace and justice movements in the 1930s and 1940s. When he died in 1949, he owned nothing and was buried in the secondhand clothing that demonstrated his view that a simple life was a Christian life.

McCLOSKEY, JOHN (10 March 1810, Brooklyn, N.Y.–10 October 1885, New York, N.Y.). *Education:* Studied at Mount St. Mary's College and Seminary, Emmitsburg, Md., 1822–34; Urban College of Propaganda, Rome, 1835–37. *Career:* Ordained, 1834; pastoral work in Diocese of New York, 1834, 1837–41; president, St. John's College (Fordham), 1841–42; rector, St. Joseph's Seminary, 1842–43; coadjutor bishop of New York, 1844–47; bishop of Albany, N.Y., 1847–64; archbishop of New York, 1864–85; cardinal, 1875–85.

John McCloskey was the first American Catholic to be created a cardinal, a dignity that symbolized Rome's acknowledgment of the growing importance and maturity of the American Catholic Church in general and of the Diocese of New York in particular. In 1864 he became the archbishop of New York, and in 1869 and 1870 he attended the First Vatican Council, where he initially opposed the definition of papal infallibility as inexpedient. McCloskey's 75 years in New York witnessed a tremendous transformation of Catholicism from a tiny minority of despised immigrants to a relatively prosperous body. The completion of St. Patrick's Cathedral on Fifth Avenue in 1879 (a project started under Bishop Hughes in 1858) was only one symbol of immigrant growth, generosity, ingenuity, and religious dedication. Catholicism in New York, moreover, passed from the aggressive and energetic internal and external antebellum battles of Bishop Hughes to the calm leadership of Archbishop McCloskey, who governed the diocese with a paternalism that provided for liberty and diversity as well as authority and unity. McCloskey's leadership provided a transition between the antebellum and late nineteenth-century ecclesiastical and civil controversies.

McGLYNN, EDWARD (27 September 1837, New York, N.Y.–7 January 1900, Newburgh, N.Y.). *Education:* S.T.D., Urban College of Propaganda, Rome, 1860. *Career:* Assistant pastor, St. Joseph's parish, New York, 1860–66; pastor, St. Stephen's parish, New York, 1866–86; president, Anti-Poverty Society, New York, 1887–92; pastor, St. Mary's parish, Newburgh, N.Y., 1894–1900.

McGlynn was a controversial activist New York City pastor. As a young priest he supported public schools for Catholics, became a member of the Accademie (a local group of former Roman students who were advocating internal reforms in the Catholic Church and a more open and accommodating stance toward American society), and protested against society's injustices toward the poor and unemployed.

In 1886, McGlynn became the center of an ecclesiastical and political controversy when he stumped for Henry George, who was running for mayor of New York and whose *Progress and Poverty* (1879) had awakened McGlynn and other social reformers such as pastor Walter Rauschenbusch to the possibilities of George's single-tax proposal. Like George, McGlynn believed that the causes of poverty were systemic and specifically related to exploitation in land ownership. Social and economic reforms like the single tax, they became convinced, were fundamental structural remedies for current economic and social injustices. A single tax on the rent of land would fairly distribute fiscal responsibility and provide economic opportunities for American workers.

In July 1886, in the midst of a controversial mayoral campaign, Archbishop Michael Corrigan suspended McGlynn from the priesthood because he violated canonical legislation by becoming involved in partisan politics. In 1887, Rome excommunicated him for ecclesiastical disobedience. From 1887 to 1892, as founder and president of the New York Anti-Poverty Society, McGlynn continued to speak out on social reforms, drawing a large following of Catholics from his former parish, St. Stephen's, to his Sunday evening talks at Cooper Union. McGlynn was reinstated in the church and priesthood in 1892, after theologians at the Catholic University of America judged his social philosophy to be in conformity with, or at least not opposed to, the social teaching in Pope Leo's *Rerum Novarum* (1891).

McQUAID, BERNARD J. (15 December 1823, New York, N.Y–18 January 1909, Rochester, N.Y.). *Education:* Studied at Chambley College, Montreal, 1839–43; St. Joseph's Seminary, Fordham, N.Y., 1843–48. *Career:* Rector, St. Vincent's Church, Madison, N.J., 1848–53; rector, St. Patrick's Cathedral, Newark, N.J., 1853–68; president, Seton Hall College, 1857, 1859–68; bishop of Rochester, N.Y., 1868–1909.

McQuaid was a forceful advocate of the construction of separate Catholic institutions, especially schools. Receiving his early education and early clerical experience under the watchful eye and forceful government of Bishop John Hughes, McQuaid developed an aggressive countercultural attitude toward American society—one that perceived the Catholic Church as the ship of religious and social stability and protection for immigrants who were tossed about in a sea of religious diversity and civil and social hostility. Although he was a native-born American, he saw himself very much like Hughes, as the protector of poor and oppressed immigrants who needed education and religious formation to be productive Americans.

As first bishop of Rochester, New York, he became a builder of Catholic educational institutions. He brought the Sisters of St. Joseph and other women religious to his diocese to teach, and he insisted that Catholics send their children to parochial schools. He also founded in Rochester: St. Andrew's Preparatory Seminary (1870), St. Bernard's Seminary (1891), a Catholic Summer Institute (1896) for training teachers and laity in general, the Nazareth Normal School (1898), and a Young Men's Catholic Institute. Although he was a strong advocate of ecclesiastical authority, he opposed the doctrine of papal infallibility during the First Vatican Council (1869–70) but affirmed it once it was promulgated as a Catholic dogma.

In the period after the Third Council of Baltimore (1884) he became allied with New York's Archbishop Michael Corrigan against the Americanist bishops. As one of the major leaders of late nineteenth-century conservative Catholicism, he opposed the founding of the Catholic University of America, all secret societies, the appointment of a Roman apostolic delegate, Archbishop Ireland's Faribault-Stillwater plan, and the ecumenical activities of Bishop John Joseph Keane. Throughout his career, he remained a consistent conservative and an effective builder of immigrant Catholic institutions.

MERTON, THOMAS (31 January 1915, Prades, France–10 December 1968, Bangkok, Thailand). *Education:* Studied at Cambridge University, 1933–34; B.A., Columbia University, 1938; M.A., 1939. *Career:* Instructor in English, St. Bonaventure College, 1940–41; member, Reformed Cistercians of the Strict Observance (Trappists), 1941–68; master of students, 1951–55; master of novices, 1955–65.

Like Isaac Hecker, Thomas Merton was a restless seeker throughout his life, searching for spiritual peace, social justice, and unity among the religions of the world. He was received into the Catholic Church in 1938. After graduating from Columbia University he taught literature at St. Bonaventure's College, and during his year of teaching he visited Catherine de Hueck's Friendship House in Harlem. He found no personal satisfaction, however, either in teaching or work for social justice, although he saw the need and benefit of both. Driven by a need for contemplation, silence, and spiritual meaning, he entered a Trappist monastery at Gethsemani, near Bardstown, Kentucky, in 1941, where he spent the next 27 years in contemplative prayer, writing 50 books and several hundred articles about the interdependence of contemplation and action in the modern world, and giving spiritual advice to Catholics and others who came to the monastery for retreats. In 1948 he published his spiritual autobiography, *The Seven Storey Mountain,* which became a best-seller, resonating as it did with a yearning for peace and security in the post–World War II era. Merton also supported the efforts of the Catholic Worker movement, the liturgical movement, Catholic pacifists, and the post–Vatican II Catholic and Christian dialogues with Eastern religions. In 1968, while at an ecumenical conference of Catholic and Buddhist monks in Bangkok, he was killed by accidental electrocution.

MICHEL, VIRGIL GEORGE (26 June 1890, St. Paul, Minn.–26 November 1938, Collegeville, Minn.). *Education:* B.A., St. John's University (Minn.), 1909; Ph.B., 1912; M.A., 1913; S.T.B., Catholic University of America, Washington, D.C., 1917; Ph.D., 1918; studied at Sant'Anselmo, Rome, 1924; Louvain, Belgium, 1924–25. *Career:* Novice, the Order of St. Benedict, St. John's Abbey, Collegeville, Minn., 1909; teacher and administrator, St. John's University, 1918–24; founding editor, *Orate Fratres,* 1926–30, 1936–38; missionary work among the Ojibuay Indians, northern Minnesota, 1930–33; teacher and administrator, St. John's University, 1933–38.

Dom Virgil (née George) Michel was the foremost spokesman for the liturgical revival in American Catholicism during the early twentieth century. Combining interests in sociology, economics, education, art, and philosophy with his study of liturgy, Michel developed a liturgical movement in the United States that differed significantly from its European Catholic precursor, emphasizing the liturgy's potential for social reform. The liturgy expressed a Christian community of justice as well as faith. For Michel this meant that a renewal of the social order must be tied to a revival of the liturgy, and that a revived concern for the liturgy demanded a corresponding concern for social reconstruction, since the liturgy expressed the divine ideal of communal living and provided the divine means for effectively reforming society.

Michel advanced the connection between liturgy and social reform during the Depression, shortly after the publication of Pius XI's *Quadragesimo Anno* (1931) and after Michel had served a three-year missionary experience (1930–33) among the economically depressed Indians in northern Minnesota. Michel and others established *Orate Fratres* and the Liturgical Press at St. John's Abbey in Collegeville, Minnesota, to publish liturgical studies and texts and promote a renewed liturgical sense among American Catholics. Michel's pragmatic and activist-oriented liturgical movement was not popular in American Catholicism, but it did eventually contribute to the renewal of the liturgical life of the church through the reforms initiated by Vatican II.

MUNDELEIN, GEORGE WILLIAM (2 July 1872, New York, N.Y.–2 October 1939, Chicago, Ill.). *Education:* B.A., Manhattan College, 1889; studied at St. Vincent's Seminary, Beatty, Pa., 1889–91; Urban College of Propaganda, Rome, 1891–95. *Career:* Ordained, 1895; pastoral work in Diocese of Brooklyn,

N.Y., 1895–97; diocesan chancellor, 1897–1909; auxiliary bishop of Brooklyn, 1909–15; archbishop of Chicago, 1915–39; cardinal, 1924–39.

In 1915, at the age of 43, George Mundelein, son of German immigrants, became the archbishop of Chicago, the largest Catholic diocese in the United States. For the next 24 years he helped build and manage a host of ecclesiastical institutions that helped to further the Americanization of Chicago's Catholic immigrants and his vision of the fusion of American and Catholic values. He was a fund-raiser, organizer, builder, and manager of an ecclesiastical bureaucracy that was known for its efficiency and effectiveness.

Mundelein was interested in big and ostentatious projects that manifested the growing prosperity of the Chicago Catholic community and his confidence that Catholics would respond to his vision of making Chicago Catholicism influential in the Midwest. He encouraged the parochial schools and diocesan high schools to be instruments of Americanization. He built Quigley Preparatory College (1918) and the Seminary of St. Mary of the Lake (1921) to provide for a native clergy and to manifest, at least in the seminary's architecture, the symbolic collaboration of American and Roman styles. Because of his financial support of the Vatican, his double allegiance to the papacy and the American political system, and the growing importance of the diocese of Chicago, he was made Chicago's first cardinal in 1924. In 1926, to draw attention to Chicago's Catholic community and raise the religious fervor of his diocese, he hosted the twenty-eighth International Eucharistic Congress, which became a massive symbolic display of corporate Catholic life and its international connections.

During the Depression, Mundelein became a strong supporter of President Roosevelt's New Deal, an early critic of Nazism, a promoter of the cause of labor, and an advocate for social justice. Mundelein stayed clear of partisan political campaigning, but he supported those local and federal politicians whom he believed upheld the freedom of the church and the rights of the poor and unemployed. His primary legacy, however, was his reorganization and restructuring of diocesan administration, providing for an efficient development of twentieth-century Chicago Catholicism.

MURRAY, JOHN COURTNEY (12 September 1904, New York, N.Y.–16 August 1967, New York, N.Y.). *Education:* B.A., Boston College, 1926; M.A., 1927; S.T.L., Woodstock Seminary (Md.), 1934; S.T.D., Gregorian University, Rome, 1937. *Career:* Ordained, 1933; instructor, Ateneo de Manila, Philippines, 1927–30; professor of theology, Woodstock Seminary, 1937–67; editor, *Theological Studies,* 1941–67; associate editor, *America,* 1945–46; adviser, Second Vatican Council, 1963–65.

John Courtney Murray was the principal twentieth-century American Catholic theoretician on religious liberty. His views on religious liberty not only gave

American Catholics a systematic way of looking at their political experience, but also influenced the official Catholic teaching at the Second Vatican Council. In the course of a number of systematic-historical studies published after 1948, Murray developed the view that the constitutional provisions for religious liberty that had developed in the Western world for the past two centuries were consistent with an evolving Catholic teaching on the dignity and freedom of the person. Catholics should accept the constitutional developments not simply on the grounds of historical expediency and beneficial historical experience, but also on the moral ground that they provided for social peace and harmony among peoples—that is, they fulfilled the state's ultimate purpose for existence. The state's function was to protect freedom, not to enforce or secure religious belief or ecclesiastical goals. Such a view, he argued, provided for the church's freedom as well as that of the individual, and such a view of the state's role was consistent with all that the church had struggled to achieve in its own past declarations. For him there was no such thing as an ideal relationship between church and state.

Murray's position was contrary to the prevailing view at the Vatican and at the Catholic University of America, where the theologian Joseph Fenton challenged Murray's orthodoxy. In the mid-1950s, Rome and Murray's Jesuit superiors silenced him on the issue, but his position was eventually vindicated at the Second Vatican Council, where he became a primary author of the *Declaration on Religious Liberty* (*Dignitatis Humanae,* 1965).

N

NEUMANN, JOHN NEPONUCENE (28 March 1811, Prachatitz, Bohemia–5 January 1860, Philadelphia, Pa.). *Education:* Diocesan seminary, Budweis, 1831–33; archepiscopal seminary, Prague, 1833–35. *Career:* Ordained priest in New York City, 25 June 1836; itinerant pastor, Buffalo-Rochester area, 1836–40; entered the Congregation of the Most Holy Redeemer (the Redemptorists), 1840; traveling Redemptorist missionary, 1842–52; bishop of Philadelphia, 1852; canonized a saint, 19 June 1977.

Before becoming the archbishop of Philadelphia, Neumann served as a missionary among the German-speaking immigrants. As archbishop of Philadelphia, a diocese that was considerably debt-ridden, he became a personal example of holiness, a defender of the rights of all immigrants, a promoter of spirituality among them (establishing in Philadelphia the Forty Hours Devotion), an author of a catechism and a text on biblical study for German-speakers, a recruiter of seven new religious orders for the diocese, a unifier of a parochial school system, and a founder of a preparatory seminary for young candidates for the priesthood. He did not like his role as episcopal administrator, however, because his talents were not in financial management, and repeatedly he requested that he be removed as bishop. Many in his diocese considered him a saint even before he died, and immediately after his death and well into the late nineteenth century people attributed miracles to his intervention. In 1977 he was canonized a saint for his works of piety and charity.

O

O'CONNELL, DENIS JOSEPH (28 January 1849, Donoughmore, Ireland–1 January 1927, Richmond, Va.). *Education:* Studied at St. Charles College (Md.), 1868–71; D.D., Urban College of Propaganda, Rome, 1877. *Career:* Assistant pastor, St. Peter's Cathedral, Richmond, 1877–83; rector, North American Coll., Rome, 1885–95; rector, Church of Santa Maria, Rome, 1895–1903; rector, Catholic University of America, 1903–9; auxiliary bishop of San Francisco, 1909–12; bishop of Richmond, 1912–26; retired archbishop of Mariamne, Syria, 1926–27.

O'Connell was a strong advocate of Americanism in the post–Civil War church. From 1885 to 1903, he played a major role as Roman agent for Cardinal James Gibbons and the Americanist bishops (especially John Ireland and John Keane), maneuvering at the Vatican to win approval for Americanist pastoral objectives in accommodating Catholicism to late nineteenth-century American social and political conditions. Anti-Americanist conservatives in the church considered him a pawn in the hands of the Americanizing party and sought to discredit his work as rector at the North American College. Removed as rector of the college in 1895, he continued to articulate the Americanist program in Europe, giving a major address on the subject at the International Catholic Scientific Congress (1897) in Fribourg, Switzerland. His speech, titled "A New Idea in the Life of Father Hecker," distinguished between political Americanism, which expressed the fundamental ideas of American government, and ecclesiastical Americanism, which expressed the pragmatic beneficial relationship between church and state in the United States. His advocacy of Americanism, however, was ineffective in turning the tide of European and American reaction against it.

Because of the support and protection of Cardinal Gibbons, O'Connell's ecclesiastical career was advanced even after Pope Leo XIII's condemnation of Americanism in 1899. In 1903, O'Connell was made rector of the Catholic University of America, where he rescued the fledgling university from tentative obscurity, helped to improve the faculty, expanded the university to include undergraduates, and placed it on a firm financial footing. In 1909, he was ordained a bishop, and after a short and unsatisfactory role as auxiliary bishop of San Francisco, he was named bishop of Richmond where his 14-year episcopate was generally uneventful.

O'CONNELL, WILLIAM HENRY (8 December 1859, Lowell, Mass.–22 April 1944, Boston, Mass.). *Education:* Studied at St. Charles College, Ellicot City, Md., 1879; B.A., Boston College, 1881; studied at North American College, Rome, 1881–84. *Career:* Ordained, 1884; pastoral work, Archdiocese of Boston, 1885–95; rector, North American College, Rome, 1895–1901; bishop of Portland, Maine, 1901–6; coadjutor archbishop of Boston, 1906–7; archbishop of Boston, 1907–44; cardinal, 1911–44.

William Henry O'Connell rose to ecclesiastical prominence in American Catholicism at the beginning of the Vatican campaign against prominent Americanist clergy and bishops. Roman-trained and -educated, he was appointed in 1895 as rector of the North American College in Rome, where he replaced the Americanist Denis J. O'Connell. Throughout the remaining period of the Americanist crisis, 1895–99, he continued as rector of the college and made friends with Cardinal Francesco Satolli and Archbishop Rafael Merry del Val, leaders in the Roman campaign against Americanism and later, under Pope Pius X (1903–14), against modernism.

His ideological identification with the anti-Americanist and antimodernist Roman leadership made him a prime candidate in 1901 for the episcopacy of Portland, Maine, and for the archbishopric of Boston in 1907. During his 38-year reign as archbishop of Boston, O'Connell turned away from the Americanist tendencies of his predecessor, Archbishop John Joseph Williams, centralized episcopal administrative control over the diocese, aligned his administrative policies with the antimodernist and integralist stance of Pius X, and simultaneously reaffirmed Catholic allegiance and loyalty to America. He also supported missionary activity (especially the establishment of James A. Walsh and Thomas Price's Maryknoll), the lay apostolate and street preaching methods of David Goldstein and Martha Moore Avery, the lay activism inherent in the American Federation of Catholic Societies, and President Wilson's Fourteen Points. Like Pius X, he also encouraged the retreat movement, frequent communion, and Lenten devotions. He was an accomplished organist, too, and created and translated numerous hymns. Although he was never popular among the American bishops, and although his national leadership in American Catholicism decreased after the death of Pius X in 1914, he had a significant conservative impact on the Archdiocese of Boston throughout his tenure and was a forceful public figure there. His episcopal declarations commanded the attention of the press and politicians, even when they were not appreciated. From Protestants and Jews as well as Catholics he was able to raise significant funds for charitable and educational projects.

P

PURCELL, JOHN BAPTIST (26 February 1800, Mallow, Ireland–4 July 1883, Brown County, Ohio). *Education:* Studied at Mount St. Mary's College (Md.), 1820–23; seminary of St. Suplice, Paris, 1834–27. *Career:* Professor (president after 1829), Mount St. Mary's College, 1827–33; bishop of Cincinnati, 1833–50; archbishop of Cincinnati, 1850–83.

For 50 years John Baptist Purcell presided over the phenomenal expansion of Midwestern Catholicism. During his episcopal career he saw the center of Catholic gravity shift from Bardstown, Kentucky, to St. Louis and Cincinnati, both of which were made metropolitan sees in 1847 and 1850, respectively. Irish by birth, Sulpician by education and early clerical experience, and American by choice, Purcell had the skills of an orator, the mind of a Gallican-trained professor, and the pragmatism of an American ecclesiastical builder. He met the religious and institutional needs of Midwestern German and Irish Catholic immigrants who were flooding his and other newly erected dioceses throughout the Midwest, from the Alleghenies to the Mississippi River. When he began his bishopric the diocese had 14 priests and 16 churches; when he died there were 480 priests, 510 churches, two newspapers (the *Catholic Telegraph* and *Der Wahrheitsfreund*), 3 colleges, 3 seminaries, 6 hospitals, 30 schools, and about 24 orphanages. During his episcopate, moreover, the territory north of the Ohio and east of the Mississippi River served by his diocese and that of St. Louis saw the creation of 10 new dioceses and two metropolitan sees (Milwaukee 1850; Chicago 1880).

Purcell was an apologist for Catholicism in the Midwest as well as a builder at a time when Cincinnati itself was perceived as a key to the religious struggle to win the West. He became a spokesman for a moderate post-Tridentine Catholicism open to American values. In a series of public religious debates with Alexander Campbell (1836–37) and Thomas Vickers (1867), Purcell upheld the Catholic doctrinal tradition and demonstrated that Catholic leaders could promote their traditions and institutions and simultaneously contribute to the needs of the expanding Midwest without appropriating the new measures used by Protestant evangelicals. In the midst of Nativist hostility during the early 1850s, he defended Archbishop Gaetano Bedini against the assaults of Cincinnati's free thinkers and the German revolutionaries of 1848. He also defended Catholic schools and periodically applied for public funds to support them, a measure that created considerable animosity in Ohio. During the Civil War he was a strong supporter of the Union side and advocated emancipation five months before President Lincoln announced it.

Purcell attended the First Vatican Council (1869–70), where he became an opponent of the definition of papal infallibility because he believed the doctrine was not only inopportune but also inconsistent with earlier ecclesiastical tradition. Once the council defined the doctrine, however, he, like other American opponents, accepted it. In 1878, because of his brother Father Edward Purcell's financial mismanagement of four million dollars, the diocese of Cincinnati was bankrupted. The pressures of the financial embarrassment and ill health forced Purcell to retire from public ecclesiastical life. In 1883 he died in an Ursuline convent at St. Martin's, Ohio.

R

RUDD, DANIEL (7 August 1854, Bardstown, Ky.–3 December 1933, Bardstown, Ky.). *Career:* Founder and editor, *Ohio State Tribune* (renamed *American Catholic Tribune*), Springfield, 1886–94; organizer and president, Afro-American Lay Catholic Congresses, 1889–94; member, committee of organization, Lay Catholic Congress, Baltimore, 1889; manager, lumber mill, Bolivar County, Miss., c. 1910; accountant, Madison, Ark., c. 1918–20; feed-store operator, Marion, Ark., 1920–32.

Son of Kentucky Catholic slaves, Daniel Rudd was one of the most prominent and articulate black Catholic lay journalists, lecturers, and organizers in the late nineteenth century. His *American Catholic Tribune,* the first black Catholic newspaper, focused on religious and social issues, emphasized the need for racial and religious solidarity, and fostered the idea that only the Catholic Church possessed the doctrine and will to break down all barriers of color and treat all people equally. Rudd also promoted the church's social teachings, published a translation of Pope Leo XIII's *Rerum Novarum* (seeing it as an abolitionist document), criticized other Catholic newspapers' failure to address issues of religious segregation and other racial injustices in the church, and lectured on these topics in German as well as English, not only in the diocese of Cincinnati, but throughout the United States. In 1899, he traveled to France to meet Cardinal Lavigerie and represent blacks at an international congress on slavery. While in England he lectured in Cardinal Manning's St. George's Cathedral Hall in Westminister.

Aware of the Catholic congresses in Belguim and Germany, Rudd founded and organized the first of five national Catholic Afro-American Congresses (1889–94) to promote solidarity, Catholic missionary work among blacks, and Catholic schools for blacks. Rudd's national work on behalf of racial justice in church and society waned after 1894, but he continued to promote these causes on the local level in Arkansas throughout the early twentieth century.

RYAN, JOHN AUGUSTINE (25 May 1869, Vermillion, Minn.–16 September 1945, St. Paul, Minn.). *Education:* Studied at St. Thomas College and St. Paul's Seminary (Minn.), 1892–98; S.T.D., Catholic University of America, 1906. *Career:* Professor of moral theology, St. Paul's Seminary, 1902–15; professor of political science and moral theology, Catholic University of America, 1915–39; director of the Department of Social Action, National Catholic Welfare Conference, 1919–45.

During the first half of the twentieth century, John A. Ryan became the foremost American Catholic social analyst and promoter of systematic social thought. He believed that the Catholic social ethic, as he discovered it in Pope Leo XIII's encyclical *Rerum Novarum,* had to be wedded to the empirical and theoretical study of economics. After writing his two most important theoretical works on economic justice in the industrial order, *A Living Wage* (1906) and *Distributive Justice* (1916), Ryan became an active promoter of minimum wage legislation and a lobbyist in state and federal legislatures for protective laws for workers. He also propagated Catholic social thought among clergy and laity through the activities of the National Catholic Welfare Conference's Social Action Department, his classes on moral theology at the Catholic University, the *Catholic Charities Review,* which he founded and edited (1917–20), and through lectures at summer schools of social action at various Catholic universities and colleges.

In 1919 he wrote the "Bishops' Program for Social Reconstruction," a detailed outline of progressive legislation in favor of workers and wage earners. During the 1920s, he became an active member of the Catholic Association for International Peace, American Civil Liberties Union, and Federal Council of Churches, hoping to advance the cause of universal liberty and justice through these institutions. In the 1930s, he supported President Roosevelt's economic initiatives and programs, earning for himself the sobriquet "Right Reverend New Dealer." He also publicly criticized the economic nostrums and anti-Semitism of the radical radio priest Charles Coughlin.

S

SERRA, JUNÍPERO (24 November 1717, Petra, Majorca, Spain–28 August 1784, near Monterey, Calif.). *Education:* Entered the novitiate for the Order of Friars Mendicant, 1730; doctorate in theology, Lullian University, Palma, Majorca, 1743. *Career:* Lecturer in philosophy at St. Francis Friary, Palma, 1738; professor of philosophy, Lullian University, 1743–49; teacher, Apostolic College of San Fernando, Mexico, 1750; missionary in Sierra Gorda, 1750–58; administrator and missionary, Apostolic College, 1758–67; missionary in Lower Calif., 1767–69; missionary in Upper Calif., 1769–84.

Junípero Serra was the first major Franciscan missionary to California. Because of his administrative skills he was appointed superior of the Franciscan missionary effort in Lower California in 1767, when the Jesuits were expelled from that territory. In 1769 he joined a Spanish expedition into Upper California and founded San Diego mission, the first of nine Indian missions he would establish between San Diego and San Francisco during his life. Under his ecclesiastical jurisdiction, which was periodically challenged by Spanish civil authorities, he sent Franciscan missionaries to the Indians, built the missions as centers of Spanish Catholic evangelization, and organized them into prosperous agricultural and farming institutions. Using religious education and at times Spanish military force and rigorous discipline, he tried to convert the Indians and make them productive members of a sedentary Spanish Catholic culture. According to his own accounts, he was responsible for 6,000 baptisms and 5,300 confirmations in Upper California. In 1934 his cause for beatification was started in Rome but was seriously challenged in the 1980s by activists for Native American cultural independence and by critics of the Spanish cultural devastation of Indian life.

SETON, ELIZABETH ANN BAYLEY (28 August 1774, New York, N.Y.–4 January 1821, Emmitsburg, Md.). *Career:* Various teaching and boarding school projects in New York and Baltimore, 1804–9; founder and mother superior, Sisters of Charity of St. Joseph, Emmitsburg, Md., 1809–21.

Elizabeth Ann Bayley was the founder of the Sisters of Charity of St. Joseph. In 1805, shortly after her husband's death, she took instructions and was received into the Catholic Church. As a Catholic widow with five small children, she tried to make a living by running a boarding school in New York, but the project failed. In 1808, at the encouragement of a number of priests, she moved her family to Baltimore, a more Catholic city at the time, and opened a girls' school there. As her religious life deepened, so did her desire to live a common Christian life and serve the church through education. That desire was realized in 1809, when Elizabeth gathered around her a number of young women to live a common regulated religious life whose primary mission was the education of the young, establishing in Baltimore the Sisters of Charity of St. Joseph.

In June 1809 Elizabeth moved her new community to Emmitsburg, Maryland, where they had been offered land and a house close to a newly established Catholic college for young men. During the next 12 years she raised her children, built the new convent, enlisted new members from prominent New York and Philadelphia families, and took on the additional mission of nursing the sick. By 1814 the new community had grown to such an extent that she was able to send some of her sisters to Philadelphia to establish schools and hospitals, and in 1817 she expanded to New York. Although periodically embattled with clerics over the administration of her new religious community and in the midst of personal tragedies (two of her children died in the convent) and weak health, she managed to develop a spirit of common Christian life and service among her sisters. In 1821, at the age of 46, she died at Emmitsburg. She was declared venerable in 1959, beatified in 1963, and in 1975 she became the first native-born American to be canonized a saint.

SHEEN, FULTON J. (8 May 1895, El Paso, Ill.–9 December 1979, New York, N.Y.). *Education:* B.A., M.A., St. Viator's College, Bourbonnais, Ill., 1917; studied at St. Paul Seminary (Minn.), 1917–20; J.C.B., S.T.D., Catholic University of America, 1920; Ph.D., University of Louvain, Belgium, 1923; *agrégé* in philosophy, Louvain, 1925. *Career:* Ordained, 1919; theology professor, St. Edmund's College, Ware, England, 1925; assistant pastor, St. Patrick's Church, Peoria, 1925–26; professor of philosophy, Catholic University of America, 1926–50; NBC radio preacher, *The Catholic Hour,* 1930–50; national director, Society for the Propagation of the Faith, 1950–66; auxiliary bishop of New York, 1951–66; ABC television host, *Life is Worth Living,* 1952–57; bishop of Rochester, N.Y., 1966–69; retirement, 1969–79.

Fulton J. Sheen was perhaps the most visible representative of American Catholicism in the 1950s. In 1925, his bishop appointed him to a parish in Peoria and after a year sent him to teach philosophy at the Catholic University of America. Gifted with eloquence in both oral and written communication, he abandoned the pursuit of serious philosophical inquiry in the 1930s and began to popularize the Thomist intellectual revival and to address issues of political and social concern in American life. His eloquence attracted attention in the

1930s when he lectured at various churches and colleges across the country, especially at St. Patrick's Cathedral in New York, where his sermons and talks drew large audiences. In the 1930s, too, he became a regular speaker on NBC's radio program *The Catholic Hour* and became one of the first television evangelists in the 1950s when he hosted ABC's *Life is Worth Living*. He also published more than 65 books and numerous articles on Catholic views of philosophy, psychology, spirituality, politics, and social justice.

As national director of the Society for the Propagation of the Faith from 1950 to 1966, he helped raise the consciousness of American Catholics to the missionary enterprise and collected millions of dollars to support social and evangelical work in many Third World countries. His work in this office prepared him for participating in the Second Vatican Council, where he spoke out on social justice and missionary work. In 1969, moreover, he was made a member of the Vatican's Commission for Missions. Although he opposed communism and saw it as philosophically antithetical to Catholicism and Western Christian civilization, he warned Catholics that the communist criticism of social and economic injustices in modern society should not be taken lightly and that Catholics should be in the forefront of movements to eliminate such injustices.

After the Second Vatican Council, as bishop of Rochester, Sheen tried to put his notions of social justice into action by offering the U.S. government a church building and church land for housing the poor and homeless. This move created a forceful public resistance from the Catholic laity, and a few clergy and eventually forced Sheen to withdraw the offer and resign from his see in 1969. He spent the remaining 10 years of his life writing, giving lectures, and fostering the spiritual life of diocesan priests.

SPALDING, JOHN LANCASTER (2 June 1840, Lebanon, Ky.–25 August 1916, Peoria, Ill.). *Education:* Studied at St. Mary's College (Ky.), 1855–57; Mount St. Mary's College (Md.), 1857–58; B.A., Mount St. Mary's of the West (Ohio), 1859; S.T.B., American Coll., Louvain, Belgium, 1862; lic. theology, Louvain, 1864; studied in Rome, 1864–65. *Career:* Secretary to the bishop of Louisville, Ky, 1865–71; chancellor, Diocese of Louisville, 1871–73; curate at St. Michael's Church, New York, 1873–76; bishop, Diocese of Peoria, 1877–1908; retirement, 1908–16.

John Lancaster Spalding was perhaps the most intellectually gifted of the American bishops at the end of the nineteenth century. In 1877, he was made the first bishop of Peoria, an office he served for 32 years. Although the new diocese did not have the influence of the more established and much larger dioceses, Spalding had a significant impact on the larger American church through his literary efforts to bring American Catholicism in tune with modern developments in thought and literature. He was also responsible for conceiving of and promoting the idea of a Catholic University in the United States to prepare clergy to dialogue with modern patterns of thought and utilize the empirical sciences to respond to social and cultural problems. He championed, too, the causes of Prohibition, women's higher education, the franchise for women, and a just wage for workers. Although aligned with many of the Americanists in his general orientation to society, he opposed Archbishop John Ireland's Faribault-Stillwater education plan and his endorsement of a Roman apostolic delegate, Americanist hostility to German preservationists, and the second-generation Irish American tendency to identify uncritically with American values. Because of personal entanglements with the Caldwell sisters, benefactors of the Catholic University, and his public criticism of the sending of a Roman apostolic delegate, he came under a cloud of ecclesiastical suspicion in Rome and was never promoted to a large episcopal see.

SPALDING, MARTIN JOHN (23 May 1810, Rolling Fork, Ky.–7 February 1872, Baltimore, Md.). *Education:* B.A., St. Mary's College (Ky.), 1826; B.D., St. Thomas Seminary (Ky.), 1830; Urban College of Propaganda, Rome, 1834. *Career:* Rector, St. Joseph's Church, Bardstown, Ky., 1834–38, 1841–44; president, St. Joseph's College (Ky.), 1838–40; rector, Lexington, Kr., 1840–41; vicar general, Diocese of Louisville, Ky., 1844–48; auxiliary bishop and bishop, Louisville, 1848–64; archbishop of Baltimore, 1864–72.

Martin J. Spalding, a native Kentuckian and a member of a family that had a long history on American soil, was a forceful clerical and episcopal apologist for Catholicism in his native diocese of Bardstown (transferred to Louisville in 1841) for 30 years, a period when Nativism was becoming a potent force in American life and a threat to American Catholic identity and institutions. As editor of the newly established *Catholic Advocate* (1836–49), a popular lecturer, debater, preacher, and a prolific writer of apologetic and historical tracts and books, he gained a national reputation as an articulate defender of the faith.

As the seventh archbishop of Baltimore, Spalding became the most visible and influential episcopal representative of Catholicism in the United States between 1864 and 1872. During that period he continued, as he had in Louisville, to emphasize Catholic education on the parochial level, but he also became a prime supporter of the establishment of the North American College in Rome and the American College in Louvain, Belgium, and of the notion that a major Catholic university ought to be erected in the United States. During the Civil War his sympathies were with the South, but he was adamant that the church should take no stand on either side of the conflict. After the war he convoked the Second Plenary Council of Baltimore (1866) to demonstrate a united Catholicism and elicit from the nation's bishops plans for evangelizing blacks in the postwar South, but no plans were forthcoming. Like most other American bishops, he supported the conciliar approach to national ecclesiastical legislation, having previously participated in the First Plenary Council of Baltimore

(1852) and three previous provincial synods (Cincinnati, 1855, 1858, 1861). At the Vatican Council (1869–70) he became a moderate proponent of papal infallibility, seeing the definition of this doctrine as a timely antidote to various forms of Gallicanism. After the council he tried to demonstrate how the religious doctrine was not a threat to American civil and political values. Although Spalding was a native American and cherished American values, he lived at a time when he felt called on to reinforce the internal support systems within the Catholic tradition, build up the ecclesiastical institutions, and develop a religious perspective that delineated and emphasized the differences between Catholicism and Protestantism.

SPELLMAN, FRANCIS JOSEPH (4 May 1889, Whitman, Mass.–2 December 1967, New York, N.Y.). *Education:* B.A., Fordham University, 1911; S.T.D., North American College, Rome, 1916. *Career:* Curate, Roxbury, Mass., 1916–18; staff, Cathedral of the Holy Cross, Boston, 1918–22; vice chancellor, Diocese of Boston, 1922–25; attaché, Secretariate of State, Rome, 1925–32; auxiliary bishop, Boston, 1932–39; archbishop of New York, 1939–67; military vicar for the army and navy, 1940–67; cardinal, 1946–67.

Cardinal Francis Spellman was perhaps the most influential episcopal representative of Catholicism in the United States between 1939 and the end of the Second Vatican Council. Like many other pre–Vatican II, postmodernist, big-city bishops, he was thoroughly American yet utterly Roman in his allegiances. A second-generation Irish American, he was educated in the United States and Rome during the days of Pope Pius X's antimodernism. He rose to ecclesiastical leadership in the dioceses of Boston and New York because of the influence of Cardinal Eugenio Pacelli, the Vatican secretary of state (1929–39), for whom he worked in Rome between 1925 and 1932. When Cardinal Pacelli was elected Pope Pius XII in 1939, Spellman was made archbishop of New York, where he rose rapidly to national ecclesiastical prominence through his office as military vicar for the U.S. Army and Navy.

Prior to and during World War II, Spellman cultivated the friendship of prominent and influential Americans including Joseph P. Kennedy and President Roosevelt, and was an important diplomatic link between the Vatican and the Roosevelt government, helping to pave the way for Roosevelt's 1939 appointment of Myron Taylor as the president's personal representative to Pius XII. Spellman repeatedly reinforced the links between Catholicism and American governmental policies during World War II and throughout the Cold War years through his yearly trips as military ordinary to the armed forces overseas. No other postwar American prelate, with the exception of Bishop Fulton J. Sheen, traveled as extensively throughout the world, making Catholic and American influence a part of the new postwar world order.

In the United States, Spellman became a voice for Cold War Catholic anti-communism, aligning himself with Senator Joseph McCarthy. Like other American prelates, he was also a forceful voice against what he considered the growing licentiousness and pornography of popular literature and motion pictures. His battles with prominent Americans such as Eleanor Roosevelt over the issue of governmental aid to parochial schools furthermore made him a national symbol of Cold War Catholic aggressiveness in the minds of many Americans.

Because of his influence at the Vatican, he had an impact on the appointment of numerous bishops in the United States, particularly on the East Coast. Within his own diocese he was a capable builder of numerous educational institutions and an efficient administrator who encouraged and collected an enormous amount of funds for charitable institutes.

Although he was himself a theological and social conservative and not well acquainted with postwar theological developments taking place in Europe and elsewhere, he gave his episcopal protection to Catholic biblical scholars in the 1950s and to John Courtney Murray's themes of religious liberty during the Second Vatican Council. He opposed a number of new measures, especially in the liturgy, at the council, but he used his influence there to organize the American bishops in favor of a declaration on religious liberty. In fact, he made more oral and written interventions (131) than any other American bishop, was one of the presidents of the council, and was considered the titular leader of the American hierarchy there.

After the council, Spellman continued his advocacy of American governmental policies and militant objectives, supporting the war in Vietnam in his Christmas message to the troops there in 1966, at a time when the Berrigan brothers and a few other Catholics were protesting against the war. To the end of his life he gave his wholehearted allegiance to the American government and saw this support as consistent with his Roman anticommunist stance, but that kind of support was increasingly called into question in the late 1960s.

T

TANEY, ROGER BROOKE (17 March 1777, Calvert County, Md.–12 October 1864, Washington, D.C.). *Education:* Studied at Dickinson College, 1792–95; read law in the office of Judge Jeremiah Townley Chase in Md., 1796–99. *Career:* Entered law practice, 1799; state legislator, Md., 1799–1800; state senator, 1816; attorney general of Md., 1827–31; attorney general of the United States, 1831–32; interim secretary of the treasury, 1833–36; Chief Justice of the Supreme Court, 1836–64.

Educated in the postrevolutionary period, Roger B. Taney was one of a small number of prominent Maryland Catholic laymen who were significantly involved in American political life. He was a practicing lawyer after 1799, and he came to public attention in 1811 when he successfully defended General James Wilkinson, commander in chief of the army, who was charged with being an accomplice in Aaron Burr's "western conspiracy." He also participated in federalist politics at both the state and national levels and held a number of positions in both legislatures. As President Jackson's attorney general he was involved in the charter renewal fight of the Bank of the United States. He served under the same president as secretary of state and secretary of the treasury. He was nominated for the Supreme Court and was rejected twice by the Senate largely for political reasons, but in 1836 his nomination was confirmed, and he served as the first Catholic chief justice for the next 28 years. As chief justice he sustained states' rights and in this vein wrote the majority opinion in the Dred Scott decision (1857), which held that no black slave or descendant of a slave could be a citizen of the United States, that Congress had no right to prohibit slavery in the territories, and that the Missouri Compromise (1820) had been null and void from the day of its enactment.

TEKAKWITHA, CATHERINE (1656?, Gandahouhague, Mohawk territory–17 April 1680, La Prairie de la Madeleine, Canada).

Catherine Tekakwitha's short, 24-year biography reads like the lives of some early converts to primitive Christianity, with the exception that her conversion story and her four-year life as a Christian are conditioned by seventeenth-century French Catholic piety. Catherine was born in a Mohawk village in present-day upstate New York. A smallpox epidemic disfigured her when she was four and took the lives of her parents. Although she met French Jesuits as a child, she was not instructed in Christianity until she reached her late teens and was baptized on Easter 1676, at the age of about 20.

Her conversion to Catholicism and her own particular austere appropriation of it alienated her from her former traditions, and her own family and tribe ostracized her. In 1677, shortly after her baptism, she abandoned her tribe and went to live in an Indian village in Sault St. Louis in Upper Canada, where she received her first communion and continued a regular routine of prayer, fasting, and self-flagellation. She also kept a private vow of chastity and refused to marry. Her austere Christian life was admired by the Jesuits as well as by the new converts in Canada, and the Jesuits in particular spread the stories of her remarkable holiness and steadfastness in the faith. Although she was about to begin a small convent in 1679, she did not live long enough to direct it. Almost immediately on her death in 1680 her tomb became a pilgrimage site. In 1932 she was nominated for beatification, and in 1980, she was declared "Blessed," the first stage in the process toward canonization.

TOUSSAINT, PIERRE (1766, St. Domingue—30 June 1853, New York City). *Career:* a slave in Artibonite Valley in central Haiti, 1766–87; moved to New York City with the Jean-Jacques Bérard family, 1787; house-slave in New York City, 1787–1807; emancipated, New York City, 1807; hairdresser, New York City, 1787–1853.

Born a slave in Haiti, Toussaint grew up and was educated in the household of Jean-Jacques Bérard, a prominent and wealthy Haitian Catholic. Within the Bérard family he learned to read French and was particularly fond of the classical French preachers Bossuet and Massillon. During the Haitian Revolution, the Bérard family moved to New York City, taking Toussaint with them. Jean-Jacques died shortly after the move to New York, leaving his widow penniless. In response to her need, Toussaint developed a hairdressing business in the city and supported his mistress until her death in 1807, at which time he was emancipated. For the remainder of his life as a freedman, he continued his hairdressing business among the wealthy of New York, attended daily Mass, took black orphans into his own household after he married in 1811, supported other orphans by contributing his financial resources to the St. Patrick's Orphan Asylum and other charities in the city. Throughout his life he was widely known in New York City for his piety and charity, and when he died in 1853, large numbers of New Yorkers from his parish of St. Peter's and beyond attended his funeral and the New York newspapers gave more than ordinary attention to his obituary. A year after his death, Hannah Lee Sawyer published the *Memoir of Pierre Toussaint,* making his deeds of piety and charity more widely known in the American Catholic community. In 1990, Cardinal John O'Connor of New York

City introduced his cause for canonization and placed his body in the crypt beneath St. Patrick's Cathedral. In 1995 Pope John Paul II acknowledged Toussaint as a "servant of God" in a speech at St. Patrick's Cathedral, and in 1997 the pope declared Toussaint "venerable," a major first step in the process of canonization.

TURNER, THOMAS WYATT (16 March 1877, Hughesville, Charles County, Md.–21 April 1978, Washington, D.C.). *Education:* A.B., Howard University, 1901; studied at University of Rochester, 1903; M.A., biology, Cold Springs Biological Laboratory, Howard University, 1905; studied at Johns Hopkins University, 1905–6; Columbia University, 1913; Ph.D., Cornell Univ., 1921. *Career:* Teacher, Tuskegee Institute, 1901–2; Baltimore High and Training School, 1902–10, 1911–13; and St. Louis High School, 1910–11; founding member, NAACP, 1909; professor of biology, Howard University, 1913–24; acting dean, School of Education, Howard University, 1914–20; teacher, Hampton Institute, 1914; agent, National Security League of New York, 1916–17; organizer, Committee Against the Extension of Race Prejudice in the Church, 1917 (name changed to Committee for the Advancement of Colored Catholics in 1919 and to Federated Colored Catholics of the United States from 1925–58); cytologist, U.S. Department of Agriculture, and potato field investigator, Presque Isle, Maine, 1918–19; department head, Biological Sciences, Hampton Institute, 1924–45; retired from Hampton Institute, 1945; consultant, Florida Normal College, St. Augustine, 1947–48; consultant to president, organizer of biology department, professor of biology, Texas Southern University, 1949–50.

Thomas Wyatt Turner was a black lay Catholic intellectual who was actively involved the promotion of the rights and responsibilities of blacks in the church. As a result of increasing discrimination against blacks in the early twentieth century, Turner became an active participant in the NAACP in Baltimore and Washington. Because Catholic institutions like the Knights of Columbus, Catholic University of America, and Josephite seminary of Baltimore refused to accept black Catholics, Turner and others from St. Augustine's parish in Washington, D.C., organized a movement in 1919, eventually called the Federation of Colored Catholics, to protest against racism in the church, develop black Catholic solidarity, and increase their educational, social, and health-care opportunities within Catholic institutions. In 1919, as chairman of the federation, Turner wrote that black Catholics were "without voice anywhere in the Church." He and his movement intended to change that situation. The federation became active after World War I as race hatred and murders of blacks became almost epidemic.

From 1927 to 1932, Turner convoked national meetings of the federation and after each one wrote to the national hierarchy demanding more active episcopal promotion of racial justice and opportunity within Catholic institutions. In

1933, however, the movement split because of differing perceptions of the goals it should pursue. Turner and his faction emphasized racial solidarity, but the white Jesuits William Markoe and John LaFarge, participants in the federation, wanted the group to emphasize interracial Catholic activities. The Turner group remained under the title of Federated Colored Catholics until 1958, but after 1933 the group lacked the focus and strength it had had in the earlier period. Turner continued to speak out on racial justice, but he would not be a central voice in the movement. When he was 99 years old in 1976, he received an honorary degree from the Catholic University of America, a school he could not enter in the early 1900s, for his work in raising Catholic consciousness on racial justice.

W

WALSH, JAMES ANTHONY (24 February 1867, Boston, Mass.–14 April 1936, Maryknoll, N.Y.). *Education:* Studied at Boston College, 1884–85; Harvard University, 1885–86; St. John's Seminary, Brighton, Mass., 1886–92. *Career:* Ordained, 1892; curate, St. Patrick's Parish, Roxbury, Mass., 1892–1903; director, Society for the Propagation of the Faith, Boston, 1903–11; cofounder of the Catholic Missions Bureau, 1906; editor, the *Field Afar,* 1907; cofounder with Thomas F. Price, Catholic Foreign Missions Society of America (Maryknoll), 1911; superior general, Maryknoll, 1929–33; titular bishop of Syene, 1933–36.

James A. Walsh is significant in American Catholicism for his work in raising the missionary consciousness of the American Catholic people and for cofounding Maryknoll. Like the Paulists Walter Elliott and Alexander P. Doyle and the North Carolina diocesan priest Thomas F. Price, Walsh was interested in a home missionary movement that would encourage Catholic evangelical efforts among non-Catholics in the United States. Out of his association with these like-minded men, especially Price, he began to develop the idea for a new religious order that would be an American Catholic contribution to foreign missions. In 1911, he and Price won the approval of the American hierarchy and Pope Pius X to establish the Maryknoll Fathers as a religious society of diocesan priests dedicated exclusively to foreign missionary work. That same year the two began to build a seminary for the new work, and in 1917 they sent the first five Maryknoll priests to Yeungkong, China. Walsh was elected the first superior general of the new order and between 1917 and 1930 toured the rapidly growing mission fields in the Orient, where Maryknoll sisters as well as priests were active. In recognition of his missionary work, Walsh was made a titular bishop of Syene in 1933, but his failing health caused his retirement in 1934 and his death in 1936.

WEIGEL, GUSTAVE (15 January 1906, Buffalo, N.Y.–3 January 1964, New York, N.Y.). *Education:* B.A., Woodstock College (Md.), 1928; S.T.D., Gregorian University, Rome, 1938. *Career:* Ordained, 1933; professor of dogmatic theology, Catholic University of Chile, 1937–38; professor of ecclesiology, Woodstock College, 1949–64; special adviser, Secretariat for the Promotion of Christian Unity, 1960; liaison officer for non-Catholic observers at Vatican II, 1962–64.

Gustave Weigel was a pioneer ecumenist during the 1950s. He tried to awaken American Catholics to the significance of the movement toward Christian unity, which he saw as "the most striking ecclesiological event since the sixteenth century." He introduced many articulate Catholics to the ecumenical movement through his numerous books, pamphlets, and articles, and he encouraged them to study Protestant traditions from Protestant sources, a tactic he hoped would contribute to mutual understanding. He was engaged in a number of dialogues with Protestant theologians, most notably with Paul Tillich, and was an observer at the Oberlin Conference on Faith and Order (1957) and other ecumenical gatherings. He was pessimistic, though, about the immediate possibilities of Christian unity and believed that his attitude was well grounded in a realistic evaluation of American circumstances. Numerous historical, cultural, and theological differences and an apparent lack of concern for doctrinal unity within the Protestant ecumenical movement made Christian union extremely difficult, he believed.

In 1960, prior to the Second Vatican Council, he was appointed a consulter to the Vatican's new Secretariat for the Promotion of Christian Unity—a commission to help members of other religious traditions follow the council's work, assist council members in understanding other Christian bodies, mediate Protestant observers' suggestions, and guide the council on those pastoral and theological matters that bore directly and indirectly on the problem of Christian unity. Although Weigel did not contribute much to the secretariat's preparatory work, he proved invaluable once the council began in 1962, guiding journalists and Protestant observers through the daily developments and conflicting theological battles on the council floor. His personal openness to Protestants made him an effective pioneer of a changing mentality in Catholicism and helped to break down some of the historical and cultural walls that had separated American Protestants and Catholics for generations.

WILLIAMS, MICHAEL (5 February 1877, Halifax, Nova Scotia–12 October 1950, Westport, Conn.). *Career:* City editor, San Francisco *Examiner,* 1906; founder and editor, *Commonweal,* 1924–37.

Michael Williams was one of the leading Catholic laity during and immediately after World War I. After leading a vagabond existence during his early years, Williams had a religious conversion in 1912 and was led back into the Catholic Church, reporting that experience in *The Book of High Romance* (1918). The Paulist John Burke was impressed with Williams's *High Romance* and his abilities as a journalist and invited him to be the assistant director of the press department of the National Catholic War Council during World War I. Williams became acquainted with other leading Catholic clerics, bishops, and laity through his work publicizing Catholic efforts during the war. After the war, the bishops commissioned him to write *American Catholics in the War* (1921), an apologetic attempt to make a case for Catholic patriotism. Through these experiences, Williams became convinced of the need for a lay-edited intellectual Catholic weekly analogous to the influential *New Republic* and *Nation*. In the early 1920s he moved to New York, organized a group of Catholic laymen called the Calvert Association, and in 1924 established *Commonweal,* a journal by and for lay Catholic intellectuals.

From 1924 to 1937, he edited the journal, presenting a Catholic view on the major issues of his day (e.g., evolution and theology, the candidacy of Al Smith, New Deal programs, the Calles's persecution of Catholics in Mexico, the rise of Nazi Germany, and the Spanish Civil War). Although his own positions were marked by his understanding of the papal social encyclical tradition, his support for Generalissimo Franco during the Spanish civil war was not agreeable to his fellow editors, and in 1937, he gave up the editorship to a new generation of young Catholic intellectuals who were anti-Franco as well as anticommunist in their approach to Spain. After he left the editorship he continued to contribute a column, "Views and Reviews," but for all practical purposes his national influence on developments in American Catholicism ceased.

Z

ZAHM, JOHN AUGUSTINE (14 June 1851, New Lexington, Ohio–10 November 1921, Munich, Germany). *Education:* B.A., University of Notre Dame, 1871; studied at Notre Dame Seminary (Ind.), 1871–75. *Career:* Ordained, 1875; professor of chemistry and physics, University of Notre Dame, 1875–92; visiting lecturer in N.Y., Wis., Calif., Belgium, and Switzerland, 1893–97; U.S. provincial, Congregation of the Holy Cross, 1898–1905; traveler, lecturer, and author, 1906–21.

John Augustine Zahm, a priest of the Congregation of the Holy Cross, was a science professor at the University of Notre Dame who became involved in the Catholic controversies over evolution. He was one of the first American Catholic intellectuals to develop a Catholic understanding of evolution. Steering a path between special creationism and naturalistic evolutionism, he developed a view that he and others called theistic evolutionism. He opposed what he considered the unscientific literalism of those who maintained that God was immediately and directly responsible for the creation of all species and all forms of life, as well as the dogmatism of those scientists who ruled God out of creation and attributed all creation to the laws of evolution. According to Zahm, a theistic theory of evolution was compatible with a properly understood biblical account of creation and with Christian and Catholic teachings.

Zahm's position, maturely articulated in his *Evolution and Dogma* (1896), was welcomed by the Americanists and liberal Catholics of the late nineteenth century but severely criticized by the conservatives within American Catholicism. The conservatives pressured Rome to have Zahm's book condemned; rather than condemning the book publicly, however, Rome requested that Zahm withdraw it from publication in 1898. This censure was one part of the growing Roman anti-Americanist sentiment prior to Leo XIII's condemnation of Americanism in 1899. After 1898, Zahm ceased publishing anything relating to the dialogue between science and religion, became provincial of his religious order, and thereafter traveled extensively until his death in 1921.

CHRONOLOGY

1492   Christopher Columbus's first voyage to America

1542   Fray Juan de Padilla, proto-martyr of the United States, murdered by Indians on the plains of Kansas

1565   First Catholic parish of the United States founded at St. Augustine, Florida

1609   Founding of Santa Fe, future headquarters of the missions of New Mexico

1611   Pierre Biard, S.J., and Ennémond Massé, S.J., open missionary efforts among the Indians of Maine

1622   Pope Gregory XV establishes Congregation de Propaganda Fide, under whose jurisdiction American Catholics would remain until 1908

1634   The *Ark* and the *Dove* reach Maryland with first settlers

1646   Isaac Jogues, S.J., murdered by the Iroquois near Auriesville, New York

1649   Maryland's general assembly passes an act of religious toleration for all Christians

1654   Puritan regime repeals the act of religious toleration in Maryland

1671   Sieur de Lusson and Claude Allouez, S.J., at Mackinac Island take possession of the western country for France

1673   Louis Jollet and Jacques Marquette, S.J., conduct an expedition down the Mississippi River

1680   Indian rebellion destroys the missions of New Mexico

1687   Eusebio Francisco Kino, S.J., enters Pimeria Alta to inaugurate the missions of Arizona

1692   Church of England established by law in Maryland; De Vargas reconquers New Mexico, and the friars return to reopen the missions

1704   Destruction of Florida's northern missions by Governor James Moore of South Carolina

1716   Antonio Margil, O.F.M., launches his missionary career in Texas

1718   Disfranchisement of Catholics in Maryland

1727   Ursuline Sisters arrive from France to open first Catholic school in New Orleans

1763   Jesuits banished from Louisiana and the Illinois Country; Spain cedes Florida to England, and the latter gains all lands east of Mississippi River from France

1769   Junipero Serra, O.F.M., founds the first of the California missions at San Diego

1773   Charles Carroll of Carrollton publishes "First Citizen" letters against Daniel Dulany and the royal government in Maryland; Society of Jesus suppressed by Pope Clement XIV

1774   Quebec Act passes the British Parliament

1775   Continental Congress denounces Catholicism to George III and the British people; Washington suppresses the army's celebration of Guy Fawkes Day

1776   Charles Carroll appointed with Benjamin Franklin and Samuel Chase as commission of Congress to seek Canadian aid, with Father John Carroll accompanying the commissioners; Virginia the first state to vote full religious freedom in its bill of rights, followed by religious freedom for Christians in Pennsylvania and Maryland; Charles Carroll signs the Declaration of Independence

1784   Vatican appoints John Carroll as superior of the American Catholic missions

1787   Daniel Carroll of Maryland and Thomas Fitzsimmons of Pennsylvania sign the Constitution of the United States

1789   Pope Pius VI erects the Diocese of Baltimore and names John Carroll as first bishop

1791   French Sulpicians open first seminary in the United States, St. Mary's in Baltimore; Georgetown Academy begins classes; Bishop Carroll convokes first synod of his clergy; Bill of Rights ratified

1808   Baltimore made first metropolitan see of the United States, with Bardstown (Ky.), Boston, New York, and Philadelphia as first suffragan sees

1809   Mother Elizabeth Bayley Seton establishes first native American sisterhood at Emmitsburg, Md.

1822   Bishop John England founds the *United States Catholic Miscellany*, the first Catholic newspaper in the country; Society for the Propagation of the Faith founded in France

1829   First Provincial Council of Baltimore convoked; Elizabeth Lange, Marie Balas, Rosine Boegue, and Almeide Duchemin Maxis begin religious life in Baltimore as the Oblate Sisters of Providence, the first black congregation of women religious in the United States

1834   Ursuline Convent at Charlestown, Mass., burned by a Nativist mob

1836   Publication of Maria Monk's *Awful Disclosures of the Hotel Dieu Nunnery of Montreal;* President Jackson nominates Roger Brooke Taney as Chief Justice of the Supreme Court

1839   Pope Gregory XVI condemns slave trade in *In Supremo Apostolatus*

1842   Henriette Delille and Juliette Gaudin begin the Sisters of the Holy Family in New Orleans, the second black order of women religious

1844   Philadelphia rioters burn two Catholic churches and kill thirteen persons; Isaac Hecker and Orestes A. Brownson received into Catholic Church; establishment of *Brownson's Quarterly Review*

1845   Beginning of potato famine in Ireland

1846   Establishment of first Benedictine priory (Pa.)

1848   Establishment of first permanent American Trappist foundation (Ky.)

1852   First Plenary Council of Baltimore

1855   Founding of the German Catholic Central-Verein

1857   Opening of American College at Louvain, Belgium

1858   Founding of the Paulists, the first native religious community for men

1859   North American College opens in Rome

1865   Founding of *Catholic World*

1866   Second Plenary Council of Baltimore

1869   American bishops attend the First Vatican Council in Rome

1871   Arrival of Mill Hill Fathers (Josephites) in Baltimore

1874   Bureau of Catholic Indian Missions established

1875   Archbishop John McCloskey of New York becomes first American cardinal; James Augustine Healy named the first black (mulatto) bishop (for Portland, Maine)

1876   Founding of the *American Catholic Quarterly Review;* publication of James Gibbons's *Faith of Our Fathers*

1884   Third Plenary Council of Baltimore

1886   Archbishop James Gibbons of Baltimore named the second American cardinal; Augustus Tolton ordained the first black priest

1889   Opening of the Catholic University of America; first black Catholic lay congress in Washington, D.C. (others held in Cincinnati, 1890; Philadelphia, 1892; Chicago, 1893; and Baltimore, 1894)

1890   Archbishop Ireland's address on public and private schools before the National Education Association in St. Paul

1891   Mother Katharine Drexel founds the Sisters of the Blessed Sacrament for Indians and Colored People

1893   Apostolic Delegation established in Washington, D.C.; opening of College of Notre Dame of Maryland, first Catholic college for women

1899   Pope Leo XIII publishes *Testem Benevolentiae*

1904   Founding of the National Catholic Education Association

1905   Founding of the Catholic Church Extension Society for home missions

1907   Publication of the first volume of the *Catholic Encyclopedia*

1908   Pope Pius X publishes *Pascendi Dominici Gregis* against modernism; American Catholicism removed from jurisdiction of the Congregation de Propaganda Fide; William O'Connell becomes bishop of Boston

1911   Establishment of Catholic Foreign Mission Society of America (Maryknoll)

1917   Founding of the National Catholic War Council

1919   Publication of the *Bishops' Program of Social Reconstruction;* founding of the National Catholic Welfare Council

1924   Federated Colored Catholics of the United States established

1925   Supreme Court declares Oregon school law unconstitutional

1926   Twenty-eighth International Eucharistic Congress held in Chicago

1934   John LaFarge, S.J., founds first Catholic Interracial Council in New York

1939   Myron C. Taylor named personal representative of President Roosevelt to Pope Pius XII

1948   Protestants and Other Americans United for the Separation of Church and State (POAU) organized

1951   President Truman nominates General Mark Clark as American ambassador to Vatican City

1954   Establishment of the Sister Formation Conference

1955   Publication of John Tracy Ellis's "American Catholics and the Intellectual Life"

1958   Christopher Dawson named first occupant of the Chauney Stillman Chair of Roman Catholic Studies in the Divinity School of Harvard University

1959   Pope John XXIII announces convocation of the Second Vatican Council

1960   John F. Kennedy becomes the first Catholic president

1962   Opening of the Second Vatican Council; Vatican appoints Gustave Weigel, S.J., as one of five Catholic observers at the third general assembly of the World Council of Churches at New Delhi; Archbishop Joseph F. Rummel of New Orleans announces integration of Catholic schools; organization of National Farm Workers Association

1963   Catholic University of America prohibits Godfrey Diekmann, O.S.B., Hans Kung, John Courtney Murray, S.J., and Gustave Weigel, S.J., from speaking there; Elizabeth Seton becomes first American to be beatified; widespread discussion of Dr. John Rock's pill and birth-control methods; President Kennedy assassinated

1965   March on Selma, Alabama; visit of Pope Paul VI to United Nations; Gommar A. De Pauw organizes Catholic Traditionalist movement; academic freedom debates at St. John's University, Jamaica, N.Y.; Roger LaPorte immolated before United Nations Building

1966   Organization of the NCCB/USCC; Harold Perry, S.V.D., becomes second black to be ordained a bishop

1967   Land O' Lakes Statement; beginning of Catholic Charismatic movement

1968   Pope Paul VI publishes *Humanae Vitae* against artificial means of birth control; Richard Nixon elected president; formation of the National Black Catholic Clergy Caucus, National Black Sisters' Conference, National Black Catholic Seminarians Association, and National Federation of Priests' Council; Catonsville Trial

1969   Organization of Priests Associated for Religious, Educational, and Social Rights (PADRES); formation of Dignity

1970   Patricio Flores becomes first contemporary Hispanic to be ordained a bishop

1971   Establishment of Leadership Conference of Women Religious (formerly the Conference of Major Superiors of Women, 1956), *Consortium Perfectae Caritatis*, Las Hermanas, and Network

1972   Harrisburg Trial

1973   *Roe v. Wade*

1975   Organization of first Catholic Women's Ordination Conference (Detroit)

1976   Convocation of "Call to Action" Conference (Detroit)

1979   Pope John Paul II visits the United States

1983   Publication of NCCB's *Challenge of Peace*

1985   Vatican disciplines Seattle's Archbishop Raymond Hunthausen

1986   Publication of NCCB's *Economic Justice for All*; Vatican removes Father Charles Curran from teaching theology at the Catholic University of America

1987   Pope John Paul II's second visit to the United States; convocation of the National Black Catholic Congress (Washington, D.C.)

1989   Fall of the Iron Curtain; separation of Father George Stallings from Catholic Church and his ordination as bishop and archbishop of schismatic African-American Catholic Church

1991   Persian Gulf War; U.S. Catholic bishops called to Rome for consultation on the American episcopal pastoral on women's issues

1992   National Black Catholic Congress meets in New Orleans; NCCB published "Resolution on Clergy Sex Abuse"

1993   Pope John Paul II presides over World Youth Day, Denver, Colorado; Cardinal Joseph Bernardin falsely charged with sexual abuse

1994   The Vatican publishes *Ordinatio Sacerdotalis*; the *Catechism of the Catholic Church* published in English; sexual abuse suit against Cardinal Bernardin dropped

1995   "Convocation '95," a national conference on the Hispanic presence in the United States, meets in San Antonio, Texas, celebrating the fiftieth anniversary of the establishment of the NCCB office of Hispanic Affairs; Pope John Paul II visits the United States and addresses the United Nations

1996   Cardinal Joseph Bernardin launches the Common Ground Project and dies in November from cancer

1997   Pope John Paul II declares Pierre Toussaint a "venerable servant of God"; Francis George appointed archbishop of Chicago; Synod for America held in Rome; the eighth National Black Catholic Congress meets in Baltimore; President Bill Clinton vetoes bill that prohibited partial-birth abortions

2000   NCCB/USCC becomes incorporated as the USCCB

2001   Terrorists attacks on New York City's World Trade Center and the Pentagon; U.S. war against the Taliban-protected terrorist training camps in Afghanistan

2002   *Boston Globe* publishes accounts of sexual abuse and episcopal negligence in the archdiocese of Boston; USCCB publishes *Charter for the Protection of Children and Young People*

2003   United States preemptive war against Iraq and American Catholic episcopal protests against preemptive strikes

2004   From Boston to San Francisco, a national debate on the legality of gay marriages and USCCB statements on the issue

NOTES

CHAPTER 1. Colonial Catholicism: 1492–1840

1. John F. Bannon, ed., *Bolton and the Spanish Borderlands* (Norman: University of Oklahoma Press, 1964), 48.

2. Or seventy-eight years if one considers the permanent presence of the Indian missions from the year 1715.

3. Robert Ricard, *The Spiritual Conquest of Mexico: An Essay on the Apostolate and the Evangelizing Methods of the Mendicant Orders in New Spain, 1523–1572,* trans. Lesley Byrd Simpson (Berkeley: University of California Press, 1966), 284.

4. John Gilmary Shea, *History of the Catholic Missions among the Indian Tribes of the United States, 1529–1854* (New York: P. J. Kennedy, 1882), 119.

5. John L. Kessell, *Kiva, Cross, and Crown: The Pecos Indians and New Mexico, 1540–1840* (Washington, D.C.: National Park Service, U.S. Department of the Interior, 1979), 319.

6. John J. Kessell, *Friars, Soldiers, and Reformers: Hispanic Arizona and the Sonora Mission Frontier, 1767–1856* (Tucson: University of Arizona Press, 1976), 236.

7. On this, see Cornelius J. Jaenen, *The Role of the Church in New France* (Toronto: McGraw-Hill Ryerson, 1976), viii.

8. Reuben Gold Thwaites, ed., *The Jesuit Relations and Allied Documents: Travels and Explorations of the Jesuit Missionaries in New France, 1610–1791,* 73 vols. (1896–1901; New York: Pageant Book Co., 1959), 35:273.

9. Ibid., 25:247; see also p. 249ff. for stories of these problems.

10. Ibid., 51:265.

11. Francis Parkman, *The Jesuits in North America* (Boston: Little, Brown, 1897), 216.

12. For example, *Jesuit Relations,* 34:159–95; 34:223–27; 35:201–5.

13. Ibid., 24:299–301; see also p. 281.

14. Ibid., 34:163.

15. John Tracy Ellis, ed., *Documents of American Catholic History,* 3 vols. (Wilmington, Del.: M. Glazier, 1987), 1:95.

16. R. Emmett Curran, ed., *American Jesuit Spirituality: The Maryland Tradition, 1634–1900* (New York: Paulist Press, 1988), 3.

17. R. Emmett Curran, J. T. Durkin, and G. P. Fogarty, eds., *The Maryland Jesuits, 1634–1833* (Baltimore: Corporation of the Roman Catholic Clergymen, Maryland Province, Society of Jesus, 1976), 20.

18. *JCP,* 1:179.

19. Curran, Durkin, and Fogarty, *Maryland Jesuits,* 10.

20. Thomas Hughes, *History of the Society of Jesus in North America: Colonial and Federal,* 4 vols. (New York: Longmans, Green, and Co., 1907–17), text 1:256.

21. [Richard Challoner], *The Garden of the Soul: A Manual of Spiritual Exercises and Instructions for Christians, Who, Living in the World, Aspire to Devotion* (1740, reprint, New York: D. & J. Sadlier & Co., 1869).

22. Jay P. Dolan, *The American Catholic Experience: A History from Colonial Times to the Present* (Garden City, N.Y.: Doubleday, 1985), 94–95.

23. Ellis, *Documents,* 1:98.

24. Michael James Graham, "Lord Baltimore's Pious Enterprise: Toleration and Community in Colonial Maryland, 1634–1724" (Ph.D. diss., University of Michigan, 1983), 51.

25. See Clayton Colman Hall, ed., *Narratives of Early Maryland, 1633–1684* (1946; reprint, New York: Barnes and Noble, 1967), 269–72.

26. Quoted in John D. Krugler, "Puritan and Papist: Politics and Religion in Massachusetts and Maryland before the Restoration of Charles II" (Ph.D. diss., University of Illinois, 1971), 277.

27. See Graham, "Pious Enterprise," 389; see also Gerald P. Fogarty, "Property and Religious Liberty in Colonial Maryland Catholic Thought," *CHR* 72 (October 1986): 573–600, esp., 587–92.

28. Hughes, *History,* text 2:591; John Tracy Ellis, *Catholics in Colonial America* (Baltimore: Helicon, 1965), 384; idem., *Documents,* 1:125–28.

29. Sydney H. Ahlstrom, *A Religious History of the American People* (New Haven, Conn.: Yale University Press, 1972), 361.

30. On this American problem, see Carl Bridenbaugh, *Mitre and Sceptre: Transatlantic Faiths, Ideas, Personalities, and Politics 1689–1775* (New York: Oxford University Press, 1962).

31. On this, see Peter S. Onuf, ed., *Maryland and the Empire, 1773: The Antilon–First Citizen Letters* (Baltimore: Johns Hopkins University Press, 1974).

32. See Elihu S. Riley, ed., *Correspondence of "First Citizen"—Charles Carroll of Carrollton and "Antilon"—Daniel Dulany Jr., 1773, with a History of Governor Eden's Administration in Maryland. 1769–1776* (Baltimore: King Bros., 1902), 118.

33. Ibid., 121, 230.

34. Worthington Chauncey Ford, ed., *Journals of the Continental Congress 1774–1789,* 34 vols. (Washington, D.C.: U.S. Government Printing Office, 1904–37), 1:34–35, quoted in James J. Hennesey, *American Catholics: A History of the Roman Catholic Community in the United States* (New York: Oxford University Press, 1981), 57.

35. Although some Pennsylvania Catholics joined the Tories in resisting the movement toward independence, most Catholics in Maryland and Pennsylvania supported the war effort. See Martin I. J. Griffin, *Catholics and the American Revolution,* 3 vols. (Ridley Park, Pa.: Author, 1907–11).

36. Carroll to G. W. P. Custis, February 20, 1829, quoted in Ellen Hart Smith, *Charles Carroll of Carrollton* (Cambridge, Mass.: Harvard University Press, 1942), 274.

CHAPTER 2. A Free Church in a Free State: 1776–1815

1. John Carroll to Vitaliano Borromeo, 10 November 1783, *JCP,* 1:80.

2. John Carroll to Charles Plowden, 20 February 1782, *JCP,* 1:65; on the moderate Enlightenment, see Henry May, *The Enlightenment in America* (New York: Oxford University Press, 1976), 3–105. May's description of the moderate Enlightenment did not include any Catholics, but it could have.

3. Patrick Carey, "American Catholics and the First Amendment: 1776–1840," *Pennsylvania Magazine of History and Biography* 113 (July 1989): 323–46.

4. *JCP,* 1:259–61, 365–68, 409–11. On Carroll's argumentation, see Joseph McShane, "John Carroll and the Appeal to Evidence: A Pragmatic Defense of Principle," *CH* 57 (September 1988): 298–309.

5. *JCP,* 1:180.

6. *JCP,* 3:375–466.

7. *JCP,* 1:527.

8. *JCP,* 1:68.

9. John Carroll, Robert Molyneaux, and John Ashton to Pope Pius VI, 12 March 1788, *JCP,* 1:279–80.

10. *JCP,* 1:520–21, 526–41.

11. *PL* 1:16–27.

12. *JCP,* 1:533.

13. John Carroll to Charles Plowden, [?] December 1792 [?], *JCP,* 1:548.

14. John Carroll to Charles Plowden, 26 September 1783, *JCP,* 1:78.

15. John Carroll to Leonardo Antonelli, 19 April 1788, *JCP,* 1:301.

16. Harvard, Yale, and Princeton had for years trained men for the ministry, but American Protestants did not establish the first independent divinity school until 1808 at Andover, Massachusetts. On this and the Sulpician influence on American Catholicism, see the excellent studies by Christopher J. Kauffman, *Tradition and Transformation in Catholic Culture: The Priests of Saint Sulpice in the United States from 1791 to the Present* (New York: Macmillan, 1988), 42 and passim, and Joseph M. White, *The Diocesan Seminary in the United States: A History from the 1780s to the Present* (Notre Dame, Ind.: University of Notre Dame Press, 1989).

17. For these statistics, see *JCP,* 1:181; and James F. Connelly, *The Visit of Archbishop Gaetano Bedini to the United States of America, June 1853–February 1854* (Rome: Libreria Editrice dell'Università Gregoriana, 1960), 264.

18. Ellis, *Documents,* 1:208.

19. For a social history of the new American establishments, see Barbara Misner, *"Highly Respectable and Accomplished Ladies": Catholic Women Religious in America 1790–1850* (New York: Garland Publishing, 1988). For more general histories of women religious, see Diane Bates Morrow, *Persons of Color and Religious at the Same Time: The Oblate Sisters of Providence, 1828–1860* (Chapel Hill: University of North Carolina Press, 2002); Mary Ewens, *The Role of the Nun in Nineteenth Century America* (New York: Arno Press, 1978); James Joseph Kenneally, *The History of American Catholic Women* (New York: Crossroad, 1990); and Karen Kennelly, ed., *American Catholic Women: A Historical Exploration* (New York: Macmillan, 1989).

20. Mary Ewens, "Women in the Convent," in Kennelly, *American Catholic Women,* 18.

21. Ellis, *Documents,* 1:218–19.

22. John Tracy Ellis, *American Catholicism,* 2d ed., rev. (Chicago: University of Chicago, 1969), 41–83.

23. Quoted in Annabelle M. Melville, *Jean Lefebvre de Cheverus 1768–1836* (Milwaukee: Bruce Publishing, 1958), 222.

24. On the territorial increases, see Gerald Shaughnessy, *Has the Immigrant Kept the Faith? A Study of Immigration and Catholic Growth in the United States, 1790–1920* (New York: Macmillan, 1925), 68–72. Shaughnessy's estimate that in 1803 Louisiana had

fifteen thousand white Catholics, primarily Spanish and French, out of an estimated twenty-four thousand seems to me to be a low estimate based on slim evidence.

25. John Carroll to the Congregation of Boston, 30 April 1790, *JCP*, 1:441.

26. John Carroll, Report for His Eminence Cardinal Antonelli on the Condition of Religion in the sections of the United States of America, 1 March 1785, *JCP* 1:179; see also Shaughnessy, *Has the Immigrant?* 63–73.

CHAPTER 3. Internal Conflicts, Nativism, and Immigrant Catholicism: 1815–1866

1. On trusteeism, see Patrick Carey, "The Laity's Understanding of the Trustee System," *CHR* 64 (July 1978): 357–76; and idem, *People, Priests, and Prelates: Ecclesiastical Democracy and the Tensions of Trusteeism* (Notre Dame, Ind.: University of Notre Dame Press, 1987). For a fuller examination of the antebellum development of sole corporation legislation and the anticipated liabilities as well as benefits of such legislation, see ibid., 73–74, 106.

2. On this, see James Hennesey, "Papacy and Episcopacy in Eighteenth and Nineteenth Century American Catholic Thought," *RACHS* 77 (September 1966): 175–89.

3. For figures, see Shaughnessy, *Has the Immigrant?* 125, 153.

4. For an extensive treatment of the individual characteristics of the various ethnic groups that made up nineteenth-century American Catholicism, see Dolan, *American Catholic Experience,* 127–348. Much attention has been given to the ethnic variety in American Catholicism, but little attention has been paid to the ways in which the development of American Catholicism has been affected by geography and regional sensibilities. *Catholics in the Old South: Essays on Church and Culture,* ed. Randall M. Miller and Jon L. Wakelyn (Macon, Ga.: Mercer University Press, 1983), is an exception here. During this period the fundamental outlines of regional variations in Catholicism began to emerge. East Coast Irish Catholics, for example, do not have the same sensibilities and cultural and historical experiences as do those in the South, Southwest, Midwest, or Northwest. It is beyond the scope of the present essay, however, to develop these variations.

5. Jo Ann Manfra, "The Catholic Episcopacy in America, 1789–1852" (Ph.D. diss., University of Iowa, 1975), 14.

6. On this estimate, see Dolan, *American Catholic Experience,* 130.

7. Colman J. Barry, *The Catholic Church and German Americans* (Milwaukee: Bruce Publishing Co., 1953), 44–86.

8. Ray Allen Billington, *The Protestant Crusade: 1800–1860* (1938; reprint, Chicago: Quadrangle Books, 1964).

9. William Ellery Channing, *The Works of William E. Channing, D.D.,* 3d ed., 5 vols. (Glasgow: James Hedderwick and Son, 1840), 2:271.

10. On Catholic newspapers, see Paul J. Foik, *Pioneer Catholic Journalism* (New York: United States Catholic Historical Society, 1930).

11. John Hughes, "The Decline of Protestantism, and Its Causes," in *Complete Works of the Most Rev. John Hughes, D.D., Archbishop of New York: Comprising His Sermons, Letters, Lectures, Speeches, etc.,* ed. Lawrence Kehoe, 2nd ed., rev. and corr., 2 vols. (New York: American News Co., 1865), 2:101.

12. On developments in the Midwest, see Robert Frederick Trisco, *The Holy See and the Nascent Church in the Middle Western United States, 1826–1850* (Rome: Gregorian

University Press, 1962); Timothy Walch, "Catholic Social Institutions and Urban Development: The View from Nineteenth-Century Chicago and Milwaukee," *CHR* 64 (January 1978): 16–32; and Thomas W. Spalding, "Frontier Catholicism," *CHR* 77 (July 1991): 470–84.

13. The provincial councils that met in 1829, 1833, 1837, 1840, 1843, 1846, and 1849 were in reality legally binding national synods as much as were the plenary councils that met in 1852, 1866, and 1884. After each of these meetings the bishops prepared pastoral letters for American Catholics, a practice that has continued to the present day after national episcopal meetings.

14. These figures are based on an analysis of Joseph Bernard Code, *Dictionary of the American Hierarchy* (New York: Longmans, Green and Co., 1940).

15. See, for example, Bishop John Hughes to a correspondent in Rome, 30 March 1858, quoted in John R. G. Hassard, *Life of the Most Reverend John Hughes, D.D., First Archbishop of New York* (New York: D. Appleton and Co., 1866), 389.

16. On this, see, for example, John Hughes, *Pastoral Letter of the Right Rev. Dr. Hughes to the Clergy and Laity of the Diocese of New York* (New York: George Mitchell, 1842), 5; Dale Light, "The Reformation of Philadelphia Catholicism, 1830–1860," *Pennsylvania Magazine of History and Biography* 112 (July 1988): 375–406; idem, *Rome and the New Republic: Conflict and Community in the Philadelphia Catholicism from the Revolution to the Civil War* (Notre Dame, Ind.: University of Notre Dame Press, 1996); and Paul Horgan, *Lamy of Santa Fe: His Life and Times* (New York: Farrar, Straus and Giroux, 1975), 169–251.

17. On these statistics, see Peter Guilday, *A History of the Councils of Baltimore, 1791–1884* (New York: Macmillan, 1932), 193–94.

18. Quoted in Connelly, *Visit of Archbishop Bedini,* 240.

19. This statistic is an estimate based on accounts in Thomas W. Spalding, *The Premier See: A History of the Archdiocese of Baltimore, 1789–1989* (Baltimore: Johns Hopkins University Press, 1989), 107–9; Clyde F. Crews, *An American Holy Land: A History of the Archdiocese of Louisville* (Wilmington, Del.: Michael Glazier, 1987), 88, 106; Misner, "Highly Respectable and Accomplished Ladies," 143, 166; and Ewens, *Role of the Nun,* 32. The phenomenal growth in the number of women religious is illustrated in the diocese of Bardstown, Kentucky, where the number of sisters increased from none in 1815 to 260 in 1836.

20. For statistics, see Ewens, *Role of the Nun,* 86, 201.

21. On the "sectarian" pan-Protestantism of the common schools and the anti-Catholicism of textbooks and readers, see Richard Shaw, *Dagger John: The Unquiet Life and Times of Archbishop John Hughes of New York* (New York: Paulist Press, 1977), 139–45; and *PL,* 1:141–42. Even primary spellers acquainted students with words (e.g., nunnery, abbot, monastic, papist) that would help students understand Nativist literature; on this, see Ruth Elson, *Guardians of Tradition: American Schoolbooks of the Nineteenth Century* (Lincoln: University of Nebraska Press, 1964), 53, quoted in Ewens, *Role of the Nun,* 162. Timothy L. Smith, "Protestant Schooling and American Nationality," *Journal of American History* 53 (March 1967): 679–95, is the classic treatment of Protestant religious influence on public schools.

22. *PL,* 1:111.

23. For a history of the controversy, see William Oland Bourne, *History of the Public School Society of New York* (New York: George Putnam's Sons, 1873); Shaw, *Dagger John,*

139–75; Vincent P. Lannie, *Public Money and Parochial Education: Bishop Hughes, Governor Seward, and the New York School Controversy* (Cleveland: Press of Case Western Reserve University, 1968); and Hughes, *Works,* 1:41–298.

24. See Dolan, *American Catholic Experience,* 262–93, for an account of the varieties of diocesan responses to the development of a Catholic school system.

25. Connelly, *Visit of Archbishop Bedini,* 264–65.

26. Edward J. Power, *A History of Catholic Higher Education in the United States* (Milwaukee: Bruce Publishing Co., 1958), 34, 255. See also Connelly, *Visit of Archbishop Bedini,* 264–65; and Harold A. Buetow, *Of Singular Benefit: The Story of Catholic Education in the United States* (New York: Macmillan, 1970), 117.

27. *PL,* 1:42, 72, 76.

28. Joseph P. Chinnici, *Living Stones: The History and Structure of Catholic Spiritual Life in the United States* (New York: Macmillan, 1989), 50. See also pp. 35–85 for a description of immigrant bishops' views of the spiritual life.

29. Hughes, *Works,* 2:158–69.

30. Emmet Larkin, "The Devotional Revolution in Ireland," *American Historical Review,* 77 (1972): 625–52.

31. Jay P. Dolan, *Catholic Revivalism: The American Experience, 1830–1900* (Notre Dame, Ind.: University of Notre Dame Press, 1978).

32. [Orestes A. Brownson], "Revivals and Retreats," *Brownson's Quarterly Review* 15 (July 1858): 289–322.

33. Ann Taves, *The Household of Faith: Roman Catholic Devotions in Mid-Nineteenth-Century America* (Notre Dame, Ind.: University of Notre Dame Press, 1986).

34. Orestes Augustus Brownson, *The Works of Orestes A. Brownson,* coll. and arr. Henry F. Brownson, 20 vols. (Detroit: T. Nourse, 1882–87), 8:316; see also Patrick W. Carey, ed., *Orestes A. Brownson: Selected Writings* (New York: Paulist Press, 1991), 45.

35. O. A. Brownson, "Rights of the Temporal," *Brownson's Quarterly Review* 18 (October 1860): 464–67.

36. Brownson, *Works,* 20:256, 270–71, 274.

37. Ibid., 256.

38. Patrick W. Carey, "American Catholic Romanticism, 1830–1888," *CHR* 64 (October 1988): 590–606.

39. Ahlstrom, *Religious History of the American People,* 597–632.

40. Only a few prominent lay Catholics during the antebellum period (e.g., Mathew Carey, William Gaston, Roger Brooke Taney) became actively involved in American public and political life.

41. *PL,* 1:85.

42. For more information on American Catholics and slavery, see Benjamin J. Blied, *Catholics and the Civil War* (Milwaukee: Author, 1945); Madeline Hooke Rice, *American Catholic Opinion in the Slavery Controversy* (New York: Columbia University Press, 1944); and Joseph D. Brokhage, *Francis Patrick Kenrick's Opinion on Slavery* (Washington, D.C.: Catholic University of America Press, 1955).

43. John England, *The Works of the Right Reverend John England, First Bishop of Charleston,* coll. and arr. Ignatius A. Reynolds, 5 vols. (Baltimore: John Murphy and Co., 1849), 3:112, 113–91.

44. *PL,* 1:181.

45. See Rice, *American Catholic Opinion,* 12.

46. See, for example, John England, *A Catechism of the Roman Catholic Faith* (Charleston, S.C.: Henry J. Egan, 1821), quoted in Peter Clarke, *A Free Church in a Free Society: The Ecclesiology of John England, Bishop of Charleston, 1820–1842, a Nineteenth-Century Missionary Bishop in the Southern United States,* 2nd ed. (Hartsville, S.C.: Center for John England Studies, 1982), 400.

47. Francis P. Kenrick, *Theologia Moralis,* 3 vols. (Philadelphia: Eugene Cummiskey, 1841–43), 1:255–57.

48. For a summary of these rights and their sources in the tradition, see Stafford Poole and Douglas J. Slawson, *Church and Slave in Perry County, Missouri, 1818–1865* (Lewiston, N.Y.: Edwin Mellen Press, 1986), 55–58.

49. John Mary Odin to director of the seminary at Lyons, France, 2 August 1823, quoted in ibid., 59.

50. Gaston's speech at Chapel Hill, North Carolina, "Judge Gaston on Slavery," reprinted in *American Catholic Historical Researches* 8 (April 1891): 71.

51. See Rice, *American Catholic Opinion,* 135–36.

52. Quoted in Billington, *Protestant Crusade,* 425.

53. For an account of Catholic participation in the war, see Blied, *Catholics and the Civil War.*

54. Michael V. Gannon, *Rebel Bishop: The Life and Era of Augustin Verot* (Milwaukee: Bruce Publishing Co., 1964), 31.

55. Brownson, *Works,* 17:156.

56. Hughes to Simon Cameron, 2 October 1861, quoted in Shaw, *Dagger John,* 344.

57. On the draft riots, see ibid., 360–69; and Hennesey, *American Catholics,* 154–55.

58. On Hughes's trip, see Shaw, *Dagger John,* 345–54.

59. Hennesey, *American Catholics,* 155.

60. Ewens, "Women in the Convent," in Kennelly, *American Catholic Women,* 26.

61. Spalding's journal of 5 July 1863, quoted in Thomas W. Spalding, *Martin John Spalding: American Churchman* (Washington, D.C.: Catholic University of America Press, 1973), 142.

62. Gannon, *Rebel Bishop,* 118.

63. Brownson, *Works,* 17:279.

64. Ibid., 12:509.

65. On the purpose and results of this council, see Thomas Spalding, *Martin John Spalding,* 194–237.

66. Quoted in ibid., 197.

67. Ibid., 215, 222.

68. James Parton, "Our Roman Catholic Brethren," *Atlantic Monthly* 21 (April 1868): 432–51, quoted in Dolores Liptak, *Immigrants and Their Church* (New York: Macmillan, 1989), 48.

CHAPTER 4. Reconstruction and Expansion: 1866–1884

1. Sydney E. Ahlstrom, *A Religious History of the American People,* 698.

2. Gannon, *Rebel Bishop,* 120.

3. For examples of this, see Richard C. Madden, *Catholics in South Carolina: A Record* (Lanham, Md.: University Press of America, 1985), 112–13.

4. For these statistics, see Shaughnessy, *Has the Immigrant?* 149, 159, 189.

5. These statistics are based on information in Code, *Dictionary of the American Hierarchy, 1789–1964* (New York: J. F. Wagner, 1964).

6. The best study of this phenomenon is Robert Trisco, "Bishops and Their Priests in the United States," in *The Catholic Priests in the United States: Historical Investigations,* ed. John Tracy Ellis (Collegeville, Minn.: St. John's University Press, 1971), 111–292.

7. Robert Emmet Curran, "Prelude to 'Americanism': The New York Accademia and Clerical Radicalism in the Late Nineteenth Century," *CH* 47 (March 1978): 48–65.

8. *The Conservative Reformers: German-American Catholics and the Social Order* (Notre Dame, Ind.: University of Notre Dame Press, 1968), 23, 24.

9. Some of the new national organizations included the Ancient Order of Hibernians (AOH, originally organized in 1836 in St. James Parish in New York City), which became national in 1867, the Irish Catholic Benevolent Union (1869), the Catholic Total Abstinence Union (in 1872), the Catholic Young Men's National Union (1875), and the Catholic Knights of America (1877).

10. On the Knights, see the excellent study by Christopher Kauffman, *Faith and Fraternalism: The History of the Knights of Columbus, 1882–1982* (San Francisco: Harper and Row, 1982).

11. O'Brien, *Public Catholicism,* 92.

12. Some of those involved included William McLaughlin of the Shoemakers, John Sidey of the anthracite coal miners, Hugh McLaughlin of the Iron Puddlers, and Terence Powderly, Leonora Barry, Augusta L. Troup, Elizabeth F. Rodgers, and "Mother" Mary Harris Jones of the Knights of Labor. On Catholic participation in labor and labor organizations, see ibid., 81–84, 87–88, and Mary J. Oates, "Catholic Laywomen in the Labor Force, 1850–1950," in Karen Kennelly, ed., *American Catholic Women,* 81–124.

13. T. Spalding, *Spalding,* 252. Cf. also John Gilmary Shea, "Labor Discontent," *American Catholic Quarterly Review* 7 (October 1882): 712.

14. Francis Paul Prucha, *American Indian Policy in Crisis: Christian Reformers and the Indian, 1865–1900* (Norman: University of Oklahoma Press, 1976), 31–32.

15. Quoted in ibid., 45 n. 47.

16. On American Catholic postwar reactions, particularly Brownson's, to the new sciences, see my forthcoming *An American Religious Weathervane: Orestes A. Brownson* (Grand Rapids, Mich.: Eerdmans), chap. 10.

17. For the *Syllabus,* see Colman J. Barry, ed., *Readings in Church History,* 3 vols. (Westminster, Md.: The Newman Press, 1965), 3:70–74.

18. Quoted in T. Spalding, *Spalding,* 242.

19. Brownson, *Works,* 18:219.

20. For the best account of American participation at the council, see James J. Hennesey, *The First Council of the Vatican: The American Experience* (New York: Herder and Herder, 1963). I am relying on Hennesey's account in what follows.

21. For a brief review of the contrasting preconciliar positions on papal infallibility, see my *American Catholic Religious Thought* (New York: Paulist Press, 1987), 24–30.

22. For postconciliar acceptances of papal infallibility, see Gerald Fogarty, "Archbishop Peter Kenrick's Submission to Papal Infallibility," *Archivum Historiae Pontificiae* 16 (1978): 205–23, and "Pastoral Letter of the Most Reverend Martin John Spalding, D.D., Archbishop of Baltimore, to the Clergy and Laity of the Archdiocese, on the Papal Infallibility" (19 July 1870), in M. J. Spalding, *The Evidences of Catholicity,* 6th ed. (Baltimore: John Murphy, 1876), 441–77.

23. I. T. Hecker, "An Exposition of the Church in View of the Recent Difficulties and Controversies and the Present Needs of the Age," *Catholic World* 21 (April–September 1875): 125. For a more extensive interpretation of Hecker's views, see William L. Portier, *Isaac Hecker and the First Vatican Council* (Lewiston, N.Y.: Edwin Mellen Press, 1985).

24. For historical confirmations of this interpretation, see James Turner, *Without God, Without Creed: The Origins of Unbelief in America* (Baltimore: Johns Hopkins University Press, 1985) and Philip Gleason "Baltimore III and Education," *U.S.CH* 4 (1985): 273–306.

25. *The Church and the Age: An Exposition of the Catholic Church in View of the Needs and Aspirations of the Present Age* (New York: Office of the Catholic World, 1887), 1–2.

26. For general background on the council and a discussion of the issues, see Peter Guilday, *A History of the Councils of Baltimore,* 221–49; John Tracy Ellis, *The Life of James Cardinal Gibbons, Archbishop of Baltimore, 1834–1921,* 2 vols. (Milwaukee: Bruce Publishing, 1952), 1:203–51; and idem, "Episcopal Vision in 1884 and Thereafter," *U.S.CH* 4 (1985): 197–222.

27. *Acta et Decreta Concilii Plenarii Baltimorensis Tertii* (Baltimore: John Murphy, 1886).

28. "Baltimore III and Education," 273.

CHAPTER 5. Americanism: 1884–1899

1. For discussions of Americanism, see Robert D. Cross, *The Emergence of Liberal Catholicism in America* (Cambridge, Mass.: Harvard University Press, 1958); Robert Emmett Curran, *Michael Augustine Corrigan and the Shaping of Conservative Catholicism in America, 1878–1902* (New York: Arno Press, 1978); Gerald P. Fogarty, *The Vatican and the Americanist Crisis: Denis J. O'Connell, American Agent in Rome, 1885–1903* (Rome: Università Gregoriana Editrice, 1974); Thomas T. McAvoy, *The Americanist Heresy in Roman Catholicism, 1895–1900* (Notre Dame, Ind.: University of Notre Dame Press, 1963); Margaret M. Reher, "The Church and the Kingdom of God in America: The Ecclesiology of the Americanists" (Ph.D. diss., Fordham University, 1972); idem, "Pope Leo XIII and Americanism," *TS* 34 (December 1973): 679–89; Thomas E. Wangler, "The Ecclesiology of Archbishop John Ireland: Its Nature, Development and Influence" (Ph.D. diss., Marquette University, 1968); and idem, "The Birth of Americanism: 'Westward the Apocalyptic Candlestick,' " *Harvard Theological Review* 65 (July 1972): 415–36.

2. See Wangler, "Ecclesiology of Archbishop Ireland"; idem, "Birth of Americanism"; and Reher, "Church and the Kingdom of God."

3. On these statistics, see Shaughnessy, *Has the Immigrant?* 165, 169, 175, 180.

4. For sources on the new immigrants, see Carey, *People, Priests, and Prelates,* 337 n. 12, 15; 338 n. 18, 19.

5. Barry, *Catholic Church and German Americans,* 289–96.

6. Ibid., 11.

7. Reprinted in ibid., 296–312.

8. Henry Joseph Browne, *The Catholic Church and the Knights of Labor* (Washington, D.C.: Catholic University of America Press, 1949).

9. For the petition, see Ellis, *Documents,* 2:457–60.

10. Ibid., 1:455.

11. On the school question, see Daniel F. Reilly, *The School Controversy (1891–1893)* (Washington, D.C.: Catholic University of America Press, 1943).

12. In John Ireland, *Church and Modern Society* (New York: D. H. McBride and Co., 1903), 215–32; quote is from p. 217.

13. On the whole question in some detail, see Ellis, *Life of Gibbons,* 1:595–652.

14. J. L. Spalding, "Catholicism and Apaism," *North American Review* 159 (September 1894): 282–83.

15. John J. Keane, "The Ultimate Religion," in John Henry Barrows, ed., *The World's Parliament of Religions,* 2 vols. (Chicago: Parliament Publishing Co., 1893), 2:1331. See also James F. Cleary, "Catholic Participation in the World's Parliament of Religions, Chicago, 1893," *CHR* 55 (January 1970): 585–609.

16. Letter quoted in Frederick J. Zwierlein, *The Life and Letters of Bishop McQuaid: Prefaced with the History of Catholic Rochester before His Episcopate,* 3 vols. (Rochester, N.Y.: Art Print Shop, 1927), 3:224.

17. Letter quoted in Cleary, "Catholic Participation," 605.

18. Sermon in Ellis, *Documents,* 2:461–63.

19. John L. Spalding, *Education and the Higher Life* (Chicago: A. C. McClurg and Co, 1890), 179.

20. For the encyclical, see Ellis, *Documents,* 2:499–511; quote from p. 502.

21. Joseph Schroeder, "Leo XIII and the Encyclical 'Longinqua,' " *American Catholic Quarterly Review* 20 (April 1895): 381–82.

22. On these early attempts at modernism, see R. Scott Appleby, *"Church and Age Unite!" The Modernist Impulse in American Catholicism* (Notre Dame, Ind.: University of Notre Dame Press, 1992).

23. Joseph Schroeder, "Theological Minimizers and Their Latest Defenders," *AER* 4 (February 1891): 118.

24. *Le Père Hecker Fondateur des "Paulistes" Américains, 1819–1888* (Paris, 1897).

25. On Catholic negotiations prior to the war, see Marvin R. O'Connell, *John Ireland and the American Catholic Church* (St. Paul: Minnesota Historical Society Press, 1988), 441–55.

26. O'Connell to Ireland, Rome, 24 May 1898, quoted in ibid., 455.

27. Republished in Ellis, *Documents,* 2:537–47.

28. Ireland to George Deshon, 24 February 1899, in the Paulist Fathers Archives, quoted in O'Connell, *John Ireland,* 462, and McAvoy, *Americanist Heresy,* 237.

29. Corrigan to Leo XIII, 10 March 1899, quoted in McAvoy, *Americanist Heresy,* 248–49.

30. Katzer to Leo XIII, Pentecost Sunday, 1899, quoted in ibid., 252–53.

CHAPTER 6. Catholicism in the Progressive Era: 1900–1920

1. Claudia Carlen, *The Papal Encyclicals,* 5 vols. (New York: McGrath, 1981), 3:5–10.

2. Ibid., 3:71–98.

3. On what little modernism there was, see Appleby, *"Church and Age Unite!"* For the attempts of some progressive era Catholic intellectuals to reconcile modern science and Catholic thought, see my "After *Testem Benevolentiae* and *Pascendi,"* *Catholic Southwest: A Journal of History and Culture* 7 (1996): 13–33.

4. Edward R. Kantowicz, *Corporation Sole: Cardinal Mundelein and Chicago Catholicism* (Notre Dame, Ind.: University of Notre Dame Press, 1983), 2. See also idem, "Cardinal Mundelein of Chicago and the Shaping of Twentieth-Century American Catholicism,"

Journal of American History 68 (June 1981): 52–68; James M. O'Toole, *Militant and Triumphant: William Henry O'Connell and the Catholic Church in Boston, 1859–1944* (Notre Dame, Ind.: University of Notre Dame Press, 1992); and idem, "The Name that Stood for Rome: William O'Connell and the Modern Episcopal Style," in Gerald P. Fogarty, ed., *Patterns of Episcopal Leadership* (New York: Macmillan, 1989), 171–84.

5. On this, see James M. O'Toole, "The Role of Bishops in American Catholic History: Myth and Reality in the Case of Cardinal William O'Connell," *CHR* 77 (October 1991): 595–615.

6. John J. Wynne, *America* 1 (17 April 1909), 5–6.

7. On the missionary union movement, see Thomas J. Jonas, *The Divided Mind: American Catholic Evangelists of the 1890s* (New York: Garland, 1988).

8. Debra Campbell has done the most to uncover something of this early twentieth-century lay movement in her "David Goldstein and the Lay Catholic Street Apostolate 1917–41" (Ph.D. diss., Boston University, 1982), but she has concentrated on Goldstein and his Boston-based operation; see also idem, "A Catholic Salvation Army: David Goldstein, Pioneer Lay Evangelist," *CH* 52 (September 1983): 322–32; and idem, "The Rise of the Lay Catholic Evangelist in England and America," *Harvard Theological Review* 79 (October 1986): 413–37. Other local movements still need a historian.

9. For example, the American Federation of Catholic Societies, 1901; the Catholic Educational Association, 1904; the National Conference of Catholic Charities, 1910; the Catholic Press Association, 1911; the Catholic Hospital Association, 1915; and local Catholic social settlement houses. On the latter, see Margaret M. McGuinness, "Response to Reform: The History of the Catholic Social Settlement Movement, 1897–1915" (Ph.D. dissertation, Union Theological Seminary, 1985); and idem, "A Puzzle with Missing Pieces: Catholic Women and the Social Settlement Movement, 1897–1915," Working Paper Series, Charles and Margaret Hall Cushwa Center for the Study of American Catholicism, University of Notre Dame, ser. 22, no. 2 (spring 1990).

10. Richard T. Ely, "Introduction," in John A. Ryan, *A Living Wage* (New York: Macmillan, 1906), xii–xiii.

11. On the Catholic movement, see Joan Bland, *Hibernian Crusade: The Story of the Catholic Total Abstinence Union of America* (Washington, D.C.: Catholic University of America Press, 1951).

12. On the suffragist issue, see James J. Kenneally, "A Question of Equality," in Kennelly, *American Catholic Women,* 125–51.

13. A 1906 address to the American Federation of Catholic Societies, quoted in Alfred J. Ede, *The Lay Crusade for a Christian America: A Study of the American Federation of Catholic Societies, 1900–1919* (New York: Garland, 1988), 237.

14. Quoted in ibid., 238.

15. Ellis, *Documents,* 2:540–42.

16. I am indebted to Philip Gleason for this interpretation.

17. Elizabeth McKeown, *War and Welfare: American Catholics and World War I* (New York: Garland, 1988), 74. See also Douglas J. Slawson, *The Foundation and First Decade of the National Catholic Welfare Council* (Washington, D.C.: Catholic University of America Press, 1992).

18. Ibid., 50.

19. On the program, see *PL,* 1:255–71.

20. Joseph M. McShane, *"Sufficiently Radical": Catholicism, Progressivism, and the Bishops' Program of 1919* (Washington, D.C.: Catholic University of America Press, 1986).

21. Quoted in ibid., 247.

CHAPTER 7. The Roaring Twenties, the Depression, and World War II: 1920–1945

1. John A. Ryan, *Declining Liberty and Other Papers* (New York: Macmillan, 1927), 57–58.

2. *Society of Sisters of the Holy Names, Plaintiff, v. Pierce et al., Defendants, Nos. E 8662 and 8660.* For studies and sources on the Oregon law, see David P. Tyack, "The Perils of Pluralism: The Background of the Pierce Case," *American Historical Review* 74 (October 1968): 74–98; Lloyd P. Jorgenson, "The Oregon School Law of 1922: Passage and Sequel," *CHR* 54 (October 1968): 455–66; Christopher Kauffman, *Faith and Fraternalism,* 281–85; *Oregon School Cases: A Complete Record* (Baltimore: Westminster Press, 1925); and Thomas J. Shelley, "The Oregon School Case and the National Catholic Welfare Conference," *CHR* 75 (July 1989): 439–57.

3. Charles C. Marshall, "Open Letter to the Honorable Alfred E. Smith," *Atlantic Monthly* 139 (April 1927): 540–49.

4. Alfred E. Smith, "Catholic and Patriot: Governor Smith Replies," *Atlantic Monthly* 139 (May 1927): 721–28; quoted in Hennesey, *American Catholics,* 252.

5. On these reforms, see Arnold Sparr, *To Promote, Defend, and Redeem: The Catholic Literary Revival and the Cultural Transformation of American Catholicism 1920–1960* (New York: Greenwood Press, 1990).

6. Philip Gleason, "In Search of Unity: American Catholic Thought 1920–1960," *CHR* 65 (April 1979): 185–205; William M. Halsey, *The Survival of American Innocence: Catholicism in an Era of Disillusionment, 1920–1940* (Notre Dame, Ind.: University of Notre Dame Press, 1980); Gerald A. McCool, "The Tradition of St. Thomas in North America: At 50 Years," *The Modern Schoolman* 65 (March 1988): 185–206.

7. Quoted in Pope Piux IX's *Studiorum Ducem* (29 June 1923), in Carlen, *Papal Encyclicals,* 3:256.

8. Virgil Michel, "The Mission of Catholic Thought," *American Catholic Quarterly Review* 46 (October 1921): 664.

9. Carlen, *Papal Encyclicals,* 3:252.

10. J. Edward Coffey, "Classroom Disease and the Scholastic Prescription," *AER* 69 (July 1923): 34.

11. Ibid.

12. See Marilyn Wenzke Nickels, *Black Catholic Protest and the Federated Colored Catholics, 1917–1933* (New York: Garland, 1988), 303.

13. On the exclusion of blacks from the priesthood, see Stephen Ochs, *Desegregating the Altar: The Josephites and the Struggle for Black Priests, 1871–1960* (Baton Rouge: Louisiana State University Press, 1990).

14. For the 1943 and 1958 statements, see *PL,* 2:48, 201–6.

15. On these movements, see David J. O'Brien, *American Catholics and Social Reform: The New Deal Years* (New York: Oxford University Press, 1968).

16. Edward S. Shapiro, "Catholic Agrarian Thought and the New Deal," *CHR* 65 (October 1979): 598.

17. *PL,* 1:436, 438.

18. George Q. Flynn, *American Catholics and the Roosevelt Presidency 1932–1936* (Lexington: University of Kentucky Press, 1968), xi. See also idem, *Roosevelt and Romanism: Catholics and American Diplomacy, 1937–1945* (Westport, Conn.: Greenwood Press, 1976).

19. Gerhard Lenski, *The Religious Factor: A Sociological Study of Religion's Impact on Politics, Economics, and Family Life* (Garden City, N.Y.: Doubleday, 1963), 173; and Seymour M. Lipset, "Religion and Politics in the American Past," in Robert Lee and Martin E. Marty, eds., *Religion and Social Conflict* (New York: Oxford University Press, 1964), 92–94.

20. On this, see Wilson D. Miscamble, "Catholics and American Foreign Policy from McKinley to McCarthy: A Historiographical Survey," *Diplomatic History* 4 (1980): 223–40.

21. On the different traditions in American Catholicism, see Donald F. Crosby, *God, Church, and Flag: Senator Joseph R. McCarthy and the Catholic Church, 1950–1957* (Chapel Hill: University of North Carolina Press, 1978), 3–25; and Kathleen Riley Fields, "Bishop Fulton J. Sheen: An American Catholic Response to the Twentieth Century" (Ph.D. diss., University of Notre Dame, 1988), 217–310.

22. For an account of American Catholic responses to the crises in Mexico, see James P. Gaffey, *Francis Clement Kelley and the American Catholic Dream,* 2 vols. (Bensenville, Ill.: Heritage Foundation, 1980), 2:3–73; Robert E. Quirk, *The Mexican Revolution and the Catholic Church, 1910–1929* (Bloomington: Indiana University Press, 1973); Robert H. Vinca, "The American Catholic Reaction to the Persecution of the Church in Mexico, from 1926–1936," *RACHS* 79 (March 1968): 3–38; and Ellis, *Life of Gibbons,* 2:208–21. On Curley's role, see Spalding, *Premier See,* 349–52; on the bishops' views, see *PL,* 1:337–65, 408–11; on Burke's role, see John B. Sheerin, *Never Look Back: The Career and Concerns of John J. Burke* (New York: Paulist Press, 1975), 108–54.

23. On American Catholic reactions, see J. David Valaik, "American Catholic Dissenters and the Spanish Civil War," *CHR* 53 (January 1968): 537–55; and idem, "Catholics, Neutrality, and the Spanish Embargo, 1937–1939," *Journal of American History* 54 (June 1967): 73–85.

24. Statistics quoted in J. David Valaik, "American Catholics and the Spanish Civil War, 1931–1939" (Ph.D. diss., University of Rochester, 1964), 396–97.

25. On this, see John P. Diggins, *Mussolini and Fascism: The View from America* (Princeton, N.J.: Princeton University Press, 1972), 333, 336–37.

26. Ibid., 330–31.

27. On this, see F. K. Wentz, "American Catholic Periodicals React to Nazism," *CH* 31 (December 1962): 400–20.

28. Carlen, *Papal Encyclicals,* 3:525–37.

29. On this, see Thomas M. Keefe, "The Mundelein Affair: A Reappraisal," *RACHS* 89 (1978): 74–84.

30. Alden V. Brown, *The Tablet: The First Seventy-Five Years* (Brooklyn, N.Y.: Tablet Publishing Co., 1983), 32.

31. Quoted in Fields, "Bishop Sheen," 181, 212 n. 106.

32. Kauffman, *Faith and Fraternalism,* 335–36.

33. Quoted in Saul E. Bronder, *Social Justice and Church Authority: The Public Life of Archbishop Robert E. Lucey* (Philadelphia: Temple University Press, 1982), 63.

34. *PL,* 2:32.

35. Ibid., 37.

CHAPTER 8. Catholicism in the Cold War: 1945–1965

1. For these statistics, see the *Official Catholic Directory* for 1945 and 1965; *PL*, 2:1; and Fields, "Bishop Sheen," 391.

2. *PL*, 2:74.

3. Ibid., 82.

4. I am indebted for information on these family movements to Jeffrey M. Burns, *American Catholics and the Family Crisis 1930–1962* (New York: Garland, 1988).

5. On the censorship, see Robert I. Gannon, *The Cardinal Spellman Story* (New York: Pocket Books, 1963), 423–30; and Paul Blanshard, *American Freedom and Catholic Power* (Boston: Beacon Press, 1949), 180–210.

6. For the papers of this conference, see *Man and Modern Secularism: Essays on the Conflict of the Two Cultures* (New York: National Catholic Alumni Federation, 1940), 45. On Dewey's pragmatic secularism and the American Protestant Neo-Orthodox reaction against it, see George M. Marsden, *Religion and American Culture* (San Diego: Harcourt Brace Jovanovich, 1990), 200–204.

7. John Courtney Murray, "Religious Liberty: The Concern of All," *America* 77 (7 February 1948): 513–16.

8. John Courtney Murray, "Paul Blanshard and the New Nativism," *Month*, n.s. 5 (April 1951): 214–25.

9. *PL*, 3:13.

10. John Tracy Ellis, "American Catholics and the Intellectual Life," *Thought* 30 (autumn 1955): 353–86; Walter J. Ong, *Frontiers of American Catholicism: Essays on Ideology and Culture* (New York: Macmillan, 1957); Gustave Weigel, "American Catholic Intellectualist—A Theologian's Reflection," *Review of Politics* 19 (July 1957): 275–307; and Thomas F. O'Dea, *American Catholic Dilemma: An Inquiry into the Intellectual Life* (New York: Sheed and Ward, 1958).

11. George Bull, "The Function of a Catholic Graduate School," *Thought* 13 (September 1938): 368, 378.

12. Godfrey Diekmann, "The Primary Apostolate," in Leo Richard Ward, ed., *The American Apostolate: American Catholics in the Twentieth Century* (Westminster, Md.: Newman Press, 1952), 29–46. On Diekmann, see Kathleen Hughes, *The Monk's Tale hx003A; A Biography of Godfrey Diekmann, O.S.B.* (Collegeville, Minn.: Liturgical Press, 1991).

13. On postwar developments and conflicts in biblical studies, see Gerald P. Fogarty, *American Catholic Biblical Scholarship: A History from the Early Republic to Vatican II* (San Francisco: Harper and Row, 1989), 222–350.

14. On this, see Rosemary T. Rodgers, "The Changing Concept of College Theology: A Case Study" (Ph.D. diss., Catholic University of America, 1973).

15. For discussions of Murray's stance in this debate, see Donald E. Pelotte, *John Courtney Murray: Theologian in Conflict* (New York: Paulist Press, 1975), 14–17, 152–54; and J. Leon Hooper, *The Ethics of Discourse: The Social Philosophy of John Courtney Murray* (Washington, D.C.: Georgetown University Press, 1986), 11–30.

16. Carlen, *Papal Encyclicals*, 4:175–84.

17. The other three were Gregory Baum, O.S.A., from Toronto; George Tavard, A.A., from Mount Mercy College in Pittsburgh; and Edward Hanahoe, S.A., of the Friars of the Atonement at Graymoor, New York.

18. Cited in Patrick W. Collins, "Gustave Weigel: Ecclesiologist and Ecumenist" (Ph.D. diss., Fordham University, 1972), 283–84.

19. On Spellman's position, see Gannon, *Cardinal Spellman Story*, 397. On Murray's positions, see Pelotte, *John Courtney Murray;* and Hooper, *Ethics of Discourse.*

20. *PL*, 2:173.

21. Will Herberg, *Protestant-Catholic-Jew,* rev. ed. (Garden City, N.Y.: Anchor Books, 1960), 260.

22. Andrew M. Greeley, *The Church and the Suburbs* (New York: Sheed and Ward, 1959), 149.

23. Quoted from a 1948 *Christopher News Notes* in Chinnici, *Living Stones,* 197. Some of Keller's best-selling and widely distributed pamphlets and books include *You Can Change the World: The Christopher Approach* (1948), *Three Minutes a Day: Christopher Thoughts for Daily Living* (1949), *Careers that Change Your World* (1950), and *Government Is Your Business* (1951). On Keller, see Chinnici, *Living Stones,* 194–204.

24. For Jackson's criticisms, see Chinnici, *Living Stones,* 201–2; and Peter Michaels, "It Don't Come Naturally," *Integrity* 2 (January 1949): 42–44. See also Debra Campbell, "The Nunk Controversy: A Symbolic Moment in the Search for a Lay Spirituality," *U.S.CH* 8 (winter/spring 1989): 81–89.

25. Thomas Merton, *The Seven Storey Mountain* (New York: New American Library, 1948), 408.

26. For these statistics, see Fields, "Bishop Sheen," 391.

27. For a good analysis of postwar Chicago Catholicism, see Steven M. Avella, *This Confident Church: Catholic Leadership and Life in Chicago, 1940–1965* (Notre Dame, Ind.: University of Notre Dame Press, 1992).

28. For a study of *Integrity* Catholics, see James Terence Fisher, "The Limits of Personalism: *Integrity* and the Marycrest Community, 1946–1956," in *The Catholic Counterculture in America, 1933–1962* (Chapel Hill: University of North Carolina Press, 1989), 101–29. On the Grail, see Alden V. Brown, *The Grail Movement and American Catholicism 1940–1975* (Notre Dame, Ind.: University of Notre Dame Press, 1989).

29. For background on the NCCEM, see *Social Digest* (May–June 1965): 133. The NCCEM needs a historian.

30. "A Personal Note," *Commonweal* 53 (2 February 1951): 413.

31. "What Is Commonweal?," *Commonweal* 59 (5 February 1954): 445.

32. John Cogley, "Some Things Are not Caesar's," *Today* (November 1951): 12; and Editorial, "The Catholic and Modern Literature," *Commonweal* 56 (16 May 1952): 131.

33. Philip Gleason, "A Browser's Guide to American Catholicism, 1950–1980," *Theology Today* 38 (October 1981): 375.

34. For most of the information in what follows, I am indebted to Avella's *This Confident Church,* 249–88. For the most extensive study of race and Catholicism during the period, see John T. McGreevy's *Parish Boundaries: The Catholic Encounter with Race in the Twentieth-Century Urban North* (Chicago: University of Chicago Press, 1996).

35. Quoted in Avella, *This Confident Church,* 261–62, from Report on 8 A.M. Mass at St. Ambrose, 25 June 1950, in Box 2997, Chancery Files, Stritch Papers, Archives of the Archdiocese of Chicago.

36. Ibid., 262, quoting F. J. Quinn to George Casey, Chancellor, 10 July 1950, Box 2997, Chancery Files, Stritch Papers, Archives of the Archdiocese of Chicago.

37. Ibid., 262–63, quoting Stritch to Quinn, 15 September 1950, Box 2997, Chancery Files, Stritch Papers, Archives of the Archdiocese of Chicago.

38. *PL,* 2:48.

39. Ibid., 202.

40. Ibid., 124.

41. For this assessment, see Crosby, *God, Church, and Flag,* 34–36.

42. Ibid., 243.

43. On this development, see Patrick Allitt, "American Catholics and the New Conservativism of the 1950s," *U.S.CH* 7 (winter 1988): 15–37.

44. Ibid., 15.

45. Ibid., 36.

46. For an example of this view, see "No Islands," *Commonweal* 53 (8 December 1950): 221.

47. On this, see Rodger Van Allen, *The Commonweal and American Catholicism: The Magazine, the Movement, the Meaning* (Philadelphia: Fortress Press, 1974), 107–16.

48. William Clancy, "The Liberal Catholic," *Commonweal* 56 (11 July 1952): 335–37. See also "Catholics and Liberals," *Commonweal* 51 (3 February 1950): 452–53; and "The State of Liberalism," *Commonweal* 52 (23 May 1952): 163–64.

49. Fletcher Knebel, "Democratic Forecast: A Catholic in 1960," *Look,* 3 March 1959, 17.

50. "On Questioning Catholic Candidates," *America* 100 (7 March 1959): 651.

51. Quoted in Patricia Barrett, *Religious Liberty and the American Presidency: A Study in Church–State Relations* (New York: Herder and Herder, 1963), 10.

52. Robert McAfee Brown, "Senator Kennedy's Statement," *Christianity and Crisis* 9 (16 March 1959): 25.

53. John F. Kennedy, "The Refutation of Bigotry," in *"Let the Word Go Forth": The Speeches, Statements, and Writings of John F. Kennedy,* ed. Theodore C. Sorensen (New York: Delacorte Press, 1988), 131.

54. For lay Catholic support for the acceptance of the First Amendment, see Barrett, *Religious Liberty and the American Presidency,* 164–66.

55. For this attitude, see Vincent A. Yzermans, ed., *American Participation in the Second Vatican Council* (New York: Sheed and Ward, 1967), 137, 154.

56. On the council, see, e.g., Walter M. Abbott, ed., *The Documents of Vatican II,* trans. Joseph Gallagher (New York: Crossroad, 1989); Yzermans, *American Participation;* Eugene C. Bianchi, *John XXIII and American Protestants* (Washington, D.C.: Corpus Books, 1968); Robert E. Tracy, *An American Bishop at the Vatican Council: Recollections and Projections* (New York: McGraw-Hill, 1967); Xavier Rynne, *Letters from Vatican City* (New York: Farrar, Straus, 1963); Douglas Horton, *Vatican Diary 1964: A Protestant Observes the Third Session of Vatican Council II* (Philadelphia: United Church Press, 1965); and Albert C. Outler, *Methodist Observer at Vatican II* (Westminister, Md.: Newman Press, 1967).

CHAPTER 9. Post–Vatican II Catholicism: 1965–1990

1. The resolution is printed in *PL,* 3:486.

2. "Declaration on the Relationship of the Church to Non-Christian Religions," art. 2., in Abbott, *Documents of Vatican II,* 662.

3. Douglas Horton, *Vatican Diary 1965: A Protestant Observes the Fourth Session of Vatican Council II* (Philadelphia: United Church Press, 1966), 193.

4. Dialogues with the Lutheran World Federation (1965), Anglican Communion (1966), World Methodist Council (1966), Old Catholic Churches of the Union of Utrecht (1966), World Alliance of Reformed Churches (1968), Pentecostals (1972), Disciples of Christ (1977), Evangelicals (1977), Orthodox Church (1979), and Baptist World Alliance (1984).

5. Bilateral theological conversations have been established with these churches: Eastern Orthodox (1965), Anglican (1965), Lutheran (1965), Presbyterian and Reformed (1965), United Methodist (1966), American Baptist (1967–72), Disciples of Christ (1967–73), Southern Baptist (1978), Oriental Orthodox (1978), and Polish National Catholic (1985). Theologians and bishops have met periodically with classical Pentecostals (although, as yet, there is no official national dialogue with any of the American Pentecostal churches).

6. For a collection of these statements, see Joseph A. Burgess and Jeffrey Gros, eds., *Building Unity: Ecumenical Dialogues with Roman Catholic Participation in the United States, Ecumenical Documents IV* (New York: Paulist Press, 1989). See also George A. Tavard, "Ecumenical Relations," in Adrian Hastings, ed., *Modern Catholicism: Vatican II and After* (New York: Oxford University Press, 1991), 399–421.

7. For examples of these local efforts, see William B. Greenspun and William A. Norgren, eds., *Living Room Dialogues: A Guide for Lay Discussion Catholic-Orthodox-Protestant* (Glen Rock, N.J.: National Council of the Churches of Christ in the U.S.A. and Paulist Press, 1965).

8. Burgess and Gros, *Building Unity,* 6.

9. On social mobility, see Andrew M. Greeley, *The American Catholic: A Social Portrait* (New York: Basic Books, 1977). I do not want to make too much of this social mobility, because the American Catholic population was also significantly increased by new Hispanic immigrants (from Mexico, Cuba, Spain, South and Central America, and the Dominican Republic), most of whom were, like the first waves of Irish, poor, uneducated, and without skills needed in an increasingly technological society. By the late 1980s, Hispanics constituted almost 20 percent of the American Catholic population.

10. George Gallup Jr. and Jim Castelli, *The American Catholic People: Their Beliefs, Practices and Values* (Garden City, N.Y.: Doubleday, 1987), 162–63; see also "Portrait of Religion in U.S. Holds Dozens of Surprises," *NYT,* 10 April 1991, 1.

11. Robert Wuthnow, *The Restructuring of American Religion: Society and Faith since World War II* (Princeton, N.J.: Princeton University Press, 1988), 88–90.

12. For these statistics, see "Has the Church Lost Its Soul?," *Newsweek,* 4 October 1971: 80–89.

13. For sociological studies of the clergy shortage, see Richard A. Schoenherr and Annemette Sorensen, "Decline and Change in the U.S. Catholic Church," Report no. 5, *CROS* (Madison: University of Wisconsin, 1981); idem, "Social Change in Religious Organizations: Consequences of Clergy Decline in the U.S. Catholic Church," *Sociological Analysis* 43 (spring 1982): 23–52; and Dean Hoge, *The Future of Catholic Leadership: Responses to the Priest Shortage* (Kansas City, Mo.: Sheed and Ward, 1987).

14. Andrew M. Greeley, *American Catholics since the Council: An Unauthorized Report* (Chicago: Thomas More Press, 1985), 130; Andrew M. Greeley and Peter H. Rossi, *The Education of Catholic Americans,* National Opinion Research Center, Monographs in Social Research, no. 006 (Chicago: Aldine Publishing Co., 1966); and Andrew M. Greeley,

William C. McCready, and Kathleen McCort, *Catholic Schools in a Declining Church* (Kansas City, Mo.: Sheed and Ward, 1976).

15. See *Official Catholic Directory* for these years.

16. See "Land O' Lakes Statement: The Nature of the Contemporary Catholic University," in Neil G. McCluskey, ed., *The Catholic University: A Modern Appraisal* (Notre Dame, Ind.: University of Notre Dame Press, 1970), 336–41.

17. Ibid., 336.

18. Quoted in George A. Kelly, *The Battle for the American Church* (Garden City, N.Y.: Doubleday and Co., 1979), 66.

19. *Ex Corde Ecclesiae* is published in *Origins* 20 (4 October 1990): 268–69.

20. Philip Gleason, "Changing and Remaining the Same: A Look at Higher Education," in Stephen J. Vicchio and Virginia Geiger, eds., *Perspectives on the American Catholic Church, 1789–1989* (Westminster, Md.: Christian Classics, 1989), 228.

21. On this judgment, see Conference Board of Associated Research Councils, *An Assessment of Research-Doctorate Programs in the United States,* 5 vols. (Washington, D.C.: National Academy Press, 1982); Greeley, *American Catholics Since the Council,* 145–47; Ellis, "American Catholics and the Intellectual Life"; Paul Reinert, "In Response to Father Greeley," *Jesuit Educational Quarterly* 29 (October 1966): 124–25; National Catholic Educational Association, "A Working Paper: The Future Development of Catholic Institutions of Higher Education," 15 September 1966; and Greeley, "Why Catholic Higher Learning Is Lower," *NCR,* 23 (September 1983): 5. I am indebted to William P. Leahy, *Adapting to America: Catholics, Jesuits, and Higher Education in the Twentieth Century* (Washington, D.C.: Georgetown University Press, 1991), 136–47, for these sources and his own interpretations.

22. "Justice in the World," in Austin Flannery, *Vatican Council II: More Post-conciliar Documents* (New York: Costello Publishing Co., 1983), 90.

23. On this, see *PL,* vols. 3, 4, and 5.

24. For statistics on the Catholic Left, see Charles A. Meconis, *With Clumsy Grace: The American Catholic Left 1961–1975* (New York: Seabury Press, 1979), 153–66. On the peace movement in general, see Patricia McNeal, *Harder than War: Catholic Peacemaking in Twentieth-Century America* (New Brunswick, N.J.: Rutgers University Press, 1992).

25. Richard Curtis, *The Berrigan Brothers* (New York: Hawthorn Books, 1974), 53–57.

26. For these statistics, see "Has the Church Lost Its Soul?" 89.

27. Andrew M. Greeley, "L'Affaire Berrigan," *NYT,* 19 February 1971, L:37.

28. Thomas Merton, "A Note for *Ave Maria,*" in *Thomas Merton on Peace,* ed. Gordon Zahm (New York: McCall Publishing Co., 1971), 231–33.

29. *American Catholic People,* 77–90.

30. *PL,* 4:215–26. For a list of the 182 recommendations and the NCCB's graded response to each one, see Joseph A. Varacalli, *Toward the Establishment of Liberal Catholicism in America* (Washington, D.C.: University Press of America, 1983), 263–94.

31. "To Do the Work of Justice," in *PL,* 4:243–54.

32. *The Challenge of Peace,* 1983; *Economic Justice for All,* 1986; and the first drafts of *Partners in Redemption,* 1988, 1989.

33. Michael Novak et al., *Toward the Future: Catholic Social Thought and the U.S. Economy, A Lay Letter* (Lay Commission on Catholic Social Teaching and the U.S. Economy, 1984); see also, Michael Novak, " 'Pastoral' of Lay Group Stresses Morality of Economic Systems," *Catholic Herald,* 10 January 1985, 9.

34. Gallup and Castelli, *American Catholic People,* 181.

35. Ibid., 85–87, 89.

36. Ibid., 67.

37. For example, Lawrence Lucas, a Black priest in New York, published his *Black Priest/White Church: Catholics and Racism* (New York: Random House, 1970), pointing out in some detail the racism that influenced decisions and pastoral programs.

38. Statement in Gayraud Wilmore and James Cone, eds., *Black Theology: A Documentary History, 1966–1979* (Maryknoll, N.Y.: Orbis Books, 1979), 322–24.

39. For personal accounts of the history of the NOBC, see Joseph M. Davis and Cyprian Rowe, "The Development of the National Office for Black Catholics," *U.S.CH* 7 (spring/summer 1988): 265–89.

40. These figures are based on a Gallup calculation that 70 percent of all Hispanics in the United States are Catholic (Gallup and Castelli, *American Catholic People,* 139–48) and on Hispanic population statistics supplied by Moises Sandoval, *On the Move: A History of the Hispanic Church in the United States* (Maryknoll, N.Y.: Orbis Press, 1990), 88–89.

41. Gallup and Castelli, *American Catholic People,* 139–48, 185.

42. On this definition, see Richard A. McCormick, "Moral Theology 1940–1989: An Overview," *TS* 50 (March 1989): 10.

43. Kenneally, *History of American Catholic Women,* 191, quoting Dorothy Dohen, *Women in Wonderland* (New York, 1960), 92.

44. In 1971 *Newsweek* conducted a survey that indicated that 58 percent of American Catholics believed that they could ignore the pope's condemnation of artificial contraception and remain good Catholics; only 31 percent believed the contrary. See, "Has the Church Lost Its Soul?" *Newsweek* 4 October 1971, 81. See also, Gallup and Castelli, *American Catholic People,* 50; and Greeley, *American Catholics since the Council,* 80–100.

45. In 1969, 72 percent of Catholics considered premarital sex wrong; by 1985, only 33 percent considered it wrong. On this, see Gallup and Castelli, *American Catholic People,* 50–51; and Greeley, *American Catholics since the Council,* 85.

46. Kelly, *Battle for the American Church,* 129–98.

47. Gallup and Castelli, *American Catholic People,* 91.

48. *PL,* 3:199. The NCCB has published explicit statements against abortion in 1969, 1970, 1973, 1975, 1985, and a host of other documents where abortion is not the primary focus.

49. McCormick, "Moral Theology 1940–1989," 10.

50. Kenneally, *History of American Catholic Women,* 199.

51. See Gallup and Castelli, *American Catholic People,* 91–102.

52. Anthony Kosnik et al., *Human Sexuality: New Directions in American Catholic Thought* (New York: Paulist Press, 1977), 211–16.

53. Gallup and Castelli, *American Catholic People,* 63–64.

54. "Archbishop Calls Ferraro Mistaken on Abortion Issue," *NYT,* 10 September 1984, A:1.

55. For Ferraro's position, see " '82 Letter Signed by Ferraro," *NYT,* 11 September 1984, A:26.

56. For the speech, titled, "Religious Belief and Public Morality: A Catholic Governor's Perspective," see *Notre Dame Magazine* (autumn 1984): 21–30.

57. For Hyde's speech on 24 September 1984, see "Keeping God in the Closet," in Richard McMunn, *Religion in Politics* (Milwaukee: Catholic League for Religious and Civil Rights, 1985), 39–56.

58. "U.S. Catholicism: A Church Divided," *Time,* 24 May 1976, 59.

59. Gallup and Castelli, *American Catholic People,* 42.

60. For some studies of the charismatic renewal, see Kevin and Dorothy Ranaghan, *Catholic Pentecostals* (New York: Paulist Press, 1969); Edward D. O'Connor, *The Pentecostal Movement in the Catholic Church* (Notre Dame, Ind.: Ave Maria Press, 1971); Joseph Fichter, *The Catholic Cult of the Paraclete* (New York: Sheed and Ward, 1975); Kilian McDonnell, ed., *Open the Windows: The Popes and the Charismatic Renewal* (South Bend, Ind.: Greenlawn Press, 1989); and Terrence Robert Crowe, *Pentecostal Unity: Recurring Frustration and Enduring Hopes* (Chicago: Loyola University Press, 1993).

61. For these statistics on RENEW, see Michael P. Hornsby-Smith, "RENEW: Institutional Renewal or Modernist Heresy?" *American Catholic Studies Newsletter* 18 (spring 1991).

62. Gallup and Castelli, *American Catholic People,* 43.

63. On the conservative reaction, see William Dinges, "Catholic Traditionalism in America: A Study of the Remnant Faithful" (Ph.D. diss., University of Kansas, 1983).

64. For example, James Hitchcock, *The Decline and Fall of Radical Catholicism* (New York: Herder and Herder, 1971), George A. Kelly, "The Uncertain Church: The New Catholic Problem," *Critic* (fall 1976): 14–26; idem, *The Battle for the American Church* (Garden City, N.Y.: Doubleday, 1979); Thomas Molnar, *The Church: Pilgrim of Centuries* (Grand Rapids, Mich.: W. B. Eerdmans, 1990); the publication of an *International Catholic Review: Communio* (1974) and *Catholicism in Crisis* (1982–86; later called *Crisis,* 1986–); and the organization of the Fellowship of Catholic Scholars (1978).

65. Joseph Fenton, "Rome and the Status of Catholic Theology," *AER* 143 (December 1960): 409.

66. David Tracy, *Blessed Rage for Order: The New Pluralism in Theology* (New York: Seabury Press, 1975), 3f.

67. The appeal condemned thirteen current themes it so characterized. On the appeal, see Avery Dulles, *The Resilient Church: The Necessity and Limits of Adaptation* (Garden City, N.Y.: Doubleday and Co., 1977), 191–95.

68. Tracy, *Blessed Rage,* 10, 34.

69. Philip Gleason, *Keeping the Faith: American Catholicism Past and Present* (Notre Dame, Ind.: University of Notre Dame Press, 1987), 5.

CHAPTER 10. Troubled Times: 1990–2003

1. *Ecclesia in America* (January 1999) in *Origins* 28 (4 February 1999): 565, 567–92. See paragraph no. 66.

2. For a collection of some of these statements to 1997, see *PL,* 6:9, 465–83. On 1 July 2000 the NCCB/USCC became incorporated as the USCCB. The Web site for that organization, see http://www.usccb.org., contains up-to-date information and statements produced by the conference from 1998 to 2003.

3. Rosemary Radford Ruether, "The Place of Women in the Church," in Hastings, *Modern Catholicism,* 260.

4. For Catholic reactions to the ERA, see James J. Kenneally, "Women Divided: The Catholic Struggle for an Equal Rights Amendment, 1923–1945," *CHR* 75 (April 1989): 249–63; idem, "A Question of Equality," in Kennelly, *American Catholic Women,* 125–51; and Gallup and Castelli, *American Catholic People,* 103–6.

5. On Danielou, see *Le Monde* (19–20 September 1965), quoted in George H. Tavard, *Woman in Christian Tradition* (Notre Dame, Ind.: University of Notre Dame Press, 1973), 217.

6. For a history and analysis of the conference, see Laurie Wright Garry's "The Women's Ordination Conference (1975–1994): An Introduction to a Movement" (Ph.D. dissertation, Marquette University, 2000). Some of the more prominent women associated with the WOC were Elizabeth Schüssler Fiorenza (Harvard), Rosemary Radford Ruether (Garrett Theological Seminary, Chicago), Arlene Swidler (Temple), Sandra Schneiders (Jesuit Theologate, Berkeley), Anne Carr (University of Chicago), and Margaret Farley (Yale).

7. "Women and Priestly Ministry: The New Testament Evidence," *Catholic Biblical Quarterly* 41 (October 1979): 608–13, quote on p. 613. See also *Origins* 9 (27 December 1979): 450–54.

8. For a more detailed analysis of the episcopal responses to these issues, see my introduction to the *PL,* 6:13–16, and Laurie Wright Garry, "The Women's Ordination Conference," 35–67.

9. "Minutes of the General Meeting, NCCB" (Archives of the NCCB, Washington, D.C.), Saint Paul, Minnesota, June 13–15, 1991, pp. 73–75. Hereafter references will be designated "Minutes NCCB" with place and date.

10. For the text, see "Committee Report on Women's Concerns: One in Christ Jesus (Final Text)," *Origins* 22 (31 December 1992): 489, 491–508.

11. This teaching had been articulated also in the Vatican's *Inter Insigniores* (1976). On this see, "Vatican Declaration: Women in the Ministerial Priesthood," *Origins* 6 (3 February 1977): 517, 519–24.

12. On the response to the "dubium," see "Inadmissibility of Women to Ministerial Priesthood," *Origins* 25 (30 November 1995): 401, 403–5, and "Statements on Doctrinal Congregation's Action," *Origins* 25 (30 November 1995): 406–9.

13. *Origins* 27 (19 June 1997): 74, 76–79.

14. For the statement, see *PL,* 6:863.

15. See http://www.wf-f.org/History.html for a history of the organization, for links to its annual publication, *Voices,* and for their organizing statement, "Affirmation for Catholic Women."

16. In 1974, only 29 percent favored the ordination of women, but by 1985, the favorable rating had increased to 47 percent. On this, see Gallup and Castelli, *American Catholic People,* 56. Gallup opinion polls for 1992 indicated 67 percent of Catholics supported it.

17. *Full Pews and Empty Altars: Demographics of the Priest Shortage in the United States Catholic Dioceses* (Madison: University of Wisconsin Press, 1993). The Schoenherr interpretation was challenged in Paul Sullins's "Empty Pews and Empty Altars: A Reconsideration of the Catholic Priest Shortage," *Catholic Social Science Review* 6 (October 2001): 253–69; Sullins's challenge was countered by James Davidson, "Fewer and Fewer: Is the Clergy Shortage Unique to the Catholic Church?" *America* 189 (1 December 2003): 10–13.

18. Richard A. Schoenherr, "Number's Don't Lie: A Priesthood in Irreversible Decline," *Commonweal* (7 April 1995): 13; see also *Full Pews,* xvii.

19. Between 1982 and 1992, in the estimate of Jason Berry, *Lead Us Not into Temptation: Catholic Priests and the Sexual Abuse of Children* (New York: Doubleday, 1992),

xix, about 400 of the 52,000 priests in the United States were accused of sexual abuse of minors. For 1996 estimates, see Philip Jenkins' *Pedophiles and Priests: Anatomy of a Contemporary Crisis* (New York: Oxford University Press, 1996), 80–83. For much of the information in what follows on sexual abuse among priests until 1996, I am relying on Jenkins. In 2003, the USCCB, through its National Review Board, commissioned an independent audit of sexual abuse of minors in every diocese in the United States. The report of that audit, "The Nature and Scope of the Problem of Sexual Abuse of Minors by Catholic Priests and Deacons in the United States: A Research Study Conducted by the John Jay College of Criminal Justice" (available on http://www.usccb.org/nrb/johnjaystudy/ index.htm.), indicated between 1950 and 2003, 4,392 clergy (i.e., about 4 percent of all priests and deacons active in the ministry during that period) had committed sexual abuses of minors under the age of eighteen. The dioceses and their insurance companies paid out in suits, compensations, and treatment of victims and abusers, over 600 million dollars because of the scandal.

20. Jenkins, *Pedophiles and Priests,* 16.

21. Thomas Schilling and Charles Mount, "Suit Charges Moral Misconduct by Arlington Heights Priest," *Chicago Tribune* (24 December 1982), p. B1.

22. On the revelations in that text, see Jason Berry, *Lead Us Not into Temptation,* 98–102.

23. Ibid., 98.

24. For the NCCB's history of its own reactions to sexual abuse, see "Brief History: Handling Child Sex Abuse Claims," *Origins* 23 (10 March 1994): 666–70. For episcopal reactions between 1982 and 2003, see the comprehensive chronological list of NCCB statements in http://www.usccb.org/comm/Kit2.htm.

25. For the four stories, see *NCR,* 7 June 1985.

26. Berry, *Lead Us Not into Temptation,* 32.

27. For the respective stories, see *Washington Post,* 9 June 1985, A6 and 15 October 1985, A4; *NYT,* 20 June 1985; *Time,* 1 July 1985.

28. See "Brief History: Handling Child Sex Abuse Claims," *Origins* 23 (10 March 1994): 666–70.

29. See *PL,* 5.

30. "Brief History," 667–68.

31. The General Counsel for the USCC published "USCC Pedophilia Statement," *Origins* 17 (1988): 624. Although the statement referred to "pedophilia," it was in fact a directive about all cases of sexual abuse and not just pedophilia. By 1988, "pedophilia" had become an untechnical code word, even within the USCC, for all forms of sexual abuse.

32. Seven of the eight documents are: "Brief History," "Painful Pastoral Question: Sexual Abuse of Minors," *Origins* 22 (6 August 1992): 177–78; "Child Sexual Abuse: Think Tank Recommendations," *Origins* 23 (1 July 1993): 108–11; "Statement Supporting Cardinal Bernardin," *Origins* 23 (25 November 1993): 421–22; "Policy Statement on How Dioceses are Advised to Handle Sex Abuse Cases," *Origins* 23 (10 March 1994): 669; "Twenty-eight Suggestions on Sexual Abuse Policies," *Origins* 24 (8 December 1994): 443–44; "Walk in the Light: A Pastoral Response to Child Sexual Abuse," *Origins* 25 (2 September 1995): 337, 339–43.

33. Published in *PL,* 6:484–85.

34. "Painful Pastoral Question: Sexual Abuse of Minors," 177–78.

35. Ibid., 177.

36. For a long discussion among the bishops on the importance of sharing their own collective understanding of pedophilia and on specific recommendation for improving the Church's response to problem, see "Minutes NCCB," New Orleans, Louisiana, 17–18 July 1993, pp. 49–54.

37. "Minutes NCCB," Washington, D.C., 15–18 November 1993, pp. 87–89; see also "Minutes NCCB," Washington, D.C., 14–17 November 1994, pp. 66–69.

38. For Bernardin's own account of the affair, see *The Gift of Peace: Personal Reflections* (Chicago: Loyola Press, 1997), 15–41. Bernardin died from cancer on 14 November 1996 after publishing *The Gift of Peace,* a spiritual autobiography of the last three years of his life. The book was Bernardin's touching account of his approaches to the false accusation of sexual abuse, to his diagnosis of and surgery for pancreatic cancer, to the return of cancer to his liver, and to his decision to forgo medical treatment for it. He wrote the book for those who had similar experiences in their own lives. For the national episcopal response to the accusation of sexual abuse against Bernardin, see "Statement Supporting Cardinal Bernardin," *Origins* 23 (25 November 1993): 421–22.

39. "Church Allowed Abuse by Priest," and "Geogan Preferred Preying on Poorer Children," and "In 1985, Law had Report on Repeat Abusers," in *Boston Globe* (6 January 2002): A1, (7 January 2002): A1, and (7 January 2002): A12. The *Globe* reporters also published a longer, 274-page, account in June 2002. See *Betrayal: The Crisis in the Catholic Church* (Boston: Little, Brown, 2002). The *Boston Globe* reporters eventually won the Pulitzer Prize for their reports on the Boston pedophilia stories.

40. Lisa Gentes, "Father Shanley Documents Released," *Boston Pilot* (12 April 2002): 1.

41. For two examples of Catholic responses in Boston, see Voice of the Faithful, a lay organization for reform in the church (mission statement in http://www.votf.org), and Boston College's "The Church in the 21st Century" (see http://www.bc.edu/church21/ overview), a project that applied the university's research and intellectual resources to examine the problem and suggest solutions.

42. For details of the meeting, see "Final Communiqué" (24 April 2002) in http:// vatican.va/roman_curia/cardinals/documents/rc_cardinals-20020424-fin.

43. *Charter for the Protection of Children and Young People* (Washington, D.C.: USCCB, 2002).

44. On the "Norms," see http://www.usccb.org/ocyp/norms.htm.

45. For some early 1990s conservative reactions, see Jenkins, *Pedophiles and Priests,* 101–4. For three of many early twenty-first-century conservative assessments, see George Weigel, *The Courage to be Catholic: Crisis, Reform and the Future of the Church* (New York: Basic Books, 2002); "Catholic Leader Calls Dissent Main Cause of Clergy Sex Abuse Crisis," *Catholic Herald* (Milwaukee) (11 September 2003): 1, 13, and Peggy Noonan, "What I Told the Bishops: Thoughts on the Crisis in the American Catholic Church," *Wall Street Journal* (15 September 2003): 1.

46. See, for examples, Berry, *Lead Us Not into Temptation,* 169–274, and Jenkins, *Priests and Pedophiles,* 95, 99, 101, 105–6.

47. For an example of this, see James Carroll, "Priests' Victims Victimized Twice," *Boston Globe* (8 January 2002): A13. Carroll had also suggested "massive reforms" in the *Boston Globe* during the James Porter revelations in 1992.

48. See Bernardin's brief account in *The Gift of Peace,* 129–30.

49. For this and other documents relating to the project, see *Catholic Common Ground Initiative: Foundational Documents* (New York: Crossroad Publication, 1997).

50. Joseph Cardinal Bernardin, "Faithful and Hopeful: The Catholic Common Ground Project," 24 October 1996, in http://www.geocities.com/pharsea/CommonGround. html, p. 16.

51. For an outline and description of some of the episcopal statements on these issues, see *PL,* 6:21–32, for the years 1989–1997, and *Origins* for the years 1998–2003. For some specific examples of the episcopal concerns, see "Statement on Partial-Birth Abortion Ban Veto," *Origins* 26 (4 July 1996): 110; *Critical Decisions: Genetic Testing and Its Implications* (Washington, D.C., USCC, 1996); "The Oklahoma City Bombing Case: The Church and the Death Penalty," *Origins* 27 (26 June 1997): 84; for other statements against capital punishment in general and the execution of Timothy McVeigh, see "The Church and the Death Penalty," *Origins* 27 (26 June 1997): 81, 83–85, and other episcopal protests in *Origins* 31 (21 June 21): 110–11.

52. "Political Responsibility: Choices for the 1980s," March 1984, in *PL,* 5:95, 108.

53. "Webster: Opportunity to Defend Life," *Origins* 19 (9 April 1989): 213–14.

54. See, e.g., "Election-Year Action of Tax-Exempt Organizations," *Origins* 22 (22 August 1992): 179–85, and "Activities of Tax-Exempt Catholic Organizations," *Origins* 25 (14 March 1996): 643–48.

55. "Letter to Congress on 1991 Budget," *Origins* 19 (27 March 1990): 787–88.

56. "Testimony on the Permanent Replacement of Strikers," *Origins* 20 (4 April 1991): 697, 699–700.

57. "USCC Brief in Nancy Cruzan Case," *Origins* 19 (16 October 1989): 345–51.

58. "Brief Asks Reversal of Assisted-Suicide Ruling," *Origins* 24 (1 September 1994): 214–22. A similar amicus brief was filed before the U.S. Supreme Court when the Ninth Circuit Court also found Washington State's ban unconstitutional. See "A Threat of Unforseeable Magnitude," *Origins* 25 (28 March 1996): 671–72, and "Assisted Suicide Issue Moves to Supreme Court," *Origins* 26 (12 December 1996): 421, 423–29.

59. "USCC-Led Group Opposes Assisted-Suicide Law," *Origins* 25 (8 February 1996): 553, 555–62.

60. *Origins* 20 (19 July 1990): 133–36.

61. *Origins* 23 (24 June 1993): 81–86.

62. For an introduction to the various statements on international issues between 1989 and 1997, see *PL,* 6:32–37, and *Origins* for statements between 1998 and 2003. For a chronological listing and links to the statements between 1998 and 2003, see http://www.usccb.org/chronological.htm.

63. "A Pastoral Message: Living with Faith and Hope after September 11," *Origins* 31 (29 November 2001): 413, 415–20. On debt relief, see especially "Relieving Third World Debt" (September 1989) in *PL,* 6:80–97; "Statement on President Clinton's Announcement on Debt Relief for Poor Countries" (October 1999) in http://www.nccbuscc.org/sdwp/international/debt relief.htm; and *A Jubilee Call for Debt Forgiveness* (Washington, D.C.: USCC, 1999).

64. For sample statements, see "Addressing the Needs of Refugees," *Origins* 20 (17 April 1991): 763–67; "The Injustice of Anti-Foreigner Sentiment," *Origins* 23 (25 November 1993): 422–23; "Pending Immigration Legislation's Punitive Tone," *Origins* 26 (4 July 1996): 111–12; "A Statement on the Return of Kosovar Refugees to Kosovo" (10 June 1999) in http://www.nccbuscc.org/mrs/return.htm; "Statement on African Refugees" (August 2000) in http://www.nccbuscc.org/mrs/displaced.htm; "Refugees and Displaced Persons in the Great Lakes Region of Africa and in Kenya" (5 September 2000) in http://www.nccbuscc.org/mrs/displaced.htm.

65. "Resolution on Refugee Protection," *Origins* 31 (5 July 2001): 142–43.

66. *PL*, 6:550–88.

67. See "The New Moment in Eastern and Central Europe," in *PL*, 6:200–203.

68. "Resolving Lithuania's Crisis Peacefully," *Origins* 19 (9 April 1990): 785–86.

69. "Bishops in the White House Meeting Discuss El Salvador," *Origins* 19 (4 January 4, 1990): 501, 503–4.

70. "Statement on Colombia" (16 March 2000) in http://www.nccbuscc.org/mrs/return.htm;

71. See, e.g., "Statement on the Soviet Union and Yugoslavia," *Origins* 21 (26 September 1991): 258–59.

72. "Statement on Croatia," *Origins* 21 (21 November 21, 1991): 380–81.

73. "Humanitarian Nightmare in the Balkans," *Origins* 22 (8 April 1993): 733, 735–36. See also, "On United States Intervention in Bosnia," *Origins* 23 (27 May 1993): 22–23.

74. "Clarification of Position on Aiding Bosnia," *Origins* 23 (27 May 1993): 23.

75. "Statement on Returning from Kosovo" (31 August 1998) in http://www.nccbuscc.org/comm/archives/1998/98-184a.htm.

76. See, for example, "U.S. Bishops Issue Statement on Kosovo" (25 March 1998) in "Violence in Kosovo is 'Chillingly Similar to Recent Balkan History" (1 September 1998) in http://www.nccbuscc.org/comm/archives/1998/98-184.htm; "Four Steps Toward Peace," *Origins* 28 (15 April 1999): 740–41; "Statement on Kosovo," *Origins* 28 (1 April 1999): 706; "Bishops' President Urges Implementation of Kosovo Peace Agreement" (10 June 1999) in http://www.nccbuscc.org/comm/archives/1999/99-073.htm.

77. "Letters to Presidents Milosevic and Clinton," *Origins* 28 (15 April 1999): 739–40.

78. "Statement by Most Reverend Theodore McCarrick" (8 July 1999) in http://www.nccbuscc.org/sdwp/international/yugoslavia.htm.

79. "Statement on Investing in South Africa," *Origins* 23 (21 October 1993): 338.

80. "The Unspeakable Horror Visited Upon Rwanda," *Origins* 24 (23 June 1994): 81, 83–84.

81. "The Violence in Nigeria," *Origins* 25 (11 January 1996): 495–96.

82. For some examples of these statements, see "Statement on the Congo" (27 October 1999) in http://www.nccbuscc.org/comm/archives/congo.htm; "Statement on African Refugees" (August 2000); "Sudan's Cry for Peace" (14 November 2000) *Origins* 30 (23 November 2000): 377–78; "Statement on Kenya" (5 April 2001) in http://www.nccbuscc.org/sdwp/international/kenyastatement40501.htm; "Statement on Sudan" (5 April 2001) in http://www.nccbuscc.org/sdwp/international/lawpress.htm.

83. (Washington, D.C.: USCCB, 2001).

84. "Sudan's Cry for Peace"; see also "Statement on Sudan" (5 April 2001).

85. "Statement on the Middle East: The Pursuit of Peace with Justice," *PL*, 4:276–79.

86. *PL*, 6:136–61.

87. For various episcopal statements from 1990 to 2003, see "The Cause of Peace in the Middle East," *Origins* 21 (7 November 1991): 353–54; "Statement on Cease-Fire on Israeli-Lebanese Borders," *Origins* 23 (12 August 1993): 162; "Religious Leaders Welcome Peace Accord," *Origins* 23 (23 September 1993): 254–55; "Next Steps for Israel and the Palestinians," *Origins* 25 (12 October 1995): 291–92; "Respecting and Protecting Lebanon's Integrity," *Origins* 25 (22 February 1996): 592; "Intensified Hostilities in the Middle East," *Origins* 25 (2 May 1996): 777–78; "The Holy See and the Middle East" (10 March 1999) in http://www.nccbuscc.org/bishops/tauran.htm; Bishop Joseph A. Fiorenza's letter

to President Clinton, 24 March 2000, on Lebanon and the Peace Process, in http://www.nccbuscc.org/sdwp/international/fiorenzacolo.htm; "Violence in the Holy Land: Letter to President Bush" (10 April 2002) *Origins* 31 (25 April 2002): 752–53.

88. See some of the following statements: "Returning to the Path of Peace in the Middle East" (15 November 2000), *Origins* 30 (7 December 2000): 423–24; "Resolution on the Israeli-Palestinian Crisis" (15 June 2001), *Origins* 31 (5 July 2001): 141–42; "Ending the Middle East Violence" (13 March 2002), *Origins* 31 (21 March 2002): 685–86; "Violence in the Holy Land: Letter to President Bush" (10 April 2002).

89. For the letter, see *Origins* 20 (22 November 1990): 384–86.

90. "Letter to President Bush: The Persian Gulf Crisis," *Origins* 20 (29 November 29, 1990): 397, 399–400.

91. For Roach's testimony, see "Debate on the Persian Gulf: Essential Questions," *Origins* 20 (20 December 1990): 457–60.

92. For the letter, see "Is War Justified?" *Origins* 20 (24 January 1991): 531–32.

93. "The Pope's Letters to Bush and Hussein," *Origins* 20 (24 January 1991): 534–35.

94. See Imesh's statement and that of many other bishops across the country in "Church Leaders React to the War," *Origins* 20 (7 February 1991): 572–79.

95. Anthony M. Pilla, president of NCCB/USCC, "Statement on Iraq" (19 November 1998) in *Origins* 28 (3 December 1998): 437–38. For other episcopal statements on embargoes, see "Crisis in Haiti," *Origins* 21 (11 January 1992): 495–96; "Urgent Call for Democracy and Dialogue in Haiti," *Origins* 24 (22 September 1994): 266; "Steps to Lessen Suffering in Cuba," *Origins* 22 (19 November 1992): 398–99; "President Clinton Asked to Authorize Direct Flights to Cuba," *Origins* 27 (19 June 1997): 80; "Bishop Fiorenza's Statement on Iraq," *Origins* 29 (25 November 1999): 389–90.

96. "Letter of Solidarity to Iraqi Patriarch," *Origins* 27 (27 November 1997): 412.

97. "Statement on Iraq" (19 November 1998), *Origins* 28 (3 December 1998): 437–38; "Statement on Iraq" (15 November 1999), *Origins* 29 (25 November 1999): 389–90.

98. For the immediate responses and statements, see "Day of National Tragedy," *Origins* 31 (20 September 2001): 253, 255–58.

99. "Terrorist Acts and Hate Crimes Deplored" (14 September 2001), *Origins* 31 (20 September 2001): 275–76.

100. "Responding to the Terrorism: What the National Purpose Should Be," *Origins* 31 (27 September 2001): 269, 271–72.

101. *Origins* 31 (29 November 2001): 413, 415–20.

102. "Letter to President Bush on the Iraq Situation," *Origins* 32 (26 September 2002): 261, 263–64.

103. *Origins* 31 (21 November 2002): 406–8.

104. "Serious Ethical Questions on War with Iraq" (26 February 2003), *Origins* 32 (13 March 2003): 641, 643.

105. Statement of Cardinal Pio Laghi, Papal Envoy, after Meeting with President George Bush (5 March 2003), *Origins* 32 (13 March 2003): 642.

106. See, for example, George Weigel, "Just War and Pre-emption: Three Questions," *The Tidings* (Los Angeles) (4 October 2002); Michael Novak's Vatican City speech of 10 February 2003 on the just war theory, "'Asymmetical Warfare' and Just War: A Moral Obligation" in the *National Review* On Line, www.nationalreview.com/novak/novak 021003.asp, see also *Origins* 32 (20 February 2003): 593, 595–98.

BIBLIOGRAPHY

Abell, Aaron I., ed. *American Catholic Thought on Social Questions*. Indianapolis: Bobbs-Merrill, 1968.

Allitt, Patrick. *Catholic Intellectuals and Conservative Politics in America*. Ithaca, N.Y.: Cornell University Press, 1993.

————. *Catholic Converts: British and American Intellectuals Turn to Rome*. Ithaca, N.Y.: Cornell University Press, 1993.

Appleby, Scott. *"Church and Age Unite!" The Modernist Impulse in American Catholicism*. Notre Dame, Ind.: University of Notre Dame Press, 1992.

Avella, Steven M. *This Confident Church: Catholic Leadership and Life in Chicago, 1940–1965*. Notre Dame, Ind.: University of Notre Dame Press, 1992.

————. *In the Richness of the Earth: A History of the Archdiocese of Milwaukee, 1843–1958*. Milwaukee, Wis.: Marquette University Press, 2002.

————, and Elizabeth McKeown, eds., *Public Voices: Catholics in the American Context*. Maryknoll, N.Y.: Orbis Books, 1999.

Blantz, Thomas E. *A Priest in Public Service: Francis J. Haas and the New Deal*. Notre Dame, Ind.: University of Notre Dame Press, 1982.

Carey, Patrick W., ed. *American Catholic Religious Thought*. New York: Paulist Press, 1987.

————. *People, Priests, and Prelates: Ecclesiastical Democracy and the Tensions of Trusteeism*. Notre Dame, Ind.: University of Notre Dame Press, 1987.

Carroll, Colleen. *The New Faithful: Why Young Adults are Embracing Christian Orthodoxy*. Chicago: Loyola Press, 2002.

Chinnici, Joseph P. *Living Stones: The History and Structure of Catholic Spiritual Life in the United States*. New York: Macmillan, 1989.

————, and Angelyn Dries, eds., *Prayer and Practice in the American Catholic Community*. Maryknoll, N.Y.: Orbis Books, 2000.

Crews, Clyde F. *An American Holy Land: A History of the Archdiocese of Louisville*. Wilmington, Del.: Michael Glazier, 1984.

————. *American & Catholic: A Popular History of Catholicism in the United States*. Cincinnati: St. Anthony Messenger Press, 1994.

Curran, Charles E. *American Catholic Social Ethics: Twentieth-Century Approaches*. Notre Dame, Ind.: University of Notre Dame Press, 1982.

Davidson, James. *The Search for Common Ground: What Unites and Divides Catholic Americans*. Huntington, Ind.: Our Sunday Visitor, 1997.

Davis, Cyprian. *The History of Black Catholics in the United States*. New York: Crossroad, 1990.

Dolan, Jay P. *The American Catholic Experience: A History from Colonial Times to the Present*. Garden City, N.Y.: Doubleday, 1985.

————, ed. *The American Catholic Parish: A History from 1850 to the Present*, 2 vols. New York: Paulist Press, 1987.

————. *In Search of an American Catholicism: A History of Religion and Culture in Tension.* Oxford: Oxford University Press, 2002.

Dries, Angelyn. *The Missionary Movement in American Catholic History.* Maryknoll, N.Y.: Orbis Books, 1998.

Ellis, John T., ed. *Documents of American Catholic History.* 3 vols. Wilmington, Del.: Michael Glazier, 1987.

————. *American Catholicism.* Chicago: University of Chicago Press, 1969.

Ellis, John T., and Robert Trisco. *A Guide to American Catholic History.* 2nd rev. edition and enl. Santa Barbara, Calif.: ABC-Clio, 1982.

Evans, John Whitney. *The Newman Movement: Roman Catholics in American Higher Education, 1883–1971.* Notre Dame, Ind.: University of Notre Dame Press, 1980.

Feldman, Egal. *Catholics and Jews in the Twentieth-Century America.* Urbana: Illinois University Press, 2001.

Fisher, James Terence. *The Catholic Counterculture in America, 1933–1962.* Chapel Hill: University of North Carolina Press, 1989.

Fogarty, Gerald P. *The Vatican and the American Hierarchy from 1870 to 1965.* 1982; Collegeville, Minn.: Liturgical Press, 1985.

————. *American Catholic Biblical Scholarship: A History from the Early Republic to Vatican II.* San Francisco: Harper and Row, 1989.

————, ed. *Patterns of Episcopal Leadership.* New York: Macmillan, 1989.

————. *The Vatican and the Americanist Crisis: Denis J. O'Connell, American Agent in Rome, 1885–1903.* Rome: Gregorian University, 1974.

————. *Commonwealth Catholicism: A History of the Catholic Church in Virginia.* Notre Dame, Ind.: University of Notre Dame Press, 2001.

Franchot, Jenny. *Roads to Rome: The Protestant Antebellum Encounter with Catholicism.* Berkeley: University of California Press, 1994.

Gallup, George, Jr., and Castelli, Jim. *The American Catholic People: Their Beliefs, Practices, and Values.* Garden City, N.Y.: Doubleday, 1987.

Gillis, Chester. *Roman Catholicism in America.* New York: Columbia University Press, 1999.

Gleason, Philip. *Speaking of Diversity: Essays on the Language of Ethnicity.* Baltimore: Johns Hopkins University Press, 1992.

————. *Keeping the Faith: American Catholicism Past and Present.* Notre Dame, Ind.: University of Notre Dame Press, 1987.

————. *Contending with Modernity: Catholic Higher Education in the Twentieth Century.* New York: Oxford University Press, 1995.

Greeley, Andrew M. *The American Catholic: A Social Portait.* New York: Basic Books, 1977.

————. *American Catholics Since the Council: An Unauthorized Report.* Chicago: Thomas More Press, 1985.

Hennesey, James. *American Catholics: A History of the Roman Catholic Community in the United States.* New York: Oxford University Press, 1981.

Hitchcock, James. *The Decline and Fall of Radical Catholicism.* New York: Herder and Herder, 1971.

————. *Catholicism and Modernity: Confrontation or Capitulation?.* New York: Seabury Press, 1979.

Jenkins, Philip. *Pedophiles and Priests: Anatomy of a Contemporary Crisis.* New York: Oxford University Press, 1996.

————. *The New Anti-Catholicism: The Last Acceptable Prejudice.* New York: Oxford University Press, 2003.

Kane, Paula, James Kenneally, and Karen Kennelly, eds. *Gender Identities in American Catholicism.* Maryknoll, N.Y.: Orbis Books, 2001.

Kauffman, Christopher J. *Tradition and Transformation in Catholic Culture: The Priests of Saint Sulpice in the United States from 1791 to the Present.* New York: Macmillan, 1988.

————. *Faith and Fraternalism: The History of the Knights of Columbus 1882–1982.* New York: Harper and Row, 1982.

————. *Ministry and Meaning: A Religious History of Catholic Health Care in the United States.* New York: Crossroads, 1995.

Kenneally, James K. *The History of American Catholic Women.* New York: Crossroad, 1990.

Kennelly, Karen, ed. *American Catholic Women: A Historical Exploration.* New York: Macmillan, 1989.

Leahy, William P. *Adapting to America: Catholics, Jesuits, and Higher Education in the Twentieth Century.* Washington, D.C.: Georgetown University Press, 1991.

Light, Dale. *Rome and the New Republic: Conflict and Community in the Philadelphia Catholicism from the Revolution to the Civil War.* Notre Dame, Ind.: University of Notre Dame Press, 1996.

Liptak, Dolores. *Immigrants and Their Church.* New York: Macmillan, 1989.

————. *European Immigrants and the Catholic Church in Connecticut, 1870–1920.* New York: Center for Migration Studies, 1987.

McAvoy, Thomas. *A History of the Catholic Church in the United States.* Notre Dame, Ind.: University of Notre Dame Press, 1969.

McGreevy, John T., *Parish Boundaries: The Catholic Encounter with Racism in the Twentieth Century Urban North.* Chicago: University of Chicago Press, 1996.

————. *Catholicism and American Freedom: A History.* New York: W. W. Norton, 2003.

McKeown, Elizabeth, and Dorothy M. Brown. *The Poor Belong to Us: Catholic Charities and American Welfare.* Cambridge, Mass.: Harvard University Press, 1997.

McShane, Joseph. *"Sufficiently Radical": Catholicism, Progressivism, and the Bishops' Program of 1919.* Washington, D.C.: Catholic University of America Press, 1986.

Marty, Martin. *An Invitation to American Catholic History.* Chicago: Thomas More Press, 1986.

Massa, Mark S. *Catholics and American Culture: Fulton Sheen, Dorothy Day, and the Notre Dame Football Team.* New York: Crossroad, 1999.

Mitchell, John J. *Critical Voices in American Catholic Economic Thought.* New York: Paulist Press, 1989.

Morris, Charles R. *American Catholics: The Saints and Sinners Who Built America's Most Powerful Church.* New York: Vintage Press, 1997.

Oates, Mary J. *The Catholic Philanthropic Tradition in America.* Bloomington: Indiana University Press, 1995.

O'Brien, David. *American Catholics and Social Reform: The New Deal Years.* New York: Oxford University Press, 1968.

————. *The Renewal of American Catholicism.* New York: Oxford University Press, 1972.

————. *Public Catholicism.* New York: Macmillan, 1989.

Ochs, Stephen J. *Desegrating the Altar: The Josephites and the Struggle for Black Priests, 1871–1960.* Baton Rouge: Louisiana State University Press, 1990.

Olson, James S. *Catholic Immigrants in America.* Chicago: Nelson-Hall, 1987.

Orsi, Robert Anthony. *The Madonna of 115th Street: Faith and Community in Italian Harlem,*
    1880–1950. New Haven, Conn.: Yale University Press, 1985.

———. *Thank You, St. Jude: Women's Devotion to the Patron Saint of Hopeless Causes.* New
    Haven, Conn.: Yale University Press, 1996

Piehl, Mel. *Breaking Bread: The Catholic Worker and the Origin of Catholic Radicalism in*
    America. Philadelphia: Temple University Press, 1982.

Reher, Margaret Mary. *Catholic Intellectual Life in America: A Historical Study of Persons and*
    Movements. New York: Macmillan, 1989.

Rippinger, Joel. *The Benedictine Order in the United States: An Interpretive History.* Colle-
    geville, Minn.: Liturgical Press, 1990.

Samora, Julian. *A History of the Mexican-American People.* Notre Dame, Ind.: University of
    Notre Dame Press, 1992.

Sandoval, Moises, ed. *Fronteras: A History of the Latin American Church in the USA Since*
    1513. San Antonio, Tex.: Mexican American Cultural Center, 1983.

———. *On the Move: A History of the Hispanic Church in the United States.* Maryknoll, N.Y.:
    Orbis Books, 1990.

Southern, David W. *John LaFarge and the Limits of Catholic Interracialism, 1911–1963.*
    Baton Rouge: Louisiana State University Press, 1996.

Spalding, Thomas. *The Premier See: A History of the Archdiocese of Baltimore, 1789–1989.*
    Baltimore: Johns Hopkins University Press, 1989.

Sparr, Arnold. *To Promote, Defend, and Redeem: The Catholic Literary Revival and the*
    Cultural Transformation of American Catholicism, 1920–1960. New York: Greenwood
    Press, 1990.

Stewart, George C. *Marvels of Charity: History of American Sisters and Nuns.* Huntington,
    Ind.: Our Sunday Visitor, 1994.

Taves, Ann. *The Household of Faith: Roman Catholic Devotions in Mid-Nineteenth-Century*
    America. Notre Dame, Ind.: University of Notre Dame Press, 1986.

Tentler, Leslie. *Seasons of Grace: A History of the Catholic Archdiocese of Detroit.* Detroit:
    Wayne State University Press, 1990.

Van Allen, Rodger. *The Commonweal and American Catholicism: The Magazine, the Move-
    ment, the Meaning.* Philadelphia: Fortress Press, 1974.

Varacalli, Joseph A. *Toward the Establishment of Liberal Catholicism in America.* Washing-
    ton, D.C.: University Press of America, 1983.

Vecsey, Christopher. *American Indian Catholics.* 3 vols. Notre Dame, Ind.: University of
    Notre Dame Press, 1996, 1997, 1999.

Weaver, Mary Jo. *New Catholic Women: A Contemporary Challenge to Traditional Religious*
    Authority. San Francisco: Harper and Row, 1985.

White, Joseph M. *The Diocesan Seminary in the United States: A History from the 1780s to the*
    Present. Notre Dame, Ind.: University of Notre Dame Press, 1989.

Wuthnow, Robert. *The Restructuring of American Religion: Society and Faith Since World*
    War II. Princeton, N.J.: Princeton University Press, 1988.

Yzermans, Vincent A., ed. *American Participation in the Second Vatican Council.* New York:
    Sheed and Ward, 1967.

Zanca, Kenneth J., ed. *American Catholics and Slavery, 1789–1866: An Anthology of Primary*
    Documents. Lanham, Md.: University Press of America, 1994.

Zöller, Michael. *Washington and Rome: Catholicism in American Culture.* Trans. Steven
    Rendall and Albert Wimmer. Notre Dame, Ind.: University of Notre Dame Press, 1999.

INDEX

Boldface page numbers refer to entries in the Biographical Entries section.

About the Author

PATRICK W. CAREY is Professor of Theology at Marquette University. He is a former president of the American Catholic Historical Society, and the former chair of the Department of Theology at Marquette. His work has appeared in such publications as *Church History, Catholic Historical Review, Journal of the Early American Public,* and others. Among his published books are *Theological Education in the Catholic Tradition: Contemporary Challenges* (1996), *The Roman Catholics* (Greenwood, 1993), and *People, Priests and Prelates: Ecclesiastical Democracy and the Tensions of Trusteeism* (1987).